JUSTICE

WITHOUT

VIOLENCE

edited by

Paul Wehr
Heidi Burgess
Guy Burgess

Lynne Rienner Publishers ■ Boulder & London

Published in the United States of America in 1994 by
Lynne Rienner Publishers, Inc.
1800 30th Street, Boulder, Colorado 80301

and in the United Kingdom by
Lynne Rienner Publishers, Inc.
3 Henrietta Street, Covent Garden, London WC2E 8LU

Library of Congress Cataloging-in-Publication Data
Justice without violence / edited by Paul Wehr, Heidi Burgess, and Guy
   Burgess.
      p.   cm.
   Includes bibliographical references and index.
   ISBN 1-55587-465-7 (alk. paper)
   ISBN 1-55587-491-6 (pbk.: alk. paper)
      1. Nonviolence. 2. Justice. I.Wehr, Paul Ernest, 1937–   .
II. Burgess, Heidi. III. Burgess, Guy M., 1949–   .
HM278.J87 1994
303.6'1—dc20
                                                                    93-33329
                                                                    CIP

British Cataloguing in Publication Data
A Cataloguing in Publication record for this book
is available from the British Library.

Printed and bound in the United States of America

This book is dedicated to
two dear friends and members of the Justice Without Violence
team, Elizabeth Mathiot (Moen) and Kenneth E. Boulding,
who, sadly, did not live to see its publication.
We all found Betsy's commitment to peace and justice to be both
selfless and infectious. Kenneth's brilliant insights
and, especially, his vision of the integrative system have
provided key foundations for this project and countless others.
We, and the field as a whole, will greatly miss them both.

Contents

Acknowledgments

The authors, editors, and the Conflict Resolution Consortium are grateful to the William and Flora Hewlett Foundation, the United States Institute of Peace, and the University of Colorado for providing financial support for this project. Thanks are also due to Carolyn Stephenson and Doug Bond for their reviews of and helpful comments on the manuscript and to Delinda Wunder, the Consortium secretary who helped bring the manuscript to completion.

Introduction

Heidi Burgess

This book is the first major product of the Conflict Resolution Consortium's Justice Without Violence Project. This project, which was funded by the U.S. Institute of Peace, the William and Flora Hewlett Foundation, and the University of Colorado, was one of three theory-development programs undertaken by the Consortium in its effort to find better ways of resolving difficult conflicts at the personal through international levels.

All of the contributors to this book, with two exceptions, are Consortium members who have been studying justice conflicts and approaches to resolving them in different parts of the world. Some contributors are political scientists, some are sociologists, some are economists. Each has focused his or her efforts on studying either the theory of nonviolence or a particular area of the world in which nonviolence has been used (either successfully or unsuccessfully) to confront gross injustice.

Unlike many other studies that use just one method, one case, or one region through which to examine when or how nonviolence works, this book takes a multifaceted approach, utilizing our combined theoretical and empirical expertise, to add a breadth of understanding of the problem of attaining justice without violence that was lacking in more narrow analyses.

The first four chapters of the book are theoretical. Chapter 1 was written by Guy Burgess and Heidi Burgess, who co-direct the Conflict Resolution Consortium and, with Paul Wehr, the Justice Without Violence Project as well. This chapter gives a broad overview of the related literature on justice and nonviolence, examining both the persuasive as well as the analytical literature on nonviolence as it has developed in modern times. This literature review forms the basis of the second chapter, also written by Guy Burgess and Heidi Burgess, which sets out the research questions that were developed by the project team at the outset of its investigations, guided the chapter authors as they did their research and wrote case studies.

The third chapter, written by Kenneth Boulding, gives his thoughts on the nature of justice, the causes of violence, and the applicability of various types of power to the prosecution of justice conflicts. Boulding was, until his death in March 1993, one of the leading scholars in peace research and conflict resolution for over thirty years. His chapter in this volume supplements his many other works on conflict, justice, and peace, which have deeply influenced our initial theory and approach to the research questions set out in this work.

The fourth theoretical chapter was written by Doug Bond, Director of the Program on Nonviolent Sanctions in Conflict and Defense at Harvard University. Bond's chapter sets out an interesting theory of nonviolence, relating what he calls mechanisms of action (what people actually do) to mechanisms of change (how those actions work to bring about change). Like Boulding, Bond gives readers a synopsis of an important theoretical approach to nonviolence, which, while it grows out of Gene Sharp's work, differs from Sharp in certain critical respects.

Following these four theoretical chapters are eight case studies. The first is an examination of violence, nonviolence, and justice in Sandinista Nicaragua written by Paul Wehr and sociology graduate student Sharon Erickson Nepstad. Wehr, who is one of the research directors for this project, has been studying and consulting on conflict management, nonviolence, civilian defense, and peaceful change in Central America for many years. Their chapter examines the role of both violence and nonviolence in achieving justice in Nicaragua within the context of the Sandinista/Contra conflict, as well as between the Sandinistas and the indigenous population of Nicaragua's Atlantic coast. Wehr and Nepstad describe the factors that helped to moderate conflict and limit violence within the revolutionary context. They also develop the important notion of power strategy mix— the exact combination of threat, exchange (that is, negotiation), and integrative strategies that, when combined, yields effective nonviolent social change.

The second case study, written by Joel Edelstein, a professor of political science at the University of Colorado at Denver, examines the 1989 revolutions in Eastern Europe. Although the image conveyed by the media in the United States was one of total collapse precipitated by massive nonviolent direct action, Edelstein suggests that the process was much more complex than that. Nonviolent direct action did play a role in the 1989 upheavals, of course, but other factors did as well. Edelstein describes the conditions that spurred forces for reform both within and outside the political and social elites of the Communist bloc. These forces worked together, he suggests, to bring about the widespread collapse of Communism in 1989.

The next case study was prepared by Zaven Arabajan, a Soviet economist who was visiting the University of Denver as this project was underway and then returned to Moscow, personally witnessing the events of the summer of 1992 and thereafter. Arabajan's chapter offers a historical look at the way Russia has faced justice conflicts over its long history—pointing out that the recent upheavals are but one of a series of such disruptive events that have occurred in Russia since the seventeenth century. What distinguishes the most recent series of changes is the extent to which they have come about through nonviolent action, as opposed to violent disruption, which has occurred so often in Russian history.

However, Arabajan questions the ability of Russian society to maintain this nonviolent approach to its political and economic problems over the long term. Continuing social, political, and economic chaos, as well as a lack of improvement, even after significant attempts at reform, has once again prepared Russian society, Arabajan says, "for an outburst of violence and intolerance"—an approach that would not have been tolerated in 1991, in his analysis.

Stephen Thomas, also a political scientist at the University of Colorado at Denver, examines the students' democracy movement in China, which was resoundingly if not permanently crushed in the Tiananmen Square Massacre in June 1989. Although the student democracy movement is commonly thought to be a complete failure of nonviolent direct action, Thomas suggests that it was not, because the students lost in a principled manner. Although not immediately successful, their actions may still have laid the groundwork for the reformation or even the abolition of the Communist Party in China over the long term. Whether or not this change occurs, he says, will depend on a variety of factors, including the health of the Chinese economy, the responsiveness of party leaders, and events outside of China; these factors could influence both its citizens and its leaders to work either for maintaining the status quo or for bringing about social and political change.

Following Thomas's analysis of China are two chapters on Africa. The first was prepared by James Scarritt, professor of political science at the University of Colorado at Boulder, who has spent years studying political change in Black Africa. His chapter focuses on violent and nonviolent change and compares the antecedents to each. Scarritt uses both quantitative and qualitative data analysis to develop and test many hypotheses concerning the relationship between contextual variables and both violent and nonviolent movements for social change in Black Africa.

William Kaempfer, Anton Lowenberg, H. Naci Mocan, and Lynne Bennett also contributed a chapter on Africa. William Kaempfer is a professor of economics at the University of Colorado at Boulder. Anton Lowenberg, formerly a professor of economics at the University of Colorado at Denver, has moved to California State University at Northridge since this chapter was written. H. Naci Mocan is a professor of economics at the University of Colorado at Denver, and Lynne Bennett is a graduate student. Their chapter examines the role that economic sanctions have played against apartheid in South Africa. This paper is part of a long series of studies Kaempfer and Lowenberg have done examining how signals and threats are transmitted from one nation to another in an effort to influence internal policies. Although the general perception of many economists and political scientists who have studied sanctions is that they are relatively ineffective, Kaempfer et al. suggest that sanctions can have signal and threat effects that work independently of their income effects and may be more important in bringing about social change. Using interest group analysis and public choice theory, Kaempfer et al. examine the relationships between sanctions, black strikes, black employment, black wages, and general South African economic conditions to determine the extent to which each is influenced by the other.

A chapter on the Middle East was prepared by Amin Kazak, a Lebanese political scientist now working at the University of Colorado. Kazak explores the multiple belief systems present in the Middle East and examines the extent to which these systems simultaneously support and inhibit successful nonviolent direct action in response to the Palestinian conflict. Although his chapter was written before the signing of the Palestinian–Israeli peace accord in the fall of 1993, the events now unfolding still illustrate the salience of his main points. The advocates of nonviolence are among the groups supporting the peace accord; the hardliners, who have long advocated violence as a remedy for the Palestinians, are among the groups opposing the accord and vowing to sabotage it with violent opposition.

A final case study, on development organizations in India, was written by Elizabeth Mathiot (Moen), who, until her recent death, was a University of Colorado sociologist and studied and worked among the very poor of India in conjunction with the Quaker Rights Sharing Program. Based on her extensive personal knowledge of and research on development organizations throughout India, but especially in Tamil Nadu, Moen describes the many obstacles to achieving successful nonviolent change in India. Development organizations, Moen explains, face enormous difficulties and obstacles that block their efforts to attain justice. They persist, nevertheless, and are making effective nonviolent changes for some of the poorest of the poor in India today.

In the final chapter Heidi Burgess and Guy Burgess compare the findings of these case studies to each other and to the theoretical chapters in order to develop a set of theoretical conclusions and hypotheses for further research. This effort was supplemented by a Synthesis Conference, which was held with all the authors after their cases were written and shared. At this conference, all the authors together discussed the similarities and differences they observed among their cases. The Burgesses then used this data, in addition to their own synthesis efforts, to point out the commonalities among the cases, highlight the differences, and draw conclusions about which variables appear to have the most influence on whether and when nonviolence can succeed in remedying injustice.

1

Justice Without Violence: Theoretical Foundations

Guy Burgess & Heidi Burgess

If asked which is better, peace or war, most people would choose peace. Yet most of these people are occasionally willing to go to war and are even more often willing to engage in violent conflict when the cause is something felt to be more important than peace. One value commonly considered more important is justice.

The tension between peace and justice is especially apparent in the extreme case of tyrannical governments. Such governments use the state's legal and political systems to violate fundamental economic, political, and social rights of subordinate groups. Therefore, these systems cannot be used effectively to obtain justice. Negotiation is similarly unlikely to be effective, as dominant groups will rarely voluntarily negotiate agreements that give them less power or resources than they currently have.

Very often in such asymmetrical power situations, the subordinate group concludes that the only effective strategy for pursuing justice is violent confrontation. Yet violence tends to beget more violence. The cycle often escalates quickly to the point where the ensuing struggle becomes an even greater violator of fundamental human rights than the initial injustice. Just as often, violent struggles for justice fail, as the dominant group usually has a higher capacity to inflict harm than the subordinate group.

The alternative approach to combating acute injustice is nonviolent resistance. This resistance can take many forms. One is nonviolent direct action, as characterized by Sharp.[1] This approach relies heavily on nonviolent threats or coercion to alter the power structure between the groups. Another approach is Gandhian *satyagraha*—an attempt to persuade the opponent to change its behavior largely through integrative or moral appeals. Many other forms of nonviolence exist as well. One could argue that there are far more methods of nonviolence available than there are methods of violence. What is lacking is a thorough understanding of what the options are, how they are implemented, how and when they work, and when they do not. This book is devoted to increasing our knowledge about these questions.

Definitions

Justice

Justice can be defined in many ways. Sometimes the term is used to refer to the outcome of a particular interaction of individuals or groups (commonly called distributive justice). Sometimes it refers to the procedures used for allocation (procedural justice). A third use concerns the motive underlying a particular behavior or decision.[2]

Within the context of distributive justice, further ambiguities are found. One of the most common definitions of distributive justice states that one's rewards should be proportional to one's contributions, or "inputs." This approach, commonly referred to as "equity theory," was proposed by Adams,[3] who based it on theories of relative deprivation, social exchange, dissonance, and distributive justice.

Although equity theory has many proponents, it has also come under considerable fire. Folger observed that much of the recent theoretical work on justice is a reaction against the limitations of equity theory.[4] One common critique asks what inputs are or how they are measured. Are they measured solely in economic terms? If so, critics charge, justice is relegated to economics alone.

Sampson made a distinction between equity and equality,[5] arguing that the former is justice in economic exchange, whereas equality considers noneconomic factors—interpersonal harmony and status congruence, for instance—to be important. Deutsch suggested that justice should be measured in terms of need, with personal welfare as the primary goal.[6]

Folger identified three alternative criteria for assessing distributive justice, independent of inputs. These are: equal treatment, in which everyone gets the same amount, regardless of input; leveling, in which everyone has the same cumulative amount; and social minimum, in which everyone is kept above a minimum level.

However, all of these methods for measuring justice examine distribution only and ignore questions of procedure. Procedural justice examines what distribution procedures are considered fair, and which are not. Here, criteria include who is involved in the decisionmaking process, regulations governing the manner in which information is gathered and presented, who makes the final decision, the procedures used, the role the aggrieved parties play, and who has access to the justice system.

These questions have been addressed by many authors. For our purposes, however, we agree with Reis that answering the question "what is
just?" is a "hopeless and pompous task."[7] Rather, we rely on a common-
sense definition. All of the conflicts examined in this book are ones most
observers would agree are examples of serious distributive or procedural
injustice. We chose to direct our attention to how this injustice might be
remedied without the use of violence.

Violence and Nonviolence

Although perhaps easier to define than justice, violence and nonviolence
are also tricky. Joan Bondurant, a leading proponent of nonviolence, defined violence as "the willful application of force in such a way that it is
intentionally injurious to the person or group against whom it is applied.
[Here] injury is understood to include psychological as well as physical
harm."[8] In Chapter 4 of this book, Doug Bond defines violence more narrowly as the "use of physical force against another's body, against that
person's will, and that is expected to inflict physical injury or death upon
that person." This definition seems to exclude psychological harm as well
as destruction of property, which are included in other definitions of violence. Sharp, another leading theorist of nonviolent direct action, also excluded the destruction of property from his definition of violence, although
he acknowledged that "sabotage will seriously weaken a nonviolent action
movement."[9] We agree with this statement—largely because we would
argue that destruction of property is a violent act and is likely to harm a
nonviolent movement in much the same way as other intrusions of violence into such an effort. This fact, however, can be empirically determined, and, as such, can be tested by this and other studies of nonviolent
action.

Scope of the Analysis

Given these definitions (or lack thereof), this book focuses on conflicts
that meet three criteria. The first is the presence of fundamental political,
social, or economic injustice. Examples would include clear-cut violations
of political rights such as freedom of speech, religion, and accountability
of a government to its people. Also at issue are economic rights (access to
adequate food, clothing, shelter, education, health care) and social rights
(the right to live where one desires, to pursue a chosen career or lifestyle).
   The second criterion is the disempowerment of the unjustly treated
group. The conflicts we examine here are all characterized by the failure
of political and legal institutions to protect these fundamental rights. In
some cases, authoritarian governments may have control of political and

legal institutions, which deny appeals from the disempowered segments of the population. In other cases, societies may be threatened or attacked by outside aggressors. Such rights and empowerment issues are central to many of the world's recent trouble spots: Vietnam, Iraq, Iran, South Africa, the Philippines, Israel and the occupied territories, Eastern Europe, China, Central America, and the former Soviet Union and Yugoslavia, for example.

The third criterion is that these conflicts were addressed by the low-power group primarily without using violence. Few, if any, nonviolent movements are able to maintain their nonviolent character entirely. Therefore, the aberrant use of violence within a general context of nonviolence did not exclude a case from our analysis. Neither did we reject a case because it met one definition of nonviolence but not another. Rather, we took an inclusive view of nonviolence, including, for instance, negotiation, which is generally not considered to be nonviolent action. (More on the definition of nonviolence will follow.) However, conflicts that were pursued primarily through violent means were not examined, except insofar as they provided a context to this analysis of nonviolent methods for remedying injustice.

Kenneth Boulding's Theory of Power

The most difficult problem in resolving the deeply rooted justice disputes of interest to this project is the extreme disparity of power between the dominant and subordinate groups. Because the dominant group has superior power, it has no need to alter the status quo—and, indeed, is likely to oppose any alteration. Simultaneously, the subordinate group has few methods available to it to persuade the dominant group to change. As we said before, the common assumption is that violence is the only avenue available to victims of such situations. However, violence is seldom a successful method of attaining power or structural change. There are other potentially effective approaches, however.

As a starting point for our research, we found Kenneth Boulding's analysis of power to be extremely helpful.[10] Boulding suggested that power has "three faces": threat, exchange, and love (that is, the integrative system). These principal sources of power can be employed singly or in combination, in varying degrees, and with different strategies, to effect change.

Threats

Threats, in Boulding's theory, can be violent or nonviolent. They usually take the form of "you do something I want, or I will do something you don't want."[11] They can be met with submission, flight, counterthreat, or defiance. Threats can resolve conflicts when those threatened submit or flee. This response is common, especially when the threatening party has overwhelming power, making the threat highly credible.

But if the threatened party is more powerful than the threatener, then submission is unlikely. Rather, defiance or counterthreats are the more likely response. This situation eventually forces the perpetrator of the threat either to admit the threat was a bluff or to engage in a potentially costly power contest to find out who really is more powerful.

If the threat involves violence, defiance and counterthreats are likely to escalate into a violent confrontation—with all the attendant problems previously described. Even nonviolent threats are frequently met with a violent response. Some nonviolent activists actually want such a response, as they feel it makes their own moral position look better in comparison.

The biggest problem with nonviolent threats is that they generate what we call the "backlash effect." People faced with threats seldom submit willingly or happily. If they submit, they do so grudgingly, all the while waiting for their chance to defy the threat and, if possible, get retribution. This effect means that "victories" obtained by threat tend to be highly unstable, as they create a high level of hostility in the threatened party. Hence, if the group making the threat should ever "turn its back," the prohibited behaviors are likely to return. Even if eternal vigilance can be maintained by the threatening party, those forced to do things against their will can find highly creative ways to subvert the wishes of those making the threats. This problem accounts, in large part, for the failure of economies dominated by threat and their precipitous collapse whenever the threat power is called into question. Recent events in Eastern Europe and the Soviet Union are prime examples of this dynamic.

Nevertheless, nonviolent threats can be an effective approach to confronting injustice. In this volume, we examine two types: threats exercised by the subordinate groups on their own behalf and threats exercised on behalf of these groups by outside powers.

Threats exercised by subordinates. The power that subordinate groups possess to compel the dominant group to adopt more just policies rests, paradoxically, on the unjust nature of their position. At the core of injustice there is usually a transfer of political legitimacy or economic resources from the poor to the rich. Because the rich usually become dependent on this transfer, they are vulnerable to interruptions of it. Actions designed to exploit this vulnerability can give apparently powerless groups the ability to collectively force major concessions through such means as strikes and boycotts, antigovernment demonstrations, and civil disobedience.

Despite their initial nonviolent character, nonviolent threats are a confrontational strategy that threatens the vital interests of the dominant group. As such, that group is often willing to use violent measures in response (for example, the violence used against Solidarity in Poland in the early 1980s or the Tiananmen Square suppression in China in 1989). The nonviolent group must then choose whether to revert to violence, to remain nonviolent, or to withdraw from the conflict. This book examines such decisions in terms of cause and effect. It also examines the larger question of nonviolent threat. How and when can such approaches be successfully used, and how can they be combined with other strategies to redistribute power to eliminate social injustice?

Threats exercised by external powers. Similarly, nonviolent threats can be used by outside powers to influence justice conflicts. For example, the external threat or imposition of economic, social, and political sanctions may influence the balance of power between opponents. Although sanctions are difficult to implement and, hence, may be ineffective from a purely economic point of view, the research of Kaempfer et al. (reported in this book) indicates that sanctions may have persuasive effectiveness beyond their simple economic impact.

Exchange

Exchange, as we use it here, refers to bilateral or multilateral negotiation, or "you do something I want and I'll do something you want."[12] As Fisher and Ury argued, if and when exchange works it is usually less costly and more effective than threats and power contests.[13] However, exchange strategies are dependent upon factors often absent in power and justice conflicts. The primary problem is that low-power groups have relatively little to trade.

One way around this dilemma is for the low-power group to enlist help from external or more powerful groups. But outside powers may exploit a justice conflict for selfish motives—to overthrow an unfriendly government (for example, the U.S. government's use of the Contras in Nicaragua) or to strengthen a friendly one. These are situations in which the weaker party's pursuit of outside assistance may come at a very high cost.

Exchange is potentially more useful, however, when linked with threat. For instance, low-power groups can threaten to withhold labor (that is, strike) or to withhold their political support of the government. If either their labor or their political support is sufficiently valuable to the dominant group, the latter may negotiate with the subordinate group on a more equal basis in the shadow of this threat.[14]

The Integrative System

Boulding's third source of power is what he called "love," which is shorthand for the integrative system. "In the love relationship, essentially, A says to B, 'You do something for me because you love me,'"[15] or (in our words) "I'll do something for you because I like you, not because I expect you to do something for me in exchange or fear you might hurt me if I don't." Boulding suggested that if the word *love* seems too strong, one can substitute *respect*.

Love has been largely ignored in the academic literature on power and conflict, but Boulding persuasively argued that it is the most significant source of power in his typology. "Without some sort of legitimacy," he explained, "neither threat power nor economic [that is, exchange] power can be realized in any large degree."[16]

The integrative system is especially important in justice disputes because the prevailing social order cannot be sustained unless the dominant group is morally able to justify its continued dominance. Although dominant groups can usually justify their dominant position in some moral terms, they may also believe in other universal principles of justice that are antithetical to the continuation of their dominant role.

This belief creates an opening for nonviolent strategies that confront people with these contradictions or show the superiority of the more universal standards of justice. Once the dominant group starts to believe that what they are doing is morally wrong, they must resolve what psychologists call "cognitive dissonance" by bringing their actions into line with their beliefs.[17] This was a primary strategy of both Mohandas Gandhi and Martin Luther King, Jr.

The advantage of this approach is that it persuades people to do things they eventually feel good about, rather than forcing them to do things that they do not want to do. Therefore, this approach reduces the need for continued vigilance (to make sure the group being forced does not respond by shooting the other group[s] in the back). Further, this approach sharply reduces the threat of counterrevolutionary change.

Related Theory and Research

Boulding's analysis of power provided an initial theoretical basis for our inquiry. However, his theory was supplemented by our review of the work of other nonviolence theorists. This literature can be divided into two groups: the persuasive literature and the analytical literature.

Persuasive Literature on Nonviolence

The persuasive literature generally accepts the value of nonviolence on faith. It neither examines if nonviolence works nor specifies what "works" might mean. This absence of critical examination occurs because most of the authors advocate nonviolence on moral or religious grounds. Nonviolence is seen as a more humane and civilized way of life or as a just and moral way of engaging in conflict in all circumstances. (This view is often referred to as "principled nonviolence.") Whether it works better than alternatives such as violence or disengagement is not questioned by advocates of principled nonviolence. Rather, nonviolence is seen as good in itself and is assumed to be superior to violence in all situations. Advocates of principled nonviolence include Gandhi, King, A. J. Muste, and Leo Tolstoy.

Other persuasive literature suggests that nonviolence is a means, not an end, but a means *not* subject to scientific analysis. "If it fails it must be, inevitably, because it has not been tried long enough or was not properly used."[18] Thus, the literature of persuasion "seeks to incite, to persuade, or to record; only rarely does it attempt to analyze."[19] Nevertheless, it does develop some theoretical concepts adaptable for analytical use.

Key Concepts of Principled Nonviolence

Satyagraha.   Many of the key concepts of principled nonviolence were first developed by Gandhi, the founder of modern nonviolent action. The first of these is *ahimsa*, the refusal to do harm, even if one is hurt by another. A second key concept is *satyagraha*, frequently translated as "soul-force" or "truth-force" and called by Gandhi the "law of suffering."[20]

Satyagraha and ahimsa require believers to view and treat opponents and attackers with warmth, acceptance, understanding, even love. People's humanness is seen as more important than their current beliefs or actions. Therefore, *satyagrahis* will refrain not only from violence toward their opponents, but from hating or speaking ill of them as well. In Gandhi's words,

> A *satyagrahi* must never forget the distinction between evil and the evil-doer. He must not harbor ill-will or bitterness against the latter. He may not even employ needlessly offensive language against the evil person, however unrelieved his evil might be. For it is an article of faith with every *satyagrahi* that there is no one so fallen in this world but can be converted by love. A *satyagrahi* will always try to overcome evil by good, anger by love, untruth by truth, *himsa* by *ahimsa*. There is no other way of purging the world of evil.[21]

Therefore, satyagraha forbids all violent acts, words, and even thoughts about others, calling for love and truth to bring about social change.

Conversion, not coercion.   Gene Sharp, a leader of the analytic, techniques-oriented approach to nonviolence, distinguishes between coercion and conversion. Coercion forces opponents to change their behavior because the alternatives to such a change are nonexistent or unacceptable. Conversion, on the other hand, gets people to change their behavior because they want to. They have altered their beliefs about what is right, just, or true. They have had "a change of heart."

In satyagraha, coercion is avoided as an intentional tactic because it is seen as violence in word or thought, if not deed. Although much nonviolent resistance might be interpreted as coercive, in most cases principled nonviolent activists seek to use conversion, rather than coercion, to bring about a complete change of heart in the opponent,[22] not simply a change of situation.[23]

Suffering as a strategy. There are many techniques for encouraging conversion, but most advocates of principled nonviolence believe unmerited suffering is the most forceful way to affect an opponent's conscience. Both self-imposed suffering, such as fasts, and the willing acceptance of sanctions imposed for civil disobedience or noncooperation are considered most effective for bringing about a change of heart in one's opponents, leading to social change. Again quoting Gandhi:

> Things of fundamental importance to the people are not secured by reason alone, but have to be purchased with their suffering. Suffering is the law of human beings; war is the law of the jungle. But suffering is infinitely more powerful than the law of the jungle for converting the opponent and opening his ears, which are otherwise shut, to the voice of reason.[24]

Analytical Literature on Nonviolence

Much of the analytical literature on nonviolence focuses on definitions and typologies. Many authors try to define what is and what is not "nonviolence" and to develop alternative ways of categorizing nonviolent action. Although most authors agree that an adequate definition of nonviolence goes considerably beyond simple abstinence from violence, there is little agreement on what constitutes nonviolence.

At a minimum, most agree, nonviolence means the renunciation of violence. This renunciation may be absolute (as in principled nonviolence) or limited (as in practical or strategic nonviolence).[25] Further, as Holmes suggested, definitions of nonviolence usually include a positive aspect as well, outlining what is to be done when one encounters violence or injustice. These definitions usually involve lists of techniques such as nonresistance, active reconciliation, moral resistance, selective nonviolence, satyagraha, nonviolent revolution, passive resistance, civil disobedience, direct action,[26] protest, noncooperation, and intervention without physical violence.[27] The definitions of these terms, too, vary from author to author.

Nonviolence was long equated with pacifism and passive resistance. However, Stiehm suggested that more recent work distinguishes those terms, which are seen to be passive, from nonviolent behavior, which is seen to be active.[28] This distinction agrees with Sharp's view that nonviolent action is active, not passive, and is action, not inaction.[29]

To further distinguish nonviolent action from other forms of action in conflicts, Sharp contended first that nonviolent action is not verbal.[30] In his view, it is meant to persuade not through words, but through social, economic, and political acts. Second, in Sharp's opinion, nonviolent action does not involve negotiation or compromise, as these are traditional techniques that work within, rather than outside, the system.[31] Other authors, however, have stated that negotiation is indeed a part of nonviolent action. Martin Luther King, Jr., wrote that "negotiation is the purpose of direct action."[32]

Third, Sharp considered nonviolent action to be massive or group action.[33] This view differs from that of Stiehm, who distinguished between individual and group nonviolence;[34] Sharp claimed that nonviolence is only a group phenomenon. Fourth, Sharp thought that nonviolence must involve active protest, noncooperation, or intervention. Fifth, nonviolence is extraconstitutional. It does not rely on institutional procedures of the state, but circumvents or violates these procedures to bring about social change.[35]

Typologies of Nonviolence

Closely related to the definitions of nonviolence are alternative typologies of nonviolent action developed for analysis by different authors. Stiehm identified the following seven schemes used to develop such typologies.[36]

1. *Categorization by resister's motive.* Stiehm differentiated between two motives—the desire to act morally and the desire to act effectively. Here she seemed to be referring to the distinction between principled and strategic nonviolence made by many authors. Advocates of principled nonviolence see nonviolence as an end in itself and as the appropriate response in all situations to violent attack or injustice. Advocates of strategic nonviolence see it as simply a means to an end, which may or may not be effective and, therefore, appropriate.

2. *Categorization by resister's intentions toward opponent.* Is the resister's approach intended to change the opponent's mind about what is right or just (as in Sharp's conversion) or to force the opponent to change behavior without changing his or her beliefs (as in Sharp's coercion)? Sharp[37] also included a third category—accommodation. Accommodation is the middle ground, where the opponents change their behavior because it is easier to do so than not, but not because they have changed their mind about the fundamental issue nor because they have been forced to change by threat. Both Sharp and Bond termed these distinctions "mechanisms of change," differentiating them from "mechanisms of action," which are the techniques themselves.[38]

3. *Categorization based on the nature of the intended target.* Stiehm set out two possible targets of nonviolent action: the opposing party, and unaligned outside, or "third," parties that might either join the opposition

group or otherwise aid its cause. To illustrate the latter, Stiehm cited U.S. civil rights activists who tried to provoke violence that would be witnessed by the media and hence the world and then called on the federal government to intervene with force to protect the "nonviolent" protesters. This approach, Stiehm maintained, was not intended to change the nature of the relationship between the protesters and their opponents. Rather, the tactic was designed to make that relationship obvious while maintaining a high level of legitimacy for the protesters' actions and their cause.

McCarthy categorized further by describing three groups and twelve subgroups that might be influenced by a nonviolent action.[39] The first group, direct beneficiaries, are those who are supposed to benefit from the action. They include the core action group, "waverers and peripheral activists," the uncommitted, and those afraid of change. The second group includes opponents: core adversaries, sympathizers, uncommitted and passive beneficiaries of the status quo, and those hostile toward change. The third group includes significant third-party subgroups: powerful outsider groups (such as nongovernmental organizations), conscience constituencies that support a struggle on behalf of others, potential indirect beneficiaries, and potential indirect losers.

Nonviolent action may be directed at any of these groups, McCarthy wrote, and the method chosen should differ depending on which group is the target. However, choice of target and the goal of the action are often not adequately clarified, which impairs effectiveness.

4. *Categorization by technique.* Sharp, Kuper, Seifert, and others used this approach.[40] An example is Sharp's unequaled identification of 198 techniques of nonviolent action.[41]

5. *Categorization by parties involved.* Does the conflict involve two individuals, two groups, a group and the state, or two states? Stiehm used a simplified version of this scheme, distinguishing primarily between individual nonviolence, which she saw as based on principle, and group nonviolence, which she argued is generally strategic and of a very different character than individual nonviolence.

6. *Categorization by amount of preplanning.* Was the action spontaneous, tactical, or strategic? Miller based this classification scheme on the distinction between principled and pragmatic nonviolence.[42] Tactical nonviolence is used as an expedient technique. Strategic nonviolence is used as a generally applicable, ethically based approach. Spontaneous nonviolence can be either principled or pragmatic but is unplanned. Sharp distinguished between improvised nonviolent struggle without preparation and civilian-based defense that involves extensive training and planning. Although improvised struggle has been successful on occasion, Sharp argued that it is significantly weaker than civilian-based defense.[43]

7. *Classification by goal.* Stiehm suggested that the goal of the action may be nonviolence itself or some more limited goal in which nonviolence

is seen as a means to that goal.[44] McCarthy distinguished three levels of goals.[45] First are ultimate goals, the changes an action group wishes ultimately to achieve. Second are process goals, which are the actions necessary to achieve ultimate goals. Third are achievement goals, which can be either immediate "hoped-for effects of a single action or group of actions"[46] or intermediate changes that contribute directly to reaching the final goal.

Positive/negative distinction. Boserup and Mack[47] made a useful distinction between positive and negative approaches to waging conflict. Although this distinction divides nonviolent actors in largely the same way as does the distinction between principled and practical nonviolence, the differentiation is made for a different reason. The negative approach views conflict as simply a struggle, and utilizes compulsion (that is, coercion) and power freely to bring about social change. Appeals to the moral or human qualities of an opponent play only a secondary role in this approach, which stresses effectiveness. Negative conflict advocates see coercion as more effective than conversion.

The positive approach, typical of principled nonviolence and clearly formulated in Gandhi's work, seeks mutually acceptable, rather than unilaterally imposed solutions. This approach makes strong appeals to the moral and human qualities of the opponent, and regards trust, openness, and love as highly important.

Boserup and Mack saw this distinction as more useful than the more common distinctions between techniques (because the same action can be labeled differently) and less ambiguous than typologies based on how methods are supposed to function. (As an example, they noted that Gandhi's noncooperation and Sharp's noncooperation are very different.) The simple positive/negative distinction, they claimed, is much more theoretically useful because of its simplicity and clarity. (They then went on at length to demonstrate why negative approaches are generally superior to positive ones for developing civilian defense.)

How Nonviolence Works

A smaller portion of the literature on nonviolence seeks to analyze how it works. The most analysis in this area has been done by Gene Sharp, viewed by many as the founder of the pragmatic, techniques-oriented approach to nonviolence, just as Gandhi is seen to be the major conceptualizer and practitioner of modern principled nonviolence. Sharp's key ideas were set out in his book *The Politics of Nonviolent Action* and have been adopted by most pragmatic nonviolence theorists.

Sharp's central concept is that all government, no matter how tyrannical, is based on popular consent. When this consent is withdrawn, the power of the leader is destroyed.[48] Gandhi and most advocates of principled nonviolence would likely agree with this, but the concept of power is more central in Sharp's theory of nonviolence than in Gandhi's, where truth might be its counterpart.

Sharp identified six sources of power: authority, human resources, skills and knowledge, intangible psychological and ideological factors, material resources, and sanctions.[49] The extent, quality, and availability of these factors determines the power a regime can wield. The authority a regime commands, the amount and quality of human and material resources at its disposal, and the forcefulness of sanctions it can use determine its power capacity, and consequently its ability to influence three groups—its agents and helpers, the general population, and foreign governments and people. If a regime's power capacity is high, then its ability to elicit cooperation from these three groups will be high. Otherwise, the amount of cooperation they will give may be low, further decreasing the regime's sources of power.

Nonviolent action diminishes a ruler's sources of power, Sharp suggested, through "political jiu-jitsu,"[50] an extension of Gregg's concept of moral jiu-jitsu.[51] Both concepts refer to the Oriental martial art in which an aggressor is thrown off balance when his victim fails to counter a physical attack. In Gregg's formulation, the nonviolence and goodwill of the victim cause the opponent to

> lose his moral balance. . . . He suddenly and unexpectedly loses the moral support which the usual violent resistance of most victims would render him. He plunges forward, as it were, into a new world of values. He feels insecure because of the novelty of the situation and his ignorance of how to handle it. He loses his poise and self-confidence. . . . [In this way, the nonviolent activist] uses the leverage of a superior wisdom to subdue the rough direct force of his opponent.[52]

Sharp extended this concept to include political and social imbalance as well.

> The nonviolent actionists deliberately refuse to challenge the opponent on his own level of violence. Violence against violence is reinforcing. The nonviolent group not only does not need to use violence, but they must not do so lest they strengthen their opponent and weaken themselves. They must adhere to their own nonviolent "weapons system" [which includes a variety of techniques of persuasion, manipulation, and coercion]. . . . Nonviolent action tends to turn the opponent's violence and repression against his own power position, weakening it and at the same time strengthening the nonviolent group. Because violent action and nonviolent action possess quite different mechanisms, and induce differing forces of change in the society, the opponent's repression . . . can never really come to grips with the kind of power wielded by the nonviolent actionists. Gandhi has compared the situation with that of a

man violently striking water with a sword: it was the man's arm which was dislocated.[53]

Thus, Sharp saw nonviolence upsetting traditional social and political processes as well as the opponents' sense of morality. This can be done, Sharp contended, in three ways: nonviolent protest and persuasion, noncooperation, and nonviolent intervention.[54] Nonviolent protest and persuasion is the mildest form of action in Sharp's theory. It includes symbolic acts such as parades, vigils, picketing, and teach-ins, and any action to voice peaceful opposition to a policy or law, or to persuade others to a particular view or action. Such acts go beyond verbal expression or negotiation, but stop short of noncooperation or nonviolent intervention.

Sharp's second category of nonviolent action is noncooperation, the refusal to do what one normally does to assist a person, group, institution, or regime with whom the activist is in conflict. For instance, people may stop or slow down their work; they may disobey laws they regard as immoral; they may refuse to pay taxes. The intent is to discontinue or defy certain existing relationships. Sharp further divided such actions into social, political, and economic noncooperation according to the type of relationship being discontinued.

Nonviolent intervention, Sharp's third category, is stronger yet, in that it involves direct intervention (and usually the disruption of an activity). These methods, Sharp maintained,

> pose a more direct and immediate challenge. *If successful,* the victory is likely to come quicker by the use of methods of this class than with the use of methods of the previous classes, because the disruptive effects of intervention are harder to tolerate or withstand for a considerable period of time. . . . However, . . . speedier and more severe repression may be a first result—which of course, does not necessarily mean defeat.[55]

Included in this category are physical interventions such as sit-ins, ride-ins (as in the "Freedom Rides" during segregation in the southern United States), nonviolent incursions into forbidden areas, and nonviolent obstruction. Sharp also included "psychological interventions"—self-inflicted suffering such as fasting, and "reverse trials" where defendants charge the state with violating a higher ethical code. Also included in this category is social intervention where activists establish alternative social patterns, institutions, communication systems, even governments. In all three categories, Sharp documented 198 different forms of nonviolent action.[56]

Also important in Sharp's theory is the concept of mechanisms of change. Protest and persuasion, noncooperation, and intervention (called mechanisms of action by Bond)[57] produce change in one of four ways—through conversion, accommodation, coercion, or disintegration of the opponent. These are what Sharp and Bond call mechanisms of change.

Conversion is the most difficult to achieve because it requires the highest level of internalization of values. In conversion, opponents become convinced that their behavior or beliefs are wrong and should be changed. Here the change of policy or behavior is made because the actor *wants* to change, not because he or she is *forced* to change.

By contrast, coercion involves no internalized change of values and beliefs and is therefore easier to accomplish, according to many theorists. Opponents are forced to change their policy because nonviolent resistance has so eroded their sources of power that they can no longer maintain the policy in question. Thus, "the opponent has not changed his mind on the issues and he wants to continue the struggle, but is unable to do so."[58]

Accommodation, the most common mechanism of change, lies between these two extremes. In accommodation, the opponent does not agree with the changes demanded (that is, he or she has not been converted) and he still has the power to resist (that is, he or she has not been coerced), but he chooses to accede because doing so seems easier or cheaper than holding firm.

Sharp has recently added a fourth mechanism—disintegration.[59] This state occurs when a ruler's sources of power are almost eliminated, to the point that the government simply collapses. There is no longer anyone to coerce.

Related Theories of How Nonviolence Works

Others have developed schemes similar to Sharp's but differing in minor respects. For instance, Lakey thought that nonviolent change can be induced through conversion, coercion, or persuasion. His concept of persuasion is similar to Sharp's accommodation in that opponents do not accept the actionists' view. Here opponents retain the ability to fight but choose not to fight. In Lakey's words, "The opponents can be overheard saying, 'Let them have what they want; it's too much of a nuisance to continue the fight.'"[60]

But beyond the notion of nuisance, Lakey described how persuasion comes about when opponents come to see actionists as human, and therefore, part of their group.

> All men, no matter how debased they may seem, treat well the members of their own group. . . . [It] is easy to be violent against those who are seen as either inhuman ("mad dogs") or non-human (foreign slaves, unseen faces). The task of the nonviolent campaigners, then, is to get the opponent to see them as human beings.[61]

Bond[62] combines Sharp's approach with the theories of Rummel[63] and other social science theories of opinion change, power, and conflict. Bond identifies eight mechanisms of action: physical and coercive force, discrete manipulation, public coercion, authoritative, intellectual, and altruistic appeals, and exchange. These mechanisms are used singly and in combination to bring about change through conversion, accommodation, compliance (equivalent to Sharp's coercion), or disintegration. These terms are all defined and explained in Chapter 4 of this volume.

The Positive Approach to Nonviolent Change

As noted earlier, Boserup and Mack[64] distinguished between the positive nonviolence theorists, such as Mohandas Gandhi and Johan Galtung, and the negative theorists, such as Gene Sharp, Doug Bond, George Lakey, and Clarence Case. Although the latter four might object to the label "negative," they do stress the utility of threat- and coercion-based approaches to conflict much more than Gandhi and Galtung, who seem to have a more positive or perhaps optimistic view of humankind's susceptibility to moral and intellectual appeals.

Neither Gandhi nor Galtung developed the theory of positive nonviolence as much as Sharp and his colleagues have developed their theory of change, but the notion that people respond better to positive influences than to negative ones needs to be considered. Gandhi wrote:

> We can only win over the opponent by love, never by hate. Hate is the subtlest form of violence. We cannot be really non-violent and yet have hate in us. . . . Violent non-co-operation only multiplies evil. . . . As evil can only be sustained by violence, withdrawal of support of evil requires complete abstention from violence.[65]

Even though Gandhi advocated the use of noncooperation and civil disobedience, for him those activities are not to *force* the opponent to change their behavior (that is, coercion), but rather to strongly *influence them psychologically* to change their mind about the morality or correctness of that behavior. Thus, although the so-called negative theorists see noncooperation and civil disobedience as coercive, Gandhi saw them as persuasive and advocated their use as conversion, not coercion.

In addition to stressing noncooperation and civil disobedience aimed at unjust laws, Gandhi also directed his followers to undertake "constructive work," which often involved the creation of parallel social, economic, and political structures to undermine the unjust ones.

Feminist Approaches to Nonviolence

A third perspective on nonviolence, feminist theory, both supports and contradicts other nonviolence theories. Power is a central concept in feminist theory, though it is defined differently than traditional concepts. Meyerding distinguished between *personal* power—the power each person has to control her own life—and *power-over-others,* the power to force others to do something.[66] Woehrle referred to *power-over* and *power-with;*[67] Bell and Kurtz used *power-over* and *power-to.*[68] *Power-over* involves the ability to control others and is a "limited commodity owned only by an elite."[69] *Power-with* is a "resource gained through cooperation [and involves] the ability 'to be' rather than 'to have' or 'to do.'"[70] Bell and Kurtz defined *power-to* in terms of capacity, rather than as force, coercion, authority, or violence.[71] *Power-to* can be held simultaneously and equally by all parties, and it expands when it is shared.[72] Readers familiar with game theory might see these terms corresponding to zero-sum and positive-sum views of power.

Feminist theory also envisions power as a group phenomenon, not a personal attribute. Personal empowerment is directly linked to community empowerment, which is then translated into political action and social change. (The feminist phrase for this approach is that the "personal is political.") "By changing perceptions of power in this way," Bell and Kurtz argued, "individuals are able to envision and actually begin to live in a way that denies the inevitability of domination."[73]

Assessing Effectiveness

Obstacles

Studies that analyze the effectiveness of nonviolence comparatively across cases are rare. A number of case studies assess effectiveness in one case, but few compare effectiveness across cases. The reasons for this are four-fold.

First, much of the literature is written to persuade, not analyze. Second, there is the common assumption that studying the effectiveness of nonviolence is utilitarian, amoral, or even immoral. Nonviolence is judged superior for so many philosophical and ethical reasons that an assessment of practical goal attainment is viewed as a useless determination of the obvious—the goodness of nonviolence.

Others (including ourselves) disagree with this view. We think that nonviolence, although difficult to define, is an empirically observable process to be examined objectively just as other social processes. Nonviolent actionists have goals and objectives, the attainment of which can be measured. Some nonviolent actionists may choose nonviolence for ethical reasons, but many more are likely to be practically motivated. These actionists need to know whether nonviolence will work as they hope, how to make it work better, and when its costs are likely to exceed the benefits to be gained. It is towards this end that this book is addressed.

A third reason why analyses of effectiveness are rare is that they are difficult to accomplish. Controlled experiments in the field are impossible. Experiments in the laboratory are of dubious value when extrapolated to the societal level. Analyses of a few cases such as ours can only be suggestive, as far too many variables are uncontrolled—hence, too many "what ifs" remain.

Some empirically based studies are underway (most notably those by Sharp and his colleagues at Harvard), but the work is extremely expensive and slow.[74] Few researchers have been willing or able to undertake such exhaustive research.

A fourth obstacle to such analysis is the indeterminate nature of the term *effectiveness*. Is nonviolence effective only if it brings about complete revolution? Is it effective if it brings about only minor social change? What if it brings about changes in particular individuals, but not in society as a whole? Is it more effective than violence or disengagement? How can one measure it?

The simplest response to this problem is to examine the goals of those using nonviolence to determine their intentions. It should then be possible to assess whether or not those goals are met. As McCarthy pointed out, however, goals are not always clear and can vary from one participant (or group) to another. He agreed that effectiveness is directly linked to one's goals. A group can have success, he wrote, in any of three ways. First, a group can achieve its process goals (that is, it can successfully conduct an action). Second, it can succeed or fail in reaching intermediate goals or intervening steps toward its ultimate goal. Third, it can reach its ultimate goal or not. "Groups conducting nonviolent action must be aware that success has these three aspects and that satisfaction with taking a step along the road does not end the journey."[75] Neither does failure to achieve the ultimate goal in one step mean an action is a failure on all counts.

Although goal attainment is the most common measure of success, Sharp[76] noted two other important factors. One is the increase or decrease in the absolute and relative power of the contending groups. The second is change in each group's sphere of influence and the level of outside sympathy felt for its objectives.

Factors Contributing to or Limiting Effectiveness

Sharp has written the most on determinants of effectiveness also. In Volume III of *The Politics of Nonviolent Action*, Sharp listed thirty-four factors that determine the outcome of nonviolent struggles. These include factors in the social context, characteristics of the contending groups, and factors associated with third parties.

Elements in the social situation that influence the success of nonviolent action, according to Sharp, include: the degree of conflict of interest between the parties (the greater the conflict, the smaller the chance of success); the social distance between the groups (again, an inverse relationship); the number of shared beliefs (a positive relationship); and the degree to which power is dispersed throughout the groups and society as a whole (greater dispersion of power brings higher chances for success).

Opponent group characteristics that are important are: the degree to which the opponent group is dependent upon the action group (the greater the dependence, the greater the likelihood of the nonviolent group's success); the degree of dissent that is normally tolerated (the less dissent is tolerated, the greater the impact of dissent); the degree to which the opponent group is convinced it is right; the means of control and repression available to the opponent; the degree to which the opponent's supporters (including its agents and the general population) support the opponent's position and the repression used against the nonviolent group (if they do not, the repression may break down); and the opponent's estimate of the chances of success of the movement and the consequences success would have.

Characteristics of the nonviolent group that Sharp viewed as critical include: the degree to which the nonviolent group is convinced it is right; the level of confidence the nonviolent group has in nonviolent action; the soundness of the group's strategy and tactics; the level of discipline within the nonviolent group; the number of nonviolent resisters and their proportion in the general population (generally, the higher the better); the degree to which the actionists are willing to continue in the face of repression; the ability of the actionists to keep the struggle nonviolent; the presence and quality of effective leadership; and the degree to which the nonviolent group controls its own sources of power (for instance, the degree to which they have alternative organizations to bypass repressive governmental institutions and the degree to which the former can work together).

In his book *Civilian-based Defense*, Sharp added some items to those listed above. Some refer specifically to civilian-based defense, and others apply more generally to nonviolent action as a whole. These factors include: the desire of the subordinate group to resist; the internal strength of the subordinate group; knowledge of nonviolent theory and methods; the skill of the nonviolent resisters in applying the technique; and the degree of sympathy and support for the resisters from third parties.

Other hypotheses concerning the effectiveness of nonviolent action include those of McCarthy, Bond, Kuper, Oppenheimer, and Wehr. McCarthy agreed with Sharp that nonviolent action is a struggle. Therefore, he argued, strategy and tactics "assume immense importance."[77] Also important to success are an understanding of the technique, personal commitment, creativity, and spontaneity. Of these four, he implied that understanding of the technique is of highest importance. The latter three

> alone, or backed only by false assumptions about the technique, . . . have led to avoidable suffering and failures and to premature abandonment of nonviolent means. Evidence is mounting that knowledge of the technique contributes to success.[78]

He cited Kruegler[79] as the source of such evidence. Other factors contributing to success, McCarthy suggested, include knowledge of the opponents' strong and weak points, clarity about goals, the opponents' position, and their likely response.

Most other academic analyses of effectiveness have been done through individual case studies. A few are worth noting because of the explicit hypotheses they make. For instance, Oppenheimer listed six independent variables that are likely to affect the outcome of nonviolent resistance efforts.[80] Much of this was drawn from Kuper's analysis of racial conflict in South Africa.[81] The six variables are as follows.

1. *Relative size of opposing groups.* Contrary to Sharp, Kuper and Oppenheimer argued that nonviolence is usually more successful if the subordinate group is relatively small. If it is large, they postulated, fear within the dominant group will increase and social change will become more difficult. Further, even nonviolent techniques will be perceived by the dominant group to be violent because the scale on which they are used pose such a serious threat.

2. *The differences in culture of opposing groups.* If cultural differences are great, Oppenheimer asserted, the nonviolent challenge group will be perceived as "foreign, strange, subhuman or uncivilized."[82] Common religion or culture will facilitate communication with the dominant group and will also facilitate Lakey's "persuasion."

3. *Differences in culture within the subordinate group.* If "leaders use techniques [that are] strange to the masses . . . [then there is a danger that] they may get a 'crackpot' reputation among potential followers."[83] Even without such problems, significant cultural differences within the subordinate group would make the sense of group identity and cohesiveness more difficult to maintain.

4. *Threshold of resistance.* Persuasion or conversion through voluntary or unmerited suffering is a common tactic of philosophically motivated nonviolent resisters. Oppenheimer and Kuper suggested that the success of this approach varies according to the "threshold of resistance" of the dominant group. This threshold will be higher if:

a. The dominant group's culture places a premium on violence. If so, nonviolence may be seen as cowardice or contemptible behavior.
b. The dominant group perceives the nonviolent group as inherently inferior or nonhuman (as was true for blacks in South Africa or Jews in Nazi Germany). Then even voluntary suffering may be seen as merited.
c. The dominant group sees voluntary suffering as "ill-willed masochism" and hence deserved.[84]
d. The dominant group has a monopoly on violence and thinks that constitutes a monopoly on power. Sharp maintained that such a

view, though common, is clearly wrong and can be overcome with political jiu-jitsu. However, Oppenheimer suggested that a monopoly on violence may lead the dominant group to feel that its "prerogative should never be challenged, hence any voluntary suffering undertaken by the subordinate group is seen as a usurpation of the ruler's function" (and hence, is not to be tolerated).[85]

e. The suffering is not very visible. Totalitarian regimes can easily block media coverage of self-suffering or otherwise prevent the nonviolent actionists' message from getting to the people.

f. The dominant group is simply resistant. Some societies may be more tolerant of the suffering of others, hence willing to hold out or continue to inflict violence upon the sufferers until they finally give up.

5. *Attack versus defense.* Nonviolence was seen by both Oppenheimer and Kuper to work better offensively (that is, to change existing customs) than defensively (to prevent alteration of the status quo). The literature does suggest, however, that this principle may not apply to civilian-based defense.[86]

6. *Psychological differentials.* Some populations, Kuper and Oppenheimer asserted, may be more psychologically fit for nonviolent action than others. Those populations would include cultures that tend to repress or sublimate hostility and aggression. Cultures that permit or encourage violent response to aggression are less likely to be successful nonviolent resisters. (Although this hypothesis seems intuitively obvious, it has been challenged by other analysts, for instance, Zielonka—discussed below.)

Another analysis, done by Wehr, analyzed Norwegian and Czechoslovakian nonviolent resistance to occupation.[87] The success of such resistance, Wehr wrote, depends on the following factors.

1. *Perception of the invaders as the enemy.* A strong in-group/out-group dichotomy is essential, Wehr argued, to maintain a nonviolent resistance to occupation. Other analysts of civilian-based defense have agreed. Boserup and Mack, for instance, used this reasoning to support the idea that negative influence techniques (for example, noncooperation and nonviolent intervention) are much more successful for civilian defense than are positive (that is, integrative) techniques that tend to break down the in-group/out-group distinction.[88]

2. *Clear leadership.* In order to be successful, the nonviolent resistance must have on-site, clearly identifiable, legitimate, and popular leadership. Without such leadership, organization of strategy and tactics becomes very difficult, as does maintenance of the opposition group itself.

3. *Effective communication.* The leadership must have access to an effective communication system. This communication system is important for the development and maintenance of the leaders' authority. All social

movements, Wehr observed, can be viewed as developmental processes by which "communications networks are modified and built—to mobilize and sustain popular resistance."[89]

4. *Interpersonal communication networks.* In addition to the mass media, strong interpersonal communication networks can also help resistance movements considerably. These networks operate even when access to mass media is blocked, and they not only work to transmit information but also help to integrate the resistance movement.

5. *Clarification of indigenous values.* Military occupation by outside forces, according to Wehr, creates a "temporary anomie" in which traditional, indigenous values and norms may become questioned or ill defined.[90] Resistance values must be redefined and reactivated and norms of acceptable behavior must be established under the new conditions, so that resisters know what they should and should not do in response to changing circumstances and demands.

6. *Resistance of subnational organizations.* Resistance activities undertaken by voluntary and professional associations as well as professional groupings within organizations help to "merge sub-group and national identities and loyalties and activate them on behalf of [the] resistance."[91] These activities also contribute to the resistance communications and decisionmaking systems.

7. *Geographical, political, and sociocultural factors.* Variations in these factors can determine both the propensity for nonviolent resistance to develop and also the group's ability to maintain discipline and organization and eventually succeed in achieving its goals. Among the factors listed (drawn specifically from the Czechoslovakian and Norwegian cases) are literacy, behavior of the occupying force, character of the social structure, cultural propensity toward violence, and the futility of armed resistance.[92]

A third case of interest is Zielonka's study of nonviolence in Poland. One of his main concerns was why Solidarity chose nonviolence over violence in its struggle for social change, despite several factors militating against the use of nonviolence.

> Violence abounds in modern Polish history, and the Polish people have given widespread support to armed resistance, especially where it counters military invasion by a foreign power. One could even say that armed resistance was, in a way, cultivated by Polish culture and tradition. For instance, although during World War II there were many examples of civil disobedience and the successful application of various nonviolent actions by the Poles, the *armed* opposition to the Nazis enjoyed the greatest esteem and the support of the Polish population. The postwar history of social upheavals [in Poland] is also discouraging from the perspective of nonviolence.[93]

A second factor discouraging nonviolence is that "deep philosophical considerations about nonviolence never developed in Poland, and only a few examples of direct identification with the tradition of nonviolence can be found."[94] However, the lack of a tradition of nonviolence in Poland "does not differ dramatically from other historical cases of nonviolent action. Both Gandhi's India and Thoreau's America have rich traditions of violence."[95]

Zielonka attributed Solidarity's use of nonviolence to three factors: tactical considerations, doctrinal issues, and ethics. The most important tactical consideration was the belief that violent resistance would dramatically increase casualties, without bringing Solidarity closer to its objectives. Nonviolence was chosen, in a sense, because it was the only option left.

Second, Zielonka noted, "Solidarity's struggle is aimed at the creation of a political system based on self-government and grassroots participation. . . . From the doctrinal point of view, Solidarity could not use a means of struggle that would contradict its social goals."[96]

Third, Solidarity's choice of nonviolence was closely associated with the Christian concepts of love and social justice, promoted by Pope John Paul II and parish priests across Poland. Although these factors are case specific, Zielonka suggested that explanations for nonviolence must include social, ideological, and tactical factors that are far more important in the choice of nonviolence over violence than are history and tradition. These conclusions were echoed by Crow and Grant in their analysis of nonviolence in the Middle East.[97] Nonviolent struggle is not commonly associated with the Middle East, but it has been used occasionally with success and has been a primary tactic of the intifada.

Although a few in the Middle East, notably Mubarak Awad,[98] have advocated nonviolence out of principle, its use has been mostly practical: It was the only choice available that was consistent with the intifada's long-term goals. Like Solidarity before it, the intifada is working toward self-determination. Nonviolence has strengthened grassroots participation and self-reliance and may better prepare the Palestinians for autonomy than could violence. As Grant wrote:

> One of the most remarkable accomplishments of the *Intifada* has been the growth of confidence among Palestinians in their ability to resist the occupation. The practical experience in standing up to the Israelis has significantly contributed to a growing sense of "nationhood," which in turn has led to important changes in Palestinian political, social, and economic relations. . . . [As] in other popular revolutions, the success of the struggle has created a practical understanding of the meaning of "citizenship" in an emerging Palestinian state.[99]

The intifada, Grant stated, has altered social relations between the sexes, parents, and children as well as between traditional leaders and followers.

Women, children, and "ordinary people" have been empowered and have become more independent of traditional leadership. The intifada has also increasingly developed functional indigenous organizations to supplant Israeli institutions.

In analyzing the future of the intifada, Grant listed several factors necessary for the success of that or similar movements. These factors include: (1) the conviction that nonviolent struggle, alone, can succeed; (2) a disciplined leadership capable of quelling spontaneous violence; (3) strategic thinking; (4) development of functioning, indigenous institutions capable of supporting resistance and fulfilling societal needs; and (5) an understanding of how nonviolence works and its likely effects on target populations. Writing in 1990, Grant thought these elements were not sufficiently strong for the intifada to succeed.

Still, the pursuit of nonviolence was far preferable to further violent struggle. As noted by Ibrahim,

> although nonviolent political struggle has been less sensational [than the violent conflicts in the Middle East], it has proven at least as effective as armed struggle in resolving conflicts in the region. The fact that violent means have settled no major Middle Eastern conflicts of the last four decades strengthens the case for serious examination of an alternative nonviolent course.[100]

Although one might argue that the 1991 Gulf War did temporarily settle one conflict, its costs were so heavy and so many problems were left unresolved that the case for nonviolence in the Middle East remains strong.

In his analysis of the Solidarity movement, Zielonka critiqued the strategies and tactics it used from 1980 to 1985. He suggested that some nonviolent sanctions can actually be counterproductive for the goals of the action group. Others, although "successful" in the sense of being well organized and increasing popular support, will not meet even the group's short-term objectives. Thus, nonviolent actionists must consider their choice of tactics carefully. He noted that much more research is needed to determine appropriate sanctions for particular circumstances and objectives. This research will require examination of successful and unsuccessful uses of various sanctions, their long- and short-term costs and benefits, and the complex relationship between the sanctions, strategies, and objectives of the nonviolent resister.[101] The task is huge but a necessary next step in building nonviolence analysis and theory. This book, we hope, is part of that theory-building process.

Notes

1. Sharp, *The Politics of Nonviolent Action,* Part I, Part II, Part III.
2. Folger, *The Sense of Injustice*; Reis, "The Multidimensionality of Justice."

3. Adams, "Inequity in Social Exchange."
4. Folger, *The Sense of Injustice.*
5. Sampson, "Studies in Status Congruence."
6. Deutsch, "Equity, Equality, and Need."
7. Reis, "The Multidimensionality of Justice," p. 38.
8. Bondurant, *Conquest of Violence*, p. 9.
9. Sharp, *The Politics of Nonviolent Action*, Part III, p. 609.
10. Boulding, *Three Faces of Power.*
11. Ibid., p. 25.
12. Ibid., p. 27.
13. Fisher and Ury, *Getting to Yes.*
14. Boserup and Mack, *War Without Weapons.*
15. Boulding, *Three Faces of Power*, p. 29.
16. Ibid., p. 109.
17. Festinger, *Theory of Cognitive Dissonance.*
18. Oppenheimer, "Towards a Sociological Understanding of Nonviolence," p. 123.
19. Stiehm, *Nonviolent Power*, p. 19.
20. Seifert, *Conquest by Suffering.*
21. Gandhi, "Non-Violence," p. 95.
22. Oppenheimer, "Towards a Sociological Understanding of Nonviolence."
23. Despite their philosophical statements favoring conversion over coercion, many advocates of principled nonviolence, including Gandhi and King, on occasion advocated or used at least mild coercion in their campaigns. However, a strong preference for what we will later call integrative techniques distinguishes most principled nonviolence advocates from the pragmatic school of nonviolence, which relies much more heavily on coercion to bring about social change.
24. Gandhi, "Non-Violence," p. 94.
25. Holmes, *Nonviolence in Theory and Practice.*
26. See Stiehm, *Nonviolent Power*; Holmes, *Nonviolence in Theory and Practice*; Kuper, *Passive Resistance in South Africa*; Seifert, *Conquest by Suffering.*
27. Sharp, *The Politics of Nonviolent Action*, Part II.
28. Stiehm, *Nonviolent Power.*
29. Sharp, *The Politics of Nonviolent Action*, Part I.
30. Ibid.
31. Ibid.
32. King, "Letter from a Birmingham Jail," p. 69.
33. Sharp, *The Politics of Nonviolent Action*, Part I.
34. Stiehm, *Nonviolent Power.*
35. Sharp, *The Politics of Nonviolent Action*, Part I.
36. Stiehm, *Nonviolent Power.*
37. Sharp, *The Politics of Nonviolent Action*, Part III.
38. Sharp, *The Politics of Nonviolent Action*, Part III; Bond, Chapter 4 in this book.
39. McCarthy, "The Techniques of Nonviolent Action."
40. Kuper, *Passive Resistance in South Africa*; Seifert, *Conquest by Suffering.*
41. Sharp, *The Politics of Nonviolent Action*, Part II.
42. Miller, *Nonviolence: A Christian Interpretation.*
43. Sharp, *Civilian-based Defense.*
44. This distinction seems very similar to her first categorization scheme, although she maintains they are different.
45. McCarthy, "The Techniques of Nonviolent Action."
46. Ibid., p. 116.
47. Boserup and Mack, *War Without Weapons.*

48. Sharp, *The Politics of Nonviolent Action,* Part I.
49. Ibid.
50. Sharp, *The Politics of Nonviolent Action,* Part II.
51. Gregg, *The Power of Nonviolence.*
52. Ibid., p. 44.
53. Sharp, *The Politics of Nonviolent Action,* Part II, pp. 111–113.
54. Ibid.
55. Ibid., pp. 357–358.
56. Sharp, *The Politics of Nonviolent Action,* Part II.
57. See Bond, Chapter 4 in this book.
58. Sharp, *The Politics of Nonviolent Action,* Part III, p. 706.
59. Sharp, *Civilian-based Defense.*
60. Lakey, "The Mechanisms of Nonviolent Action," p. 385.
61. Ibid., p. 388.
62. Bond, Chapter 4 in this volume.
63. Rummel, *Understanding Conflict and War*; Rummel, *The Conflict Helix Principles.*
64. Boserup and Mack, *War Without Weapons.*
65. Gandhi, "Non-Violence," p. 96.
66. Meyerding, "Reclaiming Nonviolence."
67. Woerhle, *Social Constructions of Power.*
68. Bell and Kurtz, *Social Theory and Nonviolent Revolutions.*
69. Woehrle, *Social Constructions of Power and Empowerment,* p. 3.
70. Ibid.
71. Bell and Kurtz, *Social Theory and Nonviolent Revolutions.*
72. Ibid.
73. Ibid, p. 7.
74. Sharp's major work, *The Politics of Nonviolent Action,* represents years of research and uses a huge volume of case study data analyzed with largely qualitative methods. Doug Bond, research director at Harvard's Program on Nonviolent Sanctions, is now undertaking an equally massive quantitative study of mechanisms of action and change. However, the project is proceeding slowly, and findings are not yet available.
75. McCarthy, "The Techniques of Nonviolent Action," p. 117.
76. Sharp, *Civilian-based Defense.*
77. McCarthy, "The Techniques of Nonviolent Action."
78. Ibid., p. 111.
79. Kruegler, "Implications of Prototypical Nonviolent Resistance."
80. Oppenheimer, "Towards a Sociological Understanding of Nonviolence."
81. Kuper, *Passive Resistance in South Africa.*
82. Oppenheimer, "Towards a Sociological Understanding of Nonviolence."
83. Ibid., p. 129.
84. Ibid., p. 129.
85. Ibid., p. 129.
86. Sharp, *Civilian-based Defense.*
87. Wehr, "Nonviolent Resistance to Occupation."
88. Boserup and Mack, *War Without Weapons.*
89. Wehr, "Nonviolent Resistance to Occupation," p. 217.
90. Ibid., p. 227.
91. Ibid., p. 227.
92. Ibid., p. 227.
93. Zielonka, "Strengths and Weaknesses of Nonviolent Action," p. 93.

94. Ibid., p. 93.
95. Ibid., p. 93.
96. Ibid., p. 95.
97. Crow and Grant, "Questions and Controversies About Nonviolent Struggle."
98. Awad, "Nonviolent Resistance."
99. Grant, "Nonviolent Political Struggle."
100. Ibrahim, "Why Nonviolent Political Struggle?"
101. Zielonka, "Strengths and Weaknesses of Nonviolent Action," p. 103.

Bibliography

Adams, J. S. "Inequity in Social Exchange," in L. Berkowitz (ed.), *Advances in Experimental Social Psychology* (New York: Academic Press, 1965).
Awad, Mubarak E. "Nonviolent Resistance: A Strategy for the Occupied Territories," in Robert L. Holmes (ed.), *Nonviolence in Theory and Practice* (Belmont, CA: Wadsworth Publishing Co., 1990).
Bell, Nancy, and Lester R. Kurtz. *Social Theory and Nonviolent Revolutions: Rethinking Domination and Rebellion* (Austin, TX: University of Texas at Austin Press, 1992).
Bondurant, Joan V. *Conquest of Violence: The Gandhian Philosophy of Conflict* (New Revised Edition) (Princeton, NJ: Princeton University Press, 1988).
Boserup, Anders, and Andrew Mack. *War Without Weapons: Non-Violence in National Defence* (New York: Schocken Books, 1975).
Boulding, Kenneth. *Three Faces of Power* (Newbury Park, CA: Sage Publications, 1989).
Crow, Ralph E., and Philip Grant. "Questions and Controversies About Nonviolent Struggle in the Middle East," in Ralph E. Crow, Philip Grant, and Saad E. Ibrahim (eds.), *Arab Nonviolent Political Struggle in the Middle East* (Boulder, CO: Lynne Rienner Publishers, 1990).
Deutsch, M. "Equity, Equality, and Need: What Determines Which Value Will Be Used as the Basis of Distributive Justice?" *Journal of Social Issues* 31 (1975): 137–149.
Festinger, Leon. *Theory of Cognitive Dissonance* (Stanford: Stanford University Press, 1962, 1957).
Fisher, Roger, and William Ury. *Getting to Yes: Negotiating Agreement Without Giving In* (Boston: Beacon Press, 1981).
Folger, Robert (ed.). *The Senses of Injustice: Social Psychological Perspectives* (New York: Plenum Press, 1984).
Gandhi, Mohandas K. "Non-Violence," in Jeffrie G. Murphy (ed.), *Civil Disobedience and Violence* (Belmont, CA: Wadsworth Publishing Co., 1971).
Grant, Philip. "Nonviolent Political Struggle in the Occupied Territories," in Ralph E. Crow, Philip Grant, and Saad E. Ibrahim (eds.), *Arab Nonviolent Political Struggle in the Middle East* (Boulder, CO: Lynne Rienner Publishers, 1990).
Gregg, Richard B. *The Power of Nonviolence, Revised Edition* (New York: Schocken Books, 1966).
Holmes, Robert L. (ed.). *Nonviolence in Theory and Practice* (Belmont, CA: Wadsworth Publishing Co, 1990).
Homans, G. C. "Commentary," in L. Berkowitz (ed.), *Advances in Experimental Social Psychology* (New York: Academic Press, 1965).
Ibrahim, Saad E. "Why Nonviolent Political Struggle in the Middle East?" in Ralph E. Crow, Philip Grant, and Saad E. Ibrahim (eds.), *Arab Nonviolent*

Political Struggle in the Middle East (Boulder, CO: Lynne Rienner Publishers, 1990).

King, Martin Luther, Jr. "Letter from a Birmingham Jail," in Robert L. Holmes (ed.), *Nonviolence in Theory and Practice* (Belmont, CA: Wadsworth Publishing Co, 1990).

Kruegler, Christopher. "Implications of Prototypical Nonviolent Resistance for the Conduct of Civilian-Based Defense." Paper presented at the annual convention of the International Studies Association, 1987.

Kuper, Leo. *Passive Resistance in South Africa* (New Haven: Yale University Press, 1957).

Lakey, George. "The Mechanisms of Nonviolent Action," in A. Paul Hare and Herbert H. Blumberg (eds.), *Nonviolent Direct Action American Cases: Socio-Psychological Analyses* (Washington, DC: Corpus Books, 1968).

Lerner, M. J. "The Justice Motive: Some Hypotheses as to Its Origins and Forms." *Journal of Personality* 45 (1977): 1–52.

Mark, M. M. *Justice in the Aggregate: The Perceived Fairness of the Distribution of Income* (Ph.D. diss., Northwestern University, 1980).

McCarthy, Ronald M. "The Techniques of Nonviolent Action: Some Principles of Its Nature, Use, and Effects," in Ralph E. Crow, Philip Grant, and Saad E. Ibrahim (eds.), *Arab Nonviolent Political Struggle in the Middle East* (Boulder, CO: Lynne Rienner Publishers, 1990).

Meyerding, Jane. "Reclaiming Nonviolence: Some Thoughts for Feminist Womyn Who Used to Be Nonviolent, and Vice Versa," in Pam McCallister (ed.), *Reweaving the Web of Life: Feminism and Nonviolence* (Philadelphia: New Society Publishers, 1982).

Miller, William Robert. *Nonviolence: A Christian Interpretation* (New York: Schocken Books, 1966).

Oppenheimer, Martin. "Towards a Sociological Understanding of Nonviolence." *Sociological Inquiry* 35 (1965): 123–131.

Pruitt, D. G. "Methods for Resolving Differences of Interest: A Theoretical Analysis." *Journal of Social Issues* 28 (1972): 133–154.

Reis, Harry T. "The Multidimensionality of Justice," in Robert Folger (ed.), *The Senses of Injustice: Social Psychological Perspectives* (New York: Plenum Press, 1984).

Rummel, R. J. *Understanding Conflict and War: Volume 2, The Conflict Helix* (New York: John Wiley and Sons, Halsted Press Division, 1976).

————. *The Conflict Helix: Principles and Practices of Interpersonal, Social, and International Conflict and Cooperation* (New Brunswick, NJ, Transaction, 1991; originally published in 1984).

Sampson, E. E. "Studies in Status Congruence," in L. Berkowitz (ed.), *Advances in Experimental Social Psychology* (New York: Academic Press, 1965).

Seifert, Harvey. *Conquest by Suffering: The Process and Prospects of Nonviolent Resistance* (Philadelphia: Westminster Press, 1965).

Sharp, Gene. *The Politics of Nonviolent Action* (Boston, MA: Extending Horizon Books, Porter Sargent Publishers, 1973).

————. *Civilian-based Defense: A Post-Military Weapons System* (Princeton: Princeton University Press, 1990).

————. "The Role of Power in Nonviolent Political Struggle," in Ralph E. Crow, Philip Grant, and Saad E. Ibrahim (eds.), *Arab Nonviolent Political Struggle in the Middle East* (Boulder, CO: Lynne Rienner Publishers, 1990).

Stiehm, Judith. *Nonviolent Power: Active and Passive Resistance in America* (Lexington, MA, and Toronto: D.C. Heath and Company, 1972).

Wehr, Paul. "Nonviolent Resistance to Occupation: Norway and Czechoslovakia," in S. Bruyn and P. Raman (eds.), *Nonviolent Action and Social Change* (Irvington, NY: Wiley, 1979).

Woehrle, Lynne M. *Social Constructions of Power and Empowerment: Thoughts from Feminist Approaches to Peace Research and Peace-making* (Syracuse: Syracuse University Press, 1992).

Zielonka, Jan. "Strengths and Weaknesses of Nonviolent Action: The Polish Case." *Orbis* 30 (Spring 1986): 91-110.

2

Research Questions
and Hypotheses

Guy Burgess & Heidi Burgess

From the preceding review of the literature, and especially Boulding's theory of power, we developed a set of questions and hypotheses to form the basis for this research effort. These initial questions and hypotheses fall into several categories that were further developed and expanded during the course of the project. Our initial categories, questions, and hypotheses are delineated in this chapter.

Nature of the Injustice

The literature suggests that injustice can take several forms. One distinction is between economic injustice and political injustice. Economic injustice exists when there is a large disparity of wealth and income within a society. This situation can be further subdivided into cases in which poverty is a function of the maldistribution of the wealth of society and cases in which the society has little wealth to distribute overall. (Technically, this might not be considered injustice, as everyone is poor together. This may be true, but the people suffering usually consider the situation to be unjust, nevertheless.)

Political injustice, involves what we in the West usually mean when we speak of injustice—such things as voting rights, due process, freedom of speech and religion, and protection from cruel and unusual punishments. Although the literature does not directly address the implications of these differences for nonviolence, we should ask whether some types of injustice are more easily addressed with nonviolence than are others. We would hypothesize, for instance, that nonviolence would not be as successful against society-wide poverty as it would be against the other two types of injustice because, in the former case, the dominant group does not have the power or the resources to remedy the situation, even if it wants to.

Characteristics of the Dominant and Subordinate Groups

Relative power. The initial relative power of protest and dominant groups is clearly important, though the direction of the effect is unclear. Small, relatively powerless protest groups are likely to be viewed by the dominant group as harmless. The latter may, therefore, conclude that efforts to repress these protests are not worth the trouble. On the other hand, if protest groups are stronger, they may invite repression. But they may also be more likely to generate the power necessary for success.

Dominant group power base. Another likely determinant of the success of various nonviolent strategies is the nature of the dominant group's power. To what extent does it rely upon popular support? Widely believed moral principles? Violent repression? Outside military or economic support? Although none of these bases of power are unassailable, they imply different "Achilles heels," which should be targeted by nonviolent actionists for greatest impact.

Legitimacy. One factor that appears to be an extremely important aspect of power is legitimacy—for both the dominant group and the subordinate group. If a group's leaders, structure, policies, and actions are viewed as legitimate by most of their members, this is likely to contribute greatly to their power and effectiveness. On the other hand, weak legitimacy is likely to be detrimental to effective action.

Thus, we hypothesize, nonviolent action will likely be more effective when the challenge group leader(s), goals, and tactics are viewed as legitimate—both by the group's members and by outside third parties. Likewise, if a dominant group's leaders, policies, or actions are viewed as illegitimate by much of the population, this factor will detract from the dominant group's power and make them more vulnerable to a nonviolent challenge.

Sources of support. Successful resistance is also likely to depend upon the subordinate group's sources of support. Does it include only the victims of injustice or does it include sympathizers within powerful elements of the unjust society, outside powers, or international legal and political structures? To the extent such external sources of support or power can be mobilized, the higher the chances are for the challenge group's success. Likewise, is the dominant regime supported by outside powers or other external sources of support? If it is, this is likely to make it more difficult to challenge successfully. If these outside sources of support can be removed, however, then a nonviolent resistance is more likely to succeed.

Commitment. The strength of virtually all subordinate groups lies in collective action. Collective resistance, however, requires broadly based, grassroots support. This fact suggests a hypothesis that effective resistance only occurs when commitment to resistance is intense and widespread.

Organizational skills. Nonviolent actions tend to involve large numbers of people. As such, the probability of their success is likely to depend on strong organizational skills, including the ability to plan, the ability to influence and control the membership, and the ability to resolve internal conflicts. To the extent that a challenge group has such skills, its likelihood of success should be greater; to the extent they are lacking, the likelihood of success is expected to diminish.

Historical Context

History of previous nonviolent action and/or awareness of nonviolence options. We would expect nonviolent resistance to be similar to other complex human activities with respect to learning from the past. If a culture or a group within a society has used nonviolent action successfully in the past, it might be expected that they would choose such a strategy again. Likewise, if they had only relied on violence in past struggles, it seems less likely that the group or culture would turn to nonviolence in their future conflicts—unless, of course, the past violence had been unsuccessful at achieving their goals, or was considered too costly in terms of human suffering. In that case a group might, indeed, turn to nonviolence for the first time.

In such cases, the awareness of others' efforts in nonviolent action and a thorough understanding of how such actions work are likely to contribute to success. Without such understanding, the subordinate group would be forced to reinvent not only the wheel, but the entire automobile. Under such circumstances they can be expected to create a much lower performance machine.

Credibility of nonviolent alternatives. The probability of successful nonviolent resistance may also depend upon the degree to which the potential success of these options has been demonstrated. People believe that military confrontation works—even though a large percentage of military campaigns are unsuccessful. In the case of military endeavors, most people assume that any failure is attributable to either inadequate force or poor tactics—never the inherent limitations of violent confrontation.

All too often, the failure of nonviolent resistance is interpreted in the opposite way. Failure is seen to result from the inherent limitations of the technique, rather than simply poor tactics or inadequate power mobilization. This perception suggests that nonviolent resistance is more likely to succeed where subordinate groups are convinced of the inherent power of nonviolence and are, therefore, willing to be persistent in their efforts to build their base of power and identify the most effective tactics, even after initial "defeat."

Culture gap. It is easier to repress people if they are seen to be significantly different from oneself. Perception of difference tends to make it easier to justify unequal treatment. This view suggests that nonviolent resisters are likely to benefit from efforts to minimize the differences between themselves and the opposing group—to encourage the opponents to see the commonalities between them. It may further suggest that nonviolent resistance is more likely to be successful within rather than across racial or ethnic lines because perceptions of such differences seem to be very deeply ingrained in many people.

Structural Factors

Structural factors in the society, independent of the action group, are also likely to have significant effects on the success of particular nonviolent actions. Some social structures are likely to inhibit successful nonviolent action; others might enhance it. At the same time, corrupt and inefficient regimes may simply collapse under their own weight—without requiring subordinate groups to mount an effective challenge. Such passive change may be without violence, but it is not the result of power mobilized through nonviolent action.

Protest Group Objectives

The objectives of protest groups can also be expected to have a profound effect on the success of any resistance effort. Those whose objective is vengeance—death (or at least exile) for the oppressors—have, by seeking a violent resolution, abandoned nonviolence in favor of a fight to the death. Even those who nonviolently seek what amounts to an exchange of elites (with the deportation or subjugation of the dominant group) are likely to find their opponents willing to do whatever it takes to resist them. Our hypothesis, then, is that those who offer a vision of a more just society that offers the dominant group a livable alternative have real advantages over the group that advocates revenge or elimination of the group currently in power.

Tactical Considerations

Principled versus practical nonviolence. Commitment to nonviolence can be based on moral principles or pragmatic necessity. Although most of the literature in the field addresses principled nonviolence, we suspect that nonviolence will be most appealing to those attracted by its pragmatic effectiveness. A similar hypothesis is that those practicing nonviolence would do well to understand the pragmatic "nuts and bolts" of how and when nonviolence works best, rather than taking its superiority as given and pursuing a particular strategy or tactic on the basis of principle or faith alone. However, a reverse argument could be made that only those who believe in principled nonviolence will be willing to stick with the approach long enough to attain success. Others are more likely to be quickly deterred by one or two short-term setbacks, and revert to violence before they give nonviolence an adequate chance to succeed.

Resistance triggers. Effective resistance requires that people actively challenge social relationships that have often been accepted (though resented) for long periods of time. How does this happen? Does it require some sort of triggering event or sequence of events, which causes people who have accepted their condition before to suddenly (or not so suddenly) rebel? If triggers are necessary (or just helpful), what is their nature? Do they involve specific instances of outrage on the part of the dominant group? Or, perhaps, the emergence of a charismatic leader? Or the alteration of external public opinion or pressure?

Dependency. Another likely determinant of success is dependency—the degree to which the dominant group is dependent on the subordinate group and vice versa. Are there things that the subordinate group can withhold that are sufficiently important to the dominant group to persuade it to change its ways? Is the subordinate group sufficiently independent that it can function successfully if the dominant group withholds certain important services and functions? For instance, does it have its own system of communication or does it rely on the dominant media? Has it developed parallel social and political structures, independent of those of mainstream society? To the extent that it has, the more likely the resistance is to succeed.

Power-with versus power-over. The literature suggests that it will be easier to achieve broad-based grassroots support with the "power-with" rather than the "power-over" philosophy, as the "power-over" approach is likely to generate much more resistance from the dominant group. It may also be more likely to initiate conflicts within the protest group, over questions about who is going to have power over whom, should the protest succeed.

Protest strategy and tactics. Sharp identified almost two hundred types of nonviolent action. Which ones are being used under what circumstances? How does the type of action affect possible success?

Planned versus spontaneous actions. To what extent are the nonviolent actions planned or spontaneous? To the extent that actions are planned, how do the plans differ from what actually occurred? What caused the difference? Do spontaneous actions or planned actions work better?

Protest powers. The type of power relied upon by protest groups is also likely to be important. Possibilities include violent, economic, or political threats or sanctions; economic and political trade-offs; and moral appeals. We hypothesize that a mix of all three is likely to be most successful, although the mix, we suspect, should include a stronger portion of integrative power than threat power, especially when the parties must continue to live together over the long term.

Bandwagon effect. Another possible determinant of success is what might be called the "bandwagon effect." We hypothesize that once the power of the resistance reaches a critical threshold, people start to believe that change is really going to happen. At this point members of the dominant group are likely to forsake the old order and attempt to assume the mantle of "reformers." Others, who had either been neutral or had opposed the dominant regime but had been unwilling to assume the risks of protest, are likely to decide that the risks aren't so great after all and that it surely would be better to be on the winning side.

Dominant Group's Responses

Dominant group ability to remedy injustice. We suggested earlier that nonviolence is more likely to succeed when the dominant group has the power to remedy the injustice. For example, if economic injustice is the result of a failed economy that simply has no wealth to distribute, it is unlikely that nonviolence will be able to remedy that situation—except, perhaps, over the very long term, by bringing about massive system change (as is being attempted in the former Soviet Union).

Violent response. If the dominant group responds to nonviolent challengers with violence, does this effectively repress the nonviolence or is it likely to further encourage it, due to people's outrage at the violent response? What is the best way for a challenge group to deal with a violent response?

No response. If the dominant group simply ignores the nonviolent challenge, will it discourage it? Or will it encourage the challengers to intensify their actions in order to get a response? What is the best way for the challenge group to deal with no response at all from the dominant group?

Measures of Success

A step-by-step process. Nonviolent resistance, like most everything else, is a step-by-step process. Its success should, therefore, be assessed by a number of intermediate criteria in addition to its ability to deliver final victory. These intermediate measures of success include both process goals (being able to effectively carry out a nonviolent action efficiently) and short-term objectives (such as gaining members, getting media attention, or winning the support of powerful outside groups). Such intermediate goals are crucial to establishing the sense of confidence critical to building the bandwagon effect. Nonviolent groups that initially set their goals too high are likely to become frustrated and ineffective.

Long-term stability. Success is often measured over the short term because that is most obvious. But long-term effects are also important. How effective has each approach been in motivating short- and long-term change? How effective is each likely to be in the future? What determines the probable effectiveness of alternative approaches over the long term?

Change mechanisms. It is also important to determine which of Sharp's four mechanisms of social change—conversion, coercion, accommodation, or disintegration—are most likely to result from nonviolent action and most likely to produce stable, long-term change.

All of the contributors to this volume started with this list of questions and hypotheses. They then examined those that were most important for or best illustrated by their particular cases. As readers will see from the synthesis—Chapter 13—the project has made significant progress toward answering many, but not all, of these questions. Further progress will require refinement and testing of specific hypotheses and expansion of the underlying knowledge base with quantitative and qualitative studies.

3

Peace, Justice, and the Faces of Power

Kenneth E. Boulding

> Peace, of course, is more than the mere absence of war. Achieving peace
> also means eliminating starvation, poverty, violence, threats to human
> rights, refugee problems, global environmental pollution, and the many
> other threats to peace, and it means creating a climate in which people
> can live rich and rewarding lives.
> —*City of Hiroshima Peace Declaration, August 6, 1991*

There have been some attempts to create measures of overall human welfare, but they are all inadequate. Nevertheless, the concept, in a qualitative
sense, cannot be dismissed, and we could visualize a kind of field of
human welfare around the globe, with contour lines (or isomers) showing
various peaks and troughs. We could similarly imagine a measure of the
probability of violence, based perhaps on the number of violent deaths, in-
juries, and damage to property. A similar contour map of the average expectation of life would be fairly measurable and feasible. It might perhaps
be regarded as a map of the original concept of "structural violence."[1] The
peaks in the probability-of-violence map would undoubtedly show some
correspondence with the troughs of the human welfare map, though the correspondence would be by no means perfect. Nevertheless, areas like Northern Ireland, Lebanon, northern Sri Lanka, Bhutan, Ethiopia, Mozambique,
Burundi, El Salvador, Nicaragua, parts of Peru, and certain sections of New
York and Washington, D.C., would show up as peaks in the violence field
and troughs in human welfare. There would be troughs in the violence field
in, say, Switzerland, Wales, New Zealand, Japan, and so on, which also
might correspond very well to peaks in the human welfare field.

What then makes for a peak in the violence field? To misquote the fa-
mous statement from the Charter of UNESCO, "Violence begins in the
minds of men" (and, we might add, occasionally women or even children),

and it is only in the minds of men and other humans that it can be eliminated. Many of these images in people's minds interact with each other, and with the passions and feelings, in very complex ways.

One element in the human mind that is important here is the sense of power or powerlessness. This may be only loosely related to the actual power that a person has. There are many people who have very little power, especially in the poorer part of the human race, who feel that the power that they have is adequate for their own lives. For such people, the rich and the powerful are remote from their own little neighborhoods, they are not bothered very much by envy, yet they live their own lives, hard as they may be, from day to day without much thought of an alternative. It is very rare for the really poor to revolt. Oddly enough, an increase in personal power for such people, through some kind of economic development, for instance, may actually result in an increased sense of powerlessness as alternatives to their present style of life come more clearly into view. This is not, however, likely to lead to violence unless the source of powerlessness can be identified and is in some way within reach. People who feel "pushed around" are more likely to identify a pusher. This may lead to alienation.

It is one of Marx's central concepts that the development of a labor market and full-time employment of an employee by an employer leads to alienation of the employee, simply because the employer is seen as responsible for what is felt to be an inadequate wage. As a theory of alienation, this, of course, is much too simple.

Nationalism has turned out to be a much more powerful source of personal identity than class. The workers of the world will never unite. Those who do unite in labor unions discover they have much more community with their employers than they do with the workers in other industries or with unorganized workers. The relative price structure of ultimate products is a much greater potential source of economic conflict than is the division between labor income and profit. A rise in the relative price of copper will tend to benefit all those in the copper industry at the expense of others. But the rise in the proportion of national income going to labor in the Great Depression, when profits became negative (1932 and 1933), effected an enormous redistribution of income within the working class between those who were employed and the 25 percent who were not. Similarly, there was a great redistribution within the capitalist class between interest receivers and profit receivers. A class war cannot be won by the working class, as the experience of Kampuchea shows so tragically. If all the employers are killed, the workers are worse off because production collapses.

Alienation is closely related to a sense of enmity. Alienation from "others," and especially from those perceived as enemies, may be so great that it denies all humanity to them. Why this perception develops in some cases and not in others is by no means clear. It may be that the development of enmity has something to do with the extent to which childhood experiences and the general culture of learning in a society produce "approachers," who go toward what they want, as opposed to "avoiders," who go away from what they don't want. As an economist would say, some people maximize utility and others minimize disutility.

This tendency however, can produce very different kinds of personality and behavior. Approachers tend to develop what might be called a positive identity and avoiders a negative identity. Approachers know what they like, avoiders only know what they don't like. We see this difference very strikingly in Ireland, where, in the Irish Republic, Protestants are Protestants and Catholics are Catholics, and they tolerate each other and get along fairly well. In Ulster, Northern Ireland, on the other hand, a Protestant is somebody who isn't a Catholic, and a Catholic is somebody who isn't a Protestant. It becomes easy to identify the other as an enemy around which one's own personality forms. Just what it is in a society that produces such differences, however, I confess I do not understand.

An important source of enmity may be mistrust in the sense of being deceived. There is nothing that destroys legitimacy more effectively than being caught telling a lie. How lies are perceived as such, however, is a complex process. Martin Luther's discovery that the Pope's sale of indulgences had no basis in the Christian scriptures had something to do with the success of the Lutheran Reformation. The misinformation that the Communist government fed the people of the Soviet Union became so clearly contradictory to daily reality that by 1989 all respect for the government on the part of the mass of the people had been lost.

At the other end of a spectrum of power we have something that could be called "mightiness" as a source of violence. Edward Elgar's "Pomp and Circumstance" Suite echoes this perfectly (in reference to the British Empire): "Wider, and still wider/May thy bounds be set,/God who made thee mighty,/Make thee mightier yet." The French had something of this with *la mission civilisatrice,* feeling that they were called upon to civilize those who were not fortunate enough to have been born French. Mightiness, however, can often become very expensive for the mighty and can quite suddenly collapse, as we saw in the case of the European empires and as we are seeing today in the Soviet Union. The extraordinary collapse of the legitimacy of the Communist parties, in the Soviet Union and around the world, has something to do with the fact that they made promises that were not fulfilled, so that this created mistrust and a withdrawal of legitimacy. Another factor was their belief in mightiness and a desire to change and, in a sense, to dominate the whole world. This desire again turned to dust, as did the empires.

What, then, does all this have to do with justice, freedom, peace, and all these things that are arguments in the human welfare function? Justice is a particularly complex concept. It plays an important part in the rhetoric of conflict. Nobody can possibly come out in favor of injustice. On the other hand, justice can mean very different things to different cultures and different people.

There are at least two concepts of justice that are quite different and may even be incompatible. One is the concept that people should get what they deserve. This concept raises questions, of course, as to who is to judge what people deserve. Criminal justice is perhaps the clearest example of this principle. Here the structure of laws and of courts is set up so that if people are caught breaking a law, then they should definitely deserve—and expect—some kind of punishment. What punishment for what misdemeanor or crime is frequently, though not always, spelled out in the law. Sometimes it is determined by juries or judges. If there is a general feeling that penalties are inappropriate, social processes usually exist that can change them. Whether penalties are effective in preventing criminal behavior is, of course, another question. There has been a big argument, for instance, over capital punishment. There is a good deal of evidence suggesting that its deterrent capacity is at least obscure. On the other hand, there is a considerable body of opinion in favor of capital punishment whether it deters murder or not. This opinion is due to a sense of appropriateness of the penalty.

A real economic question is, what are the circumstances under which it is cheaper to put up with crime than it is to try to prevent it by expensive punishments, like long imprisonments? The United States, for instance, has a very large proportion of its population in prison as compared to most other countries. Yet there is not much evidence that this really diminishes crime. Indeed, over the last few decades crime has risen and the expense of the whole criminal justice system has risen in about the same proportion. This increase certainly suggests that the common assumption that punishment prevents crime at least needs to be reexamined.

At the other end of the scale we have the problem of people who do not receive the benefits that they deserve, those who suffer costs that they do not deserve. Unemployment is a good example. There is no question that 25 percent unemployment in 1932 and 1933 was unjust to the unemployed, but also unjust to the employed, who were benefiting at the expense of the unemployed, and the capitalists whose profits were negative.

The other meaning of justice, sometimes called "commensal justice," going back to the principle that everybody sitting around the table should get a fair share of the food, is related to the distribution of income and wealth and suggests that beyond a certain point the inequality of economic welfare is unjust. Where this point lies, however, is not generally agreed upon. There is fairly widespread agreement in modern societies in regard to what is sometimes called a "safety net," that there is some level of economic welfare below which people should not be allowed to fall. This agreement goes back even to Queen Elizabeth I's "poor laws" in England.

This principle is usually confined to the national state. Certainly we seem to be a long way from a world safety net, even though extreme cases of famine and destitution do tend to call forth grants from richer societies to ameliorate the suffering.

Actually the proportionate distribution of income seems to be remarkably difficult to change. In the United States, for instance, it has changed very little in the last few decades, in spite of changes in tax structures and benefit payments. Poverty fell sharply in the United States between about 1950 and the mid-seventies, after which it rose slightly and then stabilized. Ironically enough, poverty stopped falling once the "War on Poverty" got underway. These problems, obviously, are not easily solved.

Another aspect of the justice problem that is difficult to deal with is what might be called the lottery of life. Certainly everybody who buys a lottery ticket demands inequality in the hope that they will benefit from it. For a lottery is certainly a device to redistribute economic welfare more unequally. There is a fair consensus that the political structure and the tax and grant system should be devised to offset, up to a point, the lottery of life, to tax people who have good luck and subsidize people who have bad luck. How much this redistribution should be done, however, is a question that is very difficult to answer. Here again, the idea of a safety net receives a good deal of support. Beyond this, demand for equality is fairly muted.

Nevertheless, an ideology of equality has a certain power, as the Declaration of Independence suggests. Even here the principle that all men are created equal (it does not seem to include women) could have some genetic objections raised to it. There are genetic deficiencies, even if genetic excellence may be more a matter of good luck than good management, considering that each one of us is about one out of eight trillion possible genetic children our parents could have produced. The concept of equality here edges toward the question of human rights. There is wide agreement that certain rights should be recognized in the structure of society. The right to vote, of course, is an obvious one, although some people are always denied the right to vote by reason of youth or criminality or citizenship status. The Bill of Rights in the United States certainly sets forth certain ideals, which cut back, however, to prohibitions and to duties. Every right implies somebody else's duty, either to refrain from doing something or to do something. Without spelling these duties out, the rights tend to be merely rhetoric.

Another aspect of human life and society closely bound up with the concept of justice is that of freedom. Here again, this concept is multidimensional. It refers broadly to what might be called the "nature of the possibility boundary," which surrounds all of us, which divides what we can do from what we can't do. Physical obstacles are not generally regarded as an encroachment on freedom. I am free to fly to New York tomorrow if I want to, but I am not free to fly to the moon, at least at the moment. It is where the boundary between what we can do and what we can't do is determined by other humans or by laws or other institutions of society that we run into the concept of freedom. Oddly enough, freedom for one person often implies a denial of freedom for another. Freedom of speech, for instance, means that somebody might want to stop me from saying something but is not free to do it. This concept edges over into justice problems, for when we try to determine the distribution of freedom in society it is obvious that the rich have a good deal more freedom than the poor. The possibility boundary of the rich is further out.

Freedom is also closely involved with the concept of property. Property is a set of possibilities in which the owner has freedom and the nonowner does not. The establishment of mutually agreed-on property boundaries is a very important aspect of the resolution of conflict. A good deal of conflict arises over conflicting claims to property. And the legal system is very much involved with this. I once had an argument with Reinhold Niebuhr,[2] which I summed up by saying that he was afraid of freedom because he saw behind it the specter of anarchy, while I was afraid of justice because I saw behind it the specter of tyranny. It is clear that the balance between freedom and justice is a delicate matter.

All this leads up to the question of the relation of all these concepts to power and especially to the various kinds of power. In my book *Three Faces of Power*,[3] I distinguish between threat power, economic power, and integrative power. Threat power begins when A says to B, "You do something I want or I'll do something you don't want."[4] This threat again has two aspects, the more common being destructive power. A may have the power to injure B or B's property, or people or property that B perceives as part of his or her community, and the instruments of threat are very frequently the means of destruction. A and B's productive power, however, is not wholly irrelevant. A may say to B, "I won't do something nice for you" instead of saying "I'm going to do something nasty to you."

Where the system goes depends on B's response to A's threat, and there are many possible responses. One is submission, as when we pay our taxes. Another is defiance, as when we drive above the speed limit. The success or failure of defiance depends on many things—whether we get found out, as we often do not when we exceed the speed limit, or whether it costs A too much to fulfill the threat, and so on. A third response is flight, which is not uncommon. It depends on the principle that the power of threat diminishes with the distance from the threatener. A fourth response is counterthreat—"You do something nasty to me and I'll do something nasty to you." This approach may result in deterrence, which may be successful in the short run, though it can be shown that it is bound to be unstable in the long run. A fifth possibility might be called "disarming behavior," such as "we're all in this together, aren't we?" This possibility has much to do with the development of courtesy, manners, and all that.

Disarming behavior can sometimes be offset by courtesy on the part of the threatener—"You really ought to do this for both our sakes."

The second form of power, economic power, is most simply defined as what the rich have more of than the poor. A good indicator of its magnitude is some measure of net worth in accounting terms, especially if this measure includes the capital value of the person, of which it is possible to make at least rough estimates. The capital value of a person depends very much on a person's economic productivity, the capacity of a person to produce things, especially for exchange, but also the ability to hold things that are rising in relative value. Real net worth in terms of "real dollars," whatever they are, can rise for two reasons. One is that production exceeds consumption, which leads to accumulation. The other is that the things (assets) held may rise in relative value. Net worth falls, of course, when the things we hold fall in relative value. Economic power can also be increased by successful theft or by exploitation. Exploitation in this case is not easy to define. It involves something like an exchange that benefits one party to the exchange much more than it benefits the other party. Where threats are brought into play, of course, exchange may actually worsen the position of the threatened party.

The third form of power goes by a number of names, but I have called it "integrative power." This is the power of legitimacy, respect, loyalty, affection, love, and so on. It may, of course, be negative when there is illegitimacy, disloyalty, disrespect, and hatred. Integrative power, I have argued, is actually the most fundamental form of power. Illegitimate threat and illegitimate wealth are very unsuccessful as compared with legitimate threat and legitimate wealth. The loss of legitimacy has remarkable effects in producing defiance in the threat system, as recent events in the Soviet Union have shown so dramatically.

None of these forms of power is ever found in an absolutely pure form. Economic power, for instance, can be devoted to developing the means of destruction and so increase threat power. Only rich countries can afford to be "great powers" in the international threat system. On the other hand, threat often undermines economic power, as the rise and fall of empires over history has certainly demonstrated. Resources that might have been used to increase economic power have been increasingly absorbed by the military and the instruments of threat, as the twentieth century has shown very dramatically in the collapse of the old empires and the collapse of communism in the Soviet Union. There are frequent cases in which military defeat leads to economic and cultural expansion, as in the case of Germany and Japan after World War II, Vienna after 1866, Paris after 1871, and so on. Economic power can be used to enhance integrative power, in some cases by rituals like coronations and parades, and in other cases by using economic power to create an image of "doing good" by setting up foundations, redistributing income toward the poor, and so on.

How then do these three forms of power relate to the problem of violence and its incidence? It is clear that the use of threat power is much
more likely to lead to violence than the use either of economic power (exchanges tend to be fairly peaceful) or integrative power. If most people in
a society regard that society and its institutions as basically legitimate,
there is not likely to be much violence, especially political violence. We
have to distinguish between personal violence and political violence, even
though these are not unrelated.

There is no doubt that certain individuals are more prone to personal
violence than others. In its most extreme form this inclination involves
sadism and perhaps even masochism as an encouragement to violence on
the part of others. Whether this inclination has a genetic component, which
now seems to have been discovered for homosexuality, in certain aspects
of brain structure, we really do not know. If both homosexuality and
sadism were strongly genetic in their origin, sheer natural selection would
tend to eliminate them, as those individuals with these kinds of genes
would be likely to produce much fewer offspring than those with more
"normal" genetic structures.

It seems likely, therefore, that personal violence is, like most things,
a mixture of genetics, culture, and experience, and it is hard to identify the
mixture. Culture and the learning process can either suppress genetic tendencies toward violence or permit and encourage them. Obviously the
atrocities committed by armed forces are primarily the result of a culture
that legitimates violence, but they also owe something to the existence of
sadism. The same goes for civilian cultures that deplore on the one hand,
or encourage on the other, hatred and fear of "others" who do not share
some common identity.

Both personal and political violence are closely related to some kind
of breakdown or deficiency in the integrative structure. An important element in this structure is personal identification with various groups. A person's identity is very closely related to the groups with which that person
identifies. We all have different identities depending on the group in which
we are operating. Thus, I have an identity as a husband, as a father, as a
grandfather, as a citizen of Boulder, of Colorado, of the United States, and
of the world, as an economist, a professor emeritus at the University of
Colorado, as a Quaker, as a writer, and so on. I indulge very little in violence because I perceive none of these identities to be insecure or to be
threatened by anybody else. I may use slightly violent language, for instance, towards mainline economists with whom I disagree. But I would
never think of hitting them. For we both have larger identities in a subcul-
ture in which violence is regarded as illegitimate.

A great question, therefore, is how does violence become legitimated?
Virtually all violence has to be legitimated in the mind of the perpetrator

at the time when it is committed. There may, of course, be split personalities, and people may be driven by sadism or anger that is out of their control. Even here, whatever is in control of action in the perpetrator must regard violence in some sense as legitimate. This sense of legitimacy may be confined to the perpetrator alone and condemned by most others. This, indeed, is what we would identify as crime. Violence, however, can be legitimated by the group with which the perpetrator identifies, whether these are terrorists (I have sometimes described them as "soldiers without a government"), regular military personnel, the police, and so on. These people may have their sense of legitimation approved by large sections of the society. The fact that the British are now building a monument to the man who ordered the totally unnecessary destruction of Dresden in World War II is an indicator as to how long this kind of legitimacy can last.

It is hard for us to deny legitimacy to what we have already done. Legitimacies, however, do collapse, as we saw in the European empires and in communism, perhaps when expectations are sufficiently disappointed or when the critique of an established legitimacy becomes powerful enough. A particularly difficult situation arises when violence is perceived, especially by the perpetrator but also by observers, as a necessary cost of achieving justice. Much revolutionary violence and terrorism will fall into this category. The possibility that under certain circumstances violence can lead to a more just and a better world is believed very widely. Few Americans, for instance, feel that the violence of the American Revolution was unjustified. Such beliefs cannot be ruled out as erroneous automatically. Nevertheless, the case against these beliefs from empirical evidence and historical records is very strong. Canada, Australia, and New Zealand obtained their independence from Britain with virtually no violence. They did not have a civil war like the United States, and they are certainly less violent societies than the United States is today, though they may not be quite as rich. The collapse of communist regimes, almost entirely without violence except in Romania, may have something to do with the fact that violence and threat are very poor "midwives for a new society," to use Karl Marx's expression. Building a society on centralized threat leads almost inevitably to an erosion of its internal legitimacy, which gets to the point where, to use a metaphor, the whole iceberg turns over and presents a different surface to the world.

The bloodless "glorious revolution" in England in 1689 set off an extraordinary period of economic and cultural development domestically, although it was also followed by imperialist expansion around the world. The French Revolution, on the other hand, produced Napoleon and a virtual stagnation, or at least slow development, of the French economy, almost until World War II, and also a period of overseas imperialism. From the early nineteenth century, however, it was the nonimperialist countries in

Europe, especially in Scandinavia, that got rich, and the empires severely crippled the development of England, France, and the Netherlands. The Spanish Empire crippled the development of Spain much earlier. Since getting rid of their empires, European imperial powers have had a remarkable explosion of economic development, which certainly suggests that economic exploitation through threat is a poor way of getting rich.

It is hard to correlate the dynamics of violence, that is, the rate at which it increases or decreases, with the many other characteristics of societies. The "causes" of violence are obscure. The actual perpetration of violence is a fairly random property of any given system, like automobile accidents. The percentage of drivers killed in automobile accidents is certainly a function of some characteristics of the system, such as the safety features of automobiles, roads, and so on. It is virtually impossible, however, to predict the time and place of actual accidents. Similarly, the time and place of acts of violence and war are virtually impossible to predict, but the quantity of violence in a society in any given period may be related to certain characteristics of the social system. A possible clue here, noted earlier, is the distinction between positive identities and negative identities, that is, between people who know what they want and go toward it, and who think they know who they are, and people who go away from what they do not want and know who they aren't. Thus, a soldier is somebody who has to have an enemy in order to justify his identity. There can be queer mixtures here of positive and negative identities. National identities are often quite positive, but national defense, on the other hand, implies a negative identity towards at least potential enemies. As one Russian said to the Americans, "We have done you great harm, we have deprived you of an enemy."

Where there is a long established system of power among various groups, it may be legitimated simply by antiquity: just the fact that the system has been around for a long time and people are accustomed to it. The erosion of this power can potentially lead into violence. We see this phenomenon sometimes, for instance, in what might be called "outbreeding," where one group in a society is increasing its population faster than another group that may currently be more dominant. Possible examples are Fiji, Guyana, possibly Trinidad, where, thanks to the old British Empire, the East Indian population is expanding more rapidly than the original African populations. Sri Lanka is a case where a rather successful development fell apart because of the conflict between the Tamils and the Singhalese, even though the Tamils are still a minority. The economic results of this struggle seem to have been disastrous. Bhutan in the Himalayas seems to be another example. In fact, almost wherever there are refugees, some intergroup identity conflict is likely to be behind the need for refuge.

The Indian subcontinent is an example of a society that is so diverse that it seems to have achieved unity only under a foreign ruler, whether the

Moguls or the British. When the British left, the subcontinent split into Pakistan and India. Pakistan split further later on when Bangladesh became independent. It is almost a miracle that India has managed to retain its democratic institutions in the face of such enormous diversity. The recent split-up of the Soviet Union, which had not been wholly unexpected, again arises out of its great diversity of cultures and people. It was held together first by simple Russian imperialism, then since 1917 by the Communist Party, which, however, did not seem to be able to fulfill the economic promises that it made and, hence, lost legitimacy with astonishing rapidity. Having lost legitimacy, it could no longer exercise the threat power that it once commanded.

It is still a puzzling question as to why some countries, like Switzerland, after a fairly violent past, move into a long period of mutual accommodation, with diverse languages, religions, and cultures, with only an occasional murmur here and there. It is puzzling why Wales and Ireland reacted so differently to the English conquests of Edward I. For 700 years there has hardly been any record of a Welsh revolt. The Irish seem to have revolted every generation. Yet the Welsh preserved their language and culture better than did the Irish, who except for the remote Western islands, lost their language, which they are now trying to recover. They made enormous contributions to England and to literature, even going back to Jonathan Swift in the last centuries, William Butler Yeats, George Bernard Shaw, and so on. One thinks also of Adam Smith and David Hume in Edinburgh in the late eighteenth century, after Scotland had suffered severe defeat at Culloden and had lost even its parliament. There seems to be something in the proposition that the creative part of a culture tends to be at its periphery rather than at the center.

Perhaps the core of the problem of violence is to see it as a system of potential and resistance, perhaps more like a system of breakdown under a critical amount of stress. If I increase the pressure on a piece of chalk for a little while nothing happens, and then crack, the chalk breaks. Ohm's Law does not provide so much for discontinuity, but here again the current is proportional to the potential difference divided by the resistance; if the resistance is high enough no current flows. The violence equation, if there is one, is a good deal more nonlinear. In political violence, especially, stress arises out of a sense of impotence. Here the Ohm's Law parallel breaks down, when the resistance to violence, which consists largely of taboos, breaks. Then the system enters a new phase as violence creates enemies on both sides. It creates also a legitimation for further violence. The taboo on violence is of great importance here, but it is also hard to identify just when it is going to break down. When it does finally break, we pass into a new phase, a little more like the Richardson equations,[5] where A's violence toward B increases B's violence toward A, which increases A's violence toward B, and so on, until there may be a kind of equilibrium, as there almost seems to be in Northern Ireland over the long pull. Or the system radically changes, the most radical change being the extermination of one party. Sometimes, however, there is radical change in identity, as both parties come to recognize that what they are doing is ridiculous and costly to both of them, and the new integrative system takes over. Just what the circumstances are under which this happens, however, is still very obscure.

What needs to be studied here is the interaction of the different subcultures in society—familial, tribal, ethnic, religious, academic, and so on. I think it is true to say that all the world religions put a low value on violence as such, regarding it as a cost. There is perhaps a religion of nationalistic militarism that regards violence and war as a positive benefit in terms of excitement, unification of the group, and so on. But even among the military, war tends to be regarded as a means to an end rather than as an end in itself, even though there is the dilemma that the military can only justify its budget if there is a high probability of war. But this fact rarely gets expressed as a moral principle. Although all the world religions have peace as an ideal, none of them has achieved it very well. They seem to have fought more within themselves than between themselves, with the possible exception of the Crusades. There is, especially in Buddhism, Hinduism, and Christianity, a certain pattern of withdrawal from violence, for instance, into monasticism or even into the peace churches in Christianity. Karl Marx thought that violence is the midwife of the new society, but, as we saw in Kampuchea, class war is the most devastating form of violence.

Nevertheless, peace grows by an almost unconscious learning process. We see this in the spread of areas of stable peace around the world in the last 150 years. We see it in the rise of political democracy, we see it in the labor movement, we see it in Gandhi and Martin Luther King, but I think we still don't understand it very well. And the understanding of peace remains one of the greatest intellectual challenges to the human mind and, one might add, the human heart.

This understanding comes from two sources. One is an increasing realization of the human capacity for thought. The other is information, mainly from the records of the past, which thought feeds upon. The case studies of this volume are an important source of food for thought, and future thinking on this problem will undoubtedly benefit from them.

Notes

1. Galtung, "Feudal Systems," pp. 110–188.
2. See Niebuhr, "Coercion, Self-Interest, and Love," pp. 228–254.
3. Boulding, *Three Faces of Power*.
4. Ibid., p. 25.
5. Richardson, *Arms and Insecurity*.

Bibliography

Boulding, Kenneth E. *Three Faces of Power* (Newbury Park, CA: Sage Publications, 1989).

Galtung, Johan. "Feudal Systems, Structural Violence, and the Structural Theory of Revolutions," in *International Peace Research Association, 3rd Proceedings,* vol. 1 (1970).

Niebuhr, R. "Coercion, Self-Interest, and Love," and K. E. Boulding, "In Reply to Professor Niebuhr," in K. E. Boulding, *The Organizational Revolution* (New York: Harper & Brothers, 1953).

Richardson, Lewis B. *Arms and Insecurity* (Chicago: Quadrangle Books, 1960) and *Statistics of Deadly Quarrels* (Chicago: Quadrangle Books, 1960).

4

Nonviolent Direct Action and the Diffusion of Power

Doug Bond

Nonviolent action is a means of combat, as is war. It involves the match-
ing of forces and the waging of "battles," requires wise strategy and tactics, employs numerous "weapons," and demands of its "soldiers"
courage, discipline, and sacrifice. . . . This view of nonviolent action as a
technique of *active* combat is diametrically opposed to the once popular,
though uninformed, assertion that no such phenomenon really existed, or
that anything "nonviolent" was simple passivity and submission . . .
—*Gene Sharp, Post-Military Defense*

Above is the characterization of nonviolent action by one acclaimed even
by his critics as "the patron theorist of nonviolent action around the
world."[1] In the wake of the widespread popular protests of the late 1980s,
it is clear that the uninformed assertion that nonviolent action does not
exist is no longer tenable.[2] Likewise, the notion that such action is either
passivity or submission is fatally flawed in light of the historic regime
changes that followed the recent prolific "people power" revolutions, especially since 1989.

Such increased visibility of nonviolent action (NVA) should help us to
better understand it. But that understanding is hindered by a persistent and
deep division among students of nonviolence[3]—those who see NVA as a
set of "tactics" and those who view it as "a way of life."[4] (These views are
often referred to as tactical and principled nonviolence.) This division inhibits communication and collaboration among those who recognize the
active nature of NVA but differ on whether it is limited to principled actions. More important, the business of defending the respective camps has
drawn attention away from a goal that remains in common across the academic divide: to improve our understanding of how NVA works to effect
and/or resist change.

The development of NVA (either as a "tactic" or as a "way of life") into a viable alternative to violence depends upon improving our ability to articulate both its limits and potential, its outcomes and dynamics. Such an improved understanding can be based upon an explanatory framework of the mechanisms of action and change underlying NVA. This chapter outlines these mechanisms as a means of explaining how NVA works. It also offers a theoretical specification of the process of power diffusion, which is hypothesized to be operative in all nonviolent action, both principled and tactical. Through this process the power relations between antagonists engaged in nonviolent action over time are expected to tend toward democratic, decentralized political structures. In other words, *all* uses of nonviolent direct action (principled or otherwise, for status quo or anti–status quo objectives) may actually encourage, if not ensure, popular empowerment. Thus the means and ends of NVA may interact in ways not yet addressed in the divisive debate between the two academic camps.

A couple of caveats are in order here. First, although I am suggesting that NVA nurtures popular empowerment, I am not saying the process is always "peaceful" or its outcomes necessarily stable. NVA sometimes is followed by protracted instability; witness the postrevolutionary Philippines or Eastern Europe. Also, NVA may be associated with heightened levels of low-intensity violence and dampened levels of high-intensity (lethal) violence.[5] Still, I agree with Sharp when he suggested that NVA "casualty rates . . . are usually much lower than in conventional or guerrilla wars."[6] Second, I am focusing on how NVA "operates" to effect or resist change. Thus, I discuss NVA as it is used to prosecute rather than eliminate conflict to advance one's interests, even if these interests are presented as mutual or unifying. Although this presentation might appear to be heavily biased toward the nonviolence as "tactics" view,[7] I suggest it is precisely this focus on the underlying mechanisms of action and change that could provide the basis for building bridges in our fractured and underdeveloped field.

A Framework for Inquiry

One resource manual for nonviolent action begins with the admonition "People working for social change need to understand the context of their labors."[8] People *studying* social change need to do the same. Our immediate task is to reduce the conceptual confusion surrounding nonviolent action by developing explicit definitions and eliminating terminological inconsistency. To place nonviolent action in context, we can frame our inquiry by distinguishing among several key concepts.[9]

The conceptual map of the present framework begins with a situation of acute conflict brought about by competing or conflicting interests. I distinguish first between selected attributes (for example, motivating beliefs, goals, attitudes, and values)[10] and manifest behaviors; and within the behavior category, I distinguish between routine and direct political action. These distinctions are outlined in Table 4.1.

Table 4.1   A Conceptual Map

Attributes

Beliefs, attitudes, goals, and values serve to motivate and inform the choice of approach and selection of particular methods of action.

Behavior

Routine political action is typically institutionalized and always entails, at least tacitly, the compliance of all parties; outcomes are determinate in that they are always prescribed by existing practices, procedures, and/or norms

Direct political action is always unilaterally initiated, engaging, and indeterminate with respect to outcomes; it is manifested in both
   Nonviolent struggle, which works through
      coercion,
      manipulation, and
      appeals; and
   Violent struggle, which works through
      physical force and
      coercive force

Attributes

Motivating beliefs, goals, attitudes, and values, as attributes of an individual or group, influence the choice to engage in alternative behaviors, including the choice between routine and direct political action. In my effort to explain how NVA "works," I focus the present inquiry on these behaviors. I suggest that the distinctive nature of nonviolent direct action is revealed more in the dynamics and consequences of behavior than in the motivating beliefs in principled nonviolence that drives some of it. Even a strong advocate of the "way of life" view, George Lakey, acknowledged that "most pacifists do not practice nonviolent resistance, and most people who do practice nonviolent resistance are not pacifists."[11]

Behavior

Routine versus direct action. Routine and direct political action are posited to be conceptually distinct and empirically discernable. The term *direct action* generally refers to some type of protest, usually nonviolent. But Lofland cautioned us about the problem of imputing this protest label (and therefore a cause or intention) to an empirical phenomenon.[12] Nevertheless,

Wilson's distinction between "bargaining" and "protest" behavior hints at
a critical difference between determinate and indeterminate actions.[13] The
outcomes of determinate behavior are prescribed by some norm, procedure, practice, or routine. In contrast, the consequences of indeterminate
behavior are not prescribed by any procedure or practice.

Routine political action is determinate—it is prescribed by norms. Direct political action is indeterminate. That is, every direct action yields an
indeterminate outcome, an outcome that is not bound by existing practice
or procedures but is a function of its performance.

Further, direct political action is always unilaterally initiated. It never
requires the cooperation or consent of another party. Routine political action, on the other hand, is always reciprocal, if not entirely voluntary, at
least to the extent that there is compliance. Routine political action generally follows, or is in accordance with, existing practice or procedures. The
outcome of political action is bound by the system parameters for conflict
resolution and is, therefore, a function of performance only within the constraints set by existing power relations. The notion that protest poses a radical threat to the status quo or system is explained by this distinction.

Nonviolent direct action. April Carter described a context of "protest or resistance" associated with nonviolent direct action. She also noted, "There is
no necessary connection between the resort to direct action and the resort to
violence."[14] Eisinger made a similar point: "That protest may lead to violence, then, is undeniable; that the latter is just an extension of the former
does not follow, however."[15] I, too, distinguish between direct action and
violence, but find it useful to consider both nonviolent direct action and violence or violent direct action to be subsets of the more encompassing domain of direct action. The idea that nonviolent direct action can serve as a
functional substitute for violence is consistent with this framework.[16]

Conceptual clarity may be enhanced when the term *nonviolent struggle* is used in place of the more general term *nonviolent direct action.* The
term *struggle* highlights the context of manifest conflict independent, or
beyond the bounds, of the norms, customs, and procedures (both formal
and informal) prescribed for routine interactions and to resolve differences. The term also captures, though is not bound by, Carter's emphasis
on "protest or resistance" associated with nonviolent direct action.

Violence. By violence, I mean any use of physical force against another's
body, against that person's will, and that is expected[17] to inflict physical
injury or death upon that person. This definition is offered only as an analytically precise, intuitively satisfying, and empirically useful measure for
research into violent struggle, and may not be applicable in other inquiries.

The mechanisms of direct action (discussed below) differentiate between social and physical bases of power. Social powers "work" through

the human mind; but physical power "targets" bodies, treating people as if they were mere objects. Thus I contend the use of physical force (violence) represents a definitive break from the realm of politics. And contrary to the Clauswitzian maxim that war is a "political act" or a "continuation of political intercourse . . . by other means,"[18] I suggest that violence, especially war, breaks the web of community, and in this important sense, is antithetical to politics.

An Example and Some Implications

A tripartite concept of behavior is quite common in the social movement literature but is not without ambiguity.[19] The specific terms vary, but most frameworks present three categories of behavior such as "normal" politics, "protest" politics, and violence. Such frameworks highlight forms of behavior without revealing how they work differently to effect or resist change. The present tripartite framework, however, illuminates the underlying mechanisms by which all direct action operates. This division is not based on the forms of organization or action, or even on style.[20] Rather, it is based upon what Eisinger called the "basic dynamics" of action.[21]

An example may help to clarify the determinate-indeterminate criterion distinguishing nonviolent direct action from the "normal" politics entailed in routine political action. Contrast a formal petition drive to initiate an impeachment process with an election boycott to protest corruption. Both involve activities of protest and persuasion; both involve certain acts of noncooperation; and both may even involve acts of intervention (to relate these to Sharp's primary categorization of methods). Note that at this level of *manifest behavior*, the different methods of action (protest and persuasion, noncooperation, and intervention) do not distinguish direct from routine political action. But a clear divergence in their operation, or *mechanisms of action,* is evident in that the petition drive works through a set (political) process, with specified procedures and known thresholds of "success." That is, a certain number of signatures triggers a prescribed outcome. An accord, or at least tacit compliance, is operative, even though it may be broken, at any time, by any party to the conflict. An election boycott, on the other hand, no matter how "successful" in terms of number of participants, has no a priori, set, or prescribed outcome. The indeterminate outcome of such direct action is a function of the actual interaction between antagonists; more precisely, it is a function of the dynamics of the nonviolent struggle.

Direct political action, then, is usefully considered to represent a balancing of competing interests, capabilities, and wills, the outcome of which is a new, or renewed, balance of powers and structure of expectations between them.[22] The assessment of this interaction or balancing is explicit in the strategic analysis below.

The lack of a clear analytic distinction between routine and direct action has reduced the rich concept of direct action to that of a simple method or form of protest at the level of manifest behavior. Lynd's shorthand expression "tactic"[23] suffers from this deficiency. Thus it is not surprising that Sharp's methods of nonviolent action have become the symbol of his "technique" approach.[24] Indeed, it is difficult to find a serious discussion on nonviolent direct action that does not mention Sharp's "198 methods," that is, the illustrative listing included in Part II of his *Politics of Nonviolent Action*.

Unlike the discontinuity between direct action and violence, the transition between routine and direct action is virtually continuous, more a matter of analytical distinction, though clearly discernable in empirical phenomena. I find the term *parapolitical* to be helpful in highlighting the core characteristics of nonviolent direct action. The notion of parapolitical action is analytically distinct from, yet connected to, the realm of routine political action. Both routine political and parapolitical action are distinguished here from the antithetical realm of violence in that they operate through social powers; violence "works" against human bodies as objects. Consider the human digestive system as an analogy. It facilitates the conversion of food into energy for the body. But the alimentary canal is not the only route through which a body can be fed. One can bypass it altogether with an intravenous injection of nourishment or one can introduce food directly into the tract in a way that does not require the body's compliance in chewing or swallowing—this approach, called paraenteral feeding, is useful when the body rejects or is unable to take food orally. Likewise, the will of the body politic can be bypassed by the use of violence or it can be transformed via parapolitical action, without an accord or violence.

Precisely what behaviors are involved in each of the conceptual domains? A description of the manifest actions (that is, the methods) are useful "handles" to talk about the different forms of action. And, as noted above, Sharp's listing of 198 methods of nonviolent action stands as the definitive catalogue of methods of nonviolent struggle.[25] But the real value of the listing begins with his subtitle to Part II—"The Methods of Nonviolent Action: Political *Jiu-Jitsu* at Work." We need to identify the underlying mechanisms of action[26] to understand how the methods "work" to effect and/or resist change. The forms of the individual methods are context bound and of little use in explaining their operation. For example, marches, parades and motorcades are among Sharp's "methods" of protest and persuasion. But a careful reading of his examples reveals that not all marches, parades, and motorcades would be appropriately considered nonviolent struggle. For example, a Washington, D.C., parade by the National American Woman Suffrage Association in 1913 constitutes an illustration of struggle not because it was a parade per se, but because it was a direct action. It sought to effect change unilaterally and directly with, at the time, an indeterminate outcome. Thus, a focus on the manifest actions or methods serves only to describe the action, but a focus on the mechanisms of action begins to get at the ways in which methods actually operate.

Sharp's methods are organized in three categories: (1) protest and persuasion; (2) noncooperation—social, economic, and political; and (3) nonviolent intervention. I seek here to refine and extend his organizing framework by specifying *how* these different types of methods operate, or "work." Accordingly, I have developed and operationalized a typology of the mechanisms of action by which the methods operate to effect and/or resist change.

Mechanisms of Direct Action

The present delineation of mechanisms builds most directly upon Rummel's work and synthesizes a number of interconnected discussions in the social sciences focused on processes of opinion change, power and influence, and conflict.[27]

Goldhamer and Shils stimulated much of the subsequent development, including the present approach, by distinguishing the three objects toward which actions can be directed: the (human) body, the will, and the environment.[28] These authors also initiated a discussion on the measurement of power use. Other social scientists who contributed to this synthesis include Kelman, French and Raven, Parsons, Gamson, Raven and Kruglanski, Wrong, and Boulding. Baldwin, Clegg, and Lukes presented good syntheses of the various strands of this diverse research.

For the most part, this literature deals with both violent and nonviolent means, generally to effect change. Meanwhile a parallel body of literature developed with a focus limited to nonviolent action but that explicitly addressed means of both effecting and resisting change. Significant contributors here include Case, Gregg, Lakey, Miller, Seifert, and Sharp.

Like Sharp's typology of methods and like Boulding's typology of powers, the present mechanisms-of-action typology is "offered as a way of organizing an extremely complex reality in a way that perhaps will make for more realistic appraisals."[29] Indeed, the similarity is not just one of purpose; the two typologies are fundamentally compatible in their views on the bases of power and the mechanisms of action by which the powers operate. Still, some differences are evident because of the different levels of specificity presented and because the present focus is limited to direct action, thereby excluding Boulding's exchange, a reciprocal mechanism in the domain of routine as opposed to direct political action.

The present mechanisms of direct action are delineated at a level of specification that is relatively detailed and, therefore, readily operationalizable; that is, the specification of empirical indicators and coding rules for the variable can follow directly from the mechanism descriptions. Earlier versions of the mechanisms of action have actually been operationalized and employed in empirical pilot research.[30] Although Boulding's typology is presented at a higher (conceptual) level, the basic approach is similar.

I outline in Table 4.2 a typology of mechanisms of direct action. The bases of power, the immediate and ultimate "objects" or "targets" of that power, and the empirical indicators needed to identify their use in practice are detailed. The mechanisms of action are to be considered against the backdrop of the typology in Table 4.2.

Table 4.2   Mechanisms of Direct Action

As Manifested in Violence

Physical force is evident when an actionist wields physical power against another's body (an adversary), and, as a result, the adversary's body is expected to suffer bodily injury or death. Its base of power is physical power or strength. It is directed at an adversary's body

- to *displace* (by physically moving) the adversary's body,
- to *incapacitate* (by injuring) the adversary's body, and/or
- *to eliminate* (by killing) the adversary's body, thereby

   preempting the adversary, and
   enabling the actionist to directly effect its objective

Coercive force is evident when physical force either is used coercively (rather than directly) or threatened. Its base of power is physical power or strength or the credibility of the threat. It is directed, via an adversary's and/or a third party's body, at the adversary's will to cause pain (by injuring or killing the adversary or third party) to affect the adversary's interests.

As Manifested in Nonviolent Struggle

Discrete manipulation is evident when an actionist wields discrete control over the physical, social, political, and/or economic situation confronting and/or opportunities available to another, and can thereby impose a cost upon or present a risk to that person's ability to sustain his/her livelihood. Its base of power is the ability to control physical, social, political, and/or economic resources. It is directed, via the environment, at another's will to affect the other's interests.

Public coercion is evident when an actionist publicly threatens to impose material, social, political, and/or economic costs (negative interests or sanctions) on another. Its base of power is the credibility of its threats. It is directed at another's will to affect the other's interests.

Demonstrative appeals are evident

- When an actionist invokes a common authority in an attestive plea to another. Its base of power is the perceived legitimacy of the common authority. These are *authoritative appeals.*
- When an actionist employs a shared system of logic or body of knowledge to persuade another. Its base of power is the persuasive capacity of the actionist. These are *persuasive appeals.*
- When an actionist attests to a sense of unity or coupled identity with another with self-sacrifice. Its base of power is the integrative capacity of the actionist's sacrifice. These are *altruistic appeals.* These attestive appeals are all directed at another's will to affect the other's interests.

Mechanisms Manifested in Violence

The physical and coercive force mechanisms operate exclusively within the domain of violence. Physical injury or death to another is likely. Human bodies constitute the immediate "target" of such violent direct action,[31] and the underlying mechanisms of physical and coercive force are both manifested in the resultant violence. Still the two mechanisms are significantly different in that physical force works solely against physical bodies while coercive force employs violence to affect another's interests.

The "expectation" referred to in the physical force mechanism is independent of the actionist's intent; also it does not refer to the actual effects of the use. Thus the setting off of a bomb to destroy an occupied building in an urban area (a clear use of physical force against the victims and of coercive force if another party's interests were affected)[32] is appropriately distinguished from the controlled destruction of an abandoned and remote building (a discrete manipulation of a resource to affect the interests of another, presumably the owner).

A close scrutiny of physical force reveals its limited utility. Striking, beating, severing, or exploding human bodies can do little more than displace, incapacitate, or kill. But then, the actionist still must effect whatever change is desired. A common consequence of the use of physical force is the generation of a tremendous amount of hatred and bitterness among the surviving victims.

Coercive force has only slightly more utility. Because here, either the use must be continuous or the threat to use must remain credible to affect another's interests. Both constitute a constant drain on the actionist's physical resources. One need only look at the expense of maintaining order at a prison, an institution that relies almost exclusively on physical confinement and coercive force. Or note the cost of maintaining the military in a totalitarian state, where rule is based largely upon the use and threat of use of physical force.

Mechanisms Manifested in Nonviolent Struggle

General manipulation of a situation or the environment to affect the interests of another would be virtually impossible to assess empirically. Among the many obstacles, the mere presence of a party could be said to control the environment under certain conditions. Oppressive power relations also can limit opportunities for change, thereby exerting a certain amount of control. Clearly such control constitutes manipulation as defined here. But it is equally clear that empirical assessment of such omnipresent manipulation poses a serious challenge for empirical research. In the interest of developing testable theory, we focus our attention on discrete acts of manipulation. Discrete manipulation affects another's interests by discernable, discrete actions upon the environment or a specific situation. The immediate "object" of such manipulation constitutes an interest of another. Thus, the discrete manipulation affects the other's interest.

As with all direct action, discrete manipulation never requires an accord with other party, but one does need the ability to control resources—physical, social, political, or economic.

Likewise, public coercion requires the credible threat of the same, if not the actual ability. Like the discrete manipulation mechanism, a qualifier—public—is attached to the coercion mechanism to facilitate empirical assessment. This qualifier presents a reasonable threshold of clear communication that allows for social and cultural variations in the use of explicit threats. We employ our "hypothetical, informed, and impartial third-party observer" to identify the presence of a threat sufficiently communicated to be characterized as public.

It is through these two social mechanisms that many of the more coercive methods of nonviolent direct action are wielded. For example, an actionist group can control (mobilize) social resources (people) for a mass demonstration to manipulate a situation. The same actionist group might also threaten (through public coercion) to wage a general strike if their demands are not met; that is, the group would threaten to exact or impose an economic or political cost for noncompliance. Nonviolent invasions and occupations of missile sites, nuclear power plants, and proposed airports are other examples of actionists using manipulation to affect the interests of others, and election boycotts threaten to impose a (political) cost or risk that can affect another's interests.

More often than not, the use of manipulation and coercion are not separated in practice. Rather they are used together, with a threat (coercion) made credible with a demonstration of the actionist's ability to control resources (manipulation). The threat might consist of a cost to be newly imposed or an existing cost to be continued. Both could affect the interests of another, assuming they were credible. Again, the empirical assessment of these mechanisms is conducted across all of them simultaneously, yielding a profile of the analytically distinct, but empirically overlapping, mechanisms.

The three demonstrative or attestive appeals mechanisms draw upon different social powers—authoritative, intellectual, and altruistic—to affect another's interests. All three depend not only upon their performance but also upon the extent to which the other party acknowledges the common, shared, or unified interests. All appeals constitute direct action, however, because they are always unilaterally invoked and have indeterminate outcomes.

The authority to be invoked in authoritative appeals may be inherent in a situation, a role, or a person. A drowning person appealing for help may hold a situational-based authority; a president's may be role based; and a charismatic leader may possess authority based on his/her unique personality. But whatever base is invoked, it must be perceived as legitimate by the other party for the mechanism to operate effectively.

Intellectual appeals require a capacity to persuade, which is dependent upon resources, performance, and the extent of a shared system of reason. All appeals are alike in that they are invoked through attestation or an act of witnessing. For intellectual appeals, the attestation lies in the persuasiveness of the appeals.

Altruistic appeals may stand out as the epitome of nonviolent appeals with their "success" dependent upon the other party sharing the actionist's sense of unified or connected identity or interests. Like all mechanisms manifested in nonviolent struggle, the manifestation refers to the process or operation, not to the outcome of the conflict. Indeed, a classic case of an attestative altruistic appeal is the hunger strike. Yet, physical harm, if not injury and death, often result.

To be clear, the distinction between mechanisms manifested in violence and those manifested in nonviolent struggle lies not in the presence or absence of violent outcomes, but in how power is applied, either against human bodies or through human minds. All mechanisms manifested in nonviolent struggle may be characterized as social mechanisms, despite the violent outcomes that sometimes follow. Thus, the coercive use of force is distinguished from public coercion by its threatened or actual use of a human body as an immediate "target" of physical force.

As indicated above, this presentation of mechanisms is restricted to direct action. Inclusion of the domain of routine political action would require the addition of a reciprocal exchange mechanism, not unlike Boulding's use of the term.

Some Implications

Sharp has contributed to our understanding of the ways nonviolent direct action works by recasting Gregg's notion of "moral jiu-jitsu"[33] into the concept of "political jiu-jitsu."[34] Whereas Gregg referred only to the integrative capacity of altruistic appeals, Sharp outlined the dynamics of nonviolent struggle more broadly, including the use of coercion and manipulation against an opponent to undermine his/her "political balance."

A careful examination of the present mechanisms suggests the conditions under which one might be more effective than another and illuminates their particular strength and limitations. For instance, not all nonviolent direct action works through the imposition of costs or sanctions. Many of the methods of protest/persuasion actually operate through appeals. And as noted above, these appeals require some degree of common, shared or unified interests to operate. Thus, in the case of a foreign or outside aggressor, strategies drawing upon the methods of noncooperation or intervention would seem to be more effective than those employing methods of protest/persuasion alone.

The methods that operate through coercion do not require common interests to effect change. Neither do they require control over physical resources if social resources are available (mass actions have a credibility independent of the physical resources they may or may not control). A credible threat to employ coercion, therefore, stands as a special class of nonviolent direct action, a class of action that we term *nonviolent sanctions*. (But see my concluding caveat.)

The strategic use of nonviolent sanctions, then, may function as a political equivalent to violence, where the opponent's control over physical resources (including military and police forces) and lack of concern (that is, common, shared or unified interests) for the actionist does not pose an insurmountable obstacle to the nonviolent actionist.

The development of strategy involves a series of complex, contingent decisions at several levels. First, one must choose the best approach or domain(s) of action—routine or direct political action, and if direct, violent or nonviolent struggle. Next, one must relate one's goals and objectives to the available resources and make an assessment of the alternative mechanisms likely to be effective. Only then can one develop a plan of action based on the methods that are available and appropriate to the situation.

Mechanisms of Change

To understand nonviolent action, we need, ultimately, to explain why some actions "fail" and others "succeed" in the realization of their objectives. To do this I have tried to develop our understanding of how the actions work. But mechanisms of direct action specified above lead us only to the point where change is effected directly (through the use of physical force) or to the point where change is obtained by affecting another's interests, either directly, or indirectly via manipulation of the situation or the environment. Now I turn to mechanisms of change to trace the processes through which these mechanisms of action actually yield or do not yield change.

Sharp referred to his mechanisms of change as "the determining combination of influences, pressures and forces . . ." that emerge from the complex interactions to "influence the opponent and his capacity for action" in a struggle.[35] He suggested that they "determine" the outcomes of the struggle. The various mechanisms of change therefore embody distinctly different types of change, which may result from the mechanisms of action.

Mechanisms of change bring about the cessation or closure of the manifest conflict and produce an imminent resolution of the struggle, even if temporary. The mechanisms of change are arrayed in Table 4.3 along two dimensions: the capacity to effect change and the basis of change. The first represents the capacity of another to effect a viable alternative in response to the actionist's demand. This capacity to change relates to a party's willingness to adopt, accept, or comply in situations where available options may be limited. The other dimension represents the basis of change. The basis of change links action and outcome; it drives the change process and may be viewed usefully as that which is leveraged to effect the outcome.

These two dimensions interact to promote change at different levels of internalization, from the completely internalized acceptance of reciprocal or mutual interests to the extreme of noninternalization represented by the default acquiescence to another's interests. The highly internalized adoption of the specific content of another's interests and the mere compliance of another's interests stand between these two extremes of internalization.[36]

The accommodation mechanism of change bespeaks a depth of internalization that is wedded to and reinforced by the ongoing process of interaction; the mechanism yields change that is particularly stable because it is self-adjusting. The disintegration mechanism of change, on the other hand, is likely to create volatile situations with virtually no internalization of any change. It is the disintegration mechanism's inherent or definitional lack of a capability to effect a viable alternative, however, that reveals its limitation to produce stable change. This capability or lack thereof is useful in distinguishing between mechanisms that operate similarily but diverge in their outcome. It is not useful to speak of conversion if the capacity not to convert is lacking; in such a disempowered situation, *cooptation* is the more accurate term to describe the change mechanism.

A seemingly trivial but important aspect of this two-dimensional perspective on the nature of change is that adoption requires the capacity to adopt. We need to distinguish the (misleading notion of) "consent" of a party who has little if any capacity to choose a viable alternative from the consent of an informed party possessing a full capacity to choose viable alternatives. I suggest the former "choice" is appropriately considered cooptation (when positive interests are leveraged) or coercion (when negative interests are leveraged) of a subordinate party (or sometimes even a victim); the latter is appropriately considered conversion or compliance (again, with positive and negative interests, respectively) by a party fully responsible for his/her choice. Ceding to another's interests, not being tied to the specific content of the change, may be effected by both convergent (positive) and divergent (negative) interests. The "choices" embodied in cooptation or coercion do not constitute consent insofar as the "consenting" party lacks the capability to choose a viable alternative.

In discussing control over people and the environment, Boulding notes explicitly the exploitative purposes for which economic power can be

Table 4.3 Mechanisms of Change

Capacity to Effect a Viable Alternative	Basis of Change	Mechanism	Level of Internalization	Nature and Stability of Outcome
Higher Lower	Reciprocal interests	Accommodation Not applicable	Very high Not applicable	Acceptance of (reciprocal) interests, the contents of which are more or less irrelevant because they are associated with a mutually desired outcome; dynamic outcome tends to self-adjust over time
Higher Lower	Positive interests and/or desired relationship	Conversion Cooptation	High High	Adoption of the specific content of another's interests stemming from a perception of the intrinsic value of the (positive) interest and/or of the (desired) relationship; static outcome depends upon maintenance of status quo or synchronized interests
Higher Lower	Negative interests	Compliance Coercion and/or undesired relationship	Moderate Moderate	Ceding to another's interests, the contents of which are more or less irrelevant because the alternative (nonacceptance) is associated with an undesirable outcome and/or the (undesired) relationship; strained outcomes require continuous application of credible threat
Higher Lower	None	Not applicable Disintegration	Low Low	Acquiescence (by default) to another's interests; volatile outcome is inherently unstable

used.[37] In the present framework, I suggest that such exploitation is indicated by a low decisionmaking capacity. But this low capacity is not limited to the economic dimension. As discussed above, one can be coopted instead of freely adopting another's interest (as in conversion). Likewise, one can be coerced by another instead of choosing to comply with his or her wishes.

Table 4.3 identifies higher- and lower-capacity mechanisms of change, based upon reciprocal, positive, and negative interests. Sharp's change mechanisms (accommodation, conversion, coercion, and disintegration) are all evident in the present framework. However, the present framework extends and refines his analysis to account for the significant differences that varying levels of the capacity and basis of change lend to the explanation of different outcomes. The present term *compliance* is consistent with Kelman's discussion in that it implies the party has a meaningful choice,[38] even if it is between two or more negative interests.[39] The term *cooptation* evolved from Nye's discussion of the ability "to structure a situation so that other[s] . . . develop preferences or define their interests in ways consistent with one's own. . . ."[40]

Change that is not internalized is inherently unstable. Equally important is the capacity to change; as it is undermined, the potential for protracted conflict increases as does the probability of renewed manifest conflict. Manifest conflict also recurs as previous coercion-driven closures lead not to stable resolutions but to increasingly unstable situations as the balance of interests, capabilities, and wills becomes fragile. As these unstable balances of power continue through time even minor incidents or triggers can set off another round of conflict.

In addition, the phenomenon of an adversary ceasing to constitute a viable party to a conflict by way of disintegration indicates a dangerous discontinuity that is not unlike the break between the nonsocial and social mechanisms of action. That disintegration can follow from social mechanisms of action (manifested in the methods of nonviolent direct action) is significant. It confirms, at the conceptual level at least, the proposition that nonviolent action has the potential to effect radical (disintegrative) change.

The Linkage of Action and Change

As we turn to the linkage of action and change, the interconnection of power and conflict needs to be made explicit. Blalock stated, "Power and conflict processes, though possibly analytically distinct and only partially overlapping, need to be joined to provide a reasonably complete orientation."[41] The connection in the present examination is premised upon the idea that power (to effect/resist change) is not reducible to the dichotomy of violent versus nonviolent means of prosecuting a conflict. To be sure, I distinguish between nonsocial and social mechanisms of action, but the bases of power driving them are multiple and distinct. The individual social mechanisms of action have varying effects on another's will. These differences are reflected in the level of internalization as indicated by the change mechanisms. This linkage between mechanisms of action and change may be viewed as a dynamic coupling of (desired) ends and means. This linkage lays the foundation for strategic analysis of nonviolent direct action and also, I hope, for a conceptual bridge between the "NVA as a set of tactics" and "NVA as a way of life" camps.

Popular Empowerment

The preceding conceptual framework and theoretical specification of mechanisms of direct action and change are intended to serve as analytic tools to aid in our understanding of how nonviolent direct action may empower those who wield it, both as a tactic and as a way of life. Where I end this discussion is really the beginning of an assessment of the complex interaction between purpose and motivation. Purpose has been cast in the form of various mechanisms of change: To what extent does an action's goal entail internalization of the change in another party? Motivation has been woven throughout the explanatory framework in the specification of strategic alternatives. But the calculus is not fixed. Purpose and motivation interact, join together, and become what Stone (paraphrasing Burns) termed "motivation through purpose."[42] Analysis of the strategic performance of nonviolent struggle, therefore, cannot be reduced to tactical level choices.

To be sure, ends and means are intertwined dynamically and interactively through time. The longitudinal interaction of moving toward, moving away, and moving against another has been specified by Raven and Kruglanski for their typology of powers.[43] The strategic performance considerations discussed above reflect the linkage and dynamics of interaction between action and change at a single point in time. A useful next step would be to empirically assess and model this interaction over time. Does violence beget violence? Are the changes evolving from altruistic appeals longer lasting than those of appeals to authority? These are but two of an endless series of questions, the answers to which would contribute to the advancement of both the "technique" and the "way of life" camps. More important, the answers may lead to the transcendence of this ill-conceived, artificial dichotomy. I suggest that both the "technique" and "way of life" perspectives can find common ground in the hypothesized operation of diffusion of power or popular empowerment.

The very process of explication, of strategic analysis, elevates the calculations beyond individual self-interests and motivations. Just as effective leadership is transformational, so is effective strategic engagement in routine and direct action. The specification of alternative mechanisms of action identifies political opportunities for effecting/resisting change. Leaders of social movements have long recognized this important point and seek to exploit and expand existing "political opportunity structures."[44]

In his comprehensive study of community power in Atlanta over four decades, Stone suggested that power struggles concern "not control and resistance, but gaining and fusing a capacity to act—*power to*, not *power over*."[45] As Sharp wrote, one of the goals of strategic analysis of nonviolent struggle is to tap into and exploit this transformational *power to*

> reduce drastically, or remove the reliance on war and other types of violent conflict . . . with a nonviolent counterpart of war, "war without violence," by which people can defend liberty, their way of life, humanitarian principles, their institutions and society, at least as effectively against military attack as military means.[46]

A Caution

A final thought comes to mind as I reflect on this inquiry into nonviolent action and change. I am struck by the centrality of the accommodation mechanism of change. The potential to sustain reciprocal interests offers "the power of balance,"[47] a built-in correction process through which opposing parties can learn about and adjust to each other.

I remarked earlier that nonviolent sanctions occupy a unique position among the methods of action. But as powerful as they are, and as broadly applicable as they are, the theoretical limits of coercion are compelling, as summarized by Raven and Kruglanski:

> Frustration and hostility resulting from being the recipient of coercive power then leads both parties to "move against" in behavior, belief, interaction, identification. Concern about appearance before third parties and lowered self-esteem increase further the desire to influence the other by means of coercion even where other bases might conceivably prove effective. Thus, the underlying and personal bases of conflict become even greater. The power preferences of two antagonists then further increase the possibility of further use of coercion by each.[48]

If we are to optimize our strategic performance we must remain careful in our resort to coercive means of action. Only through empowerment of the other can we effect stable, internalized change and, in turn, empower ourselves. Nonviolent direct action, especially, cannot be wielded with insolence.

Notes

1. Martin, "Gene Sharp's Theory of Power," p. 217.

2. The numerous examples of nonviolent direct action throughout the world, throughout history, should have dispelled this notion long ago. An illustrative listing of such cases can be found in the second volume of Sharp's *Politics of Nonviolent Action*.

3. Actually, several divisive splits remain. Others include the division between those who focus on conflict resolution and those who focus on conflict prosecution and, with respect to civilian-based defense, implementation strategies.

4. This common shorthand, used, for example, by Lynd, *Nonviolence in America*, p. xliii, inadequately captures the conceptual underpinnings of these two intellectual camps. But for the sake of clarity, I use it until later in the paper where I qualify and expand it.

5. Bond, "Alternatives to Violence," pp. 172, 194.

6. See Sharp, "The Role of Power," p. 98.

7. Given my affiliation with the Program on Nonviolent Sanctions (founded by Gene Sharp) the appearance of bias may be quite strong. In the present examination, however, unless I cite Sharp explicitly, the interpretation is mine alone.

8. Coover, Deacon, Esser, and Moore, *Resource Manual,* p. 7.

9. Parts of this and the next section are adapted from Bond, "Research Issues."

10. These are but a few of many attributes relevant to NVA, selected to illuminate the basic and often ignored distinction between attributes and behavior.

11. Lakey, *Strategy for a Living Revolution,* p. 57.

12. Lofland, *Protest Studies,* p. 2.

13. Wilson, *Political Organizations*, p. 282.

14. Carter, *Direct Action,* p. 25.

15. Eisinger, "The Conditions of Protest Behavior," p. 14.

16. To say that NVA can serve as a functional substitute for violence does not imply that violence also can serve as a functional substitute for NVA; nor does it imply that all functions of violence are served by NVA. To be sure, NVA may serve democratizing (power-devolving) functions that are antithetical to violence. Also, functions such as group identity formation may be influenced in very different ways; for example, self-group boundaries associated with certain methods of NVA (especially noncoercive methods) are likely to be more permeable and inclusive than the dehumanizing friend/foe dichotomies typically generated by violence.

17. The expectation here is related neither to the intentions of either party to the conflict nor to their motivations. Rather, it is that of a hypothetical, informed, and impartial third-party observer to the conflict who seeks in a reasonable manner to assess the risk of physical injury or death inflicted by the use of physical force.

18. Clausewitz, *War, Politics, and Power,* p. 83.

19. See Lofland, *Protest Studies*, pp. 9–10, 257–269, for a discussion of various frameworks and their problems, including a consideration of Sharp's approach.

20. But the consideration of style is important, especially as it relates to politeness phenomena. See Chilton, "Politeness, Politics," pp. 203–227, for a discussion of texts arising from diplomatic interactions. He situates politeness strategies in the domain of social action in general.

21. Eisinger, "The Conditions of Protest Behavior," p. 13.

22. See Rummel, *Understanding Conflict ,*" pp. 265–288, for an extended discussion of this conflict (helix) process model.

23. Lynd, *Nonviolence in America.*

24. Sharp himself still characterizes nonviolent struggle as a political "technique," though his usage encompasses "the practice, dynamics, and consequences . . . upon the wielding of power. . . ." And he cautions, "This technique is not understandable without consideration of this important element in its nature." (1990a: 91)

25. Sharp, *The Politics of Nonviolent Action.*

26. In contrast to the present mechanisms of *action,* Sharp outlined mechanisms of *change* (conversion, accommodation, and coercion) in his 1973 book. He added an additional mechanism of change (disintegration) in *Civilian-based Defense.*

27. Rummel, *The Conflict Helix.*

28. Goldhamer and Shils, "Types of Power and Status."

29. Boulding, *Three Faces of Power*, p. 24.

30. The earlier version was operationalized and employed to develop a profile of the ways in which various methods of NVA operate. See Bond, "The Nature and Meanings of Nonviolent Direct Action," and "Alternatives to Violence." In that first assessment, I assessed the peak use-intensity of each mechanism for both parties to a conflict over the course of a struggle. The procedure's inter-coder reliability was good; the procedures have since been refined and are being tested again.

31. It should be noted that all violence is direct action as defined in the present framework. As a subset of direct action, all violence, like nonviolent struggle, is unilaterally initiated and never requires the compliance or consent of the other party. Likewise, the "success" of violence is a function of its application rather than any implicit or explicit accord.

32. The dual characterization of the action is called for because although the use of physical force is indicated by the expected deaths of the occupants, the destruction of the building constitutes an exercise of control over a (now destroyed) resource. It is important to note that these mechanisms do not operate in isolation. Thus we assess them simultaneously to develop a profile of their composite operation.

33. Gregg, *The Power of Nonviolence.*

34. Sharp included a chapter-length discussion of "political jiu-jitsu" in Part III of his *Politics of Nonviolent Action.* He discussed his treatment of Gregg's concept in the first footnote to that chapter, p. 698.

35. Sharp, *The Politics of Nonviolent Action*, pp. 705–706.

36. Kelman, "Compliance, Identification, and Internalization, pp. 53.

37. Boulding, *Three Faces of Power.*

38. Kelman, "Compliance, Identification, and Internalization."

39. Kelman uses the terms *compliance, identification,* and *internalization* in his typology of attitude change processes. My use of *compliance* is virtually identical to his, though I distinguish between the compliance of higher- and lower-capacity parties. I employ his concept of internalization as the adoption of the specific content of a demand but prefer to follow popular usage and call this *conversion* (for higher-capacity actors). Kelman's concept of identification is included in the present framework as part of the adoption mechanisms, conversion, and cooptation; specifically, I combine the adoption of a demand motivated by positive interests with that motivated by a desired relationship. This combining is done not to ignore the important distinction that he has drawn but because of the constraints imposed by my purpose—to develop an empirically testable theory. At the scale of action involved here (as compared with the controlled experimentation conducted by Kelman), such distinctions would not be empirically discernable.

40. Nye, *Bound to Lead*, p. 191.
41. Blalock, *Power and Conflict*, p. 5.
42. Stone, "Transactional and Transformational Leadership," p. 2.
43. Raven and Kruglanski, "Conflict and Power," pp. 77–81.
44. Eisinger in "The Conditions of Protest Behavior," p. 11, first developed this concept, which has been used recently to frame a discussion of "political space" and opportunities for mobilization in a study of the nuclear freeze movement by Meyer, *A Winter of Discontent.*
45. Stone, "Transactional and Transformational Leadership," p. 229. (Italics in the original.)
46. Sharp, *Making the Abolition of War,"* p. 6.
47. Torbet, *The Power of Balance*, p. 41.
48. Raven and Kruglanski, "Conflict and Power," p. 104.

Bibliography

Albert, David H. *People Power: Applying Nonviolence Theory* (Philadelphia: New Society Publishers, 1985).

Baldwin, David A. *Paradoxes of Power* (New York: Basil Blackwell, 1989).

Blalock, H.M., Jr. *Power and Conflict: Toward a General Theory* (Newbury Park, CA: Sage Publications, 1989).

Bond, Doug. "Alternatives to Violence: An Empirical Study of Nonviolent Direct Action" (Ph.D. diss., Dept. of Political Science, University of Hawaii, 1985).

————. "The Nature and Meanings of Nonviolent Direct Action: An Exploratory Study." *Journal of Peace Research* 25 (1) (1988): 81–89.

————. "Research Issues and Explanatory Frameworks," in *Transforming Struggle: Strategy and the Global Experience of Nonviolent Direct Action* (Cambridge, MA: Program on Nonviolent Sanctions, CFIA, Harvard University, 1992).

Boulding, Kenneth. *Three Faces of Power* (Newbury Park, CA: Sage Publications, 1989).

Carter, April. *Direct Action and Liberal Democracy* (London: Routledge & Kegan Paul, 1973).

Case, Clarence Marsh. *Non-Violent Coercion: A Study in Methods of Social Pressure* (New York: Century Co., 1923).

Chilton, Paul. "Politeness, Politics, and Diplomacy." *Discourse & Society* 1 (2) (1990): 203–227.

Clausewitz, Karl von. *War, Politics, and Power* (Chicago: Henry Regnery Co., 1970).

Clegg, Stewart R. *Frameworks of Power* (Newbury Park, CA: Sage, 1989).

Coover, Virginia, Ellen Deacon, Charles Esser, and Christopher Moore. *Resource Manual for a Living Revolution* (Philadelphia: New Society Publisher, 1985).

Eisinger, Peter K. "The Conditions of Protest Behavior in American Cities." *American Political Science Review* 67 (1) (March 1973): 11–28.

French, John R. P., and Bertram Raven. "The Bases of Social Power," in Dorwin Cartwright (ed.), *Studies in Social Power* (Ann Arbor: University of Michigan, 1959).

Gamson, William A. *Power and Discontent* (Homewood, IL: Dorsey Press, 1968).

Goldhamer, Herbert, and Edward A. Shils. "Types of Power and Status." *The American Journal of Sociology* 45 (2) (September 1939): 171–182.

Gregg, Richard. *The Power of Nonviolence, Revised Edition* (New York: Schocken Books, 1966).

Kelman, Herbert C. "Compliance, Identification, and Internalization: Three Processes of Attitude Change." *Conflict Resolution* 2 (1) (1958): 51–60.

Lakey, George."The Sociological Mechanisms of Nonviolent Action." Master's thesis reprinted in *Peace Research Reviews* 2 (6) (1968): 1–102.

———. *Strategy for a Living Revolution* (San Francisco: Freeman & Co., 1973).

Lofland, John. *Protest Studies of Collective Behavior and Social Movements* (reprint of 1985 edition) (New Brunswick: Transaction, 1991).

Lukes, Steven (ed.). *Power* (New York: New York University Press, 1986).

Lynd, Staughton. *Nonviolence in America: A Documentary History* (New York: Bobbs-Merrill, 1966).

Martin, Brian. "Gene Sharp's Theory of Power." *Journal of Peace Research* 26 (2) (1989): 217–222.

Meyer, David S. *A Winter of Discontent: The Nuclear Freeze and American Politics* (New York: Praeger, 1990).

Miller, William R. *Nonviolence: A Christian Interpretation* (New York: Schocken Books, 1964).

Nye, Joseph S. *Bound to Lead: The Changing Nature of American Power* (New York: Basic Books, 1991).

Parsons, Talcott. "The Concept of Influence." *Public Opinion Quarterly* 27 (1) (Spring 1963): 37–92.

Raven, Bertram H., and Arie W. Kruglanski. "Conflict and Power," in Paul Swingle (ed.), *The Structure of Conflict* (New York: Academic Press, 1970).

Rummel, R. J. *Understanding Conflict and War: Volume 2, The Conflict Helix* (New York: Sage Publications, 1976).

———. *The Conflict Helix: Principles and Practices of Interpersonal, Social, and International Conflict and Cooperation* (New Brunswick: Transaction, 1991; originally published in 1984).

Seifert, Harvey. *Conquest Through Suffering: The Process and Prospects of Nonviolent Resistance* (Philadelphia: Westminster Press, 1965).

Sharp, Gene. "The Technique of Nonviolent Action," in Adam Roberts (ed.), *Civilian Resistance as a National Defense* (Harrisburg, PA: Stackpole Books, 1968).

———. *The Politics of Nonviolent Action*, 3 vols. (Boston: Porter Sargent Publishers, 1973).

———. *Making the Abolition of War a Realistic Goal* (New York: World Policy Institute, 1980).

———. "The Role of Power in Nonviolent Political Struggle," in Ralph Crow, Philip Grant, and Saad E. Ibrahim (eds.), *Arab Nonviolent Political Struggle in the Middle East* (Boulder: Lynne Rienner Publishers, 1990a).

———. *Post-Military Defense* (Princeton: Princeton University Press, 1990b).

Stone, Clarence M. *Regime Politics Governing Atlanta* (Lawrence: University Press of Kansas, 1989).

———. "Transactional and Transformational Leadership: A Re-Examination." Paper presented at the annual meeting of the American Political Science Association, San Francisco, 1990.

Torbet, William R. 1991. *The Power of Balance: Transforming Self, Society, and Scientific Inquiry* (Newbury Park, CA: Sage Publications, 1991).

Wilson, James Q. *Political Organizations* (New York: Basic Books, 1973).

Wrong, Dennis D. *Power* (New York: Harper and Row, 1979).

5

Violence, Nonviolence, and Justice in Sandinista Nicaragua

Paul Wehr & Sharon Erickson Nepstad

A society undergoing massive discontinuous change such as Nicaragua in the 1980s is not where one would expect to find the achievement of justice without violence. Political revolutions have been generally characterized by considerable violence. Successful insurrections move quickly to consolidate their power, leaders compete for constituencies, scores are settled, and elements opposed to radical change may challenge the revolutionary regime. Violence in Sandinista Nicaragua was, however, unusual on two counts. First, it was stimulated and executed to a very large degree from the outside. Second, it was limited by a number of constraints on violence having both practical and theoretical implications for justice attainment.

Assessing the violence-justice relationship in Sandinista Nicaragua is considerably more difficult than in more repressive and less equitable Guatemala, for example. Social justice was a guiding principle of Sandinista policy and, since losing power in 1990, Sandinista organizations have struggled to preserve the agrarian reform and social welfare structures they put in place in the 1980s.

Despite its intention to make Nicaraguan society more just and peaceful, the Sandinista revolution did give rise to deep conflicts over perceived injustices. There were regions and groups within Nicaragua with real grievances against the Sandinista state. Where these grievances produced open conflict, those opposing the state used both violent and nonviolent means to achieve what they felt was justice. Our focus in this study is upon the nonviolent methods used on all sides.

Those justice conflicts had diverse origins. Sharp ideological divisions developed rapidly after the fall of Anastasia Somoza in 1979. Marxists of every persuasion struggled both with one another and with democratic socialists. Mainstream Catholics took on liberation theologians, and both of them had uneasy relations with Protestant groups along the Atlantic Coast. Political pluralists resisted creation of a unitary state while pacifists criticized the growth of a militarized state. Those of the privileged class who had remained fought the Sandinista government as it confiscated property, developed mass education and health programs, and organized agricultural and industrial cooperatives.

Political and economic destabilization from the outside was a second major stimulator of conflict. The U.S. government's policy to derail the Sandinista revolution may have been the most intensive national destabilization program in history. The Contra resistance, and to a much lesser degree the Yatama movement, were supplied and organized from the outside.

A third stimulator of violence was the constant militarization going on in Nicaragua in the 1980–1988 period. This factor was largely a reflection of East-West military competition in Central America—the United States in sharp opposition to Sandinism and other armed insurrections, and Cuba and the Soviet Union supporting them. Whatever their origins, political conflicts in Nicaragua rapidly became armed conflicts as weapons spread throughout the population. More military and paramilitary forces and armed civilians intensified the potential for violent challenges to state authority and equally violent responses.

A number of additional factors increased the potential for violence in Sandinista Nicaragua. There were residual class divisions. Though much of the privileged class had left Nicaragua, some remained to protect their interests. A second group of privilege was created by the revolution itself as leaders in the Sandinista party, administrative apparatus, and armed forces gained economic and social advantage. Geographical separation aggravated racial and ethnic divisions on the Atlantic Coast as the Sandinistas sought forcibly to integrate it. The general grinding poverty in Nicaragua and the unpopularity of military conscription, begun in 1983, elevated political tensions in the country, increasing the likelihood of intergroup and interpersonal violence.

Despite the estimated fifty thousand casualties resulting from the Contra war alone, there occurred less political violence than one might have predicted given the radically disparate justice goals pursued, the number of armed citizens, and the level of economic and social restructuring going on at the time. This lower-than-expected incidence of violence is explained, we think, in the violence-inhibiting, conflict-moderating, justice-producing constraints operating in Nicaraguan society. Our purpose here is to identify the more important constraints and to show how they supported resolution of the two most serious conflicts, the Contra war and the Atlantic Coast resistance. We will, in conclusion, suggest some implications of the Nicaraguan experience for justice attainment without violence.

Justice Through Nonviolent Means

We must obviously qualify our description of the two struggles as achieving justice nonviolently because both were characterized initially by armed conflict. But nonviolent means were later used, and those means did lead to settlement of justice grievances. Each conflict, however, produced only partial justice as defined by the challenging parties. The Democratic Resistance, commonly known as the Contras, did see political pluralism introduced and its forces were repatriated. But three years after repatriation, many had yet to be settled on land of their own. The indigenous peoples of the Atlantic Coast did achieve political and cultural autonomy in principle but are still pressing the national government to develop workable autonomy structures. In both cases, however, the challenge groups appear to be better off than they were when they pursued goals through violent means. In both cases, violent conflict was ended within the framework of Esquipulas, the regional peacemaking structure.

The Sandinista–Atlantic Coast Conflict

The conflict between the Nicaraguan government and the Indian and Creole peoples of the Atlantic Coast began soon after the Sandinistas came to power in Managua. The Atlantic Coast had been largely isolated from both the Somoza repression and the Sandinista insurrection. When the Sandinistas sought to integrate the region politically, economically, and administratively, there was quick local resistance. The government sent the national army to impose its control over the region. There followed extended military occupation, the harsh treatment of indigenous communities, armed rebellion by loosely allied paramilitary groups, and mass flight of thirty thousand refugees into neighboring Honduras and Costa Rica.

The grievances of the Atlantic Coast resistance groups against the government were numerous: the killing and imprisonment of community members; destruction of crops and churches; violation of traditional tribal property rights and ethnic cultures; restriction of human rights including the right to refuse military service; and the denial of local self-government.

By 1984, realizing the errors of its coercive policy, the Sandinista government began a two-track conciliation strategy. It first initiated talks with Atlantic Coast political and cultural leaders. These consultations would subsequently result in a National Autonomy Commission (1984), elected local peace and autonomy commissions (1986), the drafting of a National Autonomy Law, and its ratification by a Multi-Ethnic Assembly (1987).[1] Certain Atlantic Coast Sandinistas trusted by both the government and indigenous leaders were central figures in this autonomy-building process.[2]

The second track involved government negotiation with the Indian resistance leaders in exile. Having formed Yatama in 1987, the latter's goal was the restoration of historical territorial rights, not the multiethnic regional independence permitted in the Autonomy Law. For the Sandinista-Yatama conflict, then, the Esquipulas process provided a conflict management framework.[3] Within Esquipulas, Nicaragua created a National Reconciliation Commission to resolve the larger Sandinista-Contra conflict and a Conciliation Commission to mediate the more limited Sandinista-Yatama disputes. The Moravian Church, the primary religious organization in the East, acted as the intermediary. In the early 1980s, the Moravians had lost pastors, churches, schools, and hospitals in the Sandinista-Indian war. From 1983 on, however, the Moravian Provincial Board and the Sandinistas had worked together in arranging for cease-fires and in autonomy consultations. The Conciliation Commission consisted mainly of people from the Moravian and Mennonite churches, both known for their traditions of pacifism and conciliation.

From early 1988, the commission mediated the conflict under the most difficult conditions. Oliver North and the Central Intelligence Agency (CIA) were doing their best to inhibit a Sandinista-Indian agreement. That agreement would preclude the united resistance to the Sandinistas the United States sought to build. The mediators had to overcome kidnapping threats, assassination attempts, and competition among Yatama leaders to craft a settlement. In September 1989, a full agreement was reached with the eleventh-hour intervention of former U.S. president Jimmy Carter.

Thus, the Atlantic Coast challenge to state repression shifted from initial armed response to the nonviolent approaches of consultation, negotiation, and mediation along both the internally initiated autonomy track and the externally assisted conciliation track. Certain justice goals were achieved through that shift: refugee repatriation; regional self-government; military demobilization; and reintegration of resistance leaders into the national political system.

The Sandinista-Contra Conflict

The civil war between the Sandinistas and the Contras had quite different origins from the Atlantic Coast conflict. The Contras were not seeking ethnic justice and autonomy as were the Atlantic Coast challengers, but rather the replacement of the Sandinista state with a more conservative, pluralist one. Contra grievances were as diverse as the paths by which Contra leaders came to resist. Many were former National Guard officers seeking a return to something resembling Nicaragua under Somoza. Others were disaffected Sandinistas, fallen away over ideological differences with former insurgent colleagues. They sought a more pluralist social democracy. Most of the Contras were peasants, some forced to serve against their will.

Whatever their personal motives, all but a few of the Contra leaders were organized, armed, and paid by the U.S. government. Its policy of low-intensity warfare was designed to destabilize the Sandinista regime and end its support for other Central American insurgencies.[4] With genuine grievances against a radical government and its uncompensated property seizures, Contra leaders were bought off with large amounts of U.S. funding.

By 1983, the United States was establishing Contra bases in Honduras and Costa Rica. For the next five years, Contra troops carried economic warfare and political assassination to the Nicaraguan countryside. The Sandinista government responded with military conscription, large increases in military expenditures, and the widespread arming of civilians through local Committees for the Support of the Sandinistas. Military activity was at high levels through the end of 1986.

Three sets of external events served to reduce the level of violence in the Sandinista-Contra conflict after 1986. The first were the Iran-Contra hearings in Washington in 1986–1987, which obstructed the Reagan administration's Nicaragua policy. The Contras could no longer be supplied. Second, the growing cooperation between the United States and the USSR in arms control and conflict mitigation reduced East-West competition in Latin America. Nicaraguan proxies for that rivalry became increasingly superfluous.

Finally, the Esquipulas peace process from 1987 on was providing both impetus and framework for negotiated settlement of the conflict. Esquipulas called for a National Reconciliation Commission (NRC) to resolve each civil war in Central America. The Nicaraguan NRC was the first to become operational.

Chairing the Nicaraguan NRC was Cardinal Miguel Obando y Bravo. The Catholic Church played the same central role in the Sandinista-Contra conflict as did the Moravian Church in the Sandinista–Atlantic Coast conflict. The commission worked to implement the peace agreements negotiated in the Esquipulas summit meetings of 1988–1989. Sandinista and Contra negotiators first met under Obando's auspices early in 1988. Several months of bargaining produced the Sapoa agreement and a de facto cease-fire. Esquipulas agreements were subsequently reached for: internationally supervised elections; demobilization and reintegration of Contra forces; and United Nations (UN) and Organization of American States (OAS) monitoring. Faithful implementation of those agreements produced what we believe to be one of the most successful peacemaking cases of modern times. That process will be more fully explored below.

Although the goals of the challenge groups—local autonomy, political pluralism, demilitarization of the state, an end to conscription, and land to work—were in principle met through the 1990 elections, they had not been fully realized even two years later. In the West demobilized soldiers reverted to armed threat, as *recontras* (former Contras) and *recompas* (former Sandinista military), to press their demands for land and jobs. On the Atlantic Coast, the indigenous peoples pressing for implementation of the Autonomy Law have not generally reverted to armed threat in their conflict with the national government. By April 1992, all opponents in the East and West were resolving their disputes through negotiation and disarmament agreements.[5]

Conflictant Power Mixes

One way to analyze how these challenge groups achieved justice is to view their power strategies and those of the Sandinistas as mixes of Boulding's three forms of power—threat, exchange, and love (that is, integration). Most often challenge groups use a mix of these three strategies.[6] At any given moment, an extreme approach on the threat end may appear to eclipse integrative efforts at the other. The exchange (that is, negotiation) elements should keep the mix in workable balance—for example, the threat may be kept merely implicit or nonviolent and the integrative force incomplete or tentative.

We would argue that in a conflict, the less violent the mix of power strategies, the more successful the challengers will be in achieving justice. There must be, in such a strategic mix, sufficient threat to escalate change-producing conflict. That threat, however, need not take the form of violent action. On the other hand, the love, or integrative, inclination cannot be too strong or creative conflict will not occur. The exchange in the mix is the means by which threat and integration are kept at sufficiently moderate levels to permit movement toward justice-oriented change.

Each resistance group and the Sandinista government had a mix of power strategies they were using toward their opponent(s). The power mixes of the opponents shifted as the two wars continued. Initially, the mixes were all heavy with threat characterized by violent force. Then, over time, the exchange portions in the mixes expanded, violent sanctions in the threat sector were increasingly supplanted by nonviolent ones, and the integration portions were expanded as negotiation agreements were implemented.

We further propose that such movement toward a less violent strategic mix is encouraged or discouraged by the larger context of a conflict. In Nicaragua, that context was influencing the opponents' strategic mixes away from armed force and consequently was moving the two justice conflicts toward negotiation and settlement.

The Conflict Context

Three types of factors were instrumental in moderating conflict and limiting violence as justice was pursued in the two conflicts: (1) institutional constraints; (2) normative restraints; and (3) innovative use of conflict management.

Institutional Constraints

The political and legal systems in Sandinista Nicaragua tended to limit the coercive capacity of the state. Constitutional guarantees of human and civil rights, judicial grievance procedures, and a popular army close to the people all served to limit any inclination the state might have had to use violence. Though there were attempts at times to silence opposition and re-strict political space available to Sandinista challengers, open repression was rare. When the state did repress, the psychological and political costs to it were so great that it had to retreat and publicly apologize. The political culture of Sandinism would not tolerate much repression.

Socioeconomic structures built by the Sandinistas had violence-in-hibiting consequences. Their serious efforts at life-chance redistribution through national health, agrarian reform, education, and basic-needs programs not only measurably reduced social inequality but provided mediating organizations that could respond to individual and group justice claims. The primary intermediary organizations were the branches of the Sandinista party and its mass organizations built around rural and industrial labor, professionals, women, and students. Of special importance were the cooperatives[7] and the Base Christian Communities within the People's Church, both of which have been important mechanisms for participatory democracy throughout Latin America.[8] Such organizations provided multiple grievance channels and safety-valve mechanisms that tended to reduce violent conflict and preserve system legitimacy. These mediating organizations increased social justice, but their influence was to a degree offset by the development of a Sandinista "new class," which tended to distance national leaders from local problems. Still, the organizational density providing for two-way communication and influence between levels of Nicaraguan society probably outweighed any class alienation.

A third set of structural factors were the extensive integrative affiliations encouraged by Nicaraguan society and Sandinista organizations. There were cross-cutting religious, political, and social ties that bridged existing cleavages. Religious, family, and friendship links cut across political affiliations to moderate conflict. A notable example is the family of Violeta Chamorro, two of whose children were Sandinistas and two members of the United Nicaraguan Opposition (UNO). Chamorro used family solidarity as a base to build national solidarity as a conflict-moderating device. Nicaraguans, for her, were all members of the national family. Such safety-valve institutions and cross-cutting affiliations can lead to identification and mitigation of grievances and greater societal solidarity. Where conflict is thus limited, its associative functions can strengthen both the social system generally and specific units within it.[9]

Finally, violence was reduced in the two justice struggles in question by the relations Nicaragua developed with two external facilitators of justice and nonviolence—the regional peacemaking machinery of Esquipulas II and the international movement of solidarity with the Nicaraguan people.

Esquipulas pushed the Sandinistas and their civil war opponents toward negotiated settlement. Most important, it removed the Sandinista-Contra war from U.S.-Soviet competition. Its summit agreements, its International Commission for Verification and Support (CIAV), and its sponsorship of reconciliation commissions in member countries moved violent conflict into negotiation. The Esquipulas agreement of 1987, "Process For Establishing a Firm and Lasting Peace in Central America," created the framework for bringing signatory governments and their insurgent opponents together.[10]

The Esquipulas agreement set objectives and prescribed specific measures: demilitarization of conflict through cease-fires; refusal of support for and use of territory by insurgents; national reconciliation through negotiated settlements, amnesty for insurgents, and repatriation of refugees; democratization of political systems through free and open elections, ending states of emergency, and protection of human rights; and continuing regional consultation through periodic summits and a parliament.

The attention of the successive Esquipulas summits was almost entirely on resolving Nicaraguan conflicts. Each meeting produced additional steps toward their peaceful resolution: San José (1988), a Sandinista-Contra cease-fire and negotiations; San Salvador (1989), agreement on elections and Contra demobilization/repatriation; Tela (1989), supervision of demobilization by the ICVS and request for UN monitoring; Montelimar (1990), postelection transition and Contra disarmament procedures.[11] Nicaragua, then, was at the center of a violence-reduction, justice-production process that built a momentum for reducing threat and for increasing exchange and reconciliation in the strategic mix of the opponents.

Nicaragua was also set within an international solidarity and support network that by its very nature discouraged violence and encouraged justice. Through it came international volunteers; material, technical, and financial aid; and pressure from external support organizations on behalf of nonviolence and justice. Its North American segment pressured the U.S. Congress away from military aid. Very important was the physical presence of this network's "sympathetic third parties."[12] Working and watching throughout Nicaragua, they served to limit violence and rights violations on all sides.

We have discussed some institutional and structural characteristics of the national and regional settings where Nicaraguan justice struggles were taking place. Those dimensions were damping political violence and encouraging the mitigation of justice grievances. Those constraints were a mix of mutually reinforcing internal and external initiatives.

Normative Restraints

Conflict in Sandinista Nicaragua was also moderated by ethical commitments to reconciliation and justice within the revolution itself. Those commitments were not always honored, but sincere efforts were made to do so. Upon taking power, the Sandinistas abolished the death penalty, prohibited torture, set about to correct the worst of the social injustices, and welcomed reconciliation with dissidents. The Sandinista revolution was gentle as such movements go. Reason not coercion, conciliation not division, nonviolence not violence were to be its guiding principles for transforming society. A good faith effort was made by the Sandinistas to apply those principles. Countering such ethical restraint, however, were sharp ideological and theological conflicts. Marxism confronted conservative Christianity, and the Hispanicized West rejected the religious, political, and racial separatism of the Atlantic Coast. In the face of these sharp conflicts, two factors were particularly influential in reducing violence—religious values and the participation of women.

Religious values. Elements of both the Catholic and Protestant churches were deeply involved in the justice conflicts in question. Liberation theologians and lay Catholics helped create the Sandinista state and the theoretical, ideological, and cultural bases for transforming Nicaraguan society.[13] The values of religious solidarity, social justice, and nonviolence were therefore tempering policymaking and the state's use of force. An ethical tone was established that afforded political space for nonviolent protest.

There are numerous documented illustrations of how practicing Christians active in the revolution restrained its violence.[14] The Sandinistas acknowledged that involvement in their official statement on religion.

> [Christians were involved] to a degree unprecedented in any other revolutionary movement in Latin America and perhaps in the world. The fact opens new and interesting possibilities for the participation of Christians in revolutions elsewhere, not only in the phase of struggle for power, but in the phase of building a new society.[15]

Time and again, the spirit of reconciliation was evident in the way Sandinistas dealt with their opposition. By way of illustration, Interior Minister Tomás Borge came upon a National Guard officer who had only months before the Sandinista victory tortured, raped, and killed Borge's wife. He took the officer out of the line, who undoubtedly feared he would be executed immediately. Instead, according to the account, Borge told him, "My revenge will be to pardon you."[16]

Perhaps the most direct influence of Christianity on reducing violence and facilitating justice occurred in the Base Christian Communities. Through their overlapping membership with Sandinista mass organizations, they worked to "Christianize" the revolution at the local level.

As the Sandinista-Contra war intensified, Christians were using active nonviolence for peace and justice. Father Miguel D'Escoto, Nicaraguan foreign minister in the mid-1980s, led this nonviolence movement. In 1985, D'Escoto launched a nonviolence campaign, Evangelical Insurrection, with a month-long fast during Lent. It was an insurrection, he explained, because Christians of all persuasions could rise up against war, repression, hatred, violence, external intervention—from wherever they came. It was evangelical because he believed nonviolence to be the essence of the Gospel. After Easter, D'Escoto spread his campaign through the Via Crucis (Way of the Cross), a two-week, two-hundred-mile walk across Nicaragua. Its purposes were to heal conflict internal to Nicaragua and to move U.S. Americans to work for a conciliatory U.S. policy. As D'Escoto told one interviewer: "This uprising, this protest, uses a different arsenal, with weapons different from the traditional, conventional. . . . The weapons that the Lord wants us to use are nonviolent weapons. The most obvious ones are fasting, prayer, and walking."[17]

D'Escoto and other priests in the Sandinista government constrained revolutionary excess, constantly urging moderation and nonviolence. D'Escoto was personally intrigued with the potential of nonviolent sanctions. This interest led him to invite to Nicaragua in July 1988 a team of specialists in social defense—the use of nonviolent resistance against either external attack or internal repression. The concept, as an alternative or supplement to military defense, was discussed with government leaders, mass organizations, and the political opposition.[18]

Catholic nonviolence was matched from the Protestant side by a constant search for conciliation. In 1986, partly in response to D'Escoto's insurrection of the year before, Nicaragua's evangelical church council embarked on the "Campaign of Fasting and Prayer for Peace and Justice in Nicaragua." Prayer vigils for peace were held throughout the nation, culminating in an all-night vigil by ten thousand in Managua in October.[19]

Nicaragua's international solidarity community used nonviolent action against violence. Witness for Peace (WFP), for example, had a physical presence from 1983 onward in the war zone, where it had observed that Contra attacks were reduced when international volunteers were present. WFP representatives challenged U.S. warships off the coast in unarmed boats, sailed along border rivers to protest attacks on civilians, and obtained hostage releases.[20]

The most enduring effort to minimize violence in Nicaraguan conflict, however, was the tradition of pacifism and conciliation among the Moravians and Mennonites. The Moravian tradition of peacemaking stretches back to the Czech reformation of the fifteenth century. Their reconciliation work with the Sandinistas and among the numerous ethnic groups in the

East was a most important force for violence reduction. By 1992, the Moravian leaders in the East were once again mediating conflict, this time between the UNO government and local groups calling for implementation of the Autonomy Law.

The Mennonites' tradition of conscientious refusal to participate in war brought them into direct conflict with Sandinista military conscription. Refusal to bear arms led some Mennonites to officially sanctioned conscientious objector status, others to alternative service, some to imprisonment, and still others to flee the country. Such principled resistance to war and military service presented a complication for Sandinista militarization policy. It may have inhibited Contra recruitment as well. The Mennonites' pacifism also led them to urge that nonviolent resistance be explored as an alternative to military defense against the Contras.

The role of women. Women have been a force for conflict moderation and peacemaking in contemporary Nicaragua. They may have a natural inclination toward nonviolent personal and group relations. They have also been a disadvantaged group even during the Sandinista period and thus more sensitive to justice issues being raised by aggrieved groups generally. Such women as Violeta Chamorro, Hazel Law, and Myra Cunningham demonstrated their peacemaking and justice skills in high positions. Elsewhere, women applied those skills in cooperatives and local government and as family heads.

Women appeared to vote heavily against the Sandinistas in the 1990 elections. They did so first because they felt it would end the war. As mothers, they wished to lose no more children to it. A UNO victory, the U.S. government had promised, would end the war. Second, Nicaraguan women are often single parents and managers of the family economy. The economic decline in the later Sandinista years, whatever its causes, was particularly burdensome for women responsible for feeding their families.

Finally, women had grievances against the Sandinistas. Although they had made some gains under Sandinism, its promises of sexual equality, full political participation, and protected gender rights remained largely unfulfilled.[21] The promises of a woman-led UNO coalition to end the war and improve the economy appeared to be sufficiently compelling to women voters. Their voting in itself served to reduce violence levels, at least in the short term.

Conflict Management Experience

A third conflict-moderating force in Sandinista Nicaragua was the skill at conflict settlement that developed there. Nicaraguans learned to innovate while drawing on their own peacemaking traditions. They learned to use

third parties to negotiate settlements and to invent solutions where past experience provided none.

Third-party approaches. Nicaraguans quickly learned a good deal about
third-party intervention. Use of the insider-partial to mediate disputes appears to be a tradition in Central American societies. The insider-partial
is one chosen from within the conflict, known to be more sympathetic to
one side but trusted by both because of their personal distinction and institutional prominence.[22] Cardinal Obando began such an intermediary role
during the rebellion against Somoza. In 1974 and 1978 he mediated
hostage negotiations successfully despite his open antipathy toward the
Somoza regime.[23] Ten years later, with his hostility redirected against the
Sandinistas, he was still accepted as head of the National Reconciliation
Commission. He mediated the Sapoa cease-fire, the Toncontín demobilization agreement, and the 1990 electoral transition process.

Violeta Chamorro has played a similar insider-partial role since the
1990 elections. As UNO president, she was obviously anti-Sandinista. Yet,
she headed a family representing both sides and chose to retain Sandinista
Humberto Ortega as defense minister. In post-election Nicaragua, she built
the presidency of the republic into a mediating force, trying to lead the
Sandinista and right-wing groups into a *concertación* process to review
and negotiate the conflicting claims of expropriated landowners and those
given land titles by the revolution.[24]

One could even claim that Oscar Arias, the architect of Esquipulas,
played an insider-partial role for Nicaragua. He was known to be hostile to
Sandinism. As president of Costa Rica, then having border and refugee
problems with Nicaragua, he was a party to the conflict. Yet his stature as
Nobel Laureate and head of a traditionally neutral state made him acceptable as mediator.

The Nicaraguans also used outsider-neutral mediators—those brought
in from the outside who were ostensibly impartial in the conflict. The
United Nations Observer Group—Central America (ONUCA) monitored
the Contra demobilization process that included a precedent-setting
"swords into plowshares" weapons destruction. Jimmy Carter, representing the Council of Freely Elected Heads of State, mediated and monitored
the power transfer process after the 1990 elections.

Negotiation. Nicaraguans on all sides learned to negotiate effectively. In
both civil wars, negotiation success required that opponents conceive a preferred outcome that did not require the elimination of either side. In the
Sandinista-Contra conflict, internationally supervised elections transformed
a win-all/lose-all struggle into one where each side's goals would be at
least partially met regardless of electoral victory or defeat. In the Sandinista–Atlantic Coast conflict, the indigenous peoples retained their cultural

identity and local autonomy but within the unified national state required by the Sadinistas.

Perhaps the richest illustration of how well Nicaraguans had learned the negotiation game was the peaceful transition from Sandinista to UNO government. Georg Simmel might easily have been referring to that transition process when he wrote: "The ending of conflict is a specific enterprise. It belongs neither to war nor to peace, just as a bridge is different from either bank it connects. . . . Such forms in which a fight terminates . . . constitute interaction not to be observed under any other circumstances."[25]

In that tense and ambiguous period of March–April 1990, settlements were negotiated for a series of complex issues—Contra demobilization and reintegration, transfer of governmental power, protection of smallholder property rights, and transformation of security forces. How those agreements were achieved and implemented will be the subject for more than one doctoral dissertation.

Invention. Nicaraguans often used conventional peacemaking approaches but combined them with their own original ideas. The Atlantic Coast autonomy process and the 1990 transition procedures are cases in point. There just seemed at the time to be no historical precedents either in indigenous rights protection or in revolutions relinquishing state power peacefully. The Nicaraguans had to "write the handbook" as they went. That handbook was still being written in 1993. Atlantic Coast regional governments must resolve conflict both between themselves and the national government over autonomy and natural resources, and among leaders of ethnic minorities who continue to compete for power and influence.

The need for conflict improvisation hardly diminished in the post-Sandinista period. Class, political, and ethnic conflicts seemed to intensify with further economic decline and the trauma of a system shift. The most immediate postelection tasks were military demobilization and disarmament. The Sandinista forces, already reduced dramatically from ninety thousand to twenty-eight thousand in 1990, had to be further cut and the twenty thousand Contras disarmed. All those demobilized had to be economically reintegrated. In the initial stage, the UN disarmed fourteen thousand Contras and destroyed their weapons. By March 1992, seventy-four hundred recontras and recompas had also been disarmed through a weapons buy-back plan.

Equally difficult was the problem of civilian disarmament. In the last years of the Contra war, anticipating a U.S. invasion, the Sandinistas had distributed weapons to Sandinista defense committees around the nation. After military demobilization, an estimated one hundred twenty thousand weapons remained in civilian hands.

The Nicaraguans have experimented with different approaches to weapons collection. In 1990, thirty thousand weapons were seized through unannounced vehicle searches and destroyed in a public ceremony. Such a scheme works only once. In 1991, a plan to buy back weapons was devised with funding by the U.S. government. A national commission on disarmament was created with the disarmament plan jointly supervised by a CIAV-OAS team. Nicaragua continues to rely on external third parties for disarmament monitoring. Buy-back prices range from fifty dollars for a handgun to three thousand dollars for an antiaircraft missile—substantial hard currency incentives in a depressed economy. Those who "snitch" on others get police protection, and those who lead the government to arms caches receive 50 percent of their total value.[26]

Yet another foray into uncharted territory was concertación. UNO and the Sandinista opposition sought agreement on such issues as rights to confiscated and redistributed property, with Chamorro as insider-partial mediator. In the immediate postelection period, there developed a restructuring of political relations in which the two political forces struggled for dominance within the National Assembly and local governments. Their conflicts were and in 1993 continue to be mediated by the presidency. Each side has de facto control of part of the state—the Sandinistas the security forces and their opponents the administrative machinery.

The Sandinistas, as the political opposition, have used nonviolent sanctions to apply their power. Through strikes they have resisted government moves to dismantle the Sandinista social welfare system and to privatize state firms without worker consent. Marches and mass rallies are also frequently used. The civic strike, a total withdrawal of cooperation from a despotic regime, has often been used in Latin America, though contemporary Nicaragua does not present conditions for such an action.[27]

Will Nicaraguans use more or less violence as they continue to struggle over widely disparate justice goals and equity conceptions? Our prognosis is a mixed one. The distributive justice structures developed during the Sandinista period have been severely weakened. Economic life for the average Nicaraguan has deteriorated. Yet, citizen-government relations continue to be mediated through organizations that facilitate grievance expression. The depoliticization of the armed forces permits a milieu congenial for the use of nonviolent sanctions by aggrieved constituencies. The churches continue to work for justice and reconciliation. There has been some real progress made in weapons reduction.

The Esquipulas process and Nicaragua's global solidarity network, although they have declined in influence, continue as moderating factors. Political restructuring had, by 1993, produced a left-center-right balance and has made a conflict management forum of the National Assembly. An unrestrained press encourages creative release of tension in a political system. Add to all of this the conflict management experience accumulated in Nicaragua, and there remains potential for achieving justice without violence there. A failing economy, a high birth rate, a resurgence of class interests, and personal political rivalries, however, appear to make that increasingly difficult.

Conclusion

We have said that antagonists in Nicaragua's justice struggles learned from painful experience to shift from threat-heavy power strategies to more balanced ones. A conflict-moderating context facilitated those shifts. We have considered the power strategies of threat, exchange, and integration not as mutually exclusive but as complementary elements in an opponent's overall strategy. In theory there may be pure threat, exchange, and integrative strategies. But in practice, a mix of them operates in any relationship.

Both of the challenge movements initially responded to Sandinista policies with threat-heavy strategies that were ineffective for their pursuit of justice. By 1984 the leaders of the Atlantic Coast resistance were in exile with their forces scattered as refugees. By 1988 the Contras were essentially defeated, a fact increasingly clear as the U.S. government withdrew its support. Pure threat had been costly and ineffective for both groups.

As the element of exchange increased, and extreme threats were moderated and reconciliation first appeared, the altered strategic mix encouraged the emergence of peace and justice. On the Atlantic Coast the autonomy agreement was constructed. A Sandinista-Contra cease-fire was followed by agreement on new elections, demobilization, and reintegration. In each conflict, one side or both decided to change their strategic mix with positive consequences for peace.

It is in the exchange process that threat reduction and conciliation enhancement are actively pursued. As opponents communicate, clarify positions and interests, and trade concessions, threat is reduced. Mere civility may give way to genuine mutual respect.

We have suggested there may be certain conditions necessary for the right threat/exchange/conciliation mix to emerge. In the Nicaraguan case, we identified institutional, normative, and experiential factors in the national context encouraging such strategic mixes conducive to settlement. External intervenors from Esquipulas, the international solidarity community, the United Nations, and the OAS all reinforced internal factors.

Can we extract a "power mix" model for nonviolent justice attainment from the Nicaraguan experience? Could not societies and their governments learn to consciously structure their challenges and responses to reduce armed force in the threat component, perhaps replacing it with disciplined nonviolent sanctions? Could they not learn to enhance the role of love in the integrative element, through religious values, national solidarity, and other integrative forces? Could they not increase the exchange capacity of their nation, using both indigenous and foreign conflict resolution techniques.

It might be argued that challenge groups must initially use threat to attract attention, to define issues, to build unity, and to force negotiation. Were not the Sandinistas brought to the Esquipulas and autonomy bargaining tables by the military threats of their adversaries, one might ask? Evidence does not support that argument. The Contra and Yatama military threats had been largely neutralized when the Sandinistas began conciliatory moves. What the evidence does suggest is that exchange-heavy power mixes and contexts encouraging them are important elements in nonviolent justice attainment.

What does our analysis imply for justice struggles in developing societies? First, rapid resort to violence within a threat strategy seems counterproductive for both governments and challengers. In Nicaragua, the Sandinistas, the indigenous peoples, and the Contras all paid heavy costs in their civil wars. Such wars usually become "proxy wars," with major states using the resources of client states for their own political advantage. In Nicaragua, the Atlantic Coast resistance was somewhat successful in avoiding U.S. control. The Contras, by contrast, were not. And the Sandinistas became militarily dependent on the socialist bloc. Militarization of such conflicts, as developing nations have sadly learned, is the shortest route to external control.

In summary, what appears most important is for justice opponents to be flexible and diligent in using available conflict-moderating resources and to create them where they do not exist. The Nicaraguans used institutional constraints, normative inclinations toward conciliation, and conflict management, learning all in a timely fashion. They were quick to use Esquipulas, U.S.-Soviet détente, and international mediators to moderate their conflicts. They effectively adjusted their power strategy mixes to context-transforming events such as the Sandinista electoral defeat. While Nicaraguan conditions will hardly be reproduced elsewhere, much of their conflict-moderating experience we think may have general applicability.

Notes

1. Sollis, "The Atlantic Coast."
2. Freeland, "Nationalist Revolution and Ethnic Rights."
3. Gomariz, *Balance de una esperanza.*
4. That policy and strategy were clearly laid out in the report of the Commission on Integrated Long-Term Strategy, *Discriminate Deterrence*, pp. 16–17.
5. See "An Arms Deal" and Cuadra.
6. Boulding, *Three Faces of Power.*
7. Sandinista agricultural cooperatives are analyzed in some detail in Ortega, "La gestion de los trabajadores."
8. Berryman, "Base Christian Communities."
9. For an examination of conflict functions and limiting mechanisms see Coser, *The Functions of Social Conflict.* For a study of how such mechanisms worked for Polish Solidarity, see Wehr, "Conflict and Restraint."
10. The Esquipulas agreement in its entirety is to be found in Arias Sanchez, *El camino de la paz*, pp. 411–426.

11. Wehr and Lederach, "Mediating Conflict."
12. This unusual third-party role is discussed in Wehr and Lederach, "Third-Party Intervention." See also Everett, *Bearing Witness*.
13. See Girardi, *Faith and Revolution*.
14. Randall, *Christians in the Revolution*.
15. Berryman, "Base Christian Communities," p. 38.
16. McManus and Schlabach, *Relentless Persistence*, p. 169.
17. Ibid., p. 159.
18. The social defense team's evaluation is presented in Muller and Boubault, "Nicaragua."
19. McManus and Schlabach, *Relentless Persistence*, p. 166.
20. Griffin-Nolan, *Witness for Peace*.
21. Gottschalk, "The Nicaraguan Election."
22. For an elaboration of the insider-partial concept see Wehr and Lederach, "Mediating Conflict."
23. Christian, *Nicaragua*, p. 212.
24. Flakoll Alegria, "Cesar Legislates Instability."
25. Simmel, *Conflict and the Web*, p. 110.
26. Selser, "Plan to Disarm Civilians."
27. For a competent treatment of the civic strike see Parkman, *Nonviolent Insurrection*.

Bibliography

Arias Sanchez, O. *El camino de la paz* (San José, Costa Rica: Editorial Costa Rica, 1989).

"An Arms Deal." *Barricada Internacional* 11 (347) (March 1992): 6–8.

Berryman, P. "Base Christian Communities and the Future of Latin America." *Monthly Review* 36 (3) (1984): 27–39.

Boulding, K. *Three Faces of Power* (Newbury Park, CA: Sage Publications, 1989).

Christian, S. *Nicaragua: Revolution in the Family* (New York: Random House, 1985).

Commission on Integrated Long-Term Strategy, *Discriminate Deterrence* (Washington: USGPO, 1988).

Coser, L. *The Functions of Social Conflict* (New York: Free Press, 1956).

Cuadra, S. "Shaky Peace." *Barricada Internacional* 12 (348) (April 1992): 19–21.

Everett, M. *Bearing Witness, Building Bridges: Interviews with North Americans Living and Working in Nicaragua* (Philadelphia: New Society Publishers, 1986).

Flakoll Alegria, D. "Cesar Legislates Instability." *Barricada Internacional* 11 (341) (September 1991): 4–6.

Freeland, J. "Nationalist Revolution and Ethnic Rights: The Miskito Indians of Nicaragua's Atlantic Coast." *Third World Quarterly* 10 (4) (1989): 166–190.

Girardi, G. *Faith and Revolution in Nicaragua* (Maryknoll, NY: Orbis, 1989).

Gomariz, E. *Balance de una esperanza: Esquipulas II un ano despues* (San José, Costa Rica: FLACSO, 1988).

Gottschalk, J. "The Nicaraguan Election: An Observer's Reflections." *Network: A National Catholic Social Justice Lobby* (Washington, D.C.) (May/June 1990): 7.

Griffin-Nolan, E. *Witness for Peace: A Story of Resistance* (Louisville, KY: Westminster/John Knox, 1991).

McManus, P., and G. Schlabach. *Relentless Persistence: Nonviolent Action in Latin America* (Philadelphia: New Society Publishers, 1991).

Muller, J-M, and G. Boubault, "Nicaragua: Dialogue avec les sandinistes." *Non-Violence Actualité* 19 (November 1988).

Ortega, M. "La gestion de los trabajadores en las empresas de la Reforma Agraria." *Ciencias Sociales* 40/41 (1988): 25–37.

Parkman, P. *Nonviolent Insurrection in El Salvador* (Tucson: University of Arizona Press, 1988).

Randall, M. *Christians in the Nicaraguan Revolution* (Vancouver: New Star, 1983).

Selser, G. "Plan to Disarm Civilians." *Barricada Internacional* 11 (341) (September 1991): 9–11.

Simmel, G. *Conflict and the Web of Group Affiliations* (Glencoe, IL: Free Press, 1955).

Sollis, P. "The Atlantic Coast of Nicaragua: Development and Autonomy." *Journal of Latin American Studies* 21 (3) (October 1989): 481–520.

Wehr, P. "Conflict and Restraint: Poland, 1980–1982," in P. Wallensteen, J. Galtung, and C. Portales (eds.), *Global Militarization* (Boulder, CO: Westview Press, 1985).

Wehr, P., and J. P. Lederach, "Third-Party Intervention in Nicaragua." Unpublished monograph, Department of Sociology, University of Colorado at Boulder, 1989.

———. "Mediating Conflict in Central America." *Journal of Peace Research* 28 (1) (1991): 85–98.

6

Nonviolence and the 1989 Revolution in Eastern Europe

Joel Edelstein

In 1989, amidst mass demonstrations, strikes, and other acts of citizen noncooperation, the ruling parties in Poland, Hungary, the German Democratic Republic (GDR), Czechoslovakia, Bulgaria, and Rumania fell from power. Sympathizers and opponents of the regimes alike were taken completely by surprise. This sense of amazement persisted as a wave of popular demands for change and Communist Party capitulation moved from Poland and Hungary to the GDR and Czechoslovakia, and on to Bulgaria. Only in Rumania was violence used against a government in power.

Strikes, demonstrations, and other acts of noncooperation and protest are common in much of the world, though they rarely have a direct, visible impact on the policies of national governments. In contrast, at the end of 1989, new institutional arrangements had been adopted in Bulgaria and Rumania, under which the governments would be subjected to greater accountability through electoral competition and associated political freedoms. In the other four countries, the ruling parties had fallen from power.

Totalitarianism and Conflict

What was responsible for the wave of change in Eastern Europe? The story conveyed in the dominant print and electronic media in the United States emphasized capitulation by monolithic Communist elites before the social and economic power of massive nonviolent direct action. This explanation is based on an approach focusing on "totalitarianism." Moshe Lewin, addressing the field of Soviet studies over which this approach had "taken a firm hold," characterized totalitarianism as

the idea that a terroristic government seek[s] total control of the population by massive use of indoctrination, police and ideological brainwash-
ing, monopoly of sources of information and exercise of power as well as
direct control over the economy. According to this model, the state mar-
shals its powers to preclude any autonomy of organization and expression, cultural or other, unless authorized.[1]

In its least sophisticated form, this conception perceives states wielding unmitigated power over their respective societies. Dissent was not tolerated, and there were no reservations in using force against opposition.
The party-state was characterized by a monolithic unity, usually under
command of a single party leader. The economies had failed. The parties
were concerned only with maintaining power and privilege. Change was
pursued only when power was threatened, and then only for the purpose of
ensuring the positions of those in power. Finally, as this approach is applied to Eastern and Central Europe, the party-states were subservient
to and dependent on the Soviet Union and lacked any legitimacy among
the citizenry.

Alexander Groth's explanation that the dramatic surprises of 1989 are
in the very nature of the former Eastern bloc regimes is suggestive of the
totalitarianism model. He contended that decisions of these regimes were
inherently unpredictable because they were arbitrary.

Two features in all ruling communist parties account for the recurrence
of surprises: prerogative power and clientelism. *Prerogative power* is
power unchecked by either formal or informal devices; *clientelism* is the
practice of rewarding and promoting a subordinate for his favors, rather
than for objective professional reasons. . . . Prerogative power is characterized by lawlessness, lack of political accountability, and secrecy.
These three elements provide the basis for a politics of whim and caprice,
and hence for political surprise.[2]

Clientelism is the other source of political surprise in communist
systems. As arbitrary power eliminates the formal structures that tend to
make public actions predictable, so clientelism eliminates the substantive
goals that enhance predictability. Specifically, clientelism tends to eliminate the state as the dominant force in public actions and substitutes
those less predictable forces of private and factional interests—in other
words, corruption.[3]

Thus, Groth dismissed the possibility that change could be, in part, the
product of a search on the part of ruling parties or factions within them to
find solutions to chronic social and economic problems.[4] The totalitarian
model excludes from impact on governmental decisions the civic life outside the party-state. Further, it denies any division within the ruling structure. That leaves only two agencies of change in Eastern and Central Europe: the force of citizen nonviolent direct action, and Mikhail
Gorbachev's transformation of Soviet policy toward the region. Change

was thus the product of conflict: The party-states were fatally weakened by withdrawal of Moscow's support and were therefore unable to withstand nonviolent assault by their respective societies.

The dramatic images of tens and then hundreds of thousands of people massed in Leipzig's Karl-Marx-Platz and Prague's Wenceslas Square as well as the civilians crowding atop tanks in Bucharest placed nonviolent direct action at the center of the story. And organized nonviolent direct action did precipitate the particular moment of capitulation of the regimes in Poland, the GDR, and Czechoslovakia. However, all of these countries had experienced the development of conditions that spurred forces for reform within political and social elites. Consequently, in Hungary and Bulgaria, as in the Soviet Union, political as well as economic reform was initiated by forces within the respective ruling parties. In the absence of those conditions, government responses to nonviolent citizen protest in the GDR and Czechoslovakia might well have followed the examples of El Salvador in the late 1970s, Tiananmen Square in 1989, or Indonesia in East Timor in 1991.

In this chapter I will briefly review the aspects of the situation propelling forces for change that were more or less common to the region. This review will be followed by a capsule description of the process particular to each country.

Development of Forces for Change

Bureaucratic state socialism was imposed on East Central Europe by the Soviet Union. Consequently, its legitimacy was always somewhat tenuous. The impact of economic performance on system legitimacy varied with the level of consumption available to the respective populations. However, as Michael Buroway has pointed out, it was a system making promises of economic efficiency and equity that it could not fulfill.[5] Unlike capitalism, state socialism gave all responsibility for the welfare of the population to the state. Moreover, the form of central planning made the enterprise dependent for resources not on performance but on currying favor with those in control. As a result, work in state enterprises was an experience of irrationality, giving priority to creating the appearance of high productivity and efficiency rather than actual achievement. Another source of discontent inherent in the system was the intrusion into the work of managers, engineers, and humanistic intellectuals of poorly qualified party officials and bureaucrats. Over the years of state socialism, distribution policies resulted in a decline in the position of intellectuals relative to manual workers.

Although the economic policies and performance of East Central European states manifested important differences, they all experienced decline as the period of extensive development in relative isolation gave way to the need to achieve competitiveness through intensive development. Centralized planning proved too rigid to achieve adequate increases in productivity through technological innovation. Enterprises producing at excessive cost were not disciplined by market mechanisms. Where reforms were introduced in an effort to impose such discipline, implementation lacked the requisite political will to accept bankruptcies. Instead, the strength of more efficient enterprises was sapped to continue subsidies to high-cost producers. Economic growth faltered. Consumption levels either fell or were maintained by foreign borrowing. Moreover, increased communication with the West brought unfavorable comparisons in the quality and style of consumer goods.

Meanwhile, increasing educational levels and changes in the occupational structures enlarged the segments of the population with a lower tolerance for authoritarianism. Ronald Inglehardt and Renada Siemienska analyzed results of a national opinion survey in Poland, carried out by the Centre for Public Opinion Research of Polish Radio and Television on behalf of the Institute of Sociology at the University of Warsaw in March 1980.[6] The survey replicated others carried out in eight Western countries from 1974 to 1976. They found that at the time of the survey in March 1980, "dissatisfaction was not solely, or even primarily, based on material conditions. Like the protest which spread throughout the West in the 1960s, Polish protest in 1980 was motivated largely by postmaterialist goals. In keeping with this fact, political demands played an unprecedented large role in the 1980 crisis. . . ."[7] Inglehardt and Siemienska concluded: "Thus, it was not simply the deteriorating economy that gave rise to the crisis, but also a long-term process of underlying cultural change."[8] They also stated that this situation may suggest new problems for all the socialist states.[9]

There arose not only an increasing gap between changing cultures and political systems that did not keep up, but also the growth of an alternative culture. According to Henry Krisch:

> The established communist societies, including that in the GDR, have witnessed the emergence of an alternative political culture. Such a pattern of political culture is itself the product of the existing society of the GDR. It incorporates elements of both the traditional and official cultures, but it goes beyond them by stressing new issues and especially new forms of political activity. These new issues include environmental protection, the role of the churches in public life, military influences in GDR society, issues of peace and nuclear armaments, and broader questions of life-style and cultural style including the role of women. The new forms of action include unofficial living arrangements and non-official peace demonstrations, as well as the spread of environmental action and discussion under Church auspices. . . .
>
> Insofar as the official political culture requires restriction of political initiatives, the spread of unsanctioned, albeit not necessarily illegal, initiatives indicated that GDR political culture threatens to escape from

socio-political control. Indeed, the division of political activity into official and autonomous spheres is a pressing issue in communist states generally. . . .

The special significance of Church involvement in public life lies in its provision of an organizational shelter for the development of an alternative political culture. It is not the only such refuge—the apparent existence of a floating world of communal apartments and friendship networks, of makeshift jobs and ephemeral cultural events suggests that there is an alternative "scene" in the GDR. The Church, however, is an established, public institution with an articulated organization and some degree of political capital with the authorities. Willy-nilly it plays a role analogous to (but not identical with) that of the Solidarity union organization in Poland in 1980–81, or of the reformist party leadership around Dubcek during the Prague Spring.[10]

Dissatisfaction encompassed significant portions of the party and non-party elites as well. In part, this feeling was due to a decades-long relative decline in the standard of living of intellectuals in relation to manual workers,[11] and the poor economic condition of party members below the top levels. In their study of Poland, Inglehart and Siemienska found that party members tended to be dissatisfied because of the system's failure to fulfill socialist values such as equality.

System dissatisfaction was actually *more* intense among party members than among the rest of the general public. As a relatively well-educated, politically involved and postmaterialist segment of the public, party members were particularly sensitive to the contradictions between socialist ideals and socialism as it actually existed in Poland. A similar pattern applies to the variations in system dissatisfaction according to education and occupation: system dissatisfaction was greatest among the highly educated and among those with supervisory jobs. This is one reason why the crisis was so severe when it erupted: It was not confrontation between a united party and peripheral anti-party group; like recent protest movements in the west, criticism of the established order penetrated deeply into the ranks of the establishment.[12]

Inglehart and Siemienska also found that dissatisfaction was selective. People were more satisfied than in those in Western countries with government performance in providing employment, a good education, and guaranteeing equal rights for women. Dissatisfaction was much greater in regard to providing medical care, safety from crime, and particularly housing (35 percent), pollution (43 percent), and inequality in wealth (47 percent). There was greater dissatisfaction with inequality of wealth, even though Poland had much less inequality than any of the Western countries, and a smaller proportion of Poles said that some groups in Poland had an unduly privileged position or that there were underprivileged groups in their society. Thus, it would appear that much dissatisfaction flowed from a strong commitment to egalitarian ideals.

In summary, legitimacy was always tenuous for the regimes in East Central Europe. Economies that had performed reasonably well were in decline and in need of major change after 1980. Manual workers, technical workers, managers, and intellectuals all found the centralized, bureaucratized, political economic system a source of frustration. By 1989, cultural change had made authoritarianism increasingly obsolete and countercultures had arisen. Among those who felt dissatisfaction and a desire for reform were many party members.[13]

The Process in Hungary

According to Judy Batt, "A distinctive feature of the Hungarian crisis is the key role that was played by reformers *within* the party itself."[14] The Hungarian Socialist Workers' Party (HSWP) had embraced reform since before the 1956 Soviet invasion, although there was considerable disagreement regarding its scope and depth, and there was a temporary reversal of the 1968 reform in the early 1970s. Inclusion of political reform was of particular concern, in part because of fear of possible Soviet opposition. Still, until 1988, the party itself was the chief sponsor of reform efforts. When these proved inadequate to resolve Hungary's economic and social problems, and opposition groups grew up outside the party, the HSWP acted in a fashion consistent with the style that had evolved since the 1960s. It negotiated, sought to coopt the opposition, created institutional arrangements for power sharing or a possible transfer of power, tried to recast itself to meet the new conditions, and finally accepted the judgment of Hungarian voters.

The HWSP was helped to power by the Soviet Union following liberation by the Red Army. The first prime minister, Metyas Rakosi, was a conservative. However, following the death of Josef Stalin in 1953, reformers installed Imre Nagy in the premiership of the government. Removed by party conservatives in 1955, he was reinstated in late October 1956 as a result of demonstrations and other pressure brought by students, intellectuals, and farmers. On November 1, Nagy announced radical political reforms—restoration of a multiparty system and appointment to the Cabinet of members of formerly banned, non-Communist parties—and Hungary's withdrawal from the Warsaw Pact.

Three days later, the Soviet Union intervened with massive military force. Janos Kadar, who identified with reform, had been named first party secretary only days before when Nagy was returned to the premiership. With Soviet backing, Kadar rescinded Nagy's initiatives and purged the party of reformers. Nagy was executed in 1958. However, as described by Morton F. Goldman, "Kadar remained a moderate. He supported neither the radical democratization that Nagy had tried to put through nor the reactionary Stalinism practiced by the conservative Rakosi."[15] Judy Batt concurred, characterizing Kadar as a flexible and pragmatic politician who had been a victim of Stalinism in the early 1950s. "Having forced his fellow countrymen to submit to Soviet domination, he set about making this as comfortable as possible for them, and he also went some way towards relieving everyday life of the oppressive ideological straightjacket characteristic of neo-Stalinist regimes elsewhere in Eastern Europe."[16] George Schopflin's analysis raised this theme to the level of the political system:

> The defeated (1956) revolution created a framework for both the regime and the population, inasmuch as it was a formative experience for both. The collapse and disintegration of the Hungarian Party—membership fell from 900,000 in October, 1956, to 30,000 two months later—was as much of a trauma for the elite as the suppression of the revolutionary government of Imre Nagy was for the population. Both parties recognized that they had to operate within certain political limits to ensure survival of the Hungarian polity—this tacit agreement on the survival of the Hungarian polity being the essential common ground between the two.[17]

Schopflin noted that the HSWP achieved a workable *modus vivendi* through its rejection of Stalinist terror and its acceptance of "a measure of unsupervised individual, unorganized initiative, and thus differentiation. Hence, the leading role (of the party) would be redefined to mean a monopoly of all political and economic initiatives in society, but not a monopoly of action. . . ."[18] A variety of benefits to various sectors of the population satisfied expectations that had been "artificially lowered by the repression of 1956–61" and provided "a basis for cooperation broader than merely a shared interest in the survival of the Hungarian polity."[19]

Thus, the legitimacy of the Hungarian regime was based on what J. F. Brown has described as a "contractual relationship: . . . the regime's willingness to see society withdraw from active politics in return for its own efforts to supply adequate standards of consumer and welfare provisions."[20] Popular acceptance of the contractual relationship was reflected in F. Feher's and Laszlo Bruszt's findings with regard to concepts of democracy held by the Hungarian population, based on a survey conducted in 1985:

> To summarize, irrespective of whether we inquire about various levels of policy-making or about particular political institutions and whether or not we raised the question in a general manner, the result was always the same. People do not assess the political system, nor do they perceive the presence of democracy, on the basis of their opportunities for intervening, influencing, or appealing but rather on whether or not their interests play a certain role in policy-making.[21]

Feher and Bruszt found that, although roughly one-third of those surveyed, principally the younger and better educated, did consider the ability of citizens to have influence an important attribute of democracy, the majority favored either: (1) having one's interests considered; or (2) having "politics play no role in people's lives" (that is, maintenance of a substantial area in which private initiative would be permitted without state interference).[22]

The New Economic Mechanism introduced by Kadar in 1968 contained two policy areas corresponding to the two bases of legitimacy noted in the preceding paragraph. One thrust was an effort to reduce the degree of centralized administrative controls over the economy in favor of greater use of economic controls relying on price signals generated through interaction in a market environment. Improved economic performance was to better provide for the interests of the population, understood to mean the promise of material benefit provided by the state.[23]

The economic reform provided for the second base of legitimacy, having "politics play no role in people's lives," by permitting the rise of the "second economy," composed of millions of people engaged in their respective individual economic strategies, mostly small-scale private enterprise and improvised second jobs. In the second economy, private initiative was permitted without state interference.

Prosperity in the 1970s won considerable political credibility and popularity. However, it was not based on genuine improvement in economic performance in the state sector, but on the contribution of the second economy and on increased borrowing from the West.[24]

According to a 1988 article by Gabor Revesz, scientific department head at the Institute of Economic Sciences of the Hungarian Academy of Sciences, the reforms were promising but failed because they were not fully implemented. In the 1970s, a considerable foreign debt was undertaken as a result of efforts to maintain stable consumption levels in the face of declining terms of trade, caused by recession in the West, combined with dramatic increases in the price of petroleum. The situation was exacerbated by a failure to keep up technologically with newly industrialized countries, particularly those in Asia. Revesz attributed this to inadequacies of economic reform and the unwillingness of transnational corporations to invest in a socialist country. The immediate problem of debt in the late 1970s and early 1980s, which Revesz termed a "symptom" of the underlying structural malady, was successfully treated by reinforcing centralized control of foreign trade. However, this solution was a step backward from the expansion of use of the market as a source of discipline to improve the international competitiveness of the Hungarian economy.[25]

Writing in early 1988, F. Feher and Laszlo Bruszt noted that in the 1970s the second economy rapidly expanded to 1.5 million small economic units, of which one million afforded a supplemental income to industrial workers and intellectuals. In the 1980s growing economic difficulties brought about a change in the character of both the state and the second economy.

The continual increase in social consumption is now replaced by a continual reduction of real incomes, the augmentation of prices by leaps and bounds, increasing inflation, the general retreat of the state from the field of state-supported housing and social policies. While real wages in the first economy are gradually decreasing, the state is less and less ready and able to deliver those social services whose public provision had at least nominally justified the artificially low levels of wages in earlier periods. . . .

The retreat of the "caretaker state" also alters the function of the second economy. The burdens stemming from the crisis of the first economy now are increasingly shifted to the second, to the system of the commodification of leisure time. The state relies more and more consciously on the second economy. The half-hearted reforms of the eighties result in the introduction "from above" of such forms of production as are based on the workers' free time. What had earlier served as a basis of relative autonomy now ensures a rollback of the standard of living to one experienced five to ten years earlier through the extension of the work day to ten to twelve hours.[26]

Thus, economic decline in the 1980s eroded the bases of regime legitimacy. Revesz's critical analysis of leadership response identifies the root of the failure to achieve the necessary restructuring in an untenable emphasis on avoiding or delaying domestic conflicts. A priority on utilizing the entire existing productive capacity and avoiding unemployment resulting from bankruptcies caused an inordinate tax on efficient enterprises to subsidize those that would otherwise fail. The strong firms were further weakened by withholding their profits to cope with the ever-growing burden of a deteriorating exchange rate, rising interest rates, and debt service obligations.[27] Writing in 1988, Revesz concluded that despite deficiencies in Hungary's resource base, and despite important negative developments in the international economic environment, opportunities to embark upon a promising new course had been available. The failure to do so, he asserted, "must be attributed to a loss of direction by the leadership. . . ."[28]

The leadership must . . . curtail its commitment to its own apparatus [including the party and state bureaucracy that manages the economy and enterprise managers hired through a patronage system]: Its members have to know how to shape the apparatus in accordance with their own long-range goals, how to win members of the apparatus over to support these goals, and they must be able to contradict the particular interests of the apparatus with society's broad interests. It appears that Hungary's leaders were able to do all of the above during the 1960s, but later they themselves became subject to the (frequently retrograde) influence of the apparatus. That is largely why, either ideologically or in their actions, they are unable to live up to the requirements of decisive reform management.[29]

Feher and Bruszt, and Michael Buroway, as participant-observer and worker in a Hungarian steel mill,[30] agreed that encouragement of individual strategies in the second economy gave rise to alienation and cynicism and tended to retard a collective response to economic decline. However, when legal restrictions on creating voluntary associations were eased in 1985, groups quickly formed to protect their interests and press their programs, including associations of "urbanists," citizens with large families, associations of pensioners, Base Christian Communities,[31] a youth peace movement, an environmentalist league, an association of university colleges, professional groups, and a nudists' association at Lake Balaton.[32] A political reform was also enacted in 1985 that extended considerable autonomy to local governmental units and also required that most parliamentary and local elections have at least two candidates. According to J. F. Brown, this resulted in a "freer spirit" and the beginnings of opposition within the newly elected parliament.[33] In 1988, alternative political parties became active.[34]

According to Batt, the openness of the Kadar government and the HSWP had a self-enforcing effect:

> The regime's commitment to a more pragmatic style of rule encouraged many able young people to join it in the not unreasonable hope that reform could be promoted from within. Its failure under Kadar's leadership thus activated a substantial constituency of critically-thinking people within the party. As the economic crisis grew in the mid-1980s, they were prepared to start talking with the various oppositional groupings which had emerged, without whose support the implementation of effective economic policies was no longer possible.[35]

Failure to resolve the economic crisis led to an acceleration of political change. A special conference of the HSWP forced Kadar to retire in May 1988. In January 1989, a commission of historians established by the Central Committee in 1988 announced its conclusion that the designation of 1956 as a "counterrevolution" was unwarranted and that it would be better described as a "popular uprising," a genuine expression of the people's will, rather than "false consciousness" as held by the official explanation. In February, the Central Committee accepted not only the conclusions of the Historical Commission "but also announced that it no longer considered the HSWP's monopoly of power justifiable. The party had effectively lost confidence in its own right to rule: The communist regime underwent a psychological collapse."[36]

In October 1989, upon the HWSP vote to change its name and structure, Attila Agh of the Institute of Party History asserted that the majority of Hungary's 725,000 Communists accepted conversion to social democracy.[37]

In summarizing the transition process in Hungary, Batt described the style of the Kadar regime and its role in setting the stage for the transition of 1989:

The process of political reform in Hungary has unfolded in a significantly different way from that in other East European countries. Until 1989 reform had a gradualist, evolutionary character . . . and although the question of political reform was avoided until the mid-1980s, there was nevertheless a significant relaxation in the exercise in the Party's "leading role." Until 1988, the impetus for reform came overwhelmingly from within the ruling Hungarian Socialist Workers' Party itself. In 1989, when the pace of change accelerated dramatically and other political forces emerged, the HSWP's response was to attempt to co-opt potential competitors by negotiation and compromise in order to secure peaceful change towards greater power-sharing while preserving its own dominant position within the new more pluralistic system. The readiness of the HSWP to engage in dialogue with the new movements and emergent parties diffused social and political tension before it came to open revolt, so that mass mobilization of the population has been rather less important than in other East European countries in pushing forward the process of democratic reform.[38]

Hungary's Kadarist style, following the crushing of the 1956 uprising, was the logical solution to the conflict between what the Soviet Union demanded and what the Hungarian people would accept. Leninist forms had been retained, while civil society was permitted to function. This compromise was made unnecessary by the policy shift enacted under Gorbachev, who telegraphed his congratulations within hours of the HWSP's vote to adopt social democracy.[39]

In Poland, the GDR, and Czechoslovakia, elections also became the vehicle for the transfer of power, after extreme pressure was applied by large-scale nonviolent direct action. In those instances, the regime first had to attempt to repress the opposition. In Hungary, overt repression had long since disappeared. The transfer of power was the culmination of the unsuccessful efforts to make workable the uncompleted economic reform on which the legitimacy of party and government was based. The integrative dimension, rather than conflict, was predominant.

The Process in Poland

As in Hungary, the transition in Poland was consistent with the character of relations of state and society that had prevailed in the postwar period. However, conflict rather than integration predominated in Poland. In an article published in March 1989, Michael Buroway contrasted the two national experiences, focusing on the tendency of Polish workers toward collective confrontation:

Hungary is a particularly apt comparison; like Poland, it too has suffered national humiliation at the hands of surrounding powers, it too experienced working-class revolt in 1956, and it too has had a relatively open civil society. But there the parallels stop. For Hungary today possesses none of those characteristics that made the rise of Solidarity so distinctive. Instead of a collective memory inspired by nationalism and Catholicism, binding society into a force hostile to the state, Hungary is a fragmented society, ambivalent about its past, driven by individualism and entrepreneurship. Hungarian workers have learned to maneuver within the socialist order rather than revolt against it.[40]

With a strong national tradition, reinforced by a national church and a historic hostility toward Russia, the Polish population never accepted the postwar government. Unlike Hungary, no agreement was reached between the government of the Polish United Workers' Party (PUWP) and Polish society. Moreover, from Wladyslaw Gomulka to Edward Gierek to Wojciech Jaruzelski, the official leadership lacked political skill.[41]

Poland's size and vital geopolitical position in relation to the USSR made it an object of constant Soviet attention. While Hungary eschewed overt political reform and secured Moscow's tolerance of its economic reform, the PUWP was ever subservient to the USSR. There were reformist elements within the PUWP. Following the death of Stalin, they ousted conservatives from power, released Gomulka from a prison term he had earned for seeking to adapt the Soviet model to Polish society, and made him party secretary. Gomulka relaxed censorship and state interference in the Church and rejected collectivization of agriculture. But the PUWP did not risk further reform.

The underlying causes of Poland's economic difficulties were similar to those elsewhere in Eastern Europe. As elsewhere, centralized planning was ineffective. Also, the economy lacked flexibility to integrate technological change. These deficiencies were compounded by a general incompetence in economic management and two major policy failures. One, a major hard-currency indebtedness (by 1982 the highest as a percentage of GNP in Eastern Europe)[42] was undertaken in the first half of the 1970s in an effort to jump start the economy. In the five-year period 1971–1975, money wages increased 60 percent to boost consumption and restore social morale after fifteen years of disillusionment with stagnation under Gomulka. Simultaneously, investments rose by 130 percent,[43] particularly in the purchase of turnkey industries from the West. These were poorly planned and, in some instances, hardly planned at all. They functioned poorly because the economic environment in which they were placed could not meet their requirements. As a result, their output was below expectations. Further, the new industries were introduced into a market curtailed by international recession. Although Poland had the highest economic growth rate in Eastern Europe, both in total and per capita terms, during this five-year period, the new investment failed to generate increased foreign-exchange earnings. They were the source of a debt payment burden, which was exacerbated by ongoing requirements for imported parts and materials.

Although agriculture remained primarily in private hands, peasant farmers were subject to official hostility and discrimination. This situation resulted in a lack of machinery and inputs, and, consequently, failure to respond to rising demand for meat and a growing deficiency of grain.[44]

With the end of the debt-financed expansion effort, Poland entered a prolonged crisis that the PUWP was never able to resolve. Low productivity in agriculture was not reflected in high prices because of large state subsidies. These subsidies grew beyond what a stagnant economy could support, but attempts to reduce them met with determined opposition. Strikes and protests of 1970 and 1976 were triggered by increases in food prices, though they were motivated by a much broader dissatisfaction and distrust of government. In the 1976 strikes, some workers were brutalized by police. Intellectuals formed the Workers' Defense Committee (KOR) to support them, beginning a coalition of workers and intellectuals that grew with a new wave of strikes in the summer of 1980 and the rise of Solidarity, the first independent trade union in East Central Europe.

Economic necessity forced acceptance of the union and negotiation. But this acceptance resolved little. Demands for political liberalization grew, and after initial hesitancy the Catholic Church took a determined position of support for Solidarity. The party was divided between factions favoring conciliation as well as drastic party reform, and those advocating repression. A Party Congress in the summer of 1981 adopted changes to democratize leadership selection and other measures that departed from Soviet-style democratic centralism. But a few months later, it removed party leader Stanislaw Kania and gave that position to Premier and Defense Minister Jaruzelski, who shortly thereafter carried out a military coup and imprisoned the entire Solidarity leadership and thousands of sympathizers.

The coup and the repression of Solidarity solved nothing. With opposition leaders in prison, prices could be raised. But the economy continued to deteriorate through the 1980s. The population was sullen and apathetic. The government lacked funds to finance replacement of obsolete industrial machinery. Despite serious discussion of economic reform and the passage of ambitious plans, the will to implement them was absent. The government vacillated between broad amnesties for political prisoners and new arrests, while an alternative society grew within and along side of the official one.[45]

The role of the USSR in blocking reform and ultimately the 1981 coup is not clear, other than that Moscow had made clear its unwillingness to tolerate deviation from the Soviet political model. In 1989, the Soviet Union viewed reform favorably and, in any event, repeatedly forswore intervention. A wave of strikes and demonstrations forced the government to initiate talks on holding elections that would give the opposition a share of power. As Voytek Zubek observed, "[It] tried to lure its opponents into a coalition arrangement that would offer only minimal power while burdening them with maximum responsibility for sacrifices required by economic reform."[46]

At its Tenth Plenum in December 1988 and January 1989, the PUWP accepted the principle of political pluralism. Talks began in February and elections were held in June. It was a humiliating disaster for the PUWP, which lost all of the seats it could under the terms of the electoral agreement. The following month, General Jaruzelski's election in the National Assembly to the presidency depended on support from Solidarity members, who sought to avoid a government crisis. In mid-August, two formerly subservient junior partners of the PUWP broke away and supported the formation of a Solidarity government. In January 1990, the PUWP redefined itself as a social democratic party.

Change in the USSR and the 1989 Revolution

Of course, reformers had gained power within ruling parties in East Central Europe previously. But before 1989, the USSR had removed these governments and imposed others that were subservient to Moscow. Relations between each of the governments and the Kremlin were not identical. For example, the USSR demanded political orthodoxy from the Kadar regime, which it installed in Hungary, while simultaneously accepting economic reforms that were quite unorthodox for the period. The government established in Czechoslovakia following the ouster of Alexander Dubcek had the mission of reversing all reform. As with the government of the GDR, which was placed in power by the USSR at the end of the war to govern a largely hostile population, it was highly dependent upon its sponsor and showed little originality or independence.

The relationship between each country and the USSR might best be viewed as a triangular one. Each government was linked to Moscow; it was also linked to its domestic population. How these two linkages were balanced differed from country to country. Hungary's government served to partially buffer the population from Moscow's impositions, and it gained some legitimacy as a result. The subservience of the PUWP undermined its credibility at home. The parameters on acceptable political and economic arrangements maintained by Moscow reinforced conservative elements in the governments of East Central Europe, while influencing opposition movements. Thus, in 1980, Solidarity avoided demands that were certain to provoke direct Soviet intervention.

The precipitating development of the 1989 revolution was change in the regional hegemony, the USSR. Gorbachev's "new thinking" began two related but nonetheless separate aspects of change. First, the policy of non-intervention and acceptance of a plurality of social systems in East Central Europe virtually eliminated the limits on choices that governments in the region could make to deal with their growing problems.[47] Agreements between governments and their respective peoples, shaped in the shadow of Soviet power, were rendered unnecessary. Conservatives lost an excuse for blocking reform, and reformers within governments as well as among the citizenry lost a reason to avoid confrontation. When the dramatic events of 1989 unfolded, Gorbachev personally intervened at key moments, applying pressure against repression and for acceptance of change.

Second, Gorbachev's advocacy of glasnost and perestroika marked the rejection of the model that the Soviet Union had enforced, albeit unevenly, in its sphere of influence. Conservatives in East Central Europe were without external support.

Regional Synergy

An unusual synergy of the processes of change across national boundaries played a major role in the 1989 events in Eastern Europe. The ruling parties that lost power and dissolved in Hungary and Poland were both stimulated by their respective internal situations: declining consumption and a growing economic crisis of which foreign debt was both a manifestation and a contributing cause. The growing sense of crisis, itself, was sufficient for the HSWP to undertake change, although the opportunities and limits were initially uncertain. It took important work stoppages to move the Polish United Workers' Party to see the need to bring Solidarity into the government and to negotiate the terms.

These events in the latter half of 1988 and the first half of 1989, culminating in the June 4 election in Poland and the June 16 funeral of Imre Nagy in Hungary, tested Gorbachev's assertions that the USSR would not intervene. By midsummer of 1989, the concessions of the ruling parties in Hungary and Poland had created a sense of the arrival of a historic moment for change, which influenced both governments and the citizenry across the region.

The German Democratic Republic

Unlike Hungary and Poland, the GDR did not face an urgent economic situation in 1989. Although there had been some deterioration in material living standards, the GDR was relatively successful in modernizing its economy, utilizing automation and robotics. A number of reforms had been made[48] and economic growth continued, though slowed to under 2 percent, and debt was not burdensome. Still, when a crack opened in an enforced consensus, a wave of discontent poured out.

The direct catalyst for change was the new situation in Hungary: a September 1989 decision of the Hungarian government to permit East German vacationers to cross into Austria rather than return home. Tens of thousands of East Germans in Hungary took this route through Austria to West Germany. East German visitors to Czechoslovakia jammed the West German embassy in Prague, pressing for the same right to travel to the West. They achieved their goal.

Also in September, New Forum, the principal opposition group in the GDR, was formed by middle-aged, left-wing intellectuals and defectors from the ruling Communist Party as a popular rebuttal to the mass exodus of East Germans. Their manifesto declared that they did not want to go West; they did not want German reunification; and they did not want capitalism. They wanted to create a political platform for the "restructuring of the German Democratic Republic" into a system of democratic socialism.[49] However, New Forum lacked any means to communicate with the East German population. Its name was spread by Western media reports of East German denunciations of the organization. It did not organize the spontaneous demonstrations during the next three weeks and deliberately stayed away because of the possibility that they would turn violent.

On Saturday, October 7, and the following day, with Gorbachev in East Berlin, police waded into demonstrations there and beat hundreds of demonstrators. Violent repression also took place on Sunday, October 8, in Leipzig and Dresden. Also on October 7, party leader Erich Honecker ordered security forces to be prepared to open fire on demonstrators in Leipzig, where a large demonstration was expected the following Monday, October 9. On October 9, Egon Krenz, then Politburo member in charge of security, flew to Leipzig and canceled Honecker's order. Tens of thousands marched and the police did not interfere.

The following day, at the regular Politburo meeting, security chief Erich Mielke, 82, told Honecker, "Erich, we can't beat up hundreds of thousands of people." Honecker was intransigent. He was supported by only two of the eighteen members; most took no position. The Politburo was deadlocked. The meeting was expanded by the addition of party secretaries of the GDR's fifteen districts. It concluded on October 11 with the release of a conciliatory statement, declaring that the Politburo was ready "to discuss all basic questions of our society." From that day, communications channels opened and a liberalization began. One week later, Honecker resigned and Krenz became the new party chief.[50]

In the following two months, demonstrations grew to hundreds of thousands (a half million in East Berlin). The government declared amnesty for those arrested in previous demonstrations and for those who had emigrated illegally. It established the right to travel and opened the Berlin Wall. The demands of the protestors broadened to include abolition of the secret police and other aspects of democratization. The entire cabinet resigned and Krenz created a smaller cabinet with non-Communist participation. The Krenz government announced sweeping changes but fell nevertheless. The party then held an emergency congress at which it changed its name and its internal structure. Finally, on December 17, the party declared that it would give up the formal trappings of power and would compete in elections the following May.[51]

Czechoslovakia

The momentum of protest and regime capitulation carried from the GDR into Czechoslovakia. The country's relatively high standard of living, lack of indebtedness, and successful maintenance of economic growth[52] did not spare the conservative leadership.

Party leader Milos Jakes presented a completely intransigent posture. In January 1989, the government used force against a demonstration attended by thousands of young people in Wenceslas Square in Prague to commemorate the self-immolation by a young man in 1969 in protest against the Soviet invasion. Vaclar Havel, well-known author and a leader of the Charter 77 human rights organization, was arrested at the demonstration and sentenced to eight months in prison. When, on October 28, ten thousand people gathered in Wenceslas Square to call for change, Jakes ordered out heavily armed police officers, who bashed dozens of heads with their truncheons. Two weeks later, on November 11, Jakes told a socialist youth conference in Prague that he would not tolerate street protests or communicate with groups advocating abandonment of Czechoslovakia's form of communism.[53]

Despite Jakes's efforts, opponents of his government found reasons for hope. In late 1988, some younger and more pragmatic leaders were appointed to the Politburo. The government ceased jamming Radio Free Europe broadcasts. A demonstration commemorating the universal declaration of human rights was permitted in Prague in December 1988. In January 1989, talks began to extend recognition and a legitimate space for fourteen small groups independent of the party under the umbrella of the official Czech Peace Movement. Some modest economic reforms were also implemented, including greater autonomy for state enterprises, advocacy of workers' self-management councils, and encouragement of joint ventures with Western companies.[54]

Although new political space was being opened, those seeking reform were likely encouraged by signs of division within the party leadership. In August 1989, Ian Traynor reported:

The regime is cracking and it leaks. "We have never had so much information from senior sources as now," says Jan Urban of Charter 77; but
even if the regime is cracking, no one knows what will follow it. . . .
Everything has been put on hold pending a new leadership. Prague is
waiting for change. The tension is such that it could just take one incident
to provide the spark.[55]

In the first half of November, as the crisis was developing, but before massive demonstrations began, open disagreements were expressed.[56] In addition, heavy Soviet pressure for political liberalization began in 1988. In
the summer of 1989, additional pressure came from the changed governments in Hungary and Poland.[57]

On November 17, students participating in an officially sanctioned
march to commemorate student victims of the Nazi occupation were attacked by police. Daily demonstrations of over two hundred thousand
began the following day. On November 20, party and government officials
pointedly reaffirmed their opposition to introducing political change in the
face of protests. However, the next day, Prime Minister Ladislav Adamec
first met with Havel, leader of the newly formed Civic Forum.

On November 24, Jakes resigned. State television ceased to be a government tool and became an instrument of the opposition. The demonstrations not only continued, but grew to over half a million. As the party dissolved into factions with opposed positions regarding reform, a two-hour
general strike on November 27 was effective across the country, adding
still more pressure. The next day Adamec met with Havel and other Civic
Forum leaders and pledged to delete the constitutional provision according
the "leading role" to the party and to form a multiparty cabinet. Demonstrations ceased but were renewed on December 4 in response to the announcement of a new cabinet that the opposition found unacceptable. On
December 7, Prime Minister Adamec resigned. With threats of another
general strike, a new cabinet including some members nominated by Civic
Forum was constituted. Havel was unanimously elected president on December 29 by the still mainly Communist Parliament, to occupy the
largely symbolic post until elections for a new parliament could be held
in 1990.

The 1989 Revolution as a Regional Social Movement

Why did citizens of Poland, the GDR, and Czechoslovakia break the laws
of their respective countries seemingly without regard for possible penalties, in effect following the philosophy of the Solidarity leadership to act
without regard to state power? Sidney Tarrow identified the 1989 revolutions as a wave of mobilization, "a collective response to generally expanding political opportunities, in which the costs and risks of collective

action lowered and the potential gains increased."[58] Repression had generally declined across the region, reducing the risk of acting in defiance of government.[59] An additional sense of reduced risk may have been provided by the growth of an alternative counterculture and the rise of sheltering institutions (Solidarity in Poland and the Church in the GDR).

Probably of greater influence was Gorbachev's commitment to nonintervention and the support for policies of glasnost and perestroika that raised potential gains as the prospect of successfully challenging conservative governments became more real. Two other developments across the region also reflected an expanding political opportunity structure: (1) the varying degrees of reform with which the parties were attempting to address economic problems, and (2) divisions among party leaders with respect to reform.

A momentum developed and rolled across the region. The HSWP responded to growing economic crisis in a fashion consistent with its reformist history. The stalemated confrontation between Solidarity and the government wore on until the Polish economic crisis forced the government to share power. The catalyst in the GDR was the wave of emigration resulting from change in the Hungarian government.

On the day that the Berlin Wall was opened, Bulgarian Communist Party leader and president Todor Zhivkov resigned. The conservative who had lead Bulgaria for thirty-five years had offered policies mirroring glasnost and perestroika but had done little to implement them. The economy needed reform but was not desperate. In the week prior to his resignation, approximately five thousand people had gathered in downtown Sofia, ostensibly to protest environmental pollution—the first demonstration in Bulgaria in forty years. Zhivkov had also received a message from Gorbachev suggesting that it was time to retire.[60] According to Clyde Haberman in *The Collapse of Communism,* Zhivkov stepped down to avoid suffering the humiliation of being removed, like Kadar and Honecker.[61] When massive demonstrations began in Czechoslovakia one week later, the leadership dissolved under the weight of nonviolent direct action and external pressure.

Why Did the Revolutions of 1989 Succeed Without Violence?

Nonviolent direct action played a substantial role in Poland, the GDR, and Czechoslovakia. In Poland, nonviolence was a policy of the Solidarity leadership. For most of the 1980s, it was a strategic necessity to avoid Soviet intervention on behalf of the government. Gorbachev's statements that the USSR would no longer seek to determine the social systems of East Central Europe were not initially given credibility. And even if the Soviet leader was committed to the principle, it was not clear whether Moscow would not act when a strategically important neighbor fell into civil war.

Nonviolence gave the advantage to the opposition in these countries because the opposition had such broad support. Armed struggle would have narrowed the extent of popular participation in the movement and would probably have reduced popular support. Moreover, Adam Przeworski observed that the state lacked the instruments of repression: Although security forces did attack demonstrators, the armed forces refused.[62] Things might have been different if the state had been attacked with arms.

The opposition in both the GDR and Czechoslovakia lacked the organizational means to determine initial tactics or strategy. The massive nonviolent demonstrations were the means of communicating with the citizenry for both New Forum and Civic Forum. At the outset, leaders of both groups avoided demonstrations that they could not ensure would be peaceful. In both the GDR and Czechoslovakia, nonviolence was as spontaneous as the first demonstrations. It appeared to be a product of the same cultural development that made the old regimes obsolete.

Why did the elites step down with little more than token violence? It is probably important that suppression of the opposition would not have solved the crises confronting the governments in Hungary, Poland, or the GDR. In the former two countries, it would have aggravated the immediate crisis of debt and declining economic performance. Successful repression in the GDR would only have exacerbated the crisis caused by emigration. By way of contrast, in the spring of 1989, the Deng Xiaoping government in China led a country whose economy was growing at an annual rate of 10 percent and that appeared to have the support of the larger part of its predominantly rural population. The only immediate threats facing the Chinese government were in showing weakness to peripheral provinces by failing to control Beijing, and the unpredictable consequences of giving in to demands for an independent union of students or reducing control over the media.

As in China, the government in Czechoslovakia faced no immediate crisis other than the massive nonviolent demonstrations and the threat of a longer version of the nationally effective two-hour general strike. Nonetheless, when a police attack on a small demonstration brought two hundred thousand into the streets of Prague, the government abandoned the option of repression. Przeworski addressed two aspects of why party and state elites yielded: They lacked a rationale for maintaining power through repression, and they perceived incentives to adapt to change.

> The reasons the system collapsed so rapidly and so quietly are to be found both in the realm of ideology and in the relations of physical force. For me, the most striking aspect of this collapse is that party bureaucrats

had nothing to say to defend their power. They were simply mute: They did not speak about socialism, progress, future, prosperity, rationality, equality, the working class. They only calculated how many thousands of people they could beat up if they persevered, how many ministerial posts they would have to yield if they compromised, how many jobs they could retain if they surrendered. By 1989, party bureaucrats did not believe in their speech. And to shoot one must believe in something: When those who hold the trigger have absolutely nothing to say they have no force to pull it.[63]

Clearly, the party-states had suffered severe blows to central aspects of the ideology on which four decades of governance had been justified, a loss of the political base, and much of their legitimacy. No one, in power or out, possessed ready solutions to the problems facing these countries. In Hungary, as in the USSR, change was initiated by the ruling party itself. In the other countries, elements within the parties sought reform.

A more important reason for accepting defeat rather than undertaking large-scale violence may have been that, with the exception of some members of state security forces and a few leaders at the apex of the political structure, those who lost power did so anticipating at least a tolerable future for themselves and their families. Those controlling the respective parties and states exercised control of property constituting de facto ownership. This ownership differs from de jure ownership in that the privileges of ownership were not possessed by individuals as individuals or by families and could not be inherited. Ownership privileges could only be enjoyed by attaining a job or an institutional position to which they were attached. Individuals could pass these privileges on to their children only by using them to equip their offspring to attain similar positions. Unlike a revolution, which usurps the juridically owned property of the class in power, individual party and state bureaucrats, although anticipating considerable disruption in their lives, could expect to profitably employ their knowledge, experience, and perhaps contacts under the new regime. Organizations, rather than social classes, were overthrown in 1989.

In Bulgaria, the party initiated the introduction of open competitive elections and won at least the first. In the other countries, the parties may have held overly optimistic appraisals of their ability to coopt opposition and maintain control under new institutions of formal competition, or of how much support they would receive in competitive elections.

In summary, forces for change were very strong in East Central Europe at the end of the 1980s and these forces were present within the regimes as well as in the population. A regional social mobilization was spurred by economic crisis in Hungary and Poland, together with the new Soviet policies of Mikhail Gorbachev. Particular characteristics of elites within the regimes fostered acceptance of a loss of power, but the nonviolent character of the opposition was important in promoting change and particularly in diminishing the likelihood that violence would be used to resist it.

Notes

1. Lewin, *The Gorbachev Phenomenon*, p. 3.
2. Groth, "Communist Surprise Parties," p. 19.
3. Ibid., p. 23.
4. Montias in "National Values and Economic Reform," p. 1433, also observed resistance to change, but found its origin in elite values rather than cynicism and corruption: "the reform of economic institutions in certain types of political environment will only take place once the elites in commanding positions have come to realize that the waste and inefficiency caused by these institutions have seriously undesirable *extra-economic* effects, which endanger the survival of the political system. . . . A system that has been in existence for some time is always, to a certain extent at least, in correspondence with the dominant values of its ruling elites and . . . this relative harmony makes the system more resistant to reform."
5. Buroway, "Reflections on Class Consciousness."
6. Inglehart and Siemienska, "Changing Values."
7. Ibid., pp. 448–449.
8. As cited by Gwertzman and Kaufman in *The Collapse of Communism*, pp. 192–193, journalists' reports in 1989 frequently contained comments like that of an East German woman, interviewed while shopping in West Berlin in November 1989: "The family lives reasonably well. 'What bothered us most was that they always treated us like idiots,' she said of the government."
9. Inglehart and Siemienska, "Changing Values," p. 457; also see Rakowska-Harmstone, "Eastern Europe," and works cited therein.
10. Krisch, "Changing Political Culture," pp. 51–52. Also see Hall, "The Church and the Independent Peace Movement in Eastern Europe."
11. Frentzel-Zagorska, "East European Intellectuals," p. 94.
12. Inglehart and Siemienska, "Changing Values," p. 455.
13. Of course, as with virtually all generalizations about East Central Europe, these are accurate to differing degrees in representing each of the countries in the region.
14. Batt, "Political Reform in Hungary," p. 466. (Italics in the original)
15. Goldman, *The Soviet Union and Eastern Europe*, p. 114.
16. Batt, "Political Reform," p. 465.
17. Schopflin, "Opposition in Hungary," p. 70.
18. Ibid., p. 70.
19. Ibid., p. 71.
20. Brown, *Eastern Europe and Communist Rule*, p. 201.
21. Feher and Bruszt, "Without Us But for Us," p. 65.
22. Ibid., p. 66.
23. See, for example, Dawisha, *Eastern Europe, Gorbachev, and Reform*, p. 176.
24. See Batt, "Political Reform," p. 466.
25. Revesz, "How the Economic Reforms Were Distorted."
26. Feher and Bruszt, "Without Us but for Us," pp. 52–53.
27. Revesz, "How the Economic Reforms Were Distorted," pp. 66–73.
28. Ibid., p. 82.

29. Ibid., pp. 83–84.

30. Buroway, "Reflections on Class Consciousness."

31. See Hall, "The Church and the Independent Press Movement."

32. Feher and Bruszt, "Without Us but for Us," p. 54; Brown, *Eastern Europe and Communist Rule*, p. 223.

33. Brown, *Eastern Europe and Communist Rule*, p. 221.

34. Muravchik, "Democratic Transformations in Hungary"; Gwertzman and Kaufman, *The Collapse of Communism*, p. 139.

35. Batt, "Political Reform in Hungary," pp. 466–467.

36. Ibid., p. 474.

37. Gwertzman and Kaufman, *The Collapse of Communism*, p. 163.

38. Batt, "Political Reform," p. 464.

39. Gwertzman and Kaufman, *The Collapse of Communism*, p. 161.

40. Buroway, "Reflections on Class Consciousness," p. 7.

41. Of Gomulka, Brown wrote in *Eastern Europe and Communist Rule*, p. 161: "He possessed neither intellectual ability, nor political flair; nor administrative nor economic expertise. Scouring the whole East European scene these last forty years it is difficult to find a leader less competent."

42. Dawisha, *Eastern Europe, Gorbachev, and Reform*, p. 178.

43. Nove, *The Economics of Feasible Socialism*, p. 145.

44. Ibid., pp. 141–145.

45. Brown, *Eastern Europe and Communist Rule*, pp. 197–199.

46. Zubek, "Poland's Party Self-Destructs," p. 181.

47. Montias, "National Values and Economic Reforms," p. 1438.

48. Dawisha, *Eastern Europe, Gorbachev, and Reform*, pp. 191–192; Mcintyre, "Economic Change in Eastern Europe," pp. 5–28.

49. Serge Schmemann in Gwertzman and Kaufman, *The Collapse of Communism*, p. 166.

50. This account is drawn from Craig Whitney in Gwertzman and Kaufman, *The Collapse of Communism*, pp. 216–222.

51. Ibid., p. 327.

52. Dawisha, *Eastern Europe, Gorbachev, and Reform*, pp. 187–191.

53. Gwertzman and Kaufman, *The Collapse of Communism*, p. 200.

54. Goldman, *The Soviet Union and Eastern Europe*, p. 105.

55. Traynor, "Checked Czechs," p. 19.

56. According to Gwertzman and Kaufman in *The Collapse of Communism*, pp. 201, 204–205, at the November 11 youth conference where Jakes took a hard-line position, other speakers were unusually critical of the regime. On November 15, Prime Minister Adamec explicitly challenged Jakes's position that political reform must come after economic reform.

57. Traynor, "Checked Czechs," p. 19.

58. Tarrow, "Aiming at a Moving Target," p. 15. Timur Kuran, "The East European Revolution," pp. 121–125, offered a public choice approach, focusing on a theoretical individual utility scale for voicing private preferences publicly. He argued that two factors—reasons for reduced fear, and events serving as "turning points" that give hope of government change—alter the utility scale of the aggregate of individuals in favor of public expression of discontent and a desire for reform.

59. See Tismaneanu, "Eastern European Dissent." Repression did not decrease, however, in Rumania.

60. R. W. Apple in Gwertzman and Kaufman, *The Collapse of Communism*, p. 204.

61. Gwertzman and Kaufman, *The Collapse of Communism*, p. 185.
62. Przeworski, "The 'East' Becomes the 'South'?" p. 22.
63. Ibid., p. 22.

Bibliography

Bain, D. E. "Iron Curtain/Steel Cross: The Politics of the Eastern European Religious Nationalism." *East European Quarterly* 24 (March 1990): 113–124.

Batt, Judy. "Political Reform in Hungary." *Parliamentary Affairs* (October 1, 1990): 464–481.

Brown, J. F. *Eastern Europe and Communist Rule* (Durham, NC: Duke University Press, 1988).

Bugajski, Janusz, and Maxine Pollack. *East European Fault Lines: Dissent, Opposition, and Social Activism* (Boulder, CO: Westview Press, 1989).

Buroway, Michael. "Reflections on Class Consciousness of Hungarian Steelworkers." *Politics & Society* 17 (1) (March 1989): 1–35.

Dawisha, Karen. *Eastern Europe, Gorbachev, and Reform: The Great Challenge* (Second Edition) (Cambridge: Cambridge University Press, 1990).

Feher, F., and L. Bruszt, "Without Us but for Us." *Social Research* 55 (Spring/ Summer 1988): 43–67.

Frentzel-Zagorska, J. "East European Intellectuals on the Road of Dissent: The Old Prophesy. . . ." *Politics and Society* 17 (March 1989): 89–113.

Garton Ash, Timothy. *The Magic Lantern: The Revolution of '89 Witnessed in Warsaw, Budapest, Berlin, and Prague* (New York: Random House, 1990).

Goldman, Minton F. *The Soviet Union and Eastern Europe* (Third Edition). (Guilford, CT: The Dushkin Publishing Group, 1990).

Groth, Alexander J. "Communist Surprise Parties," *Orbis* 34 (Winter 1990): 17–32.

Gwertzman, Bernard, and Michael T. Kaufman (eds.). *The Collapse of Communism* (New York: Times Books, a division of Random House, 1990).

Hall, B. W. "The Church and the Independent Peace Movement in Eastern Europe." *Journal of Peace Research* 23 (2) (1986): 193–208.

Inglehart, R., and R. Siemienska, "Changing Values and Political Dissatisfaction in Poland and the West: A Comparative Analysis." *Government and Opposition* 23 (Autumn 1988): 440–457.

Ionescu, Dan. "Religious Denominations: Change and Resistance to Change." *Report on Eastern Europe* 1 (17) (April 27, 1990): 29–44.

Krisch, Henry. "Changing Political Culture and Political Stability in the G.D.R." *Studies in Comparative Communism* 19 (Spring 1986): 41–53.

Kuran, Timur. "The East European Revolution of 1989: Is It Surprising that We Were Surprised?" *American Economic Review* 81 (May 1991): 121–125.

Lemaitre, P. "Eastern Reform Processes and the Policy of the West." *Journal of Peace Research* 26 (November 1989): 337–340.

Lewin, Moshe. *The Gorbachev Phenomenon: A Historical Interpretation* (Expanded Edition) (Berkeley: University of California Press, 1991).

Lovenduski, Joni, and Jean Woodall. *Politics and Society in Eastern Europe* (Bloomington: Indiana University Press, 1987).

Mcintyre, Robert. "Economic Change in Eastern Europe." *Science & Society* 53 (1) (Spring 1989): 5–28.

Montias, J. M. "National Values and Economic Reforms in Socialist Economies." *World Development* 17 (1989): 1433–1442.

Muravchik, J. (ed.). "Democratic Transformations in Hungary." *World Affairs* 151 (Spring 1989): 155–227.

Nove, Alec. *The Economics of Feasible Socialism* (London: Unwin Hyman Ltd., 1983).

Nelson, D. D. "Non-Supportive Participatory Involvement in Eastern Europe." *Social Science Quarterly* 67 (September 1986): 636–644.

Panov, O. "[Bulgaria] Promoting Change." *World Marxist Review* 32 (March 1989): 25–27.

Przeworski, Adam. "The 'East' Becomes the 'South'? The 'Autumn of the People' and the Future of Eastern Europe." *PS: Political Science & Politics* (March 1991): 20–24.

Rakowska-Harmstone, T. "Eastern Europe: How to Change the System Without Changing It." *Journal of International Affairs* 41 (Summer 1988): 445–463.

Revesz, Gabor. "How the Economic Reforms Were Distorted." *Eastern European Economics* 27 (3) (Spring 1989): 61–84.

Schopflin, George. "Opposition in Hungary: 1956 and Beyond," pp. 69–81 in Jane Leftwich Curry (ed.), *Dissent in Eastern Europe* (New York: Praeger, 1983).

Staniszkis, Jadwiga. "Patterns of Change in Eastern Europe." *Eastern European Politics and Society* 4 (1) (Winter 1990): 77–79.

Tarrow, Sidney. "'Aiming at a Moving Target': Social Science and the Recent Rebellions in Eastern Europe." *PS: Political Science & Politics* (March 1991): 12–20.

Tismaneanu, V. "Eastern European Dissent in the Gorbachev Era." *Orbis* 31 (Summer 1987): 234–243.

Traynor, Ian. "Checked Czechs." *New Statesman Society* 2 (62) (August 11, 1989): 18–19.

Zinam, O. "The Revolution of Rising Expectations, Nationalism and the Prospects for Freedom in the Soviet Bloc." *Journal of Social Political Economic Study* 13 (Spring 1988): 87–96.

Zubek, Voytek. "Poland's Party Self-Destructs." *Orbis* 34 (Spring 1990): 179–193.

7

Violence Versus Nonviolence in the USSR and Its Successors

Zaven Arabajan

The history of mankind is like a train leaving the station: First its wheels spin very slowly and with great difficulty. Then it begins to pick up speed and moves faster and faster. At last it flies like an arrow shot by a skillful Scythian warrior.

It is this rapid stage that the former Union of Soviet Socialist Republics (USSR) is living through now. Tremendous changes have occurred very quickly—changes that in other epochs would take hundreds or even thousands of years to effect. The coup of August 1991, the disintegration of the Soviet Union, the end of Mikhail Gorbachev's presidency, the creation of many new independent countries, including a sovereign Russian state, the launching of radical economic reform designed to transform Russia's economic system from socialism to capitalism—all of this occurred in less than a year and a half. In Russia, these events proceeded without significant bloodshed. The same was not true, however, in other Soviet republics. A review of some of the events of the last seven years helps to explain why this is so.

Although the collapse of the USSR reached a climax in the second half of 1991, the previous six years constituted an important period in

Zaven Arabajan first wrote a draft of this chapter in May 1991, when he was serving as a visiting professor of political science at the University of Colorado at Denver. He returned to Moscow in June 1991 and was in the Parliament building during the August 1991 attempted coup. In the fall of 1992, he wrote an addendum to his chapter that described his views of the events from June 1991 and September 1992. With his permission, the editors have integrated the material from his addendum into the original chapter.

Soviet history. This was a period of bewildering changes and upheavals—
which, even before the failed coup, significantly altered the outward appearance of the country.

Among these changes were the liberalization or opening of public life
(glasnost) and the repeal of the Sixth Article of the Constitution of the
USSR. This article, adopted in 1977, declared the Communist Party of the
Soviet Union (CPSU) to be the leading and guiding force of Soviet society, thereby de jure giving it a monopoly of power. Since its repeal, the
number of political parties has expanded rapidly. At the time of the August
1991 coup they numbered about one hundred.

Other changes included the creation of new representative bodies, the
implementation of a presidential form of government, the renewal of the
religious life of the people, and the restoration of cultural and literary values, all of which occurred before the even more rapid changes of 1991.

Along with these positive changes, however, came a number of serious negative ones. For instance, there was an explosion of nationalism and
chauvinism—phenomena that had never before existed in the Soviet Union
in peacetime. By May 1991, over six hundred thousand refugees had died
as a result of this trend.

Further, the economic structure of the society was coming apart at the
seams. In 1990 Soviet farmers produced one of the best harvests ever, yet
the country was on the verge of starvation. Practically no markets existed
for consumer goods. Prices were galloping while the purchasing power of
the ruble was falling. Painful crises were affecting all the social institutions: public health, education, science, culture, and morals were all suffering. Crime swept over the country, terrorizing the population. The efforts of authorities to restrain crime brought only condescending smiles
among criminal elements. The value of human life dropped so low that the
society hardly reacted to the uninterrupted murders perpetrated for nationalistic or criminal reasons. Some years ago this country appeared to be like
a man suffering from a slight cold. Why, then, did it change to one suffering from double pneumonia with what was to be a fatal outcome?

Perestroika

Perestroika began in the spring of 1985. It was intended to reconstruct the
economic, social, cultural, psychological, and political dimensions of Soviet society smoothly and peacefully along a socialist pattern. In 1987 Soviet leaders believed that such a strategy would work. But by 1991 perestroika had been transformed into a great social upheaval.

Such an upheaval had, of course, occurred several times before in the
history of Russia. In the seventeenth century, terrible conflict accompanied
the dynastic change between the fall of the Rurikovich family and rise of

the first Romanov—Mikhail, the grandfather of Peter the Great. This was the era of Boris Godunov, Pseudo-Demitri, and the Polish invasion of Russia. The second great upheaval came after the February and October Revolutions of 1917 and the civil war that followed. The situation in 1991 in the USSR to some extent parallelled those previous times, when the political and social institutions of the society were in serious disarray.

Russia historically has been ruled by a monarchy, with practically uncontrolled power. Beginning with Peter the First, the Russian monarch was called the czar, the autocrat of all Russia. In the people's eyes the tsar was always a personification of the state, its might, and glory, designed by God Himself. The role of the monarchy in providing order, law, and justice was great. The monarch was like an axis around which society turned.

When the monarchy fell in 1917, the country was plunged into political chaos. The elimination of the monarch's traditional stabilizing influence was one contributing factor. The second was the backwardness of the Russian society that made impossible a smooth transition from the monarchy to a bourgeois-democratic republic. The continuing world war and the subversion by the Bolsheviks further destabilized the situation. Consequently, the natural course of the historical process—which might have brought the gradual maturing of a capitalist mode of production—was interrupted. All these circumstances together led to widespread social and economic failure.

Politically, the society was thrown back centuries because the Bolshevik regime that ultimately took power resembled an ancient Asiatic despotism. Unlike the Russian monarchy, which kept order through the respect and even affection of the people for the monarch, the Bolsheviks kept order through power and terror.

In April 1985 Mikhail Gorbachev initiated the policies of perestroika and glasnost. The CPSU began pursuing a policy of liberalization, which freed the people from a sense of fear. But fear had been the cement of the society for decades. So once again, the society lost its central cohesive force.

Further, in addition to its supporters, perestroika and glasnost had mighty opponents ready to resist both policies. Many of these opponents were part of the party and state bureaucratic apparatus. Perestroika and glasnost threatened the power and privilege they had provided for themselves. The struggle between these forces has resulted in a new period of upheaval in Soviet society.

In April 1991, the USSR was celebrating the sixth anniversary of perestroika. But until then, Gorbachev had not chosen between the supporters and resisters of change. His November 1987 report commemorating the seventieth anniversary of the Great October Socialist Revolution demonstrated that he did not have a true understanding of the depth and complexity of the problems to be solved if perestroika was to be carried out successfully.[1]

Today a considerable number of enterprises and associations in industry, construction, transport, and agriculture are working on the principles of self-maintenance and self-finance. From the beginning of next year enterprises producing 60 percent of our industrial output will be operating on this basis. The Law on the State Enterprise (Association) will have become effective. All this is already having an effect on practical economic activity. In the work collectives there is a noticeably growing interest in financial and economic performance. They are beginning to really count inputs and outputs, save in things big and small, and find the most effective ways of dealing with problems. Today we must once again firmly say: The party will tolerate no departures from the adopted principle of the economic reform. All the changes planned must be and will be implemented in full.[2]

Unfortunately, Gorbachev and other party leaders did not adequately plan for implementing a complex program. As a result, the economic situation of the country continued to worsen, despite the assurances from Gorbachev and other party members. They did not understand sufficiently what could be done and how. Therefore, their optimism was unfounded, and the policy did not work as promised.

The political situation regarding clashing nationalities was also much more serious than the 1987 report stated. The report said:

Comrades, we have every right to say that the national question has been solved in our country. The Revolution paved the way for the equality of our nations not only in legal, but also in socio-economic terms, having done a great deal to level up the economic, social and cultural development of all our republics, regions and peoples. One of the greatest gains of the October Revolution is the friendship of the Soviet peoples. It is, indeed, a unique thing in world history. And for us, it is one of the chief buttresses of the might and endurance of the Soviet state.[3]

This glowing picture was written shortly after the first nationalistic clashes in Alma-Ata, the capital of the Kazakh Republic. These clashes were dismissed by the authorities as the work of criminal elements, drug addicts, and drunkards. This explanation was made only three and one-half months before the beginning of the Kazakh movement, which could not be so explained. Neither union authorities nor Gorbachev recognized that the Kazakh crisis was the result of a policy of national oppression on the part of Azerbaijanian authorities, a policy pursued for many decades. Even in mid-1991 they did not consider this policy to be the cause of the unrest. However, the rigid, tough positions of higher authorities could not solve the problems of nationalism, as was proven by the series of clashes in different parts of the USSR.

The 1987 report, however, acknowledged that perestroika and the related reforms were opposed by some groups.

But it would be a mistake to take no notice of a certain increase in the resistance of the conservative forces that see perestroika simply as a threat
to their selfish interest and objectives. This resistance can be felt not only
at [the] management level but also in work collectives. Nor can one really doubt that the conservative forces will seize upon any difficulty in a
bid to discredit perestroika and provoke dissatisfaction among the people.
Even now there are those who prefer to keep ticking off the slip-ups instead of getting down to combating shortcomings and looking for new solutions. Naturally, these people never say they oppose perestroika. Rather,
they would have us believe that they are fighting against its negative
side-effects, that they are guardians of the ideological principles that sup-
posedly might be eroded by the increasing activity of the masses. . . . Nor
should we succumb to the pressure of the overly zealous and impatient—
those who refuse to accept the objective logic of perestroika, who voice
their disappointment with what they regard as a slow rate of change, who
claim that this change does not yield the necessary results fast enough. It
should be clear that one cannot leap over essential stages and try to accomplish everything in one go.[4]

In this case, as in others, Gorbachev did not name the persons he
meant, so we cannot identify opponents of the first type. But one of the
names of "overly zealous reformers" we definitely heard was Boris
Yeltsin. At the meeting of the Central Committee of the CPSU held to discuss the draft report, Yeltsin made some critical remarks in connection
with the report's optimistic estimation of the situation in the country. He
felt that promises to rapidly improve the national economy were not realistic. Yeltsin was politically attacked for his criticism—with Gorbachev's
blessing. Nevertheless, the people succeeded in expressing their will, as
they elected Yeltsin to both the Soviet and Russian parliaments, the latter
of which he chaired, even before the coup.

The USSR's foreign policy was also assessed very positively in
Gorbachev's 1987 report. Only the following minor weaknesses were
mentioned:

Naturally, not all our subsequent foreign policy efforts were successful.
We have had our share of setbacks. We did not make full use of all the
opportunities that opened before us both before and after the Second
World War. We failed to translate the enormous moral prestige with
which the Soviet Union emerged from the war into effective efforts to
consolidate the peace-loving, democratic forces and to stop those who or-
chestrated the Cold War. We did not always respond adequately to imperialist provocations.[5]

Remarkable in the report is the absence of the word *Afghanistan.* It seems,
even in 1987, that Gorbachev did not consider sending troops into
Afghanistan a mistake.

The report ended with the following:

> It is the principal definitive message of our history that all these 70 years
> our people have lived and worked under the party's leadership in the name
> of socialism, in the name of a better and more just life. This is the destiny
> of our creative, constructive people! In October 1917 we parted with the
> old world, rejecting it once and for all. We are moving towards a new
> world, the world of communism. We shall never turn off that road.[6]

Why not? If the millennial existence of a monarchy in Russia did not
prevent the necessity to create socialism in 1917, why, from Gorbachev's
point of view in 1987, was only seventy years of a communist regime
enough to prove its correctness and immutability? Further, why was a man
who was speaking about plurality and democracy simultaneously rejecting
the present generation's right to choose? It was obvious to many Russians
that if the people lacked the right to change their political system, then all
talk about a state based on law and democracy was vacuous.

By the sixth anniversary of the beginning of perestroika, it became obvious that this policy had failed to better the people's living standards.
Perestroika had a lot of bottlenecks; in some spheres, it had failed completely. These failures occurred because the policy was determined by the
old structure of political power in the country. The mechanism of decisionmaking remained the same, as did the centers of power. The old forces
were trying to remain in the shadow, to keep themselves in the background. But at the same time, it was the old forces who continued to move
the ball and use all possibilities to lower the advocates of democracy in the
eyes of the people who were tired of scarce food and consumer goods.
Therefore, until the coup, the changes in the political structure of the Soviet Union had a perfunctory character.

Changing Attitudes Toward Violence

Traditionally, beginning in the Middle Ages, social conflict in Russia was
waged with violence and accompanied by chaos and bloodshed. Examples
include the peasant uprisings under the leadership of Ivan Bolotnikov,
Stepan Razin, and Emelian Pugachev (sixteenth, seventeenth, and eighteenth centuries, respectively), when both the peasants rebelling against
feudal oppression and the ruling elite spilled rivers of blood and saw nothing wrong with doing that. This tradition caused the great nineteenth-
century Russian poet Alexander Pushkin to exclaim in despair: "God save
us from witnessing a rebellion in Russia."[7]

The horrors of past peasant uprisings paled by comparison with the
October Revolution and subsequent civil war. Assassination became the
norm during that period. Now, seventy-four years after the October Revolution, thanks to the internal evolution of Soviet society and changes in the
world generally, the Soviet people have acquired increasingly negative at-

titudes about violence and hatred. In 1990 and 1991, at least, they showed more willingness to try nonviolent solutions to problems than they had before.

In this respect, the results of an opinion poll carried out by the All-Union Center for the Study of Public Opinion in September–October 1990 are significant. The poll queried 1,848 people from seventeen regions of the country concerning the Bolsheviks' use of violence. Table 7.1 shows that a majority of people polled considered armed seizure of power (52 percent) and the creation of the Extraordinary Commission and its being given the broadest rights (51 percent) as necessary steps for the Bolsheviks. At the same time, public opinion was negative toward other violent actions by the Bolsheviks (for example, closure of opposition newspapers, execution of the tsar's family, nationalization of private property, and armed suppression of peasant uprisings). This equivocal result implies a discrepancy in the public consciousness. Respondents appeared to believe it possible to take power in a country by force and to create legitimate institutions of violence, but at the same time to refrain from bloodshed and to be humane.

Here, one of the rules of dramatic art, as expressed by the Russian writer and dramatist Anton Chekhov at the beginning of the twentieth century comes to mind: "If at the first act of play, a gun is on the wall, by the third act it definitely should be fired."[8] The same is true in politics: If apparatuses of violence and suppression have been created, they will not go unused. Nevertheless, results of this poll were reassuring, as they indicated a highly negative attitude of the Soviet people toward violence.

In analyzing the popularity of violent and nonviolent methods in the Soviet Union in the epoch of perestroika, we should divide the subject into two parts: first, violence and nonviolence in conflicts between ethnic nationalities, and second, violence in political transformation in general.

Ethnic Conflicts

Unfortunately, even before the dissolution of the Soviet Union, violent methods prevailed in attempts to solve ethnic problems and contradictions. The bloodshed from nationalist conflicts was—and continues to be—extensive. This violence was inconceivable during Leonid Brezhnev's era because the Communist powers repressed all ethnic conflicts. Massacres and assassinations of the Armenians in Azerbaijan, the slaughter of Turk-Mesks in Uzbekistan, the bloody clashes between Kirgiz and Uzbeks in the Osh district, the armed conflict between Georgians and Abkhasians in Abkhasia, the collision between Moldavians and the Russian-speaking population in Moldavia are all examples of violent ethnic struggles.

All of these struggles occurred in the southern Soviet republics and resulted in hundreds of thousands of people being deported, wounded, or killed. Much of the violence in the South was initiated by local authorities.

Table 7.1   Attitudes Toward Bolshevik Violence

"In your view, were the following actions by the Bolsheviks needed or were they unnecessary?"

	Percentage of Respondents		
Response	Needed	Unnecessary	Hard to Say
Armed seizure of power	52	28	20
Disbandment of the Constitutional Assembly	26	35	39
Closure of the other newspapers	21	56	23
Execution of the tsar's family	10	77	13
Nationalization of private property	24	53	23
The creation of the Extraordinary Commission and its being given the broadest rights	51	23	26
Armed suppression of peasant uprisings	11	64	25

Source: Moscow News 44 (November 4, 1990), pp. 8–9.

For instance, the massacre of the Turk-Mesks was carried out by young unemployed people, who were given free truckloads of alcohol and drugs and were then encouraged to attack the Turk-Mesks as a way of creating turmoil and thus blocking any forces seeking change.

At the same time, strong national movements in the Baltic republics did not lead to clashes resulting in human casualties, though distrust was present. Unlike the massacres, arson, assassinations, beatings, rapes, and other violent methods of protest characteristic in the Asian republics of the USSR, both sides in the Baltic nations chose nonviolent methods: meetings, demonstrations, strikes, making a human chain from Tallin (the capital of Estonia) to Vilnius (the capital of Lithuania).

This differing response can be explained by the higher general level of development and political culture of both sectors of the Baltic population compared with the people of Asian republics. In the Baltics, methods of instigating riots such as those used in the South were totally unacceptable. This repudiation of violence was also due, in part, to their geographical closeness to Europe, which tended to temper people's behavior.

This assessment is not meant to imply that all was well in the Baltic republics. There was significant tension between Russian and non–Russian-speaking peoples in the last months of the Soviet Union. Local Baltic authorities (who were not Russian-speaking) tried to buy Russian-speaking peoples (of which there were three million) out of their homes. But the prices offered were so low, it would have been impossible for those people to find comparable housing in Russia. So intergroup conflict continued—and continues even today, but it took a much different form from that in the South.

Political Conflicts

The use of nonviolence was also common among those groups seeking political change, especially in the largest country—Russia—and in the main centers of democracy advocates—Moscow, Leningrad, Sverdlovsk, and so on. In those places nonviolent action became the main, even the only, weapon of opposition.

One of the first organizers of protest meetings in the period of perestroika was the Democratic Union, headed by Valeria Novodvozskaia. Though small, these meetings were the first of their kind. They were held without the permission of the authorities and were broken up by the police.

Serious mass nonviolence started in early 1989, when the election campaign for the Congress of People's Deputies of the USSR had begun. At that time, significant opposition to the Soviet political system had not yet developed, and organized political parties (except CPSU) were absent. Therefore, democratic nominees were obliged to struggle on their own. However, all opposition movements require a leader. Boris Yeltsin became such a leader and a symbol. His election campaign in the Moscow national electoral district (the largest in the country), faced with fierce resistance from conservatives, created a powerful incentive to the development of opposition meetings and demonstrations throughout the country.

I participated in one such meeting in March 1989 in the center of Moscow just opposite the Moscow Soviet building. Here, three thousand to four thousand people gathered around the monument to Prince Dolgoruki, the founder of the city. Speakers, who mostly represented themselves and not political parties, called on Moscovites to give their votes to Yeltsin and described the unethical methods that the bureaucracy had used against him. From time to time, people turned to the Moscow Soviet building, a visible monument of the power of the bureaucracy, and shouted: "Shame! Shame!" The meeting was surrounded by hostile police who ordered the crowd to disperse. Units of special police, ready to attack, were concentrated in nearby side streets. Fortunately, the incident ended without violence.

Such scenes took place at many early demonstrations. Later, when authorities became convinced that the protest organizers had no intention of violence, police simply planned to keep order during the meetings and marches rather than to suppress them. In the spring of 1990, when democrats became a majority in the Moscow Soviet, the relations between police and demonstrators improved.

Also remarkable were the sites where meetings and demonstrations took place. First, such actions were only permitted near Luzhniki Stadium, far from the center of Moscow. Gradually they were transferred by organizers to the city center. Finally, they were held at Manezhnaia Square near the Kremlin wall. The granting of permission for such changes was an indication of the increasing power of the democratic movement.

Along with traditional methods of nonviolent struggle (meetings, demonstrations, strikes, and so on) characteristic of the opposition, parliamentary struggle became an important element of the process of political change in the USSR. This struggle was carried on largely by a block of leftist deputies in the Soviet Parliament who called themselves "Democratic Russia." They formed in May–June 1989 during the meeting of the First Congress of People's Deputies of the USSR and aroused a strong reaction among the conservative majority who started accusing them of mortal sins.

Another important factor for the development of the democratic movement was the authorities' granting permission for live and full radio and television coverage of the work of the Congress, in response to the urgent request of some deputies. As a result, people throughout the USSR could see, hear, and assess their deputies. For the first time, people had a chance to understand who was who. Consequently, the popularity of the opposition increased greatly.

The chances of successfully using the parliamentary process to bring about democratic change were harmed, however, when one hundred fifty representatives from the Baltic states declared their independence and left the Soviet Parliament. Their absence seriously weakened the parliamentary forces advocating democracy and, for a time, worked against the goal of independence for these states.

The period after the First Congress of the People's Deputies was very active, with many new political parties and organizations formed. Especially important for the capital was the creation of the Moscow Society of Electors, which played a significant role in the victory of leftists in elections for the Moscow Soviet and the Congress of People's Deputies of the Russian Soviet Federated Socialist Republic of Russia (RSFSR).[9]

For a time, these new parties and organizations were illegal because they were not officially registered in what was still, officially, a one-party system. However, authorities came to understand that forbidding them could not stop the process of political change. They therefore began to allow the new groups to register.

The other important step in transforming the Soviet political system was taken by Mikhail Gorbachev under strong pressure from his leftist opposition in February 1990. At that time, the Central Committee of the CPSU repealed Clause Six of the Soviet Constitution, which had granted a monopoly of political power to the CPSU. From that moment on, all political parties became formally equal in rights. But equality, in fact, was still not possible, as CPSU still controlled the mass media, the army, the KGB (Soviet intelligence agency), police, prosecutors, and lower courts as well as much party property.

Other parties, therefore, still criticized the CPSU and demanded both equal access to the mass media and the nationalization of CPSU property. They also called for depoliticization of the army, the KGB, police, prosecutors, and lower courts. These institutions, the opposition argued, should serve only the government of the state, not the interests of one political party. This demand was supported by the people as well as some military officers and police officials. In 1990, many police officers left the CPSU, declaring that they should obey only the orders of their commanders, not the will of party bosses that sometimes prevented them from discharging their professional duties.

One of the most popular parties in 1991 was the Democratic Party of Russia (DPR). It was created in late May 1990 at a conference of representatives of ninety-nine cities and eighty-five districts in Russia. Nikolay Travkin, a People's Deputy of the USSR and of the RSFSR, was elected DPR chairman. Such people as chess champion Gary Kasparov; People's Deputies of the USSR, Gennadi Burbulis and Arkadi Muzashov; People's Deputy of the RSFSR Mikhail Tolstoy; and others with strong democratic convictions were among the leaders of this new party in 1991. An analysis of the charter and program of the DPR suggested the prospects for nonviolent change in Soviet society in 1991. The very essence of the party's spirit could be derived from its motto: "Toward the flowering of Russia through human rights, civil society, economic freedom, and state sovereignty."[10]

All the DPR's program documents were permeated with the idea of society's unity on the basis of global humanitarian values. "Our world belongs to us all, interdependent, strong in our convictions, with a sense of ethnic and national belonging. Military and political-ideological confrontation have no place in it. We, with all free citizens of Russia, would like to live in [an] open and prospering society founded on [the] priority of human values."[11]

The fundamental goals of the DPR in 1991 were: (1) the creation of Russian statehood in the form of a democratic republic; (2) the creation of a multiparty system with governmental divisions of legislative, executive, and judicial branches; (3) decentralization of state authority on the basis of the sovereignty of the people and development of local self-government; (4) economic improvement of the republic through the development of market relations, the support of entrepreneurship, and free peasants' labor; (5) the development of a program for the social welfare of the people of the republic; and (6) the integration of Russia's economy into the world economy.

In its program, DPR rejected violence as a method for goal attainment: "The party does not accept violent methods of solving social, religious, national, and other conflicts or protests and is against animosity, chauvinism, religious and ideological intolerance, and infringement of personal dignity."[12]

Official declarations rejecting violence were characteristic of almost all the modern political parties in the country, but some of them took actions that belied their words. For instance, the national patriotic society (Pamiat) officially declared that it did not support violence, but the members practiced it anyway. An obvious example was their attack on a liberal writers' organization, April. Pamiat agents secretly entered the "House of Literary Man," disrupted a meeting, yelled abuses and threats, and promised to return to the next meeting with submachine guns. Under public pressure, authorities initiated a criminal investigation and convicted Smirnov-Ostashvili, one of the most active Pamiat members. In this situation, as often occurs, the person who carried out orders was convicted, but the organizers were not punished. The Russian people did not support such activities, however, and hence generally disapproved of the party. A poll taken in May 1990 showed that in Moscow, only 16 percent of the people had "positive" or "rather positive" attitudes towards Pamiat and similar organizations, while 63 percent had negative attitudes toward them.

The CPSU also condemned violence but was, nevertheless, responsible for a number of violent actions taken by authorities, which led to casualties. Examples include the tragic events in Tbilisi in April 1989, the policy of deporting Armenians from Kazakh, and clashes between the army and the people in Lithuania and Latvia in the winter of 1991. In these and other cases, reactionary factions used the state apparatus (that is, the army and the police) against Soviet citizens, not against an external threat. Thus, despite its official declarations, CPSU did use violence to achieve its goals when other methods were unsuccessful.

Other strategies used by the authorities included intimidation and scare tactics, typical of governments under pressure from opposition groups. In February 1990, as democratic forces throughout the country called people to meetings and protest demonstrations, leaders of the USSR used the mass media to spread rumors of clashes, chaos, and provocations to encourage people to stay home. Sometimes authorities collaborated with other organizations such as Pamiat and the United Workers Front to spread rumors that the Democrats were preparing a coup d'état, even though such action would counter the very essence of the democratic movement. An opinion poll taken in October 1990 asked whether there was any danger of a coup. As Table 7.2 indicates, at that time more people expected a right-wing coup than one from the left.

The events of early 1991 suggested even more that the USSR was on the brink of a military coup d'état. The removal by conservatives of Mikhail

Table 7.2   Public Expectation of a Coup d'État

"Is there any danger of a coup?"

Response	Percentage of Respondents		
	Yes	No	Hard to Say
By right-wing or conservative forces?	33	21	46
By left-wing or radical forces?	17	27	56

Source: Moscow News 49 (December 9, 1990), p. 7.

Gorbachev from the post of general secretary of the CPSU seemed imminent. Of course, the attempted coup occurred in August 1991. Although
Gorbachev was not immediately removed from power, the rate of political,
social, and economic change accelerated greatly after the failed coup.

The August 1991 Coup

The conservative forces attempted the coup because Gorbachev had refused to take a clear position on several key issues and chose unreliable
people as political allies. Further, Gorbachev knew about, and for some
time supported, the plan calling for the imposition of a state of emergency
in the country. Then, at the last moment, he rejected the plan. In so doing,
Gorbachev turned practically all the high-ranking leaders of the USSR into
enemies who then plotted against him.

The coup failed, however, because Russian society had no inclination
for violence. During all three days of the coup, I was with the defenders of
the Russian Parliament building, which was the center of the coup resistance. I talked to the soldiers in downtown Moscow—both to those who
were at least formally loyal to the plotters, and those who switched sides—
joining, in their tanks, the defenders of the Parliament building and President Yeltsin. Both groups of soldiers said that, under the circumstances,
they would never shoot at the Russian people or at one another. This attitude was a major cause of the coup's failure: The plotters had relied on the
elite military units to help capture the Parliament building. But given the
nonviolent attitude of these units, the chairman of the KGB—Vladimir
Kriuchkov—did not dare give the order to attack.

Public Opinion and Expectations

The results of an opinion poll conducted from August 24 to 26, 1991 (immediately after the coup), in fourteen cities of Russia show a change in the

attitude of the population toward the army. (See Table 7.3.) According to this poll, the conduct of the army during the coup led to an increase in the common people's trust in it.

Though the coup attempt was generally regarded as nonviolent, three people were killed and several others were wounded. This tragedy happened in the early hours of the morning of August 21, when a column of armored vehicles was about one kilometer away from the Parliament building, but was not heading in its direction. However, defenders thought the armored vehicles were about to attack and decided to stop them. They started closing the observation slits of the armored troop carriers and set one of them on fire. In the ensuing skirmish, two men were run over by the vehicles and killed, and a third who was standing some distance away was shot by random gunfire started by the frightened soldiers of the blazing vehicle.

Certainly, each human life is unique and priceless, and these were unfortunate deaths. However, the failed coup marked the end of communism—an ideology that made millions of people its victims. From this perspective, the August coup and its failure can be called almost bloodless.

For the majority of the population, the failure of the coup and the subsequent disbanding of the CPSU meant the end of communism and the rebirth of hope for a better future. A public opinion poll taken September 7, 1991, asked whether people were more or less hopeful that they would have a better future. (See Table 7.4.) At that time, almost half of the respondents were more hopeful for a better future.

But by autumn, the people's hopes for improvements in the political and economic situation began to diminish. They reached their lowest point just before the autumn meeting of the leaders of Russia, Ukraine, and Byelorussia, which occurred in Brest. At that time they announced the end of the USSR and the creation of the Commonwealth of Independent States (CIS). This announcement, together with the announcement of economic reforms (to start in January 1992), gave rise to a new wave of expectation and hope.

However, the rise of the Russian peoples' willingness to take part in protest and mass actions against the government shows their eventual increased fear and concern. In January 1992, respondents in thirteen Russian cities indicated their likely response to possible mass actions against the Russian leadership. (See Table 7.5.) Though the largest part of the population (42 percent) preferred not to interfere, the 33 percent (17 percent + 16 percent) who said they would participate would be enough to shed rivers of blood.

As the winter and spring of 1992 went on, the population became severely impoverished, unemployment spread, crime increased, and Russia itself began to disintegrate. These changes brought renewed tension, dissatisfaction, and fear for the future. By the summer of 1992, concern for

Table 7.3   Trust in the Soviet Army

"Has your trust in the Soviet Army changed recently?"

Response	Percentage of Respondents
I now have more trust in the army	30
I now have less trust in the army	12
No change	49
Hard to say	9

Source: Moscow News (September 1, 1991), p. 2.

Table 7.4   Increasing Optimism?

"Comparing your feelings early in August and now, are you more hopeful for a better future now, or less?"

Response	Percentage of Respondents
More hopeful	46
As before	32
Less hopeful	15
Hard to say	7

Source: Moscow News 37 (September 15, 1991), p. 1.

the future again became the dominant feeling of the Russian people. A poll taken in June 1992 again asked about Russians' expectations of the future. (See Table 7.6.) More than half (56 percent) viewed the future with concern or dread; only 38 percent viewed it with hope or security.

During the first six months of 1992, some significant mass actions against the government and its reforms did take place. For instance, in Moscow, protests were staged on Red Army Day (February 23) and at the end of June during the siege of the TV Center in Ostankino.

Who was coming out against the government, and how? By the end of summer 1992, a strong opposition to President Yeltsin and his government had been created. It consisted of diverse elements including, on one side, various communist parties and movements (for example, the Russian Party of Communists, the Russian Communist Workers' Party, the Working Russian, and the Working Moscow movements) and, on the other side, many patriotic parties and movements (for example, the Russian Christian Democratic Party and the Constitutional Democratic Party).

Table 7.5   Spontaneous Mass Action

"If spontaneous mass action breaks out in your city or district against the leaders of Russia, will you be among the opponents or supporters of the leadership, or would you prefer not to interfere?"

Response	Percentage of Respondents
Among the opponents	17
Among the supporters	16
Would not interfere	42
Such actions are impossible	13
Hard to say	12

Source: Moscow News 3 (January 19, 1992), p. 2.

Table 7.6   Hope for the Future

"Do you think about the future with feelings of security, hope, concern, or dread?"

Response	Percentage of Respondents
With concern	45
With dread	11
With hope	32
With security	6
Hard to say	6

Source: Moscow News 24 (June 14, 1992), p. 2.

In Gorbachev's era, patriotic organizations such as Pamiat represented national patriots. In 1992 many more parties and organizations appeared supporting the idea of civilized or enlightened patriotism. Many contradictions existed between patriots and communists. (For example, some of the patriots wanted to restore the Russian monarchy.) Both, however, decided to set aside their differences for the sake of their common aim—the dismissal of the existing government and maybe even President Yeltsin. His government's actions, they believed, would ruin Russia through economic chaos, a total disregard for the needs and interests of the people, the betrayal of Russians living outside Russian borders, and the disintegration of Russia as a state.

Despite their goal, the opposition in 1992 intended to act only by constitutional, nonviolent means such as protest rallies and parliamentary action. With the help of its supporters in Parliament, the opposition intended to press for the resignation of Egor Gaidar's government and insisted that

President Yeltsin created a government that the people could trust. If Yeltsin resisted this, they planned to press for his impeachment (which they eventually did).

On many points the opposition's criticism of the government was just. For the man on the street, the economic reforms have brought nothing but hardship and misery. In 1992, the government-caused price increases were so much above wage increases that nearly 70 percent of the population lived below the poverty line. At the same time, the new bureaucracy was so impudently plundering the country that the corruption of the communist epoch looked pale by comparison. That is why the results of a public opinion poll taken on September 24, 1992, did not look so surprising. (See Table 7.7.)

Table 7.7   Evaluation of Russian Governments

"In which period did the government in power show the greatest concern for the Russian people?"

Response	Percentage of Respondents
In the Czarist period (at the beginning of the twentieth century)	14
In the Lenin period	2
In the Stalin period	8
In the Khruschev period	5
In the Brezhnev period	21
In the Gorbachev period	1
Now	5
Hard to say	44

Source: Izvestia, 28 Sept. 1992, p. 2.

The economic polarization further intensified in 1993. While the overwhelming majority of the population continued to grow poorer, 5 to 6 percent of the population has been getting unprecedentedly rich through corruption—by plundering state property and accepting bribes. In only two to three years, some people have been able to amass a fortune comparable to that of the Rockefellers in the United States (though the Rockefellers built their fortune over a much longer period of time).

Despite the gloomy economic situation and forecasts, social discontent in 1992 was not yet rampant. Psychological tension in the society was significantly reduced through the people's family and private lives—the sphere where people least depend on the state. According to another poll

taken in September 1992 the majority of Muscovites felt happy in their
private life (65 percent), 27 percent felt unhappy, and eight percent could
not answer.

In spite of all the negative events in Russian society, the majority had
not yet become socially embittered: 48 percent of poll respondents in fall
1992 believed that in Russian society there are more good people than bad
ones; 28 percent said the number of good people in Russia equal the number of bad people; while 16 percent said that there are more bad people
than good ones (8 percent found it hard to determine).[13]

Nevertheless, discontent was rising, and the situation was only to get
worse. In 1991, after their liberation from communism, people hoped for
rapid improvement in living standards. These hopes were not fulfilled.
Difficulties of everyday life, declining living standards, uncertainty of the
future, fear of unemployment, increasing numbers of refugees, the obvious
beginning of the disintegration of Russia, and most importantly, the absence of any tendencies toward positive changes have had a depressing effect on millions of people and have created a breeding ground for a social
explosion.

The general situation was further aggravated in 1992 and 1993 by the
struggle for power between President Yeltsin and Parliament. Each tried to
override the other in a struggle of passion and pride. Formally, the Parliament
was not against the reforms. It was only criticizing the forms and methods
of implementation chosen by Yeltsin's government. Parliament members
criticized what they considered an excessive passion for monetary theory,
Yeltsin's strict adherence to the recommendations of the International
Monetary Fund (IMF), his government's disregard of the social impacts of
the reforms, and his indifference to the needs of domestic producers.

In August 1993, President Yeltsin began to prepare his secret plan for
removing the Parliament. On September 21, he published a decree that declared the Parliament dissolved and fixed the day of new elections as December 12, 1993. In turn, the Parliament declared the president deposed
and appointed Vice President Alexander Rutskoi as acting president.

When he issued his decree, Yeltsin supposed that the deputies would
be frightened by him and scatter from the Parliament building without
force. (He explained this expectation to the people on television.) But
events unfolded differently: the Parliament stood its ground for several
weeks. The longer the confrontation lasted, the more supporters of Parliament appeared in the outer regions as well as in Moscow. Who were they?
That is a very important question.

After Yeltsin's "victory" of October 4, the mass media described the
supporters of Parliament as "bandits and fascists." This was not the case.
Certainly, there may have been some miscreants among Yeltsin's opponents—such is common in all civil conflicts. But the ·overwhelming
majority of the supporters of Parliament were Russians who felt themselves

humiliated by the Yeltsin government—Russians who were being given no place in the new Russian society other than that of second-class citizens. These people saw Parliament as the single state entity that was able to defend and help them. Very often they were mistaken in this assumption, but they chose to believe in Parliament rather than Yeltsin.

Disintegration of Russia

After the era of Gorbachev and the disintegration of the Soviet Union, we are now seeing the era of Yeltsin and the disintegration of Russia. The centrifugal tendencies that tore apart the USSR are now becoming manifest in the new Russian state as various regions—for example, Tatarstan, Bahkorostan, Yakutia, North Caucasus—seek autonomy. The situation is especially volatile in North Caucasus, where under the leadership of the president of the Chechen Republic, G. Dudaev, the Confederation of the North Caucasian Peoples was created. This confederation united a multitude of nationalist groups, each with their own leaders and plans for desirable social and political changes. But they are united in seeking secession from Russia. If secession is attempted, however, it could lead to serious armed conflict unless the Russian government accepts the separation and unconditionally meets the demands of the separatists.

The threat of disintegration comes from other places as well. Governments of some remote areas of Russia with predominately ethnic Russian populations are also pressing for independence. In Siberia and the Far East, for example, certain forces advocate the creation of Enisey and the Far Eastern Republics. Although 90 percent of the population of Korelia is Russian, they do not seem to object to leaving Russia either. This situation appears to be one of the consequences of the seventy years of communist rule, which has seriously undermined the feelings of national unity, national identity, and common national interests in the Russian people.

In the spring of 1992, a large fraction of the Russian population felt that the disintegration of Russia was quite possible. Muscovites were asked in a March 1992 poll whether they expected Russia to break up. (See Table 7.8.) Those expecting the loss of autonomous state entities or the disintegration of Russia totaled 45 percent, but 39 percent expected the present borders to hold.

Russia is still trying to deal with these conflicts without violence by finding a compromise solution. This approach, however, has its limitations. With the present conditions it often leads to a paralysis of power. The government's and the president's decisions are being ignored in the provinces, and there is no legal mechanism that can remedy this situation. Yet every regional administration makes some demands on the central government and threatens secession from Russia if its demands are not met.

Table 7.8   Russian Border Expectations

"Do you believe that Russia will keep its present borders until the end of the year, or will it lose several of its autonomous state entities or fall apart into several independent states?"

Response	Percentage of Respondents
Keep its present borders	39
Lose autonomous state entities	24
Fall apart	21
Do not know	16

Smugglers, arms dealers, drug traffickers, and other criminals act openly and have no fear of the law-enforcing bodies, which are themselves afraid of the criminals. The army is so demoralized that it is often prepared to give up its arms to criminals or nationalists in the republics on their first demand. Soldiers and officers who guard ammunition depots are afraid to discharge a soldier's duty and open fire at those trying to seize weapons, because they know their commanders—either because of cowardice or corruption—would give up to nationalists if attacked.

Undoubtedly, all these phenomena are in large degree the result of the paralysis of power. People understand democracy as unbridled freedom, and the government seeks to avoid violence—even when it should be used for the sake of the interests of the society and when it is permitted by law. Yet the events of 1991–1992 clearly demonstrate that a commitment to nonviolence, especially in extraordinary circumstances, should not exclude the duty or the right of the state to uphold the law. Otherwise, nonviolence actually facilitates the emergence and manifestation of violence and lawlessness, which then leads to anarchy and chaos.

The Southern Republics

Although massive violence has been avoided so far in Russia, the same has not been true in the former Soviet republics in the south. In the last three years, the situation there has deteriorated considerably; confrontations have been transformed into full-scale wars. The most serious of these have been the conflicts between Armenia and Azerbaijan (where both sides have used artillery, tanks, and aircraft), a bloody civil war in Tajikistan, and the war between Georgia and Abkhazia.

Only within the last two years and with great difficulty were armed conflicts between South Osetia and Georgia and the Dnestr Republic and Moldova halted, with the participation of peacemaking forces from the

CIS. Before ending, these conflicts cost hundreds, if not thousands, of lives and produced as many refugees.

In these areas the dominant ethnic groups have been afflicted by their own imperial ambitions and have adopted a double standard. On the one hand, they considered their right to leave the USSR as absolutely natural and legitimate. However, they deny this right to national minorities wishing to leave their republics, even those that have national autonomy (for example, Karabakh in Azerbaijan, South Osetia, and Abkhazia in Georgia). Seeking to retain the territories populated by national minorities, the newly independent states, which regard themselves as quite democratic, have used methods far more brutal than the Communist leaders of the Soviet Union ever dared use.

Moreover, when the new states find that Russia is not willing to support them in their struggle with ethnic minorities (for example, Russia does not give them military hardware), these regimes begin to use the "Russian trump." That is, they begin to hint that the Russians in their republics could suffer, and they even threaten to carry out acts of terrorism in Russia itself.

The Baltics

Nationalism has had serious manifestations in the Baltics as well, though there it has taken a different, nonviolent, form. In an effort to eject the Russian-speaking population from their territory, Estonia and Latvia have adopted citizenship laws that divide their populations into citizens and noncitizens. Only persons who lived in these republics before 1940 (the year of the occupation of the Baltic states by Stalin) and their descendants can become citizens. Thus, practically all non-Estonians and non-Latvians have been deprived of basic civil rights.

During the Estonian parliamentary elections in September 1992, noncitizens, constituting about 40 percent of the republic's population, were deprived of the right to vote and did not have representatives in the parliament. These republics have essentially created a regime of apartheid with the aim of forcing the Russian-speaking population to emigrate.

As the recent experience has shown, whereas the social and political conflicts in the disintegrating USSR could be managed without bloodshed, the national contradictions within the former Soviet republics have turned out to be the most acute and intractable.

Notes

1. It is worth mentioning that the first clash between Gorbachev and Yeltsin took place during a CPSU Central Committee discussion about an early draft of that report.

2. Mikhail Gorbachev's report on the 70th anniversary of the October Revolution, *Moscow News Week*, Nov. 7, 1987, pp. ix–x.

3. Ibid., p. x.

4. Ibid., p. xi.

5. Ibid., p. xii.

6. Ibid., p. xii, xvi.

7. Pushkin, *Tobranie Tochinenii,* p. 393.

8. Chekhov, *Pol noe sobranie,* p. 273; *Checkhov v Vospominaniakh,* pp. 293, 663.

9. The Moscow Society of Electors is a political watchdog and lobbying group, similar in function to the United States' League of Women Voters.

10. *Demokraticheskia Rossia. Prilojenie K Vipooskoo* (1), p. 2.

11. Ibid.

12. Ibid., p. 5.

13. *Moscow News* (14) (June 1992).

Bibliography

Chekhov, Anton. *Pol noe sobranie pisem* 3 (1976).
Chekhov v Vospominaniakh Sovzemenikov (Moscow) 1986.
Pushkin, Alexander. *Tobranie Tochinenii* 4 (Moscow).

8

China's Movement to Resolve
Citizen / Government Conflicts

Stephen C. Thomas

The events surrounding the Tiananmen Square massacre in 1989 high-lighted growing conflict concerning civil and political rights in the People's Republic of China (PRC). This conflict revolved around citizen demands that the Chinese government expand its basis for legitimacy to include civil and political rights and the government's desire to be judged only for its so-cial and economic rights performance. My analysis suggests two things: First, that the failure of the student movement was as much a consequence of its social and economic rights context as of its strategy and tactics; and second, although the movement did not greatly increase civil and political rights in China, it did set the stage for a struggle that will probably be suc-cessful in bringing civil and political rights to China over the longer term.

This analysis is based on several premises concerning how the Chi-nese context has influenced the possibility for nonviolent citizen/govern-ment conflict resolution. My first premise is that despite unique aspects of their culture and history, the Chinese people generally share in the world-wide aspiration for civil and political rights. The current Chinese desire for civil and political rights has historical roots dating back to imperial China.[1] The concept of civil and political rights made some progress after the 1911 Republican revolution led by Sun Yatsen, but was suppressed during the warlord period of the 1920s and 1930s. Even after 1949, when the Chinese Communist Party (CCP) assumed power and disavowed civil and political rights as bourgeois, the popular desire for them continued. The call for such rights reemerged with the reforms of 1978 and developed full force during the 1989 student democracy movement, leading up to the Tiananmen Massacre.

My second premise is that a nonviolent approach to seeking civil and political justice is suited to China. Nonviolence failed in 1989 and in several earlier efforts, and it is unclear when it will be used again. My reading of Chinese history, however, suggests that despite its share of violence, China's cultural norms and standards for political legitimacy have valued peaceful conflict resolution highly. Nonviolent movements are, therefore, a promising path for the achievement of civil and political justice in China.[2]

At the same time, Chinese citizen movements to increase civil and political rights will probably continue to be suppressed by the Chinese Communist government and, therefore, will place movement leaders at risk. Historically, Chinese governments have not valued civil and political rights, regarding them as threats to government authority. With a need to rule a large population spread over a huge land area, Chinese governments have sought citizen agreement with the need for stability and conformity, rather than to grant civil and political rights.[3]

The broader social and economic context for Chinese civil and political rights conflicts and nonviolent movements will also have a major role in determining their outcome. For example, it may be that continued economic success will inhibit changes in government policy on civil and political rights for some years to come, a scenario that has been played out in Taiwan and South Korea. On the other hand, economic failure might bring more rapid reforms in civil and political rights policies, such as has occurred in Eastern Europe and the former Soviet Union.

The Social Context

China's civil and political rights emerge both from historical traditions and from post-1949 governmental ideology and practice.[4] I will here review China's historical approach to civil and political rights, describe the development of civil and political rights from 1911 to 1949, and address the treatment of civil and political rights by the Chinese Communist government from 1949 to the eve of the 1989 Chinese democracy movement.

Historical Criteria for Political Legitimacy and the Role of Civil and Political Rights

From the beginning of the Chinese imperial dynastic system in 221 B.C. until its end in 1911, the Chinese had minimal civil and political rights. The emperor's rule was absolute and accountable only to heaven (the "mandate of heaven"), and the average citizen had little countervailing power against the government except the "right to rebel." The only Chinese permitted to communicate with the emperor were a relatively small number of scholar-officials. Although they were supposed to advise imperial authority, they criticized the emperor only at their peril.

The emperor, however, was supposed to rule by virtue, not force. He therefore resorted less frequently to military power than leaders in some other traditional societies. In Chinese Confucian society, soldiers were not valued. Officials were supposed to subdue both problems and enemies with superior moral behavior. To draw the most talented members of Chinese society into government, an imperial examination was the method by which officials were chosen. The examination was open to all males and was based on the Confucian classics. Although the imperial system was not democratic, it did have sufficient justice to be viewed as fair and legitimate by many Chinese intellectuals. Throughout this period (221 B.C. until 1911) these intellectuals and peasant leaders called for reform and rebellion but never successfully pursued revolution. China's social, economic, and political institutions endured more or less intact from 221 B.C. until the 1911 revolution.

Beginning in the nineteenth century, there was added to the requirements for political legitimacy of the Chinese government the need to defend the country against foreign imperialism. From the 1839 First Opium War on, China faced relentless foreign interference and exploitation that the imperial system seemed unable to withstand. Because its imperial system failed to defend China from Western intervention from 1839 to 1905, and from the Japanese in 1905, Chinese intellectuals by 1911 had come reluctantly to believe in the need to overthrow it.

The Republican Period

The 1911 revolution, led by U.S.-trained and inspired Sun Yatsen, set up a Western-style republic with a president (Dr. Sun), a constitution, and civil and political rights. Unfortunately, the new government did not have sufficient national unity and military strength to protect China from continued foreign occupation or exploitation through an unequal treaty system. Nor was it able to defend the Chinese from the ravages of regional warlords. Beginning in 1921, China, therefore, saw the emergence of an indigenous revolutionary movement embracing Western socialist ideology and Leninist party-organizing principles. Among these principles was the idea that civil and political rights would weaken the ability of the country to unify to resist foreign imperialism and capitalist exploitation. President Sun complained that traditional Chinese society was too democratic, that it was like a "shifting sheet of sand." The rejection of civil and political rights was adopted by both the Chinese Communist Party (founded in 1921) and by the Nationalist Party after China's 1919 humiliation at the Versailles Conference.

Government by Mao

By 1949, the Chinese Communist government, in its social contract with the Chinese people, had adopted both traditional and Leninist antidemocratic criteria for political legitimacy. From China's political traditions had come both a desire for stability and citizen conformity and obedience and a belief that a government should be ruled by moral rectitude rather than accountability. From the party's socialist ideology, China's new government had instituted rule by the workers and peasants, a Leninist dictatorship of the proletariat, and a commitment to social and economic justice for the Chinese masses, particularly the workers. And from Mao Zedong came the idea that peasants as well as workers are the most important groups in society. This government also set the goal of enhancing the basic livelihood of the impoverished Chinese people, and it pursued what the United Nations Declaration on Human Rights calls social and economic rights—that is, basic levels of food, clothing, housing, and health care.

The government since 1949 has believed that because of the success of its social and economic policies, it enjoys the support of most of its people, particularly in the countryside. There is little tradition of legal processes or institutions for peaceful political change in China. Leninist socialism considered any challenge to its authority (such as protest literature or independent political activity) as counterrevolutionary. Thus, civil and political rights were suppressed by the dictatorship of the proletariat. As a result, victims of civil and political rights violations have had few paths to obtain relief from their repression by the Chinese Communist political and legal systems.

The official CCP view was that progress toward social and economic rights would be sufficient to gain citizen support. Anyone who would oppose them as they pursued those rights, or who dared criticize them for China's lack of civil and political liberties, was judged a rightist or counterrevolutionary.

Although civil and political rights were suppressed by both the CCP and the Nationalists (Kuomintang, or KMT), the suppression was most pronounced under the Communist Party and particularly the policies of Mao Zedong. Civil and political expression as well as the work of artists and intellectuals had to follow party policy and serve the Chinese revolution. Mao's view was clarified in his 1942 Yanan Forum on Literature and Art that explicitly called for literature and art to serve the revolution. Under the CCP, civil and political rights were extremely limited.

The model for the post-1949 suppression of civil and political rights was Stalin's Soviet Union. In 1949, Mao declared that China had finally "stood up" to imperialism and capitalist exploitation. Behind a new wall of Chinese sovereignty, Chinese Communist leaders began to construct an industrial economy with Soviet advice, experts, and political and economic models. The Chinese Communists enforced agricultural land reform and a comprehensive program to meet social and economic rights (food, clothing, housing, education, and health) at minimal levels of human needs to all Chinese citizens.

China's citizens, including intellectuals, were enlisted in support of the Chinese Communist Party's social and political goals: to eradicate opium, prostitution, and pests, and to make inoculations, basic education, jobs, and decent housing universally available. The CCP also enlisted their support for its war against the United States in Korea. In these mass campaigns, Chinese citizens were asked to "voluntarily" join and show enthusiastic support for the work of the Communist Party.

In many developing societies, civil and political rights violations have often been the consequence of vast social and economic inequalities. In China the source of such violations has been the Leninist ideology of dictatorship of the proletariat, which held that civil and political rights exist only for the workers, peasants, and their political representative, the Communist Party of China. Other classes, such as capitalists, large landowners, and (sometimes) intellectuals were to be repressed by society. Bourgeois human rights (read civil and political rights) were not to be permitted.

Periodically, the Chinese government repressed the activities of these outlaw classes, or vestiges of them, as well as of any who might seem to be falling under their influence. To maintain its monopoly of power, the government also continually repressed all non-Communist political parties and religious, economic, and social organizations. Also suppressed have been unofficial newspapers, books, magazines, recordings, broadcasts, movies, and even poetry and art. Under Mao's policy of literature and art serving politics, artists and cultural workers such as publicists and writers were prohibited from expressions not serving current party policies.[5]

For eight years after 1949, most Chinese intellectuals and artists enthusiastically supported the government and were loyal, obedient, and uncritical. Although Chinese were not permitted to organize alternative political parties, start unofficial publications, or exercise civil and political rights in other areas, intellectuals were still able to express their dissent privately among their families and friends. Beginning in 1957, in the wake of the "Hundred Flowers Movement," the Chinese government launched campaigns that took away even the private rights of dissent. During the Great Leap Forward, and later during the Cultural Revolution (1966–1976), Chinese intellectuals were forced, in weekly political study groups, to criticize their own political views and to denounce those of their fellow group members. They were also required to find the "5 percent" of the population in their groups that were counterrevolutionaries and rightists—that is, in every group of twenty, there had to be at least one rightist, usually the most Western-trained person or the one with the "worst" class background.

These campaigns against "rightist" elements in society led to the arrest and internment of hundreds of thousands of intellectuals, first in 1957 and then again during the Cultural Revolution. By 1976, when Mao Zedong died, over three million Chinese intellectuals, party members, workers, and peasants had been persecuted. Many hundreds of thousands had died—either by their own hand or from physical abuse during political criticism campaigns or in prison.[6]

Much of the party's power and legitimacy rests on its record of (1) having united the country under relatively honest leadership in 1949, (2) having carried out major industrial, economic, and social development from 1949 to 1957, and (3) its economic reforms since 1978.

Even before the reforms of 1978, China's economic development was considered by the World Bank to be a model for other developing countries. China not only had developed as fast or faster than had India, Pakistan, or the Philippines, for example, but also had better distributed that economic growth. The World Bank, in 1981, noted China's impressive economic growth even before the post-1978 reforms:

> With adjustments for international comparability, per capita GNP appears to have grown at an annual rate of 2.0–2.5% in 1957–77 and (because of a spurt in the last two years) 2.5–3.0% in 1957–79. Even the former rate is significantly above the average for other low-income developing countries (1.6% in 1960–78). . . .[7]

Concerning China's investment of its income and growth in social programs of economic justice, the World Bank noted:

> Unlike most other developing countries, whose extreme poverty and considerable affluence often occur side-by-side, China is composed of communities within which there is comparatively little inequality. . . .[8]

and:

> China's most remarkable achievement during the past three decades has been to make low-income groups far better off in terms of basic needs than their counterparts in most other poor countries. They all have work; their food supply is guaranteed through a mixture of state rationing and collective self-insurance; most of their children are not only at school, but being comparatively well taught; and the great majority have access to basic health care and family planning services. Life expectancy—whose dependency on many other economic and social variables makes it probably the best single indicator of the extent of real poverty in a country—is (at 64 years) outstandingly high for a country at China's per capita income level.[9]

In sum, from 1949 to 1978, the Chinese Communist government ruled on the basis of the criteria of unifying the country and providing for basic social and economic rights, and it permitted very little exercise of civil and political rights. Because the CCP had united China, industrialized it, carried out land reform, provided for social and economic rights, and tightly controlled civil and political activity, there was little civil and political rights advocacy among Chinese. Those who did call for more civil and political rights protection as intellectuals during the 1957 Hundred Flowers Movement were branded rightists and counterrevolutionaries and were imprisoned or lost their jobs. By 1978, however, there were both calls for economic reforms and a pent-up desire for civil and political rights among China's intellectuals and students.

Reforms After 1978

In 1978, the party leaders who had survived Mao, led by Vice Premier Deng Xiaoping, arrested and tried the remaining Maoist leaders (the Gang of Four) for massive repression and social fascism. They then set about making major economic and political reforms, what Harry Harding has called the Second Revolution.[10]

Deng proposed policies in both agriculture and industry that returned control to local government and individual producers. In the countryside, Deng introduced the responsibility system that permitted peasants to contract for land and to retain much of the benefit from increased production. Production did increase, and many peasants enjoyed increased incomes. In the cities, Chinese were given the chance to set up privately or collectively owned businesses, particularly in the service sectors. Factories were encouraged to introduce manager contract systems that made them more responsible for enterprise performance.

China's respectable pre-1978 growth rate increased to one of the highest in the world (at 9–10 percent yearly), with little diminution of social and economic rights. A 1985 comparison, using the physical quality of life index (PQLI), showed that China ranked as the most "developed" large poor country in the world in terms of life expectancy, infant mortality, and literacy (just as it had before 1978).[11]

China's economic growth before and after 1978 is all the more unique and impressive since it has occurred with little foreign debt and has been based on agricultural production of less arable land per capita than even the perpetual economic-basket-case, Bangladesh. Table 8.1 illustrates the severe agricultural limitations that a mostly mountainous and arid China faces.

Thus, the Chinese government can claim, and does, that it has met the people's basic social and economic needs when compared with other developing nations. This claim permits the government to argue that its rule rests on the "will of the people," the vast rural majority of whom are still poor by world standards, and that it enjoys the approval of the majority of Chinese citizens.

In the political realm, the post-1978 reformers, led by Deng Xiaoping, offered amnesty for persecuted intellectuals and party members, freed

Table 8.1   Cultivated Area Per Capita (of the Agricultural Population, 1978)

Country	Hectares
Japan	0.25
Netherlands	0.78
Egypt	0.15
Republic of Korea	0.14
Indonesia	0.16
Bangladesh	0.15
India	0.42
China	0.12

Source: World Bank, China: Socialist Economic Development, The Main Report (Washington, DC: Unpublished, 1981), p. 6.

political prisoners, paid people back salaries, returned them to their jobs, and "reversed the verdict" on their judgment as rightists or counterrevolutionaries. Law schools were reopened, lawyers were trained, and a new emphasis was placed on following procedures of socialist legality.

Reform leaders also initially supported the 1979 Beijing Spring Movement that included a "democracy wall," demonstrations, and numerous unofficial publications. Some intellectual leaders even called for a "fifth modernization"—democracy.

The Beijing Spring Movement was suppressed, but the suppression did not end Chinese calls for democracy. Students in 1984 and again in 1986 led movements for democratization that, though unsuccessful, nevertheless successively expanded popular support. In the 1986 movement, the students even received the tacit support of then Communist Party Secretary Hu Yaobang.

By 1989, China had made significant progress toward instituting market socialism, resulting in an economy expanding at 8 to 10 percent annually. Many Chinese had not had such prosperity since 1957, if ever. The major economic complaints concerned inflation and corruption rather than a failure of the economy. In the area of political reform, although the democratization movements had been suppressed, each had gained wider support, and the legal system was being reestablished.

The 1989 Democracy Movement

Notable but uneven progress in economic and political reforms had set the stage for the 1989 student demonstrations and subsequent Tiananmen Massacre. On the one hand, the government had politically and economically "opened the door." Over eighty thousand Chinese students had gone abroad, including the sons and daughters of many CCP leaders. The economy was overheating from rapid growth, not stagnating. The government had admitted to the most grievous political errors of the previous forty years and had made amends. And the government was establishing a legal system for a society ruled by law rather than by arbitrary political slogans or whims.

On the other hand, there were increasingly active and widespread calls for democratization. These calls were occurring with rising political and economic expectations and against a leadership that had already made great political and economic strides within a decade. The government's economic successes were impressive, both in bringing most Chinese up to a minimum survival level and in introducing world technology and markets to a China isolated for forty years.

Consequently, when students marched on the government in 1989, it was not to overthrow it but to ask for more responsiveness to corruption, inflation, and democratization—that is, to widen its legitimacy criteria to include more public accountability and civil and political rights. The substantial popular support for the students, particularly in their hunger strikes, did not mean that the government had lost its legitimacy. In fact, it continued to enjoy considerable support on the basis of measurable economic successes.

The crux of the conflict with the students was the CCP's wish to retain its monopoly of power. Neither the students nor the general population were to have the authority to change the political system but were to maintain the "four basic principles:" primacy of the party, of socialism, of Maoist-Marxist-Leninist thought, and of the dictatorship of the proletariat.

Students began their demonstrations for democracy on April 15, 1989, when former CCP General Secretary Hu Yaobang died. Over the next eleven weeks, students in China's major cities demonstrated for democracy and against corruption and inflation.

Student protests coincided with several significant events. May 4 was the seventieth anniversary of the first student movement in Chinese history, the "May 4th, 1919, Movement," which occurred during the Versailles Treaty negotiations when Chinese interests were betrayed by the Western powers. Also on May 4, the Asian Development Bank was meeting in Beijing. On May 15 Mikhail Gorbachev arrived for a state visit, and one million people demonstrated in Beijing.

On May 13, some of the students began a hunger strike. Early in the morning of May 18, Premier Li Peng and CCP Secretary General Zhao Ziyang both went to Tiananmen Square to meet with students. Li Peng met with them again the same day. By the next night, May 19, he had declared martial law. For the subsequent two weeks there was internal conflict between Zhao Ziyang and his fellow moderate reformists and Li Peng and his conservative hard-line forces.

Though many, including some army generals, opposed martial law, the government finally suppressed the student movement on the night of June 3, 1989, killing hundreds and perhaps thousands of students and their supporters. In the weeks and months that followed, many hundreds more were arrested. Some were executed.

Since those events, the government has used images of sacrificing soldiers, grateful peasants and workers, and public-spirited party members to bolster its popular support. One example is its resurrection of Cultural Revolution icon Lei Feng, the martyred soldier who died "serving the people." When normative and remunerative sanctions fail, the Chinese government has been quite willing to use violence and terror tactics to suppress civil and political rights. In 1989, Amnesty International reported

- the arrest and imprisonment of prisoners of conscience and the existence of legislation providing for their detention;
- the prolonged detention without trial of people arrested on political grounds;
- inadequate trial procedures and the absence of legal safeguards to ensure fair and open trials for people arrested on political grounds;
- the reported ill-treatment of prisoners, usually in detention centers administered by Public Security Bureaus; and
- the extensive use of the death penalty.[12]

China has resisted outside pressure to protect human rights and has been particularly offended by foreign demands that its civil and political rights practices be improved. The only outside model that China has followed so far has been that of the Soviet Union before 1960. Much of China's civil and political rights codes, according to Amnesty International, have been adapted from Stalinist legal codes.

Can the Chinese government correct injustice in civil and political rights, or are its violations of civil and political rights a necessary part of the Chinese political system? Because the Leninist view restricts civil and political rights, it seems unlikely that the Chinese government can change its suppression of civil rights unless it changes its ideology. Still, just before the 1989 repression, many officials in the government supported student demands for more freedom of speech and political activity. If the economy continues to develop over the next ten to twenty years, there will be increasing demands for civil and political rights the government must meet if it is to stay in power.

Protest Goals and Strategy

What were the goals of the protesting groups? Several protest movements have occurred since 1979, with each more broadly based than the last. In 1979, encouraged by then Vice Premier Deng Xiaoping and other communist reformists, several hundred Chinese intellectuals and workers began a democracy movement called the Beijing Spring. They established unofficial publications, protested past treatment of political dissidents, and wrote character posters to post on Beijing's "democracy wall." They also added a "fifth modernization"—democracy—to the four modernizations called for by reform leaders: industrial, agricultural, science and technology, and the military. The Beijing Spring was suppressed within a year of its inception, and many of its leaders and publishers were arrested and given long prison sentences. One of its best known leaders, Wei Jingsheng, a former electrician and editor of an unofficial publication, *Exploration*, received a sentence of fifteen years.

In 1984, a second movement was mounted by Chinese dissident intellectuals and students. It called for democratization and for the freedom to publish critical views and to start independent political parties. This movement, too, was crushed, and it led to the removal of reform leader Hu Yaobang, the Communist Party general secretary, who had been too sympathetic to students' democratic demands.

Finally, in 1989, in the most widespread prodemocracy movement in China's history, urban Chinese from all occupations and professions supported a student-led movement against corruption and for civil and political rights. As mentioned earlier, the movement was finally violently suppressed in Tiananmen Square on June 3, 1989.

All of the political movements since 1978 have called for increased civil and political rights rather than calling for an overthrow of the government or the social and economic systems. Although some leaders called for radical change, China did not resemble the Soviet Union and Eastern European countries where the Communist Party had lost its legitimacy. Until the brutal repression on June 3, 1989, most protestors would probably have settled for a reform-minded Communist Party under the leadership of Zhao Ziyang, who was willing to make some concessions concerning civil and political rights.

None of the democracy movements have had well-developed notions of what should replace the current Chinese political system. There has been little freedom to write or think about the issue since 1949, and the goal of the democratization movements has not been the destruction of the communist system, but simply increased civil and political rights, freedom of the press, and freedom to organize alternative political parties. Despite a vagueness of its objectives, Gene Sharp and others have commented on the relative success of the 1989 movement in following accepted principles of nonviolent direct action.[13] Weapons were not used, and students engaged in a highly successful hunger strike. They were also willing to meet and negotiate with government leaders.

Protestors used classic nonviolent action strategies and tactics, particularly in the mass demonstrations of 1989. These included banners, leaflets, appeals to the general population, symbols of change and reform

such as the statue "Goddess of Democracy," and songs and slogans. They
also held marches and rallies. Finally, after they had occupied Tiananmen
Square, some began hunger strikes for public sympathy and support. They
seem to have studiously avoided violence and weapons, preferring instead
to try to deter soldiers through slogans and persuasion.

Interestingly, the government also delayed for some weeks the use of
armed force. It initially met students with unarmed police, then unarmed
soldiers, and finally and only with great reluctance called in tanks and
armed units. Many military commanders had signed a petition stating that
they opposed martial law. That the demonstrations continued as long as
they did indicates, in part, the lack of unity among leaders. It may also indicate that the government had few nonlethal methods to deal with nonviolent demonstrations.

Planning strategies that focused on classical nonviolent techniques
were agreed to by students and were supported by most Chinese citizens.
Although there was some violence toward the end of the June 1989 showdown, most movement participants accepted the wisdom of not threatening
the government or the army with weapons or violence. Indeed, the ultimate
tactic was a classic hunger strike designed and carried out mostly by students seeking the sympathy of the officials and the general population
of Beijing.

Some actions were not planned, but rather spontaneous, such as the
construction of the "Goddess of Democracy." Students had to improvise
with each new government challenge and threat. Most responses and actions were planned by student groupings on Tiananmen Square. Activities
were usually carried out as planned. The planning, however, had to evolve
with the situation because the outcome of each new action was uncertain.
For example, there were efforts to meet with government leaders and to
gain their attention and support. Had the meeting between hunger-striking
students and Premier Li Peng been more successful, different plans would
have been developed.

Student leader conflict occurred during the final showdown between
the protesters and the government. Many of the Beijing student groups
were prepared to leave the square by June 3, when it seemed clear that the
government would use major military force to clear it. Students had, however, been coming to Beijing from all over the country to participate in the
demonstrations and hunger strike. It was mostly those outsiders who still
occupied Tiananmen Square when the tanks finally rolled in on the night
of June 3.

Many roles were played out in the Tiananmen Massacre. As in past
movements (going back as far as the May 4th Movement of 1919), the students of elite Beijing universities spearheaded the demonstrations. By 1989,
there was considerable popular support for student demands, particularly
concerning economic problems and corruption. By May, a considerable

percentage of Beijing's population supported the demands for increased civil and political rights and decreased official corruption. That support was fueled by growing citizen concern for the inflation that the economic reforms had brought on.

Public support stimulated the demonstrations and influenced the government to delay suppressing the movement. Students demonstrated when there were already many foreign correspondents in Beijing for the historic Gorbachev visit. Students sought out reporters and particularly television crews for increased visibility. In short, they made every effort to keep the eye of international public opinion on China.

International legal and political structures played little, if any, role in the movement or its final outcome. International human rights groups were aware of the demonstrations but had little influence over the fast-moving events. They appeared to be as unaware of the day-to-day events as were most citizens around the world, whose only access was to the press covering the story.

Power Strategies

The demonstrators did not appeal to or rely on threats of violence or sanctions. Neither did they have any way to make economic threats or impose economic sanctions; with little political power, demonstrators could not use political sanctions. However, because of the publicity given the movement in the world community, China's leaders did suffer economic and political sanctions *after the fact*—that is, in the wake of the suppression. I have seen no evidence, however, that students tried to influence government actions with reference to later possible sanctions by foreign powers. Indeed, many Chinese are ambivalent about subsequent international sanctions, which have tended to jeopardize the reform-minded Chinese intellectuals and business people more than the government.[14]

Exchange also was unsuccessful, although it seems clear that there was hope that negotiation might be possible between reform-minded political leaders and the students, who had begun to enjoy widespread support even within the government and the official media. Little economic exchange was possible or proposed, but there were many possible political trade-offs. For instance, the students might have withdrawn in exchange for policy concessions or returned to school in exchange for increased democratization or more forceful suppression of corruption. The government probably had sufficient legitimacy to have made such reform concessions and stayed in power, unlike in Eastern Europe, where the economies were failing and the governments had little popular legitimacy.

The students' primary power strategy was integrative: They appealed to moral virtue. They called for peaceful change and were consistent in mobilizing citizen support. This drew large numbers of previously quiescent

Beijing officials and citizens—including police, soldiers, bureaucrats, teachers, journalists, and middle-level officials—into supporting student demands. To gain popular support, students pointed to real problems in their appeals, such as lack of government responsiveness, official corruption, and inflation. Finally, protesters actively pursued the nonviolent tactic of the hunger strike to take and keep the highest moral ground. Students thus gained the support of growing numbers of Beijing residents. Popular support for the students further increased when the government declared martial law and began to threaten students with tanks and guns. In the end, government use of lethal force against the nonviolent protest further enhanced the status of students and their demands.

Outcomes

How effective have the 1989 demonstrations been in motivating short-term change? As is well known, the students lost the June battle. They were driven from Tiananmen Square and then from the country. Many of their leaders were expelled from the party and imprisoned. It is possible to argue, however, that by losing the battle in a principled manner, the students have set the stage for winning the war. Chinese are probably less supportive of antistudent actions by the government since the bloody suppression.

In the long term, the student demonstrations may have set the stage for the reformation, even the abolition, of the Communist Party. If the government continues to provide economic growth and resists further violent repression of its own citizens, it may yet oversee the transition of power to a more democratic system, just as has occurred in Taiwan and South Korea.[15]

If, however, the economy reverses direction, the Chinese Communist system may be overthrown as in Eastern Europe. Such radical change would probably be precipitated by yet another round of mass protests, led by students and supported by a still larger percentage of China's urban population.

Because of the partial success of student protest and the lack of realistic alternatives to continued economic reforms, many Chinese anticipate continuing reforms by emerging younger party leaders, particularly after the disappearance of the octogenarian Long March generation. Some are worried that Deng Xiaoping may not outlive military leaders, in which case China might get a military dictatorship. Were that to occur, there might be more widespread and violent protest. Many Chinese believe, however, that the changes will come gradually among top leadership.

Other factors may also affect the timing and approaches of Chinese movements in the future. Massive protest would probably be less likely if the government succeeds in keeping down inflation and continues to increase economic growth. They would also be less likely if the emerging leadership pursues political reforms, but more likely if the government fails economically or becomes more repressive.

If democracy movement leaders in China wished to be more effective, they might study successful aspects of the movements led by Gandhi or against Ferdinand Marcos. They also need to attend more to what kind of government they want were they to gain power. A more developed political and economic program might consolidate their popular support.

Conclusion

Since 1978, Communist Chinese rulers have found themselves in a dilemma. On the one hand, many, particularly the older party veterans, have resisted demands by movement leaders for more responsive political institutions, for peaceful conflict resolution through open political process—in short, for democratic reforms. They have argued that the single-party system has been necessary for national unity and social and economic justice, particularly for a poor agricultural country.

At the same time, however, those leaders have seen Leninist, centrally planned economies lead Eastern Europe and the Soviet Union to social fascism in the political arena and to economic stagnation and consequent diminution of social and economic welfare. Those leaders understand that had they continued much beyond 1978 with a traditional command economy, social and economic justice and their own political legitimacy would have been at risk. Losing political legitimacy, they would have had to increasingly turn to political repression, in turn stimulating massive political movements for radical change, as in Eastern Europe.

On the other hand, having opened their economic system to the world, Chinese leaders have become more dependent on their intellectual elite and more subject to foreign influences. Exposure to the latter seems to open the way for popular demands for democratic reforms—threatening the power base of the current leaders.

In sum, the Chinese leaders' dilemma is similar to that of leaders in South Korea, Taiwan, and other developing countries. If Chinese leaders do not keep the door open to foreign markets and technology, their economy will stagnate, leading to failing economic and social justice and massive political protest. If the door is kept open to external trade and its consequent foreign influences, leaders may be subject to increasing demands by internal political movements and to international pressures for democratic reforms, as in the industrializing countries of East Asia.

Many of China's senior leaders clearly resist democratic reforms and have been willing to resort to brutal repression. Some younger political leaders and most of China's intellectuals, however, appear to support democratization and are waiting out the expiration of their elders. They are also hopeful that Deng Xiaoping will outlast the more reactionary leaders. Other authoritarian East Asian governments present a possible model for the transition from repression to peaceful change. In South Korea and Taiwan, there have been successful and usually peaceful social and political movements evolving within the context of a successfully developing national economy.

The wild card may be the rural Chinese, who do not yet have the zeal of their urban compatriots for democratic reforms. But as the countryside continues to industrialize, and as rural peasants can clearly see that their continued economic welfare depends largely on urban China and its opening to the world, democratic reforms may find support even in the countryside.

Although democratic reforms are not inevitable in China, the experience of Taiwan and South Korea suggests that they might occur. It remains to be seen whether China as a communist state, after the fashion of Bulgaria, can reform itself politically enough to gain popular support. Because of the government's economic and social policy achievements since 1949, theoretically it could remain in power by continuing to reform itself. Given the more common experiences of industrializing countries, one can also imagine an uneven but inevitable movement toward more democratic rights and institutions that will eventually make communism obsolete in China.

Notes

1. For an excellent description of Chinese democratic traditions see Nathan, *Chinese Democracy.*
2. Ibid.
3. Ibid.
4. See Edwards, Henken, and Nathan, *Human Rights.*
5. See Mao, *Selected Works,* pp. 75–80.
6. Estimates vary, and these numbers are probably low.
7. World Bank, *China,* p. iii.
8. Ibid., p. ii.
9. Ibid., p. iii.
10. Harding, *China's Second Revolution.*
11. Cited in Thomas, "Social and Economic Rights," p. 92.
12. *People's Republic of China.*
13. Sharp, "Nonviolent Struggle," pp. 1, 3.
14. See Wasserstrom and Perry, *Popular Protest.*
15. For a discussion of this, see Nathan, *China's Crises.*

Bibliography

Edwards, R. Randall, Louis Henken, and Andrew J. Nathan. *Human Rights in Contemporary China* (New York: Columbia University Press, 1986).

Harding, Harry. *China's Second Revolution: Reform after Mao* (Washington, DC: Brookings Institution, 1987).

Mao Zedong, *Selected Works of Mao Zedong*, Volume 3 (Beijing: Foreign Languages Press, 1967).

Nathan, Andrew. *Chinese Democracy* (Berkeley, CA: University of California Press, 1986).

Nathan, Andrew J. *China's Crises: Dilemmas of Reform and Prospects for Democracy* (New York: Columbia University Press, 1990).

People's Republic of China: Preliminary Findings on Killings of Unarmed Civilians, Arbitrary Arrests, and Summary Executions Since 1989 (New York: Amnesty International USA, August 1989).

Sharp, Gene. "Nonviolent Struggle in China: An Eyewitness Account," in *Nonviolent Sanctions: News from the Albert Einstein Institution* (Fall 1989): 1, 3.

Thomas, Stephen. "Social and Economic Rights Performance in Developing Countries: The People's Republic of China in Comparative Perspective," *Policy Science Journal* 15(1) (September 1986): 92.

Wasserstrom, Jeffrey, and Elizabeth J. Perry (eds.). *Popular Protest and Political Culture in Modern China: Learning from 1989* (Boulder, CO: Westview Press, 1992).

World Bank. *China: Socialist Economic Development, the Main Report* (Washington, DC: Unpublished, 1981).

9

Nonviolent Versus Violent Ethnic Political Action in Africa

James R. Scarritt

Although there has long been a vigorous debate in the literature about the importance of ethnicity as a causal factor in African politics,[1] there is little doubt that political, economic, and social grievances—whatever their underlying causes—are very frequently articulated, and political groups—whatever the range of their actual goals—are very frequently organized along lines of ethnic identity. This organization means that ethnic identity groups or ethnopolitical groups—whatever their degree of underlying "primordial" unity—are significant categories, and their leaders and members—whatever their motives—are significant actors in struggles for democracy, human rights, and social justice in Africa south of the Sahara. Furthermore, there is a genuine ethnic component in the causes of these grievances, the goals of these groups, and the motives of their leaders and members. The flexibility of group identities in response to changing interests is limited by the persistent primordial identities that are available. Thus it is both appropriate and important to examine the relationships between the types of protest in which these groups engage and their attainment of democracy, rights, and justice. To what extent have they achieved justice without violence, justice with violence, injustice without violence, or injustice with violence?

This chapter examines relationships between three types of protest by ethnopolitical groups—nonviolent protest, riot, and rebellion—and various aspects of democracy, human rights, and social justice in Black Africa. It presents both statistical analyses and more speculative analyses of those relationships that cannot be analyzed adequately using data sets.

Although the statistics fail to eliminate substantial uncertainty about the relationships between forms of protest by ethnopolitical groups and democracy/autocracy–human rights–social justice in African polities, the findings reported below give considerable support to the following generalizations.

1. Greater democracy in the period immediately following independence in the early 1960s is positively associated with nonviolent protest and negatively associated with rebellion in subsequent years through the 1980s.

2. Once a pattern of primarily nonviolent protest becomes established in these initially relatively democratic polities, it tends to maintain itself through the politics of unstable multiethnic coalitions among groups with relatively low levels of grievances, which can be characterized as communal contenders; thus the strongest predictor of nonviolent protest in the 1980s is prior nonviolent protest.

3. On the other hand, a pattern of rebellion in initially more autocratic polities by groups with relatively high levels of grievances, which can be characterized as ethnonationalists, has also been self-reinforcing, so that the strongest predictor of rebellion in the 1980s is prior rebellion.

4. Groups that can be characterized as ethnoclasses or indigenous peoples also have relatively high levels of grievances and tend to receive autocratic treatment—even in relatively democratic polities—but infrequently engage in any form of protest because of the small size and vulnerability of their groups.

5. The direction of causality in these relationships between democracy/autocracy and forms of protest appears to be two-way, although—except for two indirectly related polity characteristics, coherence and persistence—this cannot be demonstrated statistically for technical reasons.

6. The pattern of nonviolent protest by communal contenders leads to fewer human rights violations in the 1980s than the alternative patterns of rebellion by ethnonationalists or suppressed protest by ethnoclasses and indigenous peoples.

7. Riot and communal conflict are not significantly associated with either democracy or human rights/social justice.

8. Democracy fosters human rights protection and social justice more effectively than autocracy does, providing an indirect positive link between these conditions and nonviolent protest.

9. Given the ethnic diversity of most sub-Saharan African societies and the absence of a strong tendency for societies without minorities at risk to be more democratic, nonviolent ethnopolitical protest by members of groups classified as communal contenders is often more indicative of popular political organization than is the absence of protest. Such protest is therefore probably more closely related to democracy, human rights, and social justice.

The Minorities at Risk Dataset

The Minorities at Risk (MAR) project[2] identifies a universe of ethnopolitical groups—ethnic or communal minorities (either demographic or sociological) that have persistent identities and are in situations that place them at risk of experiencing violent conflict, human rights violations, and/or social injustice. It considers minorities to be at risk if they suffer (or, in the case of advantaged minorities, benefit from) systematic discriminatory treatment—economic or political—vis-à-vis other groups in the society, or they are the focus of political mobilization and action in defense or promotion of self-defined political, economic, or social interests. Such groups are ethnopolitical because they are defined by themselves and others as having a base in ethnic identity while being constantly molded by political interaction with other groups and the state, often centered on questions of economic distribution.[3] The project identifies groups at the highest politically relevant level of aggregation within a country, ignoring objective primordial differences if necessary. (For example, it codes Native Americans in the United States as one minority rather than over four hundred tribes). It includes only countries with populations of at least one million and groups whose population is at least either one hundred thousand or one percent of a country's population. According to these criteria there are seventy-four ethnopolitical groups in the MAR sub-Saharan African population.

Although not all of these ethnopolitical minority groups have actually experienced serious violations of their human rights—including the disempowerment that so effectively facilitates other rights violations—some have had such experiences, many perceive that they have had them or soon will, and all are to some degree at risk of having them. The MAR project contains data relevant to determining the severity of rights violations during the 1980s, but not prior to that time. These data will be used in the last section of the paper to examine the relationship between prior protest, prior democracy, and related authority characteristics, and rights violations in this time period. This analysis cannot include comparisons between groups that are at risk and those that are not, because no data were collected on the latter.

In seeking explanations for groups' actual involvement in political action in the 1980s, the Minorities at Risk project codes them in terms of a small number of primordial variables—including physical appearance, language, customs, and religion—and a much larger number of "situational" variables—including geographical concentration, demographic-ecological stress (including poverty, geographical mobility, and competition for land), cohesiveness of identity, conflicts with other communal groups that do not involve the state, political/economic/social differentials, discrimination and grievances, formal legal/political status, and history of antiregime protest. Most of these variables are treated as independent, influencing the two

intervening variables—grievances and 1970s political mobilization—
which, in turn, influence the dependent variables—protest and rebellion in
the 1980s. Political action by groups in neighboring states in the 1970s facilitates subsequent protest and rebellion; various polity characteristics
shape the context of political action.[4]

Because the forms of protest are significant independent or dependent
variables in various sections of this chapter, it is important to describe the
exact way in which they are measured. Ordinal scales were created for
each of the three forms of protest, their categories representing increasing
levels of scope and intensity of that form. *Riot* ranges from scattered acts
of sabotage to serious and widespread rioting and armed attempts to seize
power locally. *Rebellion* ranges from political banditry to protracted civil
war in which rebel military units have base areas. *Nonviolent protest*
ranges from verbal opposition through political organizing activity to
small and then large demonstrations, strikes, and rallies. Each ethnopolitical group was coded on each of these scales in terms of the most severe
action it took during successive five-year periods from 1945–1949 to
1985–1989; thus, protest is analyzed in terms of the most severe levels of
nonviolent protest, riot, and rebellion engaged in by each group during
various five-year time segments or longer periods that are aggregations of
such segments. Prior mobilization is coded in terms of indices built from
the amounts of each type of protest in 1975–1979 plus the amounts in
1970–1974 given a lower weight, but unindexed prior protest produces the
same results. Conflicts with other ethnopolitical groups (ranging from individual acts of harassment not resulting in fatalities to protracted, large-
scale communal warfare) are coded in the same way as protest.

Riot, rebellion, and intergroup conflict are unquestionably violent by
definition. Nonviolent protest is nonviolent in the popular meaning of that
term, but its relation to the academic philosophical meaning is ambiguous.[5] It is not necessarily, and not usually, principled nonviolence or a
nonviolent way of life; it does not always involve a sense of unity among
antagonists, self-sacrifice on the part of the protesters, or an intentional
strategy of nonviolence; and it frequently borders on violence (and occasionally crosses that border unnoticed by our coders). In Boulding's ter-
minology,[6] it involves elements of threat and implied exchange as well
as—and sometimes in stronger doses than—love. Although it is not possible to separate these three sources of power in nonviolent protest of the
types that occur in Africa south of the Sahara, and thus to weigh their relative importance, it is certainly true that this form of protest is less violent and involves significantly less threat than riot or rebellion. Furthermore, analyses of large numbers of cases of nonviolent action broadly
defined[7] reveal that most of them depart from the philosophical ideal in at
least some of the ways that cases in the MAR dataset do. Thus, the analysis of whether the relationships between nonviolent protest as we define it

and democracy, human rights, and social justice differ from those between the other forms of protest and these variables fits within the focus of the present volume.

It is also important to discuss the selection and coding of the variable that will be used to measure violations of groups' rights in the 1980s. Three potentially appropriate variables mentioned above are coded in terms of ordinal scales, but only at one point in time—the early 1980s. Grievances depend on leaders to articulate them; differentials and discrimination are coders' judgments about comparisons among objective characteristics of groups or their relationships with the state. Differentials and grievances are scaled according to their extent without regard to cause; discrimination is scaled according to the degree to which it is the result of deliberate government policies, with historical neglect that public policies seek to correct at the low end of the scale and deliberately discriminatory policies at the high end.[8] Thus, discrimination is a better indicator of rights violations than either differentials or grievances, although an appropriate combination of discrimination and differentials in a single scale is even better. Given the exploratory nature of this analysis, both political and economic discrimination and indicators derived from adding discrimination and differentials are used as indicators of rights violations. Grievances indicate the goals of protesting groups, which must be articulated by group leaders. The variety of political, economic, and social grievances included in the MAR dataset effectively represents the diversity of the goals sought by African ethnopolitical groups.

The Polity II Dataset

The Polity II dataset[9] can be utilized in combination with the Minorities at Risk dataset to systematically examine relationships between forms of protest and authority characteristics of polities. Polities are nation-state authority patterns (regimes) that persist until they are replaced by new polities through major, abrupt changes. The dataset consists of annual codings of polities' authority characteristics and changes in these characteristics as well as the directionality of change on underlying dimensions of democracy, autocracy, and power concentration. These annual codings were aggregated into five-year periods identical to those used for coding protest and communal conflict in the Minorities at Risk project. All groups in the same polity were coded identically, so that the two datasets could be compared. The Polity II data were gathered only through 1986, so 1985–1986 was not aggregated as a separate time period but was instead aggregated with 1980–1984 into a seven-year (1980–1986) period.

In order to examine the relation of nonviolent and violent protest to all authority characteristics in the Polity II dataset that might reasonably be assumed to affect human rights protection and social justice, the following variables from that dataset were examined: the basic authority characteristics of competitiveness of executive recruitment, constraints on the executive, competitiveness of participation, scope of government functions, and civilian versus military regime; the aggregated and scaled authority dimensions of democracy, autocracy, concentration of power, and coherence; and the authority change variables of the number of polity changes (presence/absence of polity establishment and/or termination through major, abrupt change), and the number of years that a polity has persisted.

The scales for these variables are presented in the sources cited above, but the conceptual dimension involved in each basic authority characteristic variable from its lowest to its highest value is as follows.

- Competitiveness of executive recruitment varies from hereditary selection to competitive election;
- Constraints on the executive vary from unlimited executive authority to executive parity or subordination;
- Competitiveness of participation varies from total suppression to regular, peaceful competition among relatively stable and enduring political groups;
- Scope varies from totalitarian to minimal (with higher scores indicating narrower scope);
- Civilian versus military regime has an intermediate mixed type.

Democracy aggregates executive recruitment, executive constraints, and participation; autocracy does the same, but with different weights; concentration does the same, but with yet another set of weights, and adds variables not analyzed separately here; and coherence is a dichotomy, separating coherent polities that are highly democratic *or* autocratic from incoherent ones that have substantial elements of both authority dimensions. Abrupt changes are accomplished within ten years or less, and major changes are those that involve sufficiently great changes in the values of a sufficient number of authority variables.

Most Black African countries have scored relatively low on democracy and relatively high on autocracy during much of the period since their independence; the most common scores on the ten-point democracy scale are those between zero and four, while the most common scores on the ten-point autocracy scale are those between five and eight. As a result of these scores a majority of countries were coherent most of the time, but a substantial minority were incoherent because they were insufficiently authoritarian (scoring less than seven on this scale).

The measurement of autocracy and democracy in the Polity II dataset is generally consistent with other, usually less systematic, characterizations,[10] although, unlike a few measurements designed exclusively for

Africa,[11] it underestimates democratic elements in some internally competitive one-party states. It should be noted that all of these authors have strictly political definitions of democracy, which probably pay too little attention to the organization of society—especially class—in their conceptual and operational approaches.[12]

Risk, Grievances, Mobilization, and Ethnopolitical Action in Africa

As indicated above, the focus of the Minorities at Risk project is on explaining the causes of protest and rebellion in the 1980s. In order to provide a context for the following discussion of the relationships between forms of political action and democracy, human rights, and social justice, these data will be summarized first. Although the scope of this chapter does not include systematic comparisons between Black Africa and other world regions, occasional comparisons between this region and the global population of groups will help to put the explanation of African protest in context.[13] There are more ethnopolitical minorities at risk in Black Africa than in any other region, and they compose a larger proportion of that region's population, so their degree of economic risk in the 1980s—whether measured in terms of differentials, discrimination, or variations in demographic-ecological stress—is lower than in almost all other world regions. Also, their degree of political risk, whether measured in terms of differentials or discrimination, is the lowest in the Third World, although close to the global mean. A smaller percentage of minorities in this region experience discrimination than in other regions, but a greater percentage of the discrimination that does occur, especially political discrimination, is severe, indicating substantial disempowerment for some groups. Not surprisingly, the levels of political, economic, and social grievances are relatively low in this region, although the level of political grievances is the highest of the three types.

In bivariate regressions, economic differentials and discrimination are significantly related to economic, social, and political rights grievances in the 1980s. But political differentials and discrimination are not significantly related to economic grievances, and cultural differences are not significantly related to political grievances. When all of the variables that are significant in bivariate regressions are entered into multiple regressions, the only significant relationships are those between economic discrimination and both economic and political rights grievances. In spite of their relatively low levels of risk and grievances, most Black African ethnopolitical groups have a strong sense of group identity because of colonial policies fostering such identities and political mobilization based on them.

Conflicts among communal groups that do not involve the state were more widespread and severe in Black Africa than in any other region over the entire period 1945–1989, although this was no longer true in the 1980s. The large number of Black African minorities, the weakness of African states, the insecurity of unstable multiethnic coalitions, and the machinations of colonial rulers and dominant postindependence majorities and minorities all help to account for this finding. On the other hand, rebellion by communal groups against the state in both the entire 1945–1989 period and the 1980s is slightly below the global average in frequency and intensity; the levels of both nonviolent protest and riot are lower than in any region except Latin America and the Caribbean for the longer period and the lowest in the world in the 1980s. These findings indicate that the image of most Black African countries as rent by severe ethnic conflict often presented in the popular press is inaccurate. In reality, both nonviolent and violent protest are relatively infrequent, although there is a relatively strong tendency for the latter to escalate into rebellion, largely because of state weakness. In the postindependence period there has been a slight decrease in nonviolent protest and a slight increase in rebellion.

In bivariate regressions of the sub-Saharan African data, no type of grievance is significantly related (at least at the .05 level)[14] to riot, rebellion, or nonviolent protest in the 1980s; the only significant relationship between group risk and political action is that between political differentials and rebellion. In multiple regressions involving prior mobilization for protest or rebellion and all types of grievances, only mobilization is significantly associated with any form of political action in the 1980s, canceling out the effects of grievances (which does not happen at the global level). These results are analyzed more fully in Scarritt and McMillan.[15]

Although we do not have systematic data on this point, it is very likely that protest in the anticolonial nationalist and immediate postindependence periods occurred more directly in response to grievances felt at those times and that this relationship was attenuated in the 1970s and 1980s by the dynamics of mobilization and repression. However, there are two substantially different patterns within which this dynamic has operated. Some African groups do experience levels of differentials, discrimination, and relative demographic-ecological stress that are high by global standards, and they develop high levels of grievances. These groups engage in all types of protest, but disproportionally in rebellion, and to a lesser degree in riot, especially in countries such as Burundi, Chad, Ethiopia and (in the 1990s) Somalia, in which they form the majority of the population. In the Minorities at Risk project these groups are classified as ethnonationalists because they seek independence or substantial autonomy. The strong relationship of prior mobilization for rebellion to rebellion in the 1980s points to a dynamic in countries where such groups predominate in which strong grievances are unresolved during long periods of partially successful rebellion that do not significantly change the status of minorities and repression limits the effectiveness of rebellion but cannot suppress it. Other groups also experience relatively high levels of differentials, discrimination, stress and grievances, but their numbers are too small to engage effectively in any type of protest. They are classified as ethnoclasses if they are distinguished from other groups mainly by economic differentials and as indigenous peoples if they are distinguished primarily by cultural differences.

Yet, other groups have lower levels of risk and grievances but have forged strong identities through competition over political power and economic distribution in the context of unstable multiethnic coalitions—often existing within a single governing party or among officers in a military regime. Leaders of specific ethnic groups move in and out of these coalitions, and there is always some degree of fear that defections will deprive the coalition of power. Any group whose leaders are presently in the coalition but were in opposition for a substantial period of time in the past will probably be suspected by other coalition members of having oppositional tendencies. The actual opposition, in turn, may be viewed as dangerous, even if few in number, because it is a potential magnet for defectors from the governing coalition.[16] Thus a high level of protest, most frequently nonviolent, is likely to occur even though the levels of risk and grievances for all groups are relatively low, as indicated by the strong relationship between prior mobilization for nonviolent protest and nonviolent protest in the 1980s. In the Minorities at Risk project such groups are called communal contenders, and fifty-four of the seventy-four Black African minorities belong to this type of group to some degree, including thirty that belong primarily to it.

These differences among ethnonationalists, ethnoclasses/indigenous peoples, and communal contenders with regard to risk, grievances, and forms of protest receive moderate statistical support in tests utilizing *lambda,* a measure of association that is appropriate for relationships involving one or more nominal or categorical variables. Lambda measures the proportionate reduction in error in predicting the dependent variable obtained by adding knowledge of its relationship to the independent variable, and varies from 1 to 0. Table 9.1 presents the proportionate reductions in error in predicting which category a minority falls into through knowing its forms of risk and its grievances in the 1980s, and its participation in different forms of protest during the entire 1945–1989 period, along with the associated t-scores and significance levels. Prediction is significantly although not dramatically improved by knowledge of all of these variables except political differentials, political discrimination, and economic grievances. On most risk and grievance variables the greatest differences are between communal contenders and the other types; on nonviolent protest and on riot the greatest differences are between ethnoclasses/indigenous peoples and the other types; while on rebellion differences among all three types

Table 9.1   Relationships Between Risk and Grievances in the 1980s, Forms of
            Protest 1945–1989, and Group Type

Proportionate reduction of error in predicting whether groups are communal contenders,
ethnoclasses/indigenous peoples, or ethnonationalists based on knowledge of:

Total Discrimination	Political Grievances
λ .282	λ .318
T 2.512	T 3.573
Sig. .005	Sig. .001
Political Discrimination	**Economic Grievances**
λ .095	λ .162
T 1.077	T 1.194
Not sig.	Not sig.
Economic Discrimination	**Social Grievances**
λ .292	λ .250
T 2.835	T 2.275
Sig. .05	Sig. .05
Aggregate Differentials	**Nonviolent Protest**
λ .475	λ .295
T 3.621	T 2.089
Sig. .001	Sig. .05
Political Differentials	**Riot**
λ .116	λ .318
T 1.699	T 2.078
Not sig.	Sig. .05
Economic Differentials	**Rebellion**
λ .243	λ .295
T 2.461	T 3.971
Sig. .05	Sig. .0005
Cultural Differences	**Total Grievances**
λ .272	λ .279
T 2.824	T 2.997
Sig. .05	Sig. .005

are relatively great. All of these differences are in the directions described
in the preceding paragraphs.

To the extent that nonviolent protest is more likely to be precipitated
by competition among communal contenders within unstable multiethnic
coalitions, while violent protest (riot and rebellion) is more likely to be
precipitated by other types of groups having higher levels of risk and
grievances, different types of protest are likely to occur in polities with
different authority characteristics and to have different consequences for
the perpetuation and change of authority characteristics. The next analytical step is to test these hypotheses.

Relationships Between Forms of
Political Action and Authority Characteristics of Polities

Various time lags can be utilized to explore the effects of authority characteristics on subsequent political action. Bivariate and/or multiple regressions were calculated relating each of the relevant authority characteristics from the Polity II dataset in each five-year time period beginning in 1960 to each form of protest in the 1980s. Although many of these relationships are not statistically significant, those that are tend to support the existence of positive relationships between at least some components of democracy and nonviolent protest. Competitiveness of executive recruitment in 1960–1964 and 1975–1979 are significantly related to nonviolent protest in the 1980s, as are executive constraints in 1960–1964, 1970–1974, and 1975–1979 and democracy 1960–1964, 1970–1974, and 1975–1979. The counterintuitive significance of the 1960–1964 period for the 1980s in these relationships is supportive of the findings of several scholars[17] that attributes of democracy in these late colonial and initial postindependence years had long-lasting consequences. When democracy 1960–1964 is included in a multiple regression for nonviolent protest in the 1980s along with prior mobilization and grievances, its effects are not canceled out by mobilization.[18] There is a virtual absence of significant relationships between these authority characteristics and either riot or communal conflict not involving the state, the one exception being the positive relationship between democracy 1960–1964 and riot in the 1980s, which may indicate that more spontaneous violence is a frequent reaction to authoritarian regimes in formerly democratic polities.

Several components of democracy—including competitiveness of executive recruitment 1970–1974 and 1975–1979, executive constraints 1970–1974, and competitiveness of participation 1960–1964—are significantly and negatively related to rebellion in the 1980s. The last of these findings is another indication of the relationship between democratic traits at independence and stability later. Competitiveness in subsequent time segments is insignificantly but still negatively related to rebellion; apparently competitiveness inhibits rebellion. The relationships between competitiveness of participation in five-year periods and both nonviolent protest and riot are all insignificant, but they are primarily positive for the former and exclusively negative for the latter. The statistically significant relationships between components of democracy and forms of protest discussed in the last two paragraphs are reported in Table 9.2.

Autocracy in earlier time segments is not significantly related to any form of protest in the 1980s except for a negative relationship between autocracy 1975–1979 and nonviolent protest in the 1980s, although nonviolent protest's statistically insignificant relationships with autocracy are

Table 9.2 Relationships Between Prior Democracy, Its Components, and Forms of Protest in the 1980s

Bivariate regressions of forms of protest on democracy and its components:

Authority Characteristics	Forms of Protest	
	Nonviolent	Rebellion
Competitiveness of Executive Recruitment		
1960–1964	B .646 T 3.420 Sig. .001	
1970–1974		B -1.025 T -2.651 Sig. .001
1975–1979	B .865 T 3.513 Sig. .0008	B -1.010 T -2.141 Sig. .035
Constraints on the Executive		
1960–1964	B .292 T 2.943 Sig. .005	
1970–1974	B .396 T 2.917 Sig. .005	B -.507 T -2.116 Sig. .038
1975–1979	B .364 T 2.724 Sig. .008	
Competitiveness of Participation		
1960–1964		B -1.218 T -3.728 Sig. .0004
Democracy		
1960–1964	B .259 T 3.555 Sig. .0008	B .171 T 2.370 Sig. .021
1970–1974	B .296 T 2.711 Sig. .009	
1975–1979	B .400 T 3.842 Sig. .0003	

consistently negative. Concentration of power 1975–1979 is also significantly and negatively related to nonviolent protest in the 1980s; concentration in earlier periods is insignificantly and negatively related to this form of protest. The decline in nonviolent protest over the years since independence is probably related to increased autocracy and power concentration in most Black African polities.

Coherence 1960–1964 is positively related to rebellion in the 1980s; coherence in 1965–1969 and 1970–1974 maintain this positive relationship, barely missing the .05 level of significance. Because a majority of coherent regimes were highly autocratic during that time period, it can be concluded that long-lived coherent autocratic regimes are more likely to eventually engender rebellion. This interpretation is strengthened by the finding that persistence 1960–1964, 1965–1969, and 1970–1974 are positively related to rebellion in the 1980s. Persistence 1975–1979 is, however, positively related to nonviolent protest in the 1980s, as is the magnitude of polity changes 1975–1979. These findings point to rebellion occurring in long-stable autocracies in the 1980s, and nonviolent protest taking place in polities that were for the first time more long lasting than these autocracies by the late 1970s, but less stable and also more democratic during that time period. The statistically significant relationships discussed in the last two paragraphs are reported in Table 9.3.

Additional indirect evidence of the relationship between democracy in the 1960s and later forms of protest is provided by the tendency for a greater percentage of communal contenders than ethnonationalists or (to a lesser degree) ethnoclasses/indigenous peoples to be found in polities that were relatively democratic in the first years of the postindependence period. The lambda statistics for these relationships are found in Table 9.4.

When the causal-temporal ordering utilized in the previous analysis is reversed to examine the effects of various forms of prior protest on subsequent authority characteristics, the cases become polities rather than groups and the size of the population thus shrinks from seventy-four to twenty-nine. Many fewer relationships are statistically significant, apparently because of the substantially smaller number of cases. When forms of protest by different groups within the same country are aggregated by simple addition, the only significant relationships that these forms have are with coherence and persistence.

Levels of nonviolent protest, riot, and rebellion often differ—sometimes substantially—among groups in the same polity, so that contradictory forces are at work within many polities with regard to many authority characteristics but not with regard to these two, where the effects of different levels of protest are more cumulative. Nonviolent protest 1945–1979 is positively related to coherence in 1980–1986, but rebellion 1945–1979 is negatively related to this polity characteristic. Prior nonviolent protest is

Table 9.3 Relationships Between Prior Autocracy, Concentration of Power, Coherence, and Persistence and Forms of Protest in the 1980s

Bivariate regressions of forms of protest on autocracy, concentration of power, coherence and persistence.

Authority Characteristics	Forms of Protest	
	Nonviolent	Rebellion
Autocracy 1975–1979	B - .254 T -2.247 Sig. .028	
Concentration of Power 1975–1979	B -.271 T -2.393 Sig. .022	
Coherence 1960–1964		B 2.340 T 3.231 Sig. .002
Persistence 1960–1964		B .032 T 3.021 Sig. .004
1965–1969		B .032 T 3.233 Sig. .002
1970–1974		B .029 T 3.045 Sig. .003
1975–1979	B .039 T 2.826 Sig. .006	
Change 1975–1979	B .951 T 3.238 Sig. .002	

negatively related to persistence in 1980–1986, but prior riot is positively related to it. When these aggregate protest scores are divided by the number of groups at risk in each polity to obtain an average score for each type of protest in the 1945–1979 period, the relationships with coherence and persistence in 1980–1986 just described remain significant, and prior riot

Table 9.4   Relationship Between Democracy in the 1960s and Group Type

Proportionate reduction of error in predicting whether groups are communal contenders, ethnoclasses/indigenous peoples, or ethnonationalists based on:

Democracy 1960–1964	Democracy 1965–1969
λ .375	λ .351
T 3.530	T 3.421
Sig. .005	Sig. .005

is also positively related to coherence. In addition, prior nonviolent protest is positively related to constraints on the executive and negatively related to scope in the 1980s; prior rebellion is positively related to change and negatively related to scope. Statistics on these findings are found in Table 9.5.

These findings include a positive connection between prior nonviolent protest and one component of democracy in the 1980s, and, if Howard[19] is correct in making a connection between reduced scope and democracy, also include an indirect positive connection (but one that is also made between rebellion and democracy). The other findings point to the complex long- and short-term relationships between forms of protest and both coherence and persistence. Nonviolent protest in the 1980s arose from short-term instability; long-term protest of this form tended to produce unstable but coherent polities in the 1980s. Rebellion in the 1980s arose from long-term autocratic stability, and long-term protest of this form tended to produce incoherent polities of indeterminate stability in the 1980s. Riot in the 1980s is not well explained by any of the variables employed in this chapter, but long-term riot—contrary to reasonable expectations—tended to produce stable and coherent polities. These results probably indicate that short- and long-term relationships between forms of protest and polity characteristics are rather different, but may also indicate that there are important aspects of these relationships that our data do not fully capture.

It can be concluded that there are relatively strong tendencies for nonviolent protest by communal contenders operating the politics of unstable multiethnic coalitions to occur in relatively democratic (by African standards), and sometimes incoherent, polities, and for rebellion by ethnonationalists and other types of groups most at risk to be found in more coherently autocratic polities. Although both types of protest promote polity change, nonviolent protest does so by increasing coherence and decreasing persistence and scope, and the direction of change promoted by it is more likely to be toward at least some aspects of democracy, but the direction promoted by rebellion is more likely to be toward incoherence and decreased scope. Thus, the relationships described in this paper occur within two types of social context with different sources of injustice and governmental power, different governmental control over rights violations, and different degrees of disempowerment.

Table 9.5   Relationships Between Forms of Protest 1945–1979 and Coherence,
Persistence, Executive Constraints, and Scope in 1980–1986

Bivariate and multiple regressions of coherence, persistence, executive constraints, and scope on forms of protest

Forms of Protest	Coherence	Persistence	Executive Constraints	Scope
Nonviolent (aggregated by addition)	*B .019 T 2.144 Sig. .043	*B .266 T 2.021 Sig. .055		
Nonviolent (average for polity)	*B .049 T 2.221 Sig. .037	*B -.709 T -2.247 Sig. .035	B .147 T 2.119 Sig. .044	B -.128 T -2.051 Sig. .052
Riot (aggregated by addition)		*B .494 T 2.146 Sig. .043		
Riot (average for polity)	*B -.060 T -2.132 Sig. .044	*B .839 T 2.085 Sig. .048		
Rebellion (aggregated by addition)	*B -.016 T 2.328 Sig. .029			
Rebellion (average for polity)	*B -.037 T -2.096 Sig. .047			B -.149 T -2.450 Sig. .022

*Multiple regression with three forms of protest as independent variables

As indicated above, the Minorities at Risk dataset does not include minorities that are not at risk, and thus does not permit a comparison between the consequences of their failure to protest and the consequences of various forms of protest by minorities at risk. The Polity II dataset, however, permits comparison of the authority characteristics of polities with and without minorities at risk. The two types of polities do not differ significantly with regard to democracy and autocracy. As nonviolent protest tends to occur in the more democratic of the polities having minorities at risk, it is fair to infer that nonviolent protest is probably more closely related to democracy than is the absence of protest.

The Effects of Political Action, Democracy, and Persistence on Human Rights and Social Justice

The relatively detailed quantitative analysis of relationships between forms of protest and authority characteristics presented in the preceding section

cannot be duplicated for relationships between protest, authority characteristics, and human rights or social justice using the Minorities at Risk
and Polity II datasets. A more limited analysis utilizing these datasets is
possible, however, and this can be supplemented by the work of other
scholars who have related the authority characteristics of African polities
to the provision of human rights and social justice.

A sophisticated scale of the attainment of human rights and social justice by ethnopolitical groups would select those types and levels of differentials (including differential experiences with demographic and ecological stress) that involve denials of rights or clearly violate a carefully
articulated conception of justice, and would combine the extent of such
differentials with the degree to which their violation is due to deliberate
discrimination.[20] As discussed above, discrimination is the single variable
from the Minorities at Risk dataset that most closely approximates this
ideal scale, although it is not very close. No form of protest in 1945–1979
or in either half of the 1970s is significantly related to the level of political, economic, or total (political and economic) discrimination in the
1980s in either bivariate or multiple regressions, except for positive relationships of both riot 1970–1974 and nonviolent protest 1975–1979 to political discrimination. In an attempt to get a more sophisticated measure
of human rights violations/social injustice, discrimination and differentials
were aggregated additively.[21] Again, no form of prior protest is significantly related to this human rights violation variable at the .05 level, but
nonviolent protest 1945–1979 is negatively related to it at the <.10 level of
significance. More relationships might be found if we had data on prior
differentials and discrimination and could thus examine changes in both
variables over time as we have done for forms of political action and authority characteristics.

In the absence of such data on differentials and discrimination, but
knowing that there is some degree of positive relationship between nonviolent protest and democracy, we can examine relationships between authority characteristics and human rights/social justice indicators on the assumption that the former may be intervening variables between forms of
protest and human rights. Analyses relating prior authority characteristics
to discrimination reveal that competitiveness of executive recruitment
1960–1964 and democracy 1960–1964 are significantly and negatively related to total (political and economic) discrimination in the 1980s in bivariate regressions. Somewhat surprisingly, executive constraints 1975–
1979 is significantly and positively related to this human rights indicator,
as are persistence 1960–1964 and 1970–1974—which have already been
shown to be positively related to rebellion. All other five-year measures of
polity variables are insignificant for discrimination. Democracy 1960–
1964 is negatively associated with the additive human rights violation variable at the .10 level. These findings reinforce the significance of democracy
in the immediate postindependence period, but lend only limited support to

the independent influence of authority characteristics on human rights. The statistically significant relationships discussed in the last two paragraphs are reported in Table 9.6. Another way to get at the relationship between forms of protest and human rights violations indirectly is to examine differences among the three types of groups previously specified with regard to differentials, discrimination, and grievances, as is done in Table 9.1. Those findings reinforce the validity of the relationships discussed in this section.

A number of studies support the positive, although relatively weak, findings reported in the previous two paragraphs by suggesting that insti-

Table 9.6   Relationships Between Prior Forms of Protest, Democracy, Persistence, and Human Rights Violations in the 1980s

Bivariate regressions of human rights violations on forms of protest, democracy, and persistence.

| | Human Rights Violation | | |
| | Discrimination | | Differentials + |
Indicator	Political	Total	Discrimination
Riot 1970–1974	B .445 T 2.342 Sig. .025		
Nonviolent Protest 1975–1979	B .505 T 2.315 Sig. .025		
Nonviolent Protest 1945–1979	B -.201 T -1.801 Sig. .077		
Democracy 1960–1964		B -.045 T -1.966 Sig. .055	B -.374 T -1.629 Sig. .109
Competitiveness of Executive Recruitment 1960–1964		B -.157 T -2.798 Sig. .007	
Constraints on the Executive 1975–1979		B .087 T 2.024 Sig. .047	
Persistence 1960–1964		B .005 T 2.684 Sig. .010	
Persistence 1970–1974		B .004 T 2.009 Sig. .049	

tutionalized or stable democracy is positively related to the protection of human rights and the attainment of social justice and that autocracy is negatively related to these goals. There is not space here to review this entire body of literature, but several studies that concentrate on Africa can be mentioned. Berg-Schlosser[22] analyzed socialist and semicompetitive polities as separate categories that are intermediate between oligarchies and polyarchies; he found that the physical quality of life index (PQLI) disparity reduction rates tend to be substantially higher in stable nonoligarchies than in stable oligarchies or unstable (praetorian) polities, although there is little variation among the categories of stable nonoligarchies. He also found that polyarchies have by far the best records of political freedom and civil liberties (as measured by Freedom House) followed at a distance by semicompetitive polities, although there is an element of tautology in this finding because of the conceptual overlap between political freedom and polyarchy.

Sandbrook[23] found that among the wealthier African countries—although not among the poorest ones—polities in which there is greater electoral competition provide more economic rights (as measured by the PQLI) for their poorer citizens. Using data from U.S. Department of State reports, he confirmed Berg-Schlosser's finding that democracies and protodemocracies are much better than autocracies at protecting civil and political rights, with competitive one-party systems falling in between. Howard[24] stressed the extensive conceptual overlap between political rights and democracy rather than drawing an empirical connection between them. She argued that a capitalist bourgeois democracy under pressure from a politically active proletariat would provide various types of rights more effectively than present regimes dominated by state-based ruling classes.[25]

Conclusion:
Justice Without Violence for African Minorities at Risk?

The data presented in this paper indicate that nonviolent protest is more likely than riot or rebellion to be positively related to at least some aspects of greater democracy and that rebellion is least likely to be associated with this authority characteristic. These forms of political action are most closely tied to democracy in the immediate postindependence period. The effort to tie greater nonviolent protest and democracy to better human rights protection and greater social justice using Minorities at Risk and Polity II data produced limited positive results and no negative ones, even though these datasets are not well designed for this purpose, and the tie between democracy and human rights/social justice is strongly supported in the literature. It must be concluded that our data give somewhat weak and ambiguous support to the conclusion that justice is attainable without violence for many but not all sub-Saharan African minorities at risk, and much less—if any—support to the conclusion that it is attainable by any of them through violence. Unfortunately, injustice remains an all too likely outcome of all forms of protest.

Can some of Africa's fairly frequent rebellions be converted into nonviolent protests? Can the connections between nonviolent protest and democracy/human rights/social justice be strengthened? Answers to these questions will inevitably be speculative, but are nevertheless worth attempting. There is more room for optimism regarding the second question than the first. Given the fragmentation of most African societies and the weakness of many African states, rebellion and its consequences are likely to occur about as frequently as they have in the past, and in essentially the same polities, for some time. For those groups and those polities for which protest is already primarily nonviolent—mainly those having the politics of unstable multiethnic coalitions among communal contenders based on an early postindependence democratic tradition—there is a reasonably good chance that the positive outcomes of that form of protest can be enhanced under a combination of internal and external pressures for greater democracy. The attainment of greater democracy and justice in these polities without violence depends on a number of factors; the crucial institutional variables are those pertaining to the party system and central-local government/party relations. Political parties, or at least the ruling party, need to have a stronger organization with greater input from ordinary citizens than have almost all postindependence African parties. If there is competition among parties, all parties need to feel that they will continue to have a fair chance to win in the future if they lose the next election. Delegation of power to local governments and party units needs to be both substantial and institutionalized.[26] Under these conditions, which will also strengthen democracy, there will be the sense of leadership and popular political security necessary to keep a broad multiethnic coalition stable, even in situations of strong group identity and cohesion and moderately high levels of differentials.

Events in Africa during the last two and one-half years, which are not covered by the quantitative data presented in this chapter, offer qualified evidence that nonviolent protest, increased democracy, and at least modest improvements in human rights go together in the early 1990s.[27] This association will probably continue throughout the decade. It is, however, far too early to conclude that the institutions necessary to sustain effective democracy and the realization of social justice, including those discussed in the previous paragraph, will develop or survive in most countries.

Notes

1. See, for example, Barrows, "Ethnic Diversity"; Bates, "Modernization, Ethnic Competition"; Chazan et al., *Politics and Society*, pp. 102–105; Doornbos, "Linking the Future"; Kasfir, *The Shrinking Political Arena*; Mafeje, "The Ideology of 'Tribalism'"; Melson and Wolpe, "Modernization"; Molteno, "Cleavage and Conflict"; Morrison and Stevenson, "Cultural Pluralism"; Osaghae, "Redeeming the Utility"; Rothchild, "Interethnic Conflict"; Saul, "The Dialectic of Class"; Scarritt, "From Tribalism to Sectionalism?"; Shaw, "Ethnicity as the Resilient Paradigm"; Sklar, "Political Science"; van den Berghe, "Class, Race, and Ethnicity."

2. Described in Gurr and Scarritt, "Minorities Rights at Risk"; Gurr, "Why Minorities Rebel"; Gurr et al., *Minorities at Risk*; Gurr and Harff, "The Rights of Collectivities."

3. Scarritt, "The Explanation of African Politics," p. 87.

4. This explanatory model is presented in greater detail in Gurr et al., *Minorities at Risk*, Chapter 5.

5. Bond, "The Nature of Nonviolent Action," and "Nonviolent Direct Action"; Bondurant, *Conquest of Violence*, pp. 23–26; Holmes, "Violence and Non-Violence"; Sharp, *The Politics of Nonviolent Action*.

6. Boulding, *Three Faces of Power*.

7. Bond, "The Nature of Nonviolent Action"; Sharp, *The Politics of Nonviolent Action*.

8. See Gurr, "Why Minorities Rebel" for details of the entire coding scheme.

9. The theoretical framework underlying this project is presented in Eckstein and Gurr, *Patterns of Authority*, and Eckstein, "Authority Relations." The data from its predecessor—Polity—are described and analyzed in Gurr, "Persistence and Change." Also see Gurr, Jaggers, and Moore, "The Transformation of the Western State."

10. Arat, *Democracy and Human Rights;* Bollen, "Issues in the Comparative Measurement"; Gastil, *Freedom in the World*; Humana, *World Human Rights;* Lane and Ersson, "Unpacking the Political Development Concept," p. 133; Vanhanen, *The Process of Democratization*, pp. 152–157.

11. Berg-Schlosser, "African Political Systems"; Sandbrook, "Liberal Democracy in Africa."

12. Anyang' Nyong'o, *Popular Struggles for Democracy;* Beckman, "Whose Democracy?"; Cohen and Goulbourne, *Democracy and Socialism;* Scarritt and Mozaffar, "Toward Sustainable Democracy."

13. See Scarritt, "Communal Conflict"; and Gurr et al., *Minorities at Risk*, Chapters 1–4, for more complete presentations of the explanation of African protest in comparative context.

14. Although African minorities at risk and African polities are, strictly speaking, populations rather than samples of larger extant populations, tests of significance are utilized throughout this paper on the assumption that both the minorities and the polities included in this study can be treated as samples of larger hypothetical populations of all possible minorities and polities.

15. Scarritt and McMillan, "Protest and Rebellion," pp. 20–21 and Tables 1a, 3a, and 5a. The statistics reported in that paper are slightly different from those reported in this chapter because the former excludes four groups that barely fail to qualify for inclusion in the MAR dataset because of their populations.

16. Gurr and Scarritt, "Minorities Rights at Risk," pp. 387–388; Horowitz, *Ethnic Groups in Conflict*, pp. 349–440; Rothchild and Foley, "African States."

17. Collier, *Regimes in Tropical Africa*; Jackman, "The Predictability of Coups d'Etat," and "Explaining African Coups d'Etat"; Welfling, *Political Institutionalization*.

18. Scarritt and McMillan, "Protest and Rebellion," Table 12.

19. Howard, *Human Rights*.

20. Bollen, "Political Rights"; Stohl et al., "State Violation of Human Rights."

21. Since privileged minorities have negative values on both differentials and discrimination, multiplicative aggregation would produce nonsense results by converting these to positive values.

22. Berg-Schlosser, "African Political Systems," pp. 134–143, and "Typologies of Political Systems," pp. 183–194.

23. Sandbrook, "Liberal Democracy," pp. 246–250.

24. Howard, *Human Rights,* pp. 119–144.

25. Ibid., pp. 224–227.

26. Scarritt and Mozaffar, "Toward Sustainable Democracy."

27. Bratton and van de Walle, "Toward Governance."

Bibliography

Anyang' Nyong'o, Peter (ed.). *Popular Struggles for Democracy in Africa* (London: Zed Books, 1987).

Arat, Zehra F. *Democracy and Human Rights in Developing Countries* (Boulder, CO: Lynne Rienner Publishers, 1991).

Barrows, Walter L. "Ethnic Diversity and Political Instability in Black Africa," *Comparative Political Studies* 9 (2) (1976): 139–170.

Bates, Robert H. "Modernization, Ethnic Competition, and the Rationality of Politics in Contemporary Africa," in Donald Rothchild and Victor A. Olorunsola (eds.), *State Versus Ethnic Claims: African Policy Dilemmas* (Boulder, CO: Westview Press, 1983), pp. 152–171.

Beckman, Bjorn. "Whose Democracy? Bourgeois Versus Popular Democracy," *Review of African Political Economy* 45/46 (1989): 84–97.

Berg-Schlosser, Dirk. "African Political Systems: Typology and Performance," *Comparative Political Studies* 17 (1) (1984): 121–151.

———. "Typologies of Third World Political Systems," in Anton Bebler and Jim Seroka (eds.), *Contemporary Political Systems* (Boulder, CO: Lynne Rienner Publishers, 1990), pp. 173–201.

Bollen, Kenneth A. "Issues in the Comparative Measurement of Political Democracy," *American Sociological Review* 45 (2) (1980): 370–390.

———. "Political Rights and Political Liberties in Nations: An Evaluation of Human Rights Measures, 1950 to 1984," *Human Rights Quarterly* 8 (4) (1986): 567–591.

Bond, Douglas G. "The Nature and Meanings of Nonviolent Direct Action: An Exploratory Study," *Journal of Peace Research* 25 (1) (1988): 81–89.

———. "Nonviolent Direct Action and the Diffusion of Power." Paper presented to the American Political Science Association annual meetings, Washington, DC, August 1991.

Bondurant, Joan V. *Conquest of Violence: The Gandhian Philosophy of Conflict* (new revised edition) (Princeton: Princeton University Press, 1988).

Boulding, Kenneth E. *Three Faces of Power* (Newbury Park, CA: Sage Publications, 1989).

Bratton, Michael, and Nicolas van de Walle. "Toward Governance in Africa: Popular Demands and State Responses" in Goran Hyden and Michael Bratton (eds.), *Governance and Politics in Africa* (Boulder, CO: Lynne Rienner Publishers, 1992), pp. 27–55.

Chazan, Naomi, Robert Mortimer, John Ravenhill, and Donald Rothchild. *Politics and Society in Contemporary Africa* (Boulder, CO: Lynne Rienner Publishers, 1988).

Cohen, Robin. "Class in Africa: Analytical Problems and Perspectives," in Ralph Miliband and John Savile (eds.), *The Socialist Register, 1972* (London: Merlin Press, 1972), pp. 231–255.

Cohen, Robin, and Harry Goulbourne (eds.). *Democracy and Socialism in Africa* (Boulder, CO: Westview Press, 1991).

Collier, Ruth Berins. *Regimes in Tropical Africa: Changing Forms of Supremacy, 1945–1975* (Berkeley: University of California Press, 1982).

Doornbos, Martin. "Linking the Future to the Past: Ethnicity and Pluralism," *Review of African Political Economy* 52 (1991): 53–65.

Eckstein, Harry. "Authority Relations and Governmental Performance: A Theoretical Framework," *Comparative Political Studies* 2 (3) (1969): 269–325.

Eckstein, Harry, and Ted Robert Gurr. *Patterns of Authority: A Structural Basis for Political Inquiry* (New York: Wiley-Interscience, 1975).

Gastil, Raymond D. *Freedom in the World: Political Rights and Civil Liberties, 1986–1987* (Westport, CT: Greenwood Press, 1987).

Gurr, Ted Robert. "Persistence and Change in Political Systems, 1800–1971," *American Political Science Review* 68 (4) (1974): 1482–1504.

———. "Why Minorities Rebel: A Global Analysis of Communal Mobilization and Conflict Since 1945," *International Political Science Review* 14 (2) (1993): 161–201.

Gurr, Ted Robert, et al. *Minorities at Risk: A Global View of Ethnopolitical Conflicts* (Washington, DC: United States Institute of Peace Press, 1993).

Gurr, Ted Robert, and Barbara Harff. "The Rights of Collectivities: Principles and Procedures in Measuring the Human Rights Status of Communal and Political Groups," in Thomas B. Jabine and Richard P. Claude (eds.), *Human Rights and Statistics: Getting the Record Straight* (Philadelphia: University of Pennsylvania Press, 1992), pp. 159–187.

Gurr, Ted Robert, Keith Jaggers, and Will H. Moore. *Polity II Codebook* (Boulder, CO: Center for Comparative Politics, Department of Political Science, University of Colorado, 1989).

———. "The Transformation of the Western State: The Growth of Democracy, Autocracy, and State Power Since 1800," *Studies in Comparative International Development* 25 (1) (1990): 73–108.

Gurr, Ted Robert, and James R. Scarritt. "Minorities Rights at Risk: A Global Survey," *Human Rights Quarterly* 11 (3) (1989): 375–405.

Holmes, Robert L. "Violence and Non-Violence," in Jerome A. Shaffer (ed.), *Violence* (New York: David McKay, 1971), pp. 103–135.

Horowitz, Donald L. *Ethnic Groups in Conflict* (Berkeley and Los Angeles: University of California Press, 1985).

Howard, Rhoda E. *Human Rights in Commonwealth Africa.* (Totowa, NJ: Rowman & Littlefield, 1986).

Humana, Charles. *World Human Rights Guide* (London: Hutchinson, 1983).

Jackman, Robert W. "The Predictability of Coups d'Etat: A Model with African Data," *American Political Science Review* 72 (4) (1978): 1262–1275.

———. "Explaining African Coups d'Etat," *American Political Science Review* 80 (1) (1986): 225–232.

Kasfir, Nelson. *The Shrinking Political Arena: Participation and Ethnicity in African Politics with a Case Study of Uganda* (Berkeley and Los Angeles: University of California Press, 1976).

———. "Explaining Ethnic Political Participation," *World Politics* 31 (3) (1979): 365–388.

Lane, J. E., and S. Ersson. "Unpacking the Political Development Concept," *Political Geography Quarterly* 8 (2) (1989): 123–144.

Mafeje, Archie. "The Ideology of 'Tribalism,'" *Journal of Modern African Studies* 9 (2) (1971): 253–261.

Melson, Robert, and Howard Wolpe. "Modernization and the Politics of Communalism: A Theoretical Perspective," *American Political Science Review* 64 (4) (1970): 1112–1130.

Molteno, Robert. "Cleavage and Conflict in Zambian Politics: A Study in Sectionalism," in William Tordoff (ed.), *Politics in Zambia* (Berkeley and Los Angeles: University of California Press, 1974), pp. 62–106.

Morrison, Donald G., and Hugh Michael Stevenson. "Cultural Pluralism, Modernization, and Conflict: An Empirical Analysis of Sources of Political Instability in African Nations," *Canadian Journal of Political Science* 5 (1972): 82–103.

———. "Integration and Instability: Patterns of African Political Development," *American Political Science Review* 66 (3) (1972): 902–927.

Osaghae, Eghosa E. "Redeeming the Utility of the Ethnic Perspective in African Studies: Towards a New Agenda," *Journal of Ethnic Studies* 18 (2) (1990): 37–58.

Rothchild, Donald. "Interethnic Conflict and Policy Analysis in Africa," *Ethnic and Racial Studies* 9 (1) (1986): 66–86.

———. "An Interactive Model for State-Ethnic Relations," in Francis M. Deng and I. William Zartman (eds.), *Conflict Resolution in Africa* (Washington, DC: Brookings Institution, 1991), pp. 190–215.

Rothchild, Donald, and Michael Foley. "African States and the Politics of Inclusive Coalitions," in Donald Rothchild and Naomi Chazan (eds.), *The Precarious Balance* (Boulder, CO: Westview Press, 1988), pp. 233–264.

Sandbrook, Richard. "Liberal Democracy in Africa: A Socialist-Revisionist Perspective," *Canadian Journal of African Studies* 22 (2) (1988): 242.

Saul, John S. "The Dialectic of Class and Tribe," in John S. Saul, *The State and Revolution in Eastern Africa* (New York: Monthly Review Press, 1979), pp. 391–423.

Scarritt, James R. "From Tribalism to Sectionalism?: Political Cleavages in Zambia and Uganda," *Umoja* 2 (2) (1975): 1–12.

———. "The Explanation of African Politics and Society: Toward a Synthesis of Approaches," *Journal of African Studies* 13 (3) (1986): 85–93.

———. "Communal Conflict and Contention for Power in Africa South of the Sahara," in Ted Robert Gurr, Barbara Harff, Monty Marshall, and James Scarritt, *Minorities at Risk: A Global View of Ethnopolitical Conflicts* (Washington, DC: United States Institute of Peace Press, 1993).

Scarritt, James R., and Susan McMillan. "Protest and Rebellion in Africa: Explaining Conflicts Between Ethnic Minorities and the State in the 1980s." Manuscript, Institute of Behavioral Science and Center for Comparative Politics, University of Colorado, Boulder, 1993.

Scarritt, James R., and Shaheen Mozaffar. "Toward Sustainable Democracy in Africa: Can U.S. Policy Make a Difference?" in William Crotty (ed.), *Post–Cold War Policy: Foreign and Military* (New York: Nelson-Hall, 1993).

Sharp, Gene. *The Politics of Nonviolent Action* (Boston: Porter Sargent Publishers, 1973).

Shaw, Timothy. "Ethnicity as the Resilient Paradigm for Africa: From the 1960s to the 1980s," *Development and Change* 17 (4) (1986): 587–605.

Sklar, Richard L. "Political Science and National Integration—A Radical Approach," *Journal of Modern African Studies* 5 (1) (1967): 1–11.

Stohl, Michael, David Carleton, George Lopez, and Stephen Samuels. "State Violation of Human Rights: Issues and Problems of Measurement," *Human Rights Quarterly* 8 (4) (1986): 592–606.

Vail, Leroy (ed.). *The Creation of Tribalism in Southern Africa* (London: James Curry, 1989).

van den Berghe, Pierre L. "Class, Race and Ethnicity in Africa," *Ethnic and Racial Studies* 6 (2) (1983): 221–236.

Vanhanen, Tatu. *The Process of Democratization: A Comparative Study of 147 States, 1980–1988* (New York: Crane Russak, 1990).

Welfling, Mary B. *Political Institutionalization: Comparative Analyses of African Party Systems* (Beverly Hills, CA: Sage Professional Papers in Comparative Politics, 01–041, 1973).

10

Foreign Threats and Domestic Actions: Sanctions Against South Africa

William Kaempfer, Anton D. Lowenberg,
H. Naci Mocan & Lynne Bennett

Nonviolent change of an unjust political, social, or economic regime in a nation is seldom accomplished without support from a foreign government or international organization for the group seeking that change. However, how signals and threats are transmitted from one nation to another so as to influence its policies is a process that is poorly understood. In a larger research program,[1] we have investigated the use of international economic sanctions for stimulating transnational policy change.[2] In line with that program, this paper examines the movement from awareness in Nation A of an objectionable social problem in Nation B, to a response in the form of sanctions by Nation A, to the impact of those sanctions in Nation B.[3] Specifically, we search for a link from political activism and civil disobedience by antiapartheid activists in South Africa to antiapartheid sanctions by other nations and to the continuation of political activism in South Africa.

The general perception by economists and political scientists who have studied sanctions is that they are relatively ineffective instruments of foreign policy.[4] Economic sanctions are supposed to bring about policy changes in the target countries by inducing economic damage that causes their leaders to abandon their objectionable behavior. One problem with this view, however, is that sanctions seldom inflict major pain on the target economies. Except in the rare instances where most or all of the target's potential trading partners join in the sanctioning campaign, it is relatively easy for the target to find substitute buyers or suppliers in world markets.[5] Moreover, cultural and social sanctions, such as boycotts of entertainers or athletes, do not generate significant economic losses.

Still, even if sanctions create economic dislocation in the target nation, how does this lead to policy reforms there? It is conceivable, of

191

course, that the sanctions might discourage the ruling regime or reduce its political support, thus causing a capitulation to foreign pressure. But it is just as likely that the sanctions will impoverish the opponents of the regime more than the regime's supporters, thereby undermining the opposition's ability to resist. In addition, several scholars have identified a "rally-round-the-flag" effect, where the sanctions generate indignation over foreign intervention and thus intensify domestic support for the target regime's policies in the target country. In that case, the sanctions could precipitate a perverse effect on the policies of the target, reinforcing rather than discouraging its objectionable behavior. A fundamental problem with sanctions is that their economic effects on the target nation (if any) are haphazard. They do not necessarily benefit the opponents of the regime nor weaken its supporters. Sanctions that produce a general decline in economic welfare are likely to hurt the very people they are intended to help.

Given these difficulties, the increasing popularity of sanctions as instruments of foreign policy is somewhat puzzling. Why do countries routinely use sanctions to achieve foreign policy objectives when (a) their economic impacts are often weak and (b) the link of sanctions with desired political reforms in the target countries is even weaker? Despite these weaknesses, recent history suggests that sanctions might have been at least partially instrumental in bringing about political and economic liberalization in some target nations. Democratic reforms in Eastern Europe, the Soviet Union, Nicaragua, and South Africa, among other things, occurred after those countries were targets of Western sanctions of varying intensity and duration. What role, if any, did those sanctions play in precipitating these reforms?[6] Is there some mechanism through which sanctions work that has been overlooked by the conventional view?

To address these questions, we studied the sanctions imposed on South Africa over the past three decades. Our analysis is based on an interest-group theory of sanctions, derived from the public-choice school of economics. According to that approach, sanctions and other foreign policies are shaped by pressures of special-interest groups within the polities of the sanctioning countries. Those special interests seek to enhance the welfare of their members by lobbying politicians to implement certain policies, including sanctions against foreign nations. One implication of this approach is that sanctions are not entirely independent of events in the target country. Political disturbances and economic distress in the target attract media coverage, which raises the profile of the target government's actions to the forefront of world attention. The result is increased lobbying for sanctions by interest groups within the sanctioning countries whose members object to the behavior of the target government. We present evidence that sanctions against South Africa tended to follow, not lead, political disturbances and economic dislocation there. Once implemented, however, the sanctions had feedback effects on political and economic conditions in South Africa.

Interest-group analysis can also explain the political effects of sanctions and other foreign policies on target countries. Using this method, the objectionable policies of a target government are viewed as responses to interest-group pressures in the target polity. Following Kaempfer and Lowenberg,[7] we propose that sanctions and other foreign policy initiatives can change the configuration of interest-group influences within the target country by altering the abilities of interest groups to mobilize support and exert political pressure. This public-choice approach can explain how even sanctions with weak economic impacts on the target country can nevertheless induce political changes there, although not necessarily in the directions preferred by the sanctioners. Moreover, there is a direct relationship between foreign sanctions and domestic political processes in the target that may not require intervening economic damage. For example, sanctions reduce the capacity of the target government to carry out its objectionable policy if the sanctions increase the ability of opposition groups to organize collective action against it.[8]

In the South African case, an intensification of sanctions in the mid-1980s was followed a few years later by significant political reforms. To what extent were economic sanctions and other foreign pressures responsible for these changes? Although we cannot directly measure the contribution of sanctions to political reform in South Africa, we do present evidence on the relationship between sanctions and the activities of the black antiapartheid movement within South Africa. This evidence shows that although sanctions might have had an immediate positive effect on the level of antiapartheid pressure in South Africa, the longer-term effect was to depress the incomes of South African blacks and therefore diminish their capacity to wage an effective campaign of resistance against apartheid.

The Public-Choice Theory of International Sanctions

Kaempfer and Lowenberg have developed a public-choice approach to the study of international relations in general and economic sanctions in particular.[9] Public-choice theory explains policy formation by rational, maximizing choices individuals make in accordance with their opportunity-cost assessments. According to this approach, foreign and domestic policies of nations are shaped by the decisions of their individual political agents such as politicians, voters, bureaucrats, and interest groups. Nation-states themselves are viewed as artifacts of these collective choice processes, not as independent actors in international relations.

Public-choice theory treats politicians as seeking to maximize their tenure in office. Consequently, they have incentives to create policy in response to lobbying and other pressures of special-interest groups. Many government policies, justified by policymakers as serving the public interest, are actually political redistributions. These policies benefit a relative few while dispersing the costs widely over all. Many trade and investment sanctions are examples of redistributional policies. Thus, trade sanctions that restrict imports from target countries benefit producers of import substitutes in the sanctioning countries at the expense of consumers of those goods. Trade sanctions often have the same protectionist effects as specific tariffs or quotas.[10] In addition, exporters sometimes pressure their governments to impose sanctions on imports from countries accused of not opening their markets to foreign goods.[11] Producers in the sanctioning countries who use those imports in their production processes pay the price for such policies.

Some interest groups lobby for sanctions, not to obtain pecuniary gains but to enhance the "psychic" welfare of their members. Thus, anti-apartheid groups in the United States and other Western countries often sought sanctions against South Africa to support their members' dislike for South African government policies. Likewise, environmentalists and allied groups lobby for sanctions against nations that violate nuclear nonproliferation agreements. Under pressure from conservation groups, the United States recently threatened Japan with sanctions for its hunting of endangered sea turtles. On occasion, groups with a pecuniary interest in sanctions will join forces with other groups seeking sanctions for largely nonpecuniary gains. For instance, U.S. sugar producers might join anti-Castro interests in lobbying for a boycott of Cuban sugar imports to the United States. Kaempfer and Lowenberg argued that many of the antiapartheid sanctions imposed by the United States and the European Community also served protectionist interests there.[12]

Regardless of the motives of the groups lobbying for sanctions, any such restrictions on trade inevitably result in substantial costs for others in terms of higher prices and foregone trading opportunities. Given these costs of sanctions accruing to individuals and groups in the sanctioning countries, it is hardly surprising that sanctioners often deliberately apply sanctions having weak economic impacts on the target countries. Elementary trade theory suggests that a sanction that has a severe economic effect on the target trading partner will also impose substantial pain on the sanctioning partner. Therefore, sanctioning governments will try to meet the demands of interest groups pressuring for sanctions by choosing relatively innocuous sanctions, thereby avoiding the wrath of other groups that might be hurt by more severe ones. This effort helps explain why the U.S. Comprehensive Antiapartheid Act included sanctions against South African textiles, steel, and agricultural goods, none of which comprised a significant share of the U.S. market, but exempted various strategic metals of which South Africa is a major world supplier. An even better illustration of the choice of insignificant trade flow by sanctioners was the Canadian refusal of landing rights for South African Airways, which did not fly to

Canada. Politicians like to appear to be "doing something" about a foreign government's violation of moral or ideological values to satisfy interest-group pressures for sanctions without incurring substantial costs or the wrath of other influential groups within the sanctioning polity.[13]

Interest-group analysis implies that the forms and severity of sanctions applied depend on several factors, including the relative influences of interest groups within a sanctioning country, the ability of policymakers to act independently of interest-group pressures, and the information possessed by individuals and groups within the sanctioning country regarding the objectionable policy of the target country. In this chapter, we will focus on this latter issue.

The intensity with which interest groups in Country A lobby for sanctions to be applied against Country B is a positive function of the quantity of information they possess about events in the target nation. The greater the awareness of injustices practiced by Government B, the greater the momentum of the sanctioning campaign. Thus, sanctions are often imposed not so much to initiate reforms there, but as a response to unrest already begun there. Resistance against Government B by its own citizens raises the profile of their struggle in sympathetic minds abroad. This enhanced consciousness of the problem leads to increased pressure on Government A to do something.[14] Later in this chapter, we analyze data on sanctions against South Africa to determine whether the sanctions were independent causes of political and economic changes in South Africa or were at least partly induced by those changes.

Just as the pressure for sanctions in the sanctioning countries is a function of interest-group politics, so their effects in the target country depend on interest-group politics there. Following Kaempfer and Lowenberg,[15] consider a simple interest-group model—a target polity with two domestic interest groups, X and Y, and a public policy, A, sufficiently objectionable to attract foreign sanctions. (In the South African case, A would represent the level of implementation of apartheid.) Suppose that members of Group X benefit from Policy A, whereas members of Group Y are harmed by A.[16]

Politicians decide the level of A by weighing the relative influences of Group X and Group Y. The presumption here is that politicians seek only to maximize their political support, by choosing policies in accordance with the relative influences of interest groups.[17] The more resources a group allocates to political activity, the more effective its political influence, and the greater the relative weight politicians give it. Political effectiveness depends on the ability of the group to organize its members for collective action. Because most of a group's goals are public goods to its members, it follows that the free-rider incentive is the main barrier to effective collective action.[18] Groups that best discourage free riding are the most effective politically. Small groups are often more effective than larger ones because the collective benefits of group action are spread over fewer people, which means a larger private gain accruing to each member from participating in the group's activities.[19] The larger the incomes of group members, the more politically effective it will be. Political activism is what economists call a "normal good." The greater an individual's income, the more of such a good he or she will purchase.

A political equilibrium occurs where the influence of Group X is balanced against that of Group Y. The greater the political effectiveness of X relative to Y, the greater the equilibrium level of Policy A.[20] Moreover, any event that increases X's effectiveness by more than it increases Y's, *ceteris paribus,* will cause an increase in the equilibrium level of A. The pressures of Group X and Group Y can be thought of as analogous to two physical forces pushing in opposite directions against an object lying on a flat surface. If Force X is stronger than Force Y, the object will be moved to an equilibrium position closer to one edge of the surface than the other, reflecting the relative strengths of the two forces.

Such an event, which shocks the domestic political system and alters the policy equilibrium, could emanate from outside the polity, such as international sanctions, other foreign policy initiatives, and revolutions in neighboring countries. Here we focus on sanctions, although Kaempfer and Lowenberg have shown how the approach may be extended to other international phenomena.[21] Sanctions reducing the incomes of both groups by the same amount will cause reductions of equal magnitude in the political effectiveness of both groups, and the equilibrium level of the objectionable Policy A will not change. Only if the sanctions reduce the income of one group by more than that of the other will the Equilibrium A change.[22] To return to our physical analogy, if both forces are reduced, but the one is reduced by more than the other, the object will shift its equilibrium position somewhat in the direction of the force that experienced the smaller reduction. Trade embargoes and financial sanctions, however, normally have widespread impacts on all groups in the target country. It is difficult to design sanctions to have selective economic impacts on different groups, especially given the haphazard way that sanctions policies are generated out of interest-group politics in the sanctioning countries.[23]

Sanctions affect political processes in the target country not only through their income effects but perhaps more significantly through their impacts on interest-group effectiveness in organizing collective action. For example, a sanction threatening to impose substantial costs on the supporters of the regime (Group X) if the objectionable policy is not altered might cause members of Group X to reduce their support for the group. This action encourages free riding among X's members and diminishes its effectiveness. The equilibrium level of A falls. Alternatively, the sanctions might increase the ability of Group X to organize its members, out of a rally-round-the-flag effect induced by unwelcome foreign intervention.[24]

The sanctions can also change the political effectiveness of the opposition, Group Y. Because the sanctions are typically aimed at the ruling regime's policies, they could be interpreted by members of Group Y as foreign support for their struggle against X and its Policy A. Y members might also perceive that the sanctions have diminished the government's power, which enhances the private return to individuals from opposing it. In either case, members of Y might be willing to allocate more resources to political opposition, thereby diminishing free riding within Y and enhancing Y's political effectiveness. The result is a fall in Equilibrium A.

Kaempfer and Lowenberg explored the mechanism linking sanctions and other foreign policy initiatives with changes in the political influence of interest groups in a target nation.[25] Individuals' decisions about participation in interest-group activities, such as rallies and demonstrations, are determined by their private calculus of benefits and costs. The greater the proportion of the population supporting a group, the less costly it is to join with them. If a sufficiently large percentage is believed to support the group, many will be induced to support it publicly even if privately they oppose it. Failure to outwardly endorse a group having a lot of visible support can impose costs on the individual through ostracism and persecution. For each, there is some minimum "private threshold" level of population-wide support a group must have before he or she will openly identify with it. Depending on the distribution of private thresholds across the population, it is possible that a switch by one person from supporting the government to supporting an opposition interest group can create a bandwagon effect leading to majority support for the opposition to a very high level in the population.[26] Kaempfer and Lowenberg showed that sanctions and other foreign interventions can help interest groups mobilize collective action by lowering the support thresholds necessary to initiate such bandwagon effects.[27] Sanctions, for example, might stimulate opposition in the target country by signaling that the ruling regime has a diminished ability to carry out its policies, thereby lowering individuals' private costs of identifying with the opposition. As noted, however, sanctions might also enhance support for the ruling group if its leaders can use them to rally citizens behind their policies in defiance of foreign interference.

It is clear, then, that the effects of sanctions on relative interest-group influences are vitally important in determining the former's political impacts. Kaempfer and Lowenberg pointed out that sanctions' signal and threat effects work independently of their income effects and may be more important in bringing about policy changes.[28] As noted above, it is difficult to design sanctions so that their negative income effects fall selectively on the groups supporting the regime. The signal and threat effects, on the other hand, are inherently selective. In South Africa, imposition of antiapartheid economic sanctions almost inevitably generated income losses to blacks, which some argue were greater in absolute and percentage terms than those suffered by white South Africans.[29] According to interest-group analysis, this outcome from sanctions by itself would serve only to reinforce the objectionable policy of apartheid. However, were sanctions interpreted by blacks as a signal of foreign support for their resistance against the government, or if blacks believed that the sanctions would accelerate the demise of white rule, black antiapartheid groups might more easily organize collective action. "[W]hether successful or not in pressuring government economically . . . sanctions might have the symbolic effect of showing increasing opposition to apartheid."[30] Arguably, this show of support might have produced a net increase in political effectiveness of the antiapartheid movement in South Africa despite the decline in black incomes, thereby contributing to the subsequent fall in the equilibrium level of apartheid.

Whether or not apartheid is diminished by sanctions also depends on the response of proapartheid groups. If their members are discouraged by the sanctions, their political effectiveness will decline, whereas a rally-round-the-flag effect increases their political effectiveness. In the former instance, the increased effectiveness of the opposition is reinforced by diminished effectiveness of government supporters. In the latter case, the sanctions increase political polarization, with both groups' effectiveness increased, resulting in an indeterminate effect on the equilibrium policy outcome.

In the remainder of this chapter we focus on the impact of anti-apartheid sanctions on the political effectiveness of the black antiapartheid movement within South Africa. Some of these sanctions are trade or investment embargoes, having important income effects on various groups there.[31] However, many of the measures directed against South Africa were cultural or social in nature, such as sporting, artistic, scientific and educational boycotts, diplomatic isolation, and censure by churches. The only way such sanctions can affect political processes in the target country is through the signals they transmit to individuals and interest groups. Moreover, as noted, even those sanctions that are primarily economic in nature produce signal and threat effects more narrowly targeted to particular groups than the economic effects.

Our main concern is with the signal effects of antiapartheid sanctions, especially on the domestic black opposition.[32] It is necessary to examine the motivational effects of sanctions, both on the opposition movement within South Africa, and the proapartheid constituency. Our emphasis on the opposition is dictated by the nature of the available data rather than theoretical considerations. This study therefore must be viewed as only a first step in analyzing the political effects of antiapartheid sanctions.

We now move on to describe the data and variables we use in our analysis of sanctions against South Africa and discuss the results of our study. We are interested not only in the relationship between sanctions and black political opposition, but also in determining whether the sanctions themselves were induced to some extent by political and economic conditions and collective action in South Africa.

The Data

South Africa has been a target of international economic and cultural sanctions for more than three decades. This long duration of antiapartheid sanctions affords a unique opportunity to investigate their economic and political impacts with time-series data. Between June 1961 and October 1988, there were no fewer than 619 episodes of sanctions applied by governmental and nongovernmental agencies against South Africa.[33] South Africa may be the only sanctions target for which the application intensity of sanctions can be treated as a continuous variable over a significant period.

The most important variables for our study are international sanctions against South Africa and the political effectiveness of the antiapartheid movement within that nation. We measure the first of these by the number of sanctions episodes imposed by governmental and nongovernmental organizations in each year, including economic sanctions such as trade and investment embargoes and noneconomic policies.[34]

During the period studied (1965–1987), black political parties in South Africa, such as the African National Congress and the Pan African Congress, were banned, and political protest was channeled largely through militant labor unions and their umbrella organizations, such as the Congress of South African Trade Unions.[35] Therefore, we use the number of black workers involved in strikes and work stoppages annually as a measure of black political resistance against apartheid. Data on strikes were obtained from the South African Department of Information.[36]

We recognize, of course, that strikes often occur for reasons not related to political action against the government. The data available do not allow us to distinguish strikes motivated by political factors from those for economic considerations such as wages or working conditions. As long as the proportion of "political" strikers within the total is relatively constant over time, however, our results should not be biased. It should be noted that strikes by black workers in South Africa have historically been very politicized.[37]

For the causes of strike activity among black workers, we must take into account all of the conventional factors economists have identified as important determinants of strikes. Studies of strikes using U.S. data have found that the number of strikes varies inversely with the level of unemployment and that recent increases in firms' profits tend to generate more strikes.[38] The duration and frequency of strikes normally increases when real wages are low or have been rising slowly. Studies concur that strike activity is a function of the tightness of the labor market, profitability of employers, and real wages. These variables determine both the opportunity cost to workers of striking and the ability of firms to absorb their costs of strikes.[39]

Data on the black unemployment rate in South Africa are difficult to obtain because many blacks work in the informal sectors of the economy or in nominally independent homelands for which the South African government did not publish statistics for many years. From Roukens de Lange and Van Eeghen, we obtained data on total black employment in the formal sector of the South African economy (including the homelands).[40] Although these data do not measure the tightness of the black labor market, they do approximate cyclical trends in the level of economic activity as it affects black workers.

We use the real price of gold as a measure of aggregate profitability of firms in the South African economy. South Africa has a small, open economy whose exports are dominated by gold. When the gold-producing sector does well, the rest of the economy tends to follow suit.[41] Annual data on the Rand price of gold per ounce, deflated by the South African consumer price index, were obtained from the International Monetary Fund's *International Financial Statistics*.

Another variable included in our study is the real wage of black workers, measured by the average monthly wage for blacks employed in all sectors of the economy in each year, deflated by the consumer price index. These wage data were obtained from the South African Department of Statistics and the International Labour Office.[42]

All of the data are annual, covering the period 1965 to 1987. Our study of trends and correlations in them is hampered by the short period they are available. Nevertheless, even limited data are of value, so long as the analysis is understood to be preliminary given the limitations of measurement.

Inspection of the data reveals distinct trends in all of the variables of interest. Summary statistics are presented in Table 10.1. Note that in 1985 there was a substantial jump in the number of both sanctions and of black workers on strike.

We next turn to the relationships and correlations among the variables discovered in our analysis.

Empirical Findings

The empirical results presented in this section are derived from a more technical time-series study using vector-autoregression, error-correction, and structural models.[43] Some of the findings obtained from that analysis

Table 10.1 Blacks on Strike, Sanctions, Employment, and Gold Prices

	Black Workers on Strike	Sanctions	Black Employment	Real Price of Gold
1966–1976				
Mean	20,326	1.91	4,019,609	1.24
Standard dev.	28,698	1.92	285,726	0.63
1977–1985[a] Mean	85,419 (67,965)	30.22 (15.0)	4,733,444	3.35
Standard dev.	75,267 (57,804)	45.87 (4.63)	161,360	0.98

Note: a. The numbers in parentheses are the means and standard deviations for the period 1977–1984.
Sources: Based on data from A. Roukens de Lange and P. H. Van Eeghen, "Standardised Employment Series for South Africa's Formal Economy," Journal for Studies in Economics and Econometrics 14 (August 1990): 25–53; International Monetary Fund, International Financial Statistics (annual) (Washington, DC: IMF); South Africa, Department of Statistics, South African Statistics (Pretoria: Government Printer, 1986); International Labour Office, Yearbook of Labour Statistics (Geneva: ILO, 1990 and earlier editions); and Elna Schoeman, South African Sanctions Directory, 1946–1988 (South African Institute of International Affairs Bibliographical Series No. 18) (Johannesburg: SAIIA, 1988).

are summarized in Figures 10.1 to 10.6. Figure 10.1 shows the relationship between sanctions and strikes by black workers in South Africa. It is evident that these two variables moved together over the sample period, 1965–1987. There appears to be a positive relationship between sanctions and strikes. This relationship is a complex one, however. In Kaempfer, Lowenberg, Mocan, and Topyan (hereafter known as the KLMT study), it was shown that the larger the increase in sanctions, the larger the contemporaneous increase in strikes, although, after a one-year lag, an increase in sanctions produced a decrease in the strike rate of change. The KLMT study also found that an increase in black strikes generates an increase in the number of sanctions. These relationships cannot be observed directly from Figure 10.1 because this figure takes into account only two variables, sanctions and strikes. The KLMT study used a more sophisticated technique in which the influences of all variables were considered simultaneously.

The nature of the positive relationship between sanctions and strikes suggests that changes in strikes lead changes in sanctions, implying that foreign pressures to impose sanctions respond positively to increased levels of political unrest in South Africa. There is also evidence, however, that once the sanctions are implemented, they produce an immediate increase in political effectiveness of the black antiapartheid groups, as measured by their ability to organize strikes and work stoppages.

Figure 10.1   Sanctions and Black Strikes

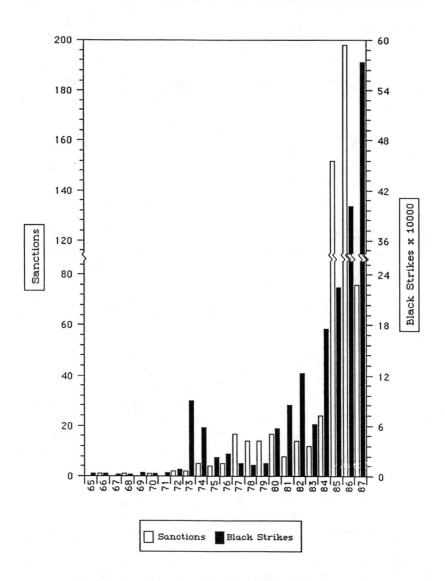

Sources: Based on data from A. Roukens de Lange and P. H. Van Eeghen, "Standardised Employment Series for South Africa's Formal Economy," *Journal for Studies in Economics and Econometrics* 14 (August 1990): 25–53; International Monetary Fund, *International Financial Statistics* (annual) (Washington, DC: IMF); South Africa, Department of Statistics, *South African Statistics* (Pretoria: Government Printer, 1986); International Labour Office, *Yearbook of Labour Statistics* (Geneva: ILO, 1990 and earlier editions); and Elna Schoeman, South African Sanctions Directory, 1946–1988 (South African Institute of International Affairs Bibliographical Series No. 18) (Johannesburg: SAIIA, 1988).

The longer-run effect is for increased sanctions to decrease strikes. This relationship might be due to a negative effect of sanctions on black incomes. If black workers are made poorer, they will be less able to engage in political strikes.

Figure 10.2 depicts the relationship between sanctions and black employment and confirms the negative effect of sanctions on black workers' incomes. The larger the increase in sanctions, the smaller the rate of increase of black employment, both contemporaneously and in the subsequent year. If sanctions have a depressing effect on the growth of black employment, then they also lower the income of the black labor force. Although not illustrated here, KLMT also found some evidence that an increase in sanctions produces a decrease in the rate of change of black wages, thus reinforcing the negative effect of sanctions on black incomes.

Figure 10.2 further reveals that a decrease in the rate of change of black employment from one year to the next generates an increase in sanctions. This result is even more strongly evident in the KLMT time-series analysis. Again, it appears that sanctions are sensitive to conditions within the target nation. In this case, worsening employment conditions in South Africa seem to heighten the proclivity of foreign interests to pressure for sanctions.

Similarly, Figure 10.3 shows that a decreasing gold price tends to produce an acceleration of sanctions, both contemporaneously and in the following year.[44] (KLMT showed that the gold price, as expected, is unaffected by sanctions or other events in South Africa, because it is determined in the world gold market.) Because the gold price broadly reflects the trend of profitability in the South African economy, this result underscores the role of declining business conditions in stimulating sanctions. This finding, together with the positive relationship between strikes and sanctions and the negative relationship between employment growth and sanctions, lends support to the interest-group theory stating that sanctions are applied more intensively when members of foreign interest groups become more aware of political and economic distress in the target country.

Figures 10.4, 10.5 and 10.6 examine the roles of conventional economic factors in determining strike behavior. Figure 10.4 plots black strikes against gold prices, the latter reflecting firms' profitability. Economic theory predicts that firms' rising profits should produce more strikes because workers perceive that firms are better able to meet their wage demands. This prediction is borne out by the evidence in Figure 10.4. Generally, the more rapid the increase in gold prices, the larger the increase in strikes.

Figure 10.5 plots black strikes against black real wages. Economic theory suggests that falling real wages should stimulate strike activity because the costs to workers of striking, in terms of earnings forgone, are

Figure 10.2   Sanctions and Black Employment

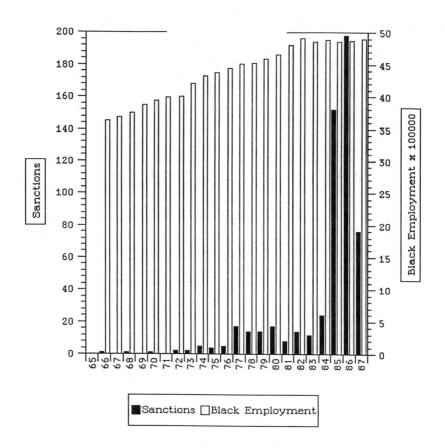

Sources: Based on data from A. Roukens de Lange and P. H. Van Eeghen, "Standardised Employment Series for South Africa's Formal Economy," *Journal for Studies in Economics and Econometrics* 14 (August 1990): 25–53; International Monetary Fund, *International Financial Statistics* (annual) (Washington, DC: IMF); South Africa, Department of Statistics, *South African Statistics* (Pretoria: Government Printer, 1986); International Labour Office, *Yearbook of Labour Statistics* (Geneva: ILO, 1990 and earlier editions); and Elna Schoeman, South African Sanctions Directory, 1946–1988 (South African Institute of International Affairs Bibliographical Series No. 18) (Johannesburg: SAIIA, 1988).

Figure 10.3   Sanctions and Real Prices of Gold

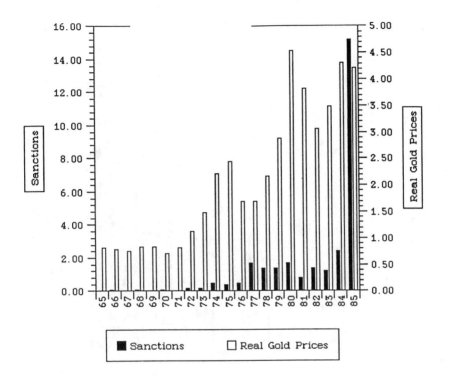

Sources: Based on data from A. Roukens de Lange and P. H. Van Eeghen, "Standardised Employment Series for South Africa's Formal Economy," *Journal for Studies in Economics and Econometrics* 14 (August 1990): 25–53; International Monetary Fund, *International Financial Statistics* (annual) (Washington, DC: IMF); South Africa, Department of Statistics, *South African Statistics* (Pretoria: Government Printer, 1986); International Labour Office, *Yearbook of Labour Statistics* (Geneva: ILO, 1990 and earlier editions); and Elna Schoeman, South African Sanctions Directory, 1946–1988 (South African Institute of International Affairs Bibliographical Series No. 18) (Johannesburg: SAIIA, 1988).

Figure 10.4 Black Strikes and Real Prices of Gold

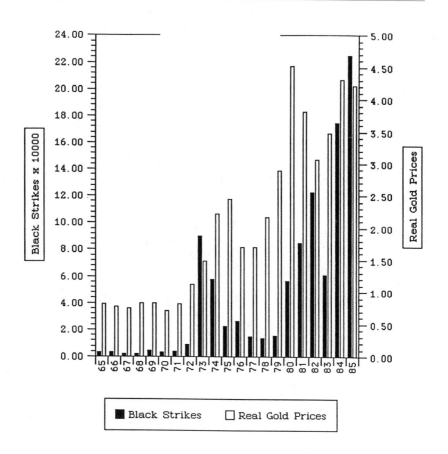

Sources: Based on data from A. Roukens de Lange and P. H. Van Eeghen, "Standardised Employment Series for South Africa's Formal Economy," *Journal for Studies in Economics and Econometrics* 14 (August 1990): 25–53; International Monetary Fund, *International Financial Statistics* (annual) (Washington, DC: IMF); South Africa, Department of Statistics, *South African Statistics* (Pretoria: Government Printer, 1986); International Labour Office, *Yearbook of Labour Statistics* (Geneva: ILO, 1990 and earlier editions); and Elna Schoeman, South African Sanctions Directory, 1946–1988 (South African Institute of International Affairs Bibliographical Series No. 18) (Johannesburg: SAIIA, 1988).

Figure 10.5   Black Strikes and Real Wages of Blacks

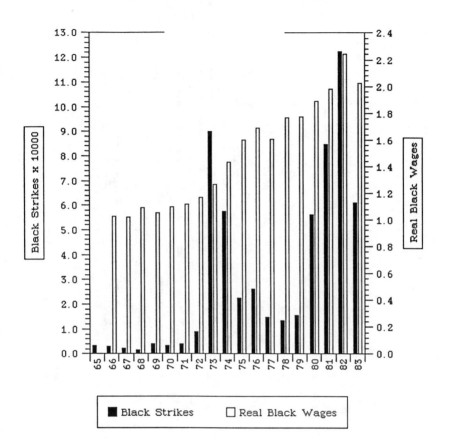

Sources: Based on data from A. Roukens de Lange and P. H. Van Eeghen, "Standardised Employment Series for South Africa's Formal Economy," *Journal for Studies in Economics and Econometrics* 14 (August 1990): 25–53; International Monetary Fund, *International Financial Statistics* (annual) (Washington, DC: IMF); South Africa, Department of Statistics, *South African Statistics* (Pretoria: Government Printer, 1986); International Labour Office, *Yearbook of Labour Statistics* (Geneva: ILO, 1990 and earlier editions); and Elna Schoeman, South African Sanctions Directory, 1946–1988 (South African Institute of International Affairs Bibliographical Series No. 18) (Johannesburg: SAIIA, 1988).

Figure 10.6   Black Strikes and Black Employment

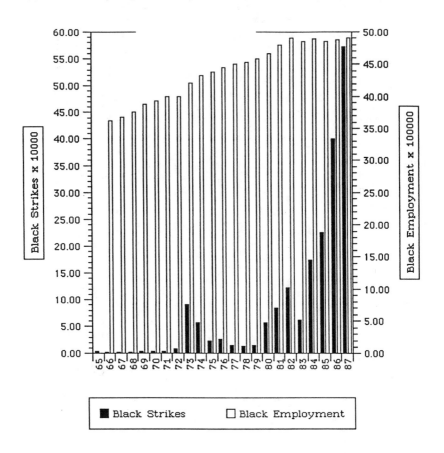

Sources: Based on data from A. Roukens de Lange and P. H. Van Eeghen, "Standardised Employment Series for South Africa's Formal Economy," *Journal for Studies in Economics and Econometrics* 14 (August 1990): 25–53; International Monetary Fund, *International Financial Statistics* (annual) (Washington, DC: IMF); South Africa, Department of Statistics, *South African Statistics* (Pretoria: Government Printer, 1986); International Labour Office, *Yearbook of Labour Statistics* (Geneva: ILO, 1990 and earlier editions); and Elna Schoeman, South African Sanctions Directory, 1946–1988 (South African Institute of International Affairs Bibliographical Series No. 18) (Johannesburg: SAIIA, 1988).

diminished by lower wages. Figure 10.5 provides some confirming evidence for this. A decline in the rate of growth of black wages tends to be followed by an increase in strikes.

Figure 10.6 shows the relationship between black employment and black strikes. Theories of strike behavior predict that strikes rise when the labor market becomes tight. Workers are more likely to strike when unemployment is low and their risk of not being able to find work if fired is correspondingly low. As already noted, total employment is not a good measure of tightness of the labor market. A measure of the rate of unemployment among black workers would be preferable for this purpose, but those data were not available over the relevant time range. Figure 10.6 provides some weak evidence that strikes by black workers rise in response to increases in the rate of growth of black employment (or falling unemployment).

Taken together, the results presented here suggest that strikes by black workers in South Africa over the period 1965–1987 were driven by both political and economic factors. Increasing foreign pressure on South Africa in the form of international economic and social sanctions had the short-term effect of stimulating black political activism, but in the longer term the negative effects of those sanctions on black employment and earnings reduced black workers' ability to participate in strikes. The foreign pressure was not independent of political unrest in South Africa. Increases in sanctions tended to follow on the heels of increases in strikes, and the sanctions then produced feedback effects on strikes. However, strikes are an imperfect measure of political effectiveness because they are also motivated by economic considerations, of which the most important are real wages, profitability, and tightness of the labor market. Our results confirm the expected relationships among these variables.

Conclusions

An interest-group analysis of international sanctions suggests that the nature and extent of the sanctions imposed by sanctioning countries is a function of interest-group pressures in those nations. One implication of this is that sanctions follow, not lead, events in the target country. An increase in visible political opposition, and perhaps a concomitant decline in economic performance in the target nation, helps to raise foreign awareness of that country's objectionable policies. This increased awareness leads to heightened pressure on national governments to impose sanctions. Our analysis of antiapartheid sanctions against South Africa leads us to conclude that these sanctions were indeed influenced by changes in political and economic conditions in South Africa. The number of sanction episodes applied in any given year tended to increase as a consequence of a rise in opposition political activity as measured by the number of black workers participating in strikes in South Africa. We also find that the annual number of episodes increased in response to declining employment growth in South Africa and, somewhat more weakly, in response to falling profitability of South African businesses, measured by the real price of gold.

Applying the interest-group theory to the target polity, we expect the impact of the sanctions to affect political processes largely through the signals or threats that the sanctions transmit to key interest groups. In this chapter we have suggested how sanctions induced changes in the political effectiveness of the antiapartheid opposition in South Africa, measured by black strikes. Our analysis shows that an increase in sanctions had an immediate positive effect on the number of black workers on strike, although, after a one-year lag, this effect became negative. Thus, there is some evidence to support the hypothesis that foreign sanctions, at least in the short run, help domestic opposition groups to organize collective action among their members. The longer-term effect of sanctions was to reduce black income, however, which then deterred strikes. We find evidence for this negative income effect in the fact that increases in sanctions were followed by reductions in both black employment and, to a lesser extent, black real wages.

Strikes are induced by both political and economic considerations, so we must take into account the purely economic factors that have been identified as important determinants of strike behavior. Our results show that, in addition to political factors such as sanctions, black strikes in South Africa were positively related to changes in firms' profitability and to changes in black employment, and negatively related to changes in black real wages. All of these findings are consistent with traditional economic theories of strike activity.

These conclusions need to be tempered, of course, by the limitations of our data and by measurement problems. Although our findings are preliminary in nature, they do suggest that sanctions are motivated partly by changes in political and economic conditions in the target country and that the sanctions themselves are not independent causes of those changes. Nevertheless, sanctions should be applied with caution because they can have an important impact on policy formation in the target country by affecting the incomes and political effectiveness of its interest groups. If sanctions are applied haphazardly, as they often are, they can be ineffective or even counterproductive by lowering the political effectiveness of the "right" groups within the target polity.

Notes

1. Kaempfer and Lowenberg, "The Theory of Sanctions"; "Analyzing Economic Sanctions"; "Using Threshold Models"; and *International Economic Sanctions*.

2. International sanctions are an increasingly important part of foreign policy. The number of major intergovernmental sanctions episodes has grown, from 9 in the 1940s to 25 in the 1980s (Hufbauer, Schott, and Elliott, *Economic Sanctions Reconsidered*). Among the major sanctions-applying nations, the United States has become increasingly dominant. In the 1940s, 56 percent of international sanctions episodes were applied by the U.S. government. By the 1980s, this share had risen to 80 percent (Kaempfer and Lowenberg, *International Economic Sanctions*).

3. This chapter presents a revision of work appearing in Kaempfer, Lowenberg, Mocan, and Bennett, "The Impact of Foreign Economic Pressure."

4. See Doxey, *Economic Sanctions;* Doxey, *International Sanctions;* Knorr, *The Power of Nations*; Losman, *International Economic Sanctions*; and Hufbauer, Schott, and Elliott, *Economic Sanctions Reconsidered*. The latter study examines 115 cases of economic sanctions applied since the 1920s, and finds that only 30 percent of these were successful in achieving their political objectives.

5. In the jargon of economists, the residual world demand and supply of most goods is sufficiently price-elastic that the withdrawal of the sanctioners' trade usually does not cause significant deterioration of the target's terms of trade. The greater the number of sanctioners relative to nonsanctioners and the more inelastic the world demand and supply of the traded goods, the greater is the loss in welfare to the target country. See Bayard, Pelzman, and Perez-Lopez, "Stakes and Risks"; Willett and Jalalighajar, "U.S. Trade Policy"; and Kaempfer and Lowenberg, "Determinants of Economic Effects."

6. Much of the debate about whether sanctions are effective hinges on definitions of appropriate time frames for analysis. Thus, many scholars argue that the sanctions against white-ruled Rhodesia were a failure because the Smith government remained in power for fourteen years, whereas others argue that the sanctions were successful in raising the costs of pursuing white rule, ultimately leading to its demise. See Knorr, *The Power of Nations*, and Baldwin, *Economic Statecraft*.

7. Kaempfer and Lowenberg, "The Theory of Sanctions."

8. Kaempfer and Lowenberg, "Using Threshold Models."

9. Kaempfer and Lowenberg, "The Theory of Sanctions"; "Analyzing Economic Sanctions"; and "Using Threshold Models."

10. Kaempfer and Lowenberg, "Sanctioning South Africa."

11. Recent examples include U.S. trade restrictions against Brazil for its refusal to allow the importation of U.S. computer products and against European Community agricultural products in reprisal for its prohibitions on U.S. hormone-fed beef exports. See Kaempfer and Lowenberg, *International Economic Sanctions*.

12. Kaempfer and Lowenberg, "Sanctioning South Africa."

13. For more on this process see Kaempfer and Lowenberg, "Sanctioning South Africa" and *International Economic Sanctions*.

14. Thus, after the Tiananmen repression, the U.S. government faced increased pressure to impose sanctions against China.

15. Kaempfer and Lowenberg, "The Theory of Sanctions."

16. If Policy A is interpreted as apartheid, in the South African context, then Group X comprises white workers and farmers who benefited from apartheid in its traditional form; Group Y consists of white capital owners and professionals as well as black workers, who were the prime losers from traditional apartheid. See Lowenberg, "An Economic Theory of Apartheid."

17. According to this conception of the political process, the government acts as a more or less impartial broker of interest-group pressures. See Becker, "A Theory of Competition"; "Public Policies, Pressure Groups"; and Kaempfer and Lowenberg, "The Theory of Sanctions." Typically, interest groups deliver support to politicians with votes or funds that can be used to finance campaigns. In this

model, however, other forms of political expression, such as demonstrations and insurrection, are also effective ways of pressuring politicians or imposing costs on their policies.

18. See Olson, *The Logic of Collective Action.* Free riding refers to the tendency for individuals to abstain from collective action for public goods, which are jointly consumed by everyone in the community regardless of whether or not they have worked for them.

19. It is also easier for a small group to monitor the behavior of its members and to penalize free riders. See Olson, *The Logic of Collective Action.*

20. In terms of the geometry of microeconomic analysis, Group X's preference for Policy A is revealed in the form of a downward sloping demand curve. The height of this curve at any given value of A is Group X's marginal willingness to pay for Policy A. This willingness to pay can be interpreted as a willingness to allocate resources to lobbying and political pressure to persuade the government to supply more A. Similarly, Group Y reveals a downward sloping demand curve for *reduced* levels of A, or alternatively, an upward sloping "supply" curve for increased levels of A. Members of Group Y are willing to allocate increasingly large amounts of resources at the margin in order to prevent A from increasing. Thus the height of their willingness-to-pay curve represents the "supply price" that politicians must incur, in terms of increased opposition from Group Y, as a consequence of allowing A to increase. The political equilibrium occurs at the intersection of the demand and supply curves. Support-maximizing politicians will supply A up to the point where X's marginal willingness to pay for an increase in A is equal to Y's marginal willingness to pay for a decrease in A. See Peltzman, "Toward a Theory of Regulation." An increase in either group's political effectiveness will cause an upward shift of its willingness-to-pay curve. Thus, for example, an increase in X's effectiveness relative to Y's effectiveness will cause X's demand curve to shift up relative to Y's, and the equilibrium value of A will increase.

21. Kaempfer and Lowenberg, "Using Threshold Models."

22. We are assuming here that sanctions are, in general, income reducing for both Groups X and Y. It is possible, of course, that members of one group might actually receive net pecuniary gains as a consequence of sanctions.

23. See Carter, *International Economic Sanctions.*

24. Kaempfer and Lowenberg, "The Theory of Sanctions."

25. Kaempfer and Lowenberg, "Using Threshold Models."

26. The "reputational utility" that an individual receives from participation in a group can offset to some extent the incentive to ride free in contributing to collective outcomes. See Kuran, "Preference Falsification" and "The East European Revolution."

27. Kaempfer and Lowenberg, "Using Threshold Models."

28. Kaempfer and Lowenberg, "The Theory of Sanctions."

29. Lewis, *The Economics of Apartheid,* p. 118.

30. General Accounting Office, "South Africa."

31. See Porter, "International Trade"; Lundahl, "Economic Effects of a Boycott"; Becker and Pollard, "The Vulnerability of South Africa"; and Khan, *The Political Economy of Sanctions* for general equilibrium models of these income effects.

32. "[T]he reaction of others [apart from the government] in South Africa, particularly the black majority, and whites actively opposed to apartheid, will be extremely important in determining the effects of further economic pressures, as they have been important in the events of the past three decades" (Lewis, *The Economics of Apartheid,* p. 116).

33. The first sanction applied against South Africa was India's trade embargo implemented in July 1946. In 1956, South Africa was forced to withdraw from the United Nations Educational, Scientific, and Cultural Organisation (UNESCO) as a consequence of its racial policies. Starting in the early 1960s, sanctions against South Africa mounted with increasing intensity. This tendency accelerated throughout the 1970s and 1980s. The majority of sanctions episodes, however, occurred in the mid-1980s. See Schoeman, *South Africa Sanctions Directory*, for a detailed chronology.

34. Schoeman, *South African Sanctions Directory*.

35. See Kendall and Louw, *After Apartheid*, pp. 107–108.

36. See South Africa, Department of Information, *Official Yearbook*.

37. See Backer, "Manpower Development," pp. 130, 148; and Denoon and Nyeko, *South Africa Since 1800*, pp. 194, 215–217.

38. See Ashenfelter and Johnson's classic political model of strike activity, "Bargaining Theory."

39. Winning concessions from management, through strike or threat of a strike, depends on the costs the union is able to impose on the firm, the firm's profits and ability to withstand losses, and whether union members can survive without their wage income for the duration of the strike. See Farber, "Bargaining Theory"; Tracy, "An Investigation into U.S. Strike Activity"; and McConnell, "Strikes, Wages and Private Information" on the role of other variables such as share of total sales, variance of profits, and the unpredicted component of wages. Seasonal factors are also important. For example, strikes are often more effective during periods of peak production.

40. Roukens de Lange and Van Eeghen, "Standardised Employment Series."

41. According to Grundy, *South Africa*, p. 70, during the 1970s every ten-dollar increase in the average annual price of gold translated into a 1 percent increase in South Africa's GNP. See also Nattrass, *The South African Economy*, pp. 145–148.

42. South Africa, Department of Statistics, *South African Statistics*; International Labour Office, *Yearbook of Labour Statistics*.

43. Kaempfer, Lowenberg, Mocan, and Topyan, "International Sanctions." (Hereafter cited in the text as KLMT)

44. In a more comprehensive model encompassing all variables, this relationship between the gold price and sanctions is not statistically significant, however. See Kaempfer, Lowenberg, Mocan, and Topyan, "International Sanctions."

Bibliography

Ashenfelter, Orley, and George E. Johnson. "Bargaining Theory, Trade Unions and Industrial Strikes." *American Economic Review* (March 1969): 59.

Backer, W. "Manpower Development," in D. J. van Vuuren, N. E. Wiehahn, J. A. Lombard, and N. J. Rhoodie (eds.), *South Africa: A Plural Society in Transition* (Durban: Butterworth, 1985), pp. 120–172.

Baldwin, David A. *Economic Statecraft* (Princeton: Princeton University Press, 1985).

Bayard, Thomas O., Joseph Pelzman, and Jorge Perez-Lopez. "Stakes and Risks in Economic Sanctions." *The World Economy* 6 (March 1983): 73–87.

Becker, Charles M., and Patricia S. Pollard. "The Vulnerability of South Africa to Economic Sanctions: An Input-Output Analysis," in Charles M. Becker,

Trevor Bell, Haider Ali Khan, and Patricia S. Pollard (eds.), *The Impact of Sanctions on South Africa* (Washington, DC: Investor Responsibility Research Center, 1990).

Becker, Gary S. "A Theory of Competition Among Pressure Groups for Political Influence." *Quarterly Journal of Economics* 98 (August 1983): 371–400.

———. "Public Policies, Pressure Groups and Dead Weight Costs." *Journal of Public Economics* 28 (December 1985): 329–347.

Carter, Barry E. *International Economic Sanctions: Improving the Haphazard U.S. Legal Regime* (Cambridge: Cambridge University Press, 1988).

Denoon, Donald, and Balam Nyeko. *Southern Africa Since 1800* (New Edition) (London: Longman, 1984).

Doxey, Margaret P. *Economic Sanctions and International Enforcement* (Second Edition). (New York: Oxford University Press, 1980).

———. *International Sanctions in Contemporary Perspective* (New York: St. Martin's Press, 1987).

Farber, Henry S. "Bargaining Theory, Wage Outcomes and the Occurrence of Strikes: An Econometric Analysis." *American Economic Review* 68 (June 1978): 262–271.

General Accounting Office. "South Africa: Feasibility of Imposing Additional Sanctions on Gold." GAO/NSIAD-89-232 (Washington, DC: GAO, September 1989).

Grundy, Kenneth W. *South Africa: Domestic Crisis and Global Challenge* (Boulder, CO: Westview Press, 1991).

Hufbauer, Gary Clyde, Jeffrey J. Schott, and Kimberly Ann Elliott. *Economic Sanctions Reconsidered: History and Current Policy* (Second Edition). (Washington, DC: Institute for International Economics, 1990).

International Labour Office. *Yearbook of Labour Statistics* (Geneva: International Labour Office, 1990 and earlier editions).

International Monetary Fund. *International Financial Statistics* (annual). (Washington, DC: IMF).

Kaempfer, William H., and Anton D. Lowenberg. "The Theory of International Economic Sanctions: A Public Choice Approach." *American Economic Review* 78 (September 1988): 786–793.

———. "Determinants of the Economic and Political Effects of Trade Sanctions." *South African Journal of Economics* 56 (December 1988): 270–277.

———. "Sanctioning South Africa: The Politics Behind the Policies." *The Cato Journal* 8 (3) (1989): 713–727.

———. "Analyzing Economic Sanctions: Toward a Public Choice Framework," in John S. Odell and Thomas D. Willett (eds.), *International Trade Policies: Gains from Exchange Between Economics and Political Science* (Ann Arbor, MI: University of Michigan Press, 1990), 173–192.

———. "Using Threshold Models to Explain International Relations." *Public Choice* 73 (4) (1992): 419–443.

———. *International Economic Sanctions: A Public Choice Study* (Boulder, CO: Westview Press, 1992).

Kaempfer, William H., Anton D Lowenberg, H. Naci Mocan, and Lynne Bennett. "The Impact of Foreign Economic Pressure on Domestic Politics: The Case of South Africa," Working Paper, University of Colorado, Denver, 1991.

Kaempfer, William H., Anton D. Lowenberg, H. Naci Mocan, and Kudret Topyan. "International Sanctions and Antiapartheid Politics in South Africa: An Empirical Investigation," Working Paper, University of Colorado, Denver, 1991.

Kendall, Frances, and Leon Louw. *After Apartheid: The Solution for South Africa* (San Francisco: Institute for Contemporary Studies, 1987).

Khan, Haider Ali. *The Political Economy of Sanctions Against Apartheid* (Boulder and London: Lynne Rienner Publishers, 1989).

Knorr, Klaus. *The Power of Nations: The Political Economy of International Relations* (New York: Basic Books, 1975).

Kuran, Timur. "Preference Falsification, Policy Continuity and Collective Conservatism." *Economic Journal* 97 (September 1987): 642–665.

———. "The East European Revolution of 1989: Is It Surprising that We Were Surprised?" *American Economic Review* 81 (May 1991): 121–125.

Lewis, Stephen R., Jr. *The Economics of Apartheid* (New York: Council on Foreign Relations Press, 1990).

Losman, Donald L. *International Economic Sanctions: The Cases of Cuba, Israel, and Rhodesia* (Albuquerque, NM: University of New Mexico Press, 1979).

Lowenberg, Anton D. "An Economic Theory of Apartheid." *Economic Inquiry* 27 (January 1989): 57–74.

Lundahl, Mats. "Economic Effects of a Trade and Investment Boycott Against South Africa." *Scandinavian Journal of Economics* 86 (1984): 68–83.

McConnell, Sheena. "Strikes, Wages and Private Information." *American Economic Review* 79 (September 1989): 801–815.

Nattrass, Jill. *The South African Economy: Its Growth and Change* (Cape Town: Oxford University Press, 1981).

Olson, Mancur. *The Logic of Collective Action: Public Goods and the Theory of Groups* (Cambridge: Harvard University Press, 1965).

Peltzman, Sam. "Toward a More General Theory of Regulation." *Journal of Law and Economics* 19 (August 1976): 211–240.

Porter, Richard C. "International Trade and Investment Sanctions: Potential Impact on the South African Economy." *Journal of Conflict Resolution* 23 (December 1979): 579–612.

Roukens de Lange, A., and P. H. Van Eeghen. "Standardised Employment Series for South Africa's Formal Economy." *Journal for Studies in Economics and Econometrics* 14 (August 1990): 25–53.

Schoeman, Elna. *South African Sanctions Directory, 1946–1988* (South African Institute of International Affairs Bibliographical Series No. 18) (Johannesburg: South African Institute of International Affairs, 1988).

South Africa, Department of Information. *Official Yearbook of the Republic of South Africa* (Cape Town: CTP Book Printers, 1989/90 and earlier editions).

South Africa, Department of Statistics. *South African Statistics* (Pretoria: Government Printer, 1986).

Tracy, Joseph. "An Investigation into the Determinants of U.S. Strike Activity." *American Economic Review* 76 (June 1986): 423–436.

Willett, Thomas D., and Mehrdad Jalalighajar. "U.S. Trade Policy and National Security." *Cato Journal* 3 (Winter 1983/84): 717–727.

11

Belief Systems and
Justice Without Violence
in the Middle East

Amin M. Kazak

Combating injustice has been a universal theme throughout human history. Inevitably, the failure to attain justice has led underprivileged and oppressed peoples to consider their condition a justification for rebellion and resistance. Although the struggle for justice and equal rights is not a new phenomenon, our awareness of it since World War II has grown. In that time, the quest for justice through armed conflict and violence has been responsible for great loss of human life.[1]

The Palestinian uprising—the intifada—in the West Bank and Gaza against Israeli occupation; the struggle of the Kurds for self-determination in Turkey, Iraq, and Iran; the enduring bitterness between the Greek majority and the Turkish minorities in Cyprus; the Serbian conflict in former Yugoslavia; the struggle of the Tamils for liberation from Sinhalese domination in Sri Lanka; the feud of the Punjabi Sikhs with Hindus in India; the Eritrean struggle against the Amharas of Ethiopia; and the unfinished episode of the indigenous Native American search for identity are some contemporary examples of indigenous and ethnic peoples seeking justice.

What are the sources of injustice? Are there specific protest strategies that are especially useful or successful for achieving justice? What methods and modes of resistance appeal most to justice seekers? Nonviolence is one alternative for pursuing justice. Is it the first choice? To what extent is nonviolent action effective for combating injustice? In what contexts does nonviolent action appeal to protesters? And above all, how do norms, values, and beliefs inspire justice seekers to pursue justice without violence?

Most studies of nonviolence emphasize the philosophical and ideological origins of nonviolent struggle. Relatively little attention has been paid to the influence of sociopsychological factors. An examination of the ideological and sociopsychological patterns of different cultures suggests that each culture promotes and nurtures different violent or nonviolent attitudes and behavior.[2]

This chapter discusses whether cultural belief systems are factors in achieving justice without violence in the Middle East, and, if so, to what extent? Given the popular myth of the Middle East as a region of violence, my intention is to explore the possibility that belief systems in the Middle East can make a positive contribution toward nonviolent solutions to the region's conflicts. Special emphasis is given here to the intifada and the Israeli reaction to it. The Israeli-Palestinian dispute is a significant illustration of justice conflict. What fuels such conflicts?

Sources of Injustice

The substance of justice is a difficult but unavoidable subject. Inevitably, the issue comes down to the question: What is just or unjust? How can a set of conditions be perceived as just for some when perceived as unjust to others? The world is too diverse to apply one universal paradigm of justice. Still, it is also impossible to list all forms of injustice that have been the subject of scholarly debate. Therefore, there is no reason to restrict ourselves to any particular set of abstract interpretations of justice or injustice. The variability of global cultural differences leads us to attempt to understand the ethos of cultural communities in terms of what they consider to be just for them.

The idea that all people have a right to choose their own sovereignty and territorial identity has been elucidated as one basis for justice. The right of self-determination has been recognized as a moral imperative both in the writings of philosophers and political theorists and in the declared values of social activists and national leaders.[3]

In principle, any renunciation of a nation's right to self-determination is equivalent to the denial of an individual's right to basic liberty. Rawls stated that each person has an equal right to the most extensive basic liberty compatible with a similar liberty for others.[4] If we admit that the individual right to liberty is a basic principle of justice, we must also accept the notion of a nation's right to liberty and self-determination.

The principle of self-determination has become a cornerstone of contemporary international law. The right to self-determination entails freedom of choice, which, in turn, implies free will in making decisions and choosing one's own representatives.[5] There is a logical coherence between freedom of choice and peace. Political history clearly demonstrates that preservation of peace is impossible without recognition and strict implementation of the right to self-determination.[6] A people's right to self-determination and freedom of choice is a prerequisite for a just, genuine, and lasting peace.

In the Israeli-Palestinian conflict, identifying the source of injustice is not easy because the issues in conflict have been obscured by cultural myths.[7] Although the dispute is often cast in the rhetoric of historical memories and interpretations, one of its dimensions centers around the Palestinian right to self-determination. Three distinct dimensions of that Palestinian right can be discerned: the Palestinians' national and territorial identity, the Palestinian right to national independence, and the right to self-determination.[8]

Beyond a doubt, denying the Palestinian people's right to both self-determination and the freedom to choose their political identity constitutes a situation of injustice and a fundamental human-rights violation. The National Conference of Catholic Bishops unequivocally asserted that the Palestinians' right to self-determination and their option for an independent homeland is a bedrock foundation for a just peace in the Middle East.[9] It cannot be denied that displacement of the Palestinians from their homeland four decades ago has been at the center of the turmoil and instability in the region and an enduring threat to international peace since that time.

If other ethnonationals have the right to security and self-rule, so do the Palestinians. Clearly, justice is not the privilege of a few, but of every group. Claiming that the concept of self-determination is not applicable to the Palestinians, as is sometimes argued, is simply ignoring the heart of the problem.[10] Clearly, in admitting that justice must be applicable to all, we cannot favor one nation or one people to the exclusion of another.

Many discussions of the Arab-Israeli conflict have been based on erroneous assumptions about real causes and have therefore addressed the wrong issues. Attempting to redirect discussion toward the right issues, an enlightened Palestinian perspective agrees that much of the conflict is about mutual recognition, security, terrorism, and other thorny issues. But the heart of the problem is, still, the displacement of the Palestinian people. All other issues are consequences, rather than causes, of that basic conflict.[11] In the same way, a reasonable Israeli view argues that although "Zionism is a constructive movement that seeks to provide the Jewish people with the resources necessary for national self-being and self-determination, the implementation of Zionism did in some way dispossess another group, the Palestinians."[12] Michael Lerner, a prominent Israeli commentator and editor of *Tikkun* admits that the Palestinians have an absolute right to statehood just as the Israelis do. There are two "right" sides, but now Israelis are denying to Palestinians what was previously denied to them: legitimate national identity.[13]

Placing the Palestinians' rights at the forefront of Jewish concern, three facts have been acknowledged within the Jewish community: first, the displacement of the Palestinians from their homeland is an obvious source of injustice; second, the call for Palestinian rights to statehood is

undeniably legitimate and just; third, the Palestinian tragedy has created
dissent among Jews over the contradiction of the tradition of Jewish ethics
with the power of Zionist ideology.[14] Unless the rights of self-determination and justice of the Palestinian people are given genuine recognition,
conflict and instability in the region will endure.

Belief Systems in the Middle East

In the face of injustice, the need for a strategy to resolve this conflict is
compelling. For such a resolution, it is essential to understand the Middle
East's value and belief systems. It is posited that belief systems are formed
through interaction of "cognitive maps," or sets of images, representing a
complex linkage of ideological beliefs and shared subjective culture.[15] The
interpretation of belief systems is necessary for understanding the basic
political concepts and behavior of a community. Sebastian de Grazia argued that concepts such as state, ruler, citizen, law, authority, alienation,
identity, and socialization are defined by a political community in terms of
certain beliefs related to a particular complex of sociopsychological functions and theological interpretations. This definition is what makes one society differ from another in its political behavior and in the way it sustains
itself. Holding a community together is a system of beliefs, flexible bands
weaving through and around it.[16] Communities in one society cling to their
ideas and behavior whether or not they are acceptable to other societies.

No nation operates without a belief system. Belief systems move nations into actions that ultimately help them to make national decisions and
policy. These systems contain both rational and irrational, formal and informal elements. On the one hand they restrict options; on the other they
rationalize policies. In other words, options are made clear and simple and
a nation is simply asked to act according to whether those choices seem
right or wrong. Most important, a belief system serves as a catalyst that
perpetually shapes a society's feelings of distinctiveness. In that sense, belief systems influence a society or nation to behave not only differently,
but often with superiority or hostility, to those with opposing belief systems. We must, therefore, understand Middle Eastern belief systems to determine effective approaches for combating injustice or resolving conflicts
nonviolently.

What are the competing norms, truths, and moralities of Middle Eastern belief systems? Above all, does the Middle East have norms and values that lend themselves effectively to problem solving and nonviolent
conflict resolution?

More than any region of the world, the Middle East has unique and complex features. Its historical, cultural, ethnic, and religious roots are interwo-
ven into a peculiar tapestry of belief systems, one difficult to understand.

Even more than socioeconomic and political development in Middle Eastern societies, religion (particularly Islam) has profoundly influenced the norms, values, beliefs, and behavior of the region's people. Religion continues to regulate and shape their daily lives. Religion in the Middle East ordains temporal lives with transcendental values, setting forth a code of behavior and practices. For example, Judaism has been a major factor in the formation of Israel's political culture; Islam has influenced political attitudes on such matters as political legitimacy, justice, political obligations of ruler and ruled, and ways of making decisions.[17] Observing recent political events and movements in the Middle East, one sees how much religious fanaticism still shapes beliefs and values there. The impact of that fanaticism upon politics in the Middle East might be seen in a number of factors: the outburst of religious radicalism of the 1979 Islamic Revolution in Iran; the mounting influence of Gush Emunim (Bloc of Faithful) and the ultraorthodox (Haredi) Jewish movements in Israeli politics; the spread of Muslim radical groups in Egypt; and the unchallenged soar of Hamas (zealots), or the Fundamentalist Islamic movement, in the West Bank and Gaza.

From a theoretical perspective there are differences in how the three main monotheistic religions—Judaism, Christianity, and Islam—perceive the truth of norms, values, beliefs, and behavior. Christianity observes such truth through a theological lens, but Judaism and Islam are more concerned about regulating human behavior by emphasizing religious laws over theology. In the same way that the Hebrew bible represents the constitution of Judaism, and the Halakah is the corpus of laws that explicate it, the Qur'an, the Holy Book of Muslims, is also considered as the constitution of Islam and the Shari'a is the jurisprudence that interprets the commands of the Qur'an. In this sense, both the Halakah and the Shari'a profoundly influence Jewish and Muslim behavior.[18]

Above all, the three main religions differently resolve conflicts and injustice. Christianity, in particular Christian liberalism, understands that love is the ultimate moral response to opposing action. Jeffrey Stout summarized one Christian perception:

> Christianity holds that love means doing unto others as you would have them do unto you. You should, therefore, act in ways that would produce the best overall result if everyone acted similarly. Clearly, the world would be a better place if no one used force or committed injustices against others. And if no one ever used force or committed injustices, there would be no need to use force in order to preserve and protect the common good. Hence, according to this view, thou shalt never use force against others.[19]

In contrast, Solomonow wrote that "while Judaism does not appear to require a commitment to nonviolence in order to fulfill its precepts, it so sharply curtails the use of violence that nonviolence becomes more often than not the only meaningful way to fulfill a life dedicated to truth, justice and peace."[20] According to this view, believing truth in the Jewish context means living that truth. The search for truth will ultimately lead to justice and peace. Thus, the status of truth within Judaism is that any departure from it is a violation of the commitment to the spirit of truth and a deceit of God, and no deceit shall stand in the way of God.[21]

In Islam, action against injustice appears more closely related with the concept of jihad. Though the word *jihad* is translated in the West as "holy war," two orientations on its meaning can be discerned in Islamic theology. One orientation is revolutionary, which views jihad as a criterion of conduct that follows the spirit of Islam in fighting for the cause of God. During the Umayyad Dynasty (A.D. 661–749), the Khawarij (seceders) were among the first Muslim predecessors to use jihad as a revolutionary method to fight injustice or to "impose their opinion on the rest of the Muslims."[22] The Khawarij believed that leaders are required to submit only to the will of God and to strictly conform to His laws. It is the responsibility of Muslims to fight and overthrow tyrant leaders who do not rule according to Islamic law and Qur'anic commands. They base their belief on the Qur'anic verse "And barter not My revelations for little gain. Whoso judgeth not by that which Allah [God] hath revealed: such are disbelievers" (Surah 5–44). Unequivocally, this rule means that any leader who breaks the law of God is a loser according to the Qur'anic dictum: "Those who break the Covenant of Allah after ratifying it, and sever that which Allah ordered to be joined, and [who] make mischief in the Earth: Those are they who are the losers" (Surah 2–27). Adhering to the Khawarij basic principles and guidelines, contemporary Shi'ite extremist groups in Iran, Iraq, and Lebanon and the Sunni zealots in Egypt, Algeria, Tunisia, the West Bank, and Gaza are at the forefront of recent social and revolutionary protest movement, demonstrating time and time again that theological fanaticism remains a powerful conviction in the Middle East.

The second meaning often given to jihad is a conciliatory one, quite contrary to the common and ambiguous translation of it as "holy war." According to this second view, jihad can be thought of as a struggle within the individual who accepts some form of spiritual guidance to purify him- or herself. This view means that the term *jihad* in Islam should be understood as resisting self-willed and seditious behavior and actions. Also, jihad need not be associated with violence in the striving for justice and truth.

It is argued that the concept of jihad should be given a moral connotation, and that its purpose ultimately is to put an end to structural violence.[23] Sheikh Mahmud Shaltut, a leading Islamic scholar and jurist of al-Azhar University, "the Islamic establishment in Egypt," made it clear in *The Koran and Fighting:* "People would do well to learn the Qur'anic rules with regard to fighting, its causes and its ends, and so come to recognize the wisdom of the Koran in this respect: Its desire for peace and its aversion against bloodshed and killing for the sake of the vanities of the world and out of sheer greediness and lust."[24] To another scholar "Islam does not give lofty exhortations to peace, but, rather, a living example."[25]

This discussion of Middle East belief systems suggests the possible utility of nonviolence as a strategy for achieving both justice and rights for the Palestinians and peace and security for the Jews. Although some argue against nonviolent strategy and express their skepticism about its feasibility in a volatile region like the Middle East, others argue for a nonviolent approach and believe it could be highly advantageous to both Palestinians and Israelis.

Skepticism of and Faith in Nonviolence

Examining attitudes toward the concept and strategy of nonviolence in the Middle East, we can distinguish between negative reactions, based largely on ideological grounds, and positive views based on ethical reasons. Rejection of nonviolence is rooted in the belief that the suggested use of nonviolent techniques is another dogma of Western subversion wrapped with a new label. Often this view is held by both radical and nationalist groups and by zealous religious movements.

Radical groups, in particular leftists and Arab nationalists, often see nonviolent strategy as imported from the West to deflect the revolutionary potential of the Arab people. In other words, Arab radicals believe that "engaging in nonviolent struggle would deprive the Arabs of their right to wage wars of national liberation in an effort to throw off the last shackles of their colonial legacy."[26] To them, nonviolent struggle is not compatible with the goals and dynamics of Arab social movements. It is argued that the revolutionary Arab social movement, to gain momentum, must first divorce itself from the cultural hegemony of capitalist Western values.

Every social movement has its own features and passes through different phases; such is the case with Arab movements. Still in its infancy, the Arab liberation movement is not yet ready to adapt itself to a new belief, especially one with Western roots. Because of historical experience with Western neocolonial hegemony with its gradual cultural penetration, Arab radicals suspect Western ideas and propositions. They strongly believe that the crisis and dependency of the Arabs follows from the political, economic, military, and, above all, the cultural intrusions of the West.[27]

Thus, radical Arab leftists and nationalists consider nonviolent struggle as a Western technique incompatible with the state of the Arab mind. The Arabs, they argue, have not yet achieved mental decolonization that would permit them to accept such an ideological apparatus of the still-dominant West.[28] Instead, for peoples seeking self-determination, armed struggle is the choice. The resort to armed struggle for national liberation and justice is legitimate and just. Leftist Arab radicals, borrowing from Vladimir Lenin's dictum, consider that armed struggles and revolutions are celebrations of the oppressed and the exploited.

As the influence of religious fundamentalism grows, critics of the nonviolent approach appear more appealing to the fundamental concerns of the masses. To these critics, religious dogma is a source of strength for resisting Western ideas such as nationalism, which have not solved the problems of Muslim societies. The humiliating defeat of Arab armies in the 1967 war demonstrated to radical Muslims that the path of salvation is pan-Islamic solidarity capable of carrying out the required solution. To them, jihad is the method because its militant character will end Arab weaknesses and defeats. Radical Muslims emphasize not the spiritual notion of jihad but its revolutionary character. They argue that the idea of jihad as a struggle for self-control against evil temptation is not authentically Islamic and is in fact spread deliberately by Westerners in order to weaken the Muslims' will to fight.[29]

To Islamic fundamentalists, nonviolence has a negative connotation for the will and dignity of a true Muslim. It means to surrender to political realities and to accept what was denied to Muslims in the first place. It is the duty of a truly devoted Muslim to struggle and fight for what he believes. Above all, for radical Islamicists, pacifism and nonviolent action are alike and acceptance of either would mean God's surrender to evil. This radical view would mean that religion is now placed at the service of struggle (jihad) against the enemy of Islam. It would also mean, to extremist religious groups, that peace with "Satan" is unacceptable.[30] In summary, both radical leftists and nationalists and the religious extremists believe that the oppressor will listen to nothing but the language of violent force.

Advocates of nonviolent resistance, to the contrary, believe that nonviolence, in many cases, saves life and helps repressed people. Confronted with superior force, one has few options. Either one builds one's own forces to achieve superiority, one is destroyed, or one neutralizes the superior force by using nonviolent techniques. The Palestinian uprising, the intifada, has done this by partially neutralizing the might of the Israeli army and reducing its military efficiency.[31] Martin van Creveld, who frequently writes on Israeli and Middle East military affairs, emphasizes that the questionable legitimacy of Israeli operations in the Occupied Territories and the disparity between the power of the Israeli Defence Forces (IDF) and that of the Palestinians puts the IDF in an untenable position. IDF attempts to suppress unarmed Palestinians and end the intifada, some argue, have reduced one of the world's finest fighting forces to a fourth-class police organization.[32]

Most importantly, nonviolent struggle evokes the sympathy of international public opinion and thus provides moral and material support for its users. The purpose of nonviolent struggle is to mobilize people's lives, to inspire them. Nonviolent activists believe if their kind of struggle becomes part of a nation's political culture, future conflicts will be more likely to occur in a manner that respects human dignity. Participating fully in resistance activities, oppressed citizens will realize they can bring to heel even the mightiest of tyrants, thus changing the political formula for governing.

Nonviolence advocates argue that nonviolence is not novel in the Arab struggle for justice. The Palestinian six-month strike in 1936 against British rule is one example of nonviolence. The Arab sect called the Druze in the occupied Golan Heights also used classic nonviolent tactics against the Israeli annexation of their land. They were successful in sending their message to the world that the Israelis could kill them but not their identity.[33] Is the nonviolent approach feasible for attaining justice in the Middle East? Does the existing system of beliefs support nonviolence as the first choice in combating injustice? Let us examine whether nonviolent struggle has a relevance to the Palestinian uprising, and if so, what lessons the intifada can provide.

Lessons from the Intifada

Does the intifada as resistance against injustice generate a new understanding of the struggle for justice without violence? Certainly it is much too early to develop a general set of conclusions about the intifada, but tentative ideas about the Palestinian uprising are possible. Our concern here is not to discuss its roots and causes, nor is it our attempt to explain whether the intifada fits the various theoretical explanations for why people revolt. The intifada is neither a revolution, in the sense of being the work of subversives who provoke the masses into revolution, nor is it a "periodic eruption of social-psychological tensions that boil up in human groups like lava under the earth's crust or steam in a geyser."[34] Farsoun and Landis correctly noted that "given the duration and the level of deprivations, human rights violations, and humiliations suffered by the Palestinians under Israeli rule," the intifada cannot be viewed simply as a "spontaneous outburst of mass anger and hostilities resulting from the sum of individual deprivations and frustrations."[35]

Our intention here is to discern what the intifada teaches us rather than to theorize why it came into existence. Though it has its own historical matrix and character, the intifada represents to some extent the learning of previous national resistance movements. Its significance, however, is that it sets new attitudes and behavior in the daily life of the Palestinian. The intifada has become a way of life and a state of mind for the Palestinian people.

What is distinctive about the intifada is its self-conscious and disciplined strategy. It draws upon both pacifist and religious values. It responds to both the main principles of the belief system of the Palestinian masses and the dictum of nonviolence. These values are expressed with an array of protest tactics of which the most violent is stone throwing.[36]

Stone throwing raises the issue of whether the intifada's leaders can restrain their constituents from using violence, a central concern of the Palestinian community. Critics argue that when violence of any kind is used, the movement ceases to be nonviolent, even though the majority of its participants and its most prominent leaders remain so. Furthermore, the strong participation of radical Muslims (Hamas) in the uprising has created a radical wing within the intifada. Those radicals take the militant view of jihad and put pressure upon intifada leaders to adopt an aggressive attitude toward the Israelis.

Both violent and nonviolent resistance require well-disciplined participants, but nonviolence can prevail only when a large proportion of the constituency accepts the discipline of the movement. Violence, on the other hand, can operate with a small disciplined group. Two additional requisites for successful nonviolent movement are some sympathy for its cause within the opposing group and the presence within its own constituency of an ethos making nonviolence and self-sacrifice admirable traits.

Though the intifada does not conform to the strict definition of a nonviolent movement, it has used many classic nonviolent techniques: the refusal to cooperate with the Israeli military and administrative officials; refusal to pay income taxes; commercial shutdowns; strikes; economic boycotts; hoisting Palestinian flags on top of buildings; demonstrative funerals; general civil disobedience; collective resignation from Israeli civil administration; social boycotts of Palestinian collaborators; and the development of self-reliant educational, social, and political institutions. The Palestinian uprising is not yet a fully nonviolent movement, but it offers us an opportunity to reconsider the impact of nonviolent values and beliefs on the strategic approach to resistance in the Middle East, and it gives a new understanding of the Palestinian-Israeli conflict.

The intifada sets a tone for Middle Eastern peoples, differentiating reality from illusion. It is awakening minds to new vision and a new spirit of change, one not carried away by nationalistic rhetoric. For a long time, the conflict between Palestinians and Israelis has been clouded by illusions that favor transitory gains over permanent assets. It is not an overstatement to say that the recent trend toward a peaceful negotiation between Israel and its neighbors is largely a result of the intifada. First and foremost, the Palestinian uprising tends to change perceptions on all sides, to dispel hatred, and to break the spiral of frenetic retaliation. The Palestinian uprising has created a new awareness of possible scenarios for attaining a just peace for both the Jewish and Palestinian peoples. Though peace and justice seem to be interlinked, one can argue that they are different. Chomsky noted that when conflicting parties speak of peace, the definition of what they mean is usually similar. When they speak of justice, however, matters are not so simple, as justice is much harder to define. The just demands of conflicting nations often seem quite incompatible.[37]

Nevertheless, the search for justice through the intifada has brought the Palestinian-Israeli conflict to the forefront of the consciousness of the two peoples. The search for justice has brought numerous and often incompatible suggestions. One idea is that the search for justice must transcend national lines, that attaining justice requires abolishing national divisions.[38] Adopting this theme, a Palestinian radical leftist group suggested that the Palestinians have already suffered a severe historical injustice. Therefore, it would be right to rectify it by establishing a democratic secular state in all the historical land of Palestine where all the Jewish and Palestinian peoples would equally share one unitary nation-state. It is argued that such a democratic secular "homeland" is the only way to heal the Palestinians' suffering and provide an absolute and lasting security for the Jewish people. Put differently, the creation of one homeland with two nonterritorial nations seems the logical way to prepare Jews and Palestinians for the logic of coexistence to replace that of dogmatic nationalism.

Supporting the validity of the single-state/dual-nation view is the reality of global migration of human groups crossing national borders, transcending ethnic divisions, and subverting the claim of one state for each ethnonational and racial group. Some ask, "Is not, in fact, every land, every nation, today a microcosm of many nations, many peoples?"[39] Thus, it is argued that nations must limit their claims of distinctiveness in order to accommodate the rights of others to live side by side with them. This is the fundamental biblical ethic of "loving thy neighbor as oneself."[40] The one-homeland scenario, however, has some problematic implications. Is not one searching for something almost unattainable or an illusion of political romanticism?

Establishing one homeland for Jews and Palestinians is difficult in the absence of a common goal or a program of social reconstruction for both peoples. A program of social reconstruction is usually a complex, long-term process. Some argue that a program of social change implemented by Arabs and Israelis acting in concert is impossible. Such a program would inevitably require both the elimination of the institutional infrastructure of Israel and the ending of the historical Palestinian identity with the Arab nations. The two peoples participating in a common effort of one homeland is still remote and would need a great will.[41]

An additional obstacle to the one-state proposal is that the Palestinian uprising has consolidated the communal and cultural self-identity of the Arab Palestinians, making it difficult to reverse. Such historical circumstances have also created in the Jewish tradition a separate cultural identity. It is true to life to love one's neighbor as oneself. But the historical circumstances producing cultural identity also means that one cannot love everyone equally. The finiteness of cultural communities presents a challenge to that biblical ethic.[42] Nations often, unfortunately, write and interpret history to present themselves as good and the other as bad. That inclination keeps people apart and challenges the vision of universalism. Thus, the vision of one land, one state for Jews and Palestinians, is still beyond reality and remains a moral challenge for both peoples.

A less desirable but more realistic alternative is the so-called two-state solution, establishment of a Palestinian state in the currently occupied West Bank and Gaza.[43] This appears to be the direction being pursued with the fall 1993 Israeli-Palestinian peace accord. Though that accord may not hold, some version of the two-state solution appears more pragmatic than the single-state approach. Even the two-state solution faces many political, social, and economic obstacles, however, and raises many questions.[44]

Considering the implications of those two scenarios, one must ask if there are better alternatives? The creation of Israel more than four decades ago in Palestine has inflicted injustice on the Palestinians. They demand and deserve a timely rectification of an unjust situation.

There exists now the suggestion of real movement of opponents down the road toward coexistence and an honorable settlement. That movement would include Israeli concessions and security and an end to Palestinian suffering. No matter how long the journey takes, clearly the Palestinian cause has been reborn, brought once again to the world's attention. It is a problem that seems certain to play a critical role in the events of the present and the upcoming decade. In the hope of clarifying our distorted vision, the test of coexistence for the sake of life is the just scenario.

Conclusion

What lesson does this conflict in the Middle East offer us? The search for justice without violence must focus on peaceful coexistence based in the light of the historical circumstances and the cultural "makeup" of each of the societies in conflict. Creating justice and peace between two people claiming one land is difficult and limits the options for settlement. It is difficult because those who would choose a nonviolent protest strategy must be aware that nonviolent action may lead to violent actions by ultranationalist and religious groups. But the struggle offers us a vision that beyond the ring of fear and hate there is still the light of hope and reason.

Notes

1. In a recent survey on armed conflicts, particularly in the Third World countries, it is estimated that between 1.6 and 3.9 million unarmed civilians have died

as result of intrastate conflicts, that is, conflicts involving one government and an opposition group demanding autonomy or secession for a particular ethnic group or region. See Stavenhagen, "Ethnic Conflicts." See also Wallensteen, *States in Armed Conflict.*

2. On the theme of the psychological and sociological perspectives of nonviolence see Kool, *Perspectives on Nonviolence.* For more on the subject see "Nonviolent Action," a special issue of *Sociological Inquiry.*

3. Although the concept of self-determination is difficult to define precisely, Przetacznik argued that such imprecision does not discredit this right for all peoples and nations. For an extensive review of the concept and recognition of the right to self-determination by political thinkers and national leaders, see his "Basic Collective Human Right."

4. See extracts from the writings of Rawls in *The Great Political Theories,* Volume 2, edited by Curtis. See also Rawls, *A Theory of Justice.*

5. The freedom of a nation to practice its affairs independently means also that it has the right to decide its sovereign identity through local autonomy and confederative relations with other states as an independent state and full-fledged member of the international community.

6. Przetacznik, "The Basic Collective Human Right," p. 49.

7. The National Conference of the American Catholic Bishops entitled "Towards Peace in the Middle East," held in Baltimore, Maryland, on November 9, 1989, concluded that the different memories and interpretations of recent history by both parties in the dispute provide conflicting contexts for discussion of how to pursue peace and justice in the region. For details, see "The National Conference of Catholic Bishops, Policy Statement."

8. For more discussion of the Palestinian right to self-determination see Abu-Lughod, "Retrieving Palestinian National Rights."

9. Ibid., p. 178.

10. See, for example, Halberston's argument about the concept of self-determination and the Palestinians, "Self-Determination," pp. 465–487.

11. Hallaj, "Breaking the Stalemate."

12. Gotlieb, *Self-Determination in the Middle East,* p. 9.

13. Quoted in Ellis, "The Task Before Us," p. 60. See also Lerner, "The Occupation."

14. For a discussion of Jewish ethics and Israeli power see Feuerlicht, *The Fate of the Jews.*

15. For a methodological survey of the linkage between ideology, culture, and belief systems, see Szalay and Kelly, "Political Ideology."

16. Drawing his argument from psychological, anthropological, theological, and sociological perspectives, de Grazia tried to bridge the gap between traditional political philosophy and modern empiricism in understanding community behavior. See extracts from de Grazia's writings cited in Curtis (ed.), *The Great Political Theories, Volume 2.* See also de Grazia, *The Political Community.*

17. On the impact of religion on politics in the Middle East see Razi, "Legitimacy, Religion, and Nationalism."

18. In contrast with Christianity, which teaches that the path of truth and salvation lies through the acceptance and imitation of Christ, Judaism and Islam believe the path of truth and salvation lie through acceptance and obedience to God's law. This law came to be the essence of Halakah in Judaism and the substance of Shari'a in Islam: the way of life ordained by God for humankind.

19. However this approach should not be seen as the only perception of attaining justice in Christian thinking. Stout demonstrated the varieties of the Christian pacifist values of justice in his chapter "Justice and Resort to War," pp. 3–33.

20. Solomonow, "Living Truth," p. 154.

21. Ibid.

22. Satha-Anand, "The Nonviolent Crescent," p. 28.

23. Ibid.

24. Quoted in Kelsay, "Islam and the Distinction," pp. 209–210.

25. Laila, "Islam and Peace," p. 62.

26. Crow and Grant, "Questions and Controversies," p. 75.

27. Hisham Sharabi argued that "dependency in the Third World countries is more than a mere result of aggression, domination, repression, despoliation and dispossession by external forces; it is more than political, economic and military hegemony practiced by the center over the periphery. It is also a relationship of cultural domination." Cited in Boullata, *Trends and Issues,* p. 90.

28. Ibid., p. 114.

29. See Sonn, *Between Qur'an and Crown,* p. 203.

30. For example, in a letter sent to the Palestine National Council (PNC), Hamas, the Palestinian radical Muslim group, stated clearly that the voices calling for peace with the assassins, while they occupy the land of Palestine and persecute the people, are nothing more than bait whose objective is to destroy the gains made by the intifada. For Hamas, the leading Islamic movement in the Palestinian uprising, the spirit of jihad must be spread throughout Islam. For more on the Palestinian Islamic groups in the West Bank and Gaza, see Legrain, "The Islamic Movement," pp. 175–189. See also Taraki, who in "The Islamic Resistance" concluded that Hamas Islamic ideology should be taken seriously,

31. See Cobban's interview with Faissal Husseini, "Gunless in Gaza."

32. See Peretz, *Intifada,* p. 134.

33. See Awad, "Nonviolent Resistance."

34. Aya, "Theories of Revolution," p. 49. See his extensive discussion on why peoples revolt.

35. See Farsoun and Landis, "The Sociology of an Uprising," p. 17.

36. Galtung, *Nonviolence and Israel/Palestine,* p. 62. Galtung discussed several methods of nonviolence used by the intifada in the Occupied Territories.

37. Chomsky, *Peace in the Middle East,* p. 97.

38. Ibid.

39. Ruether and Ruether, *The Wrath of Jonah,* p. 245.

40. Ibid.

41. Ibid., p. 103.

42. Ibid., p. 245.

43. Chomsky in *Peace in the Middle East* suspected that only extreme pressure from the United States and other great powers could lead Israel to accept a truly independent Palestinian state. The result, however, will be "Balkanization" producing a hostile and suspicious relationship between the two societies. Therefore, Chomsky believed that the two-state solution could be shaped within a federal framework, perhaps in the form of two federated republics with parity, a guarantee of a high degree of autonomy combined with significant economic integration and highly permeable boundaries (pp. 101–102).

44. For a discussion of these political and social implications see Segal, *Creating the Palestinian State.*

Bibliography

Abu-Lughod, Ibrahim. "Retrieving Palestinian National Rights," in Ibrahim Abu-Lughod (ed.), *Palestinian Rights: Affirmation and Denial* (Illinois: Medina Press, 1982).

Awad, Mubarak E. "Nonviolent Resistance: A Strategy for the Occupied Territories," in Robert L. Holmes (ed.), *Nonviolence in Theory and Practice* (Belmont, CA: Wadsworth, 1990).

Aya, Rod. "Theories of Revolution Reconsidered: Contrasting Models of Collective Violence." *Theory and Society* 8 (1) (July 1979): 39–99.

Boullata, Issa J. *Trends and Issues in Contemporary Arab Thought* (New York: State University of New York Press, 1990).

Chomsky, Noam. *Peace in the Middle East: Reflections on Justice and Nationhood* (New York: Random House, 1969).

Cobban, Helena. "Gunless in Gaza: As Israeli Debates the Uses of Military Force, Palestinians Debate the Uses of Nonviolence." *World Monitor* 3 (3) (March 1, 1990): 57–64.

Crow, Ralph E., and Philip Grant. "Questions and Controversies About Nonviolent Struggle in the Middle East," in Ralph E. Crow and Philip Grant (eds.), *Arab Nonviolent Political Struggle in The Middle East* (Boulder, CO: Lynne Rienner Publishers, 1990).

Curtis, Michael (ed.). The Great Political Theories, Volume 2 (New York: Adiscus Book, 1981).

Ellis, Marc H. "The Task Before Us: Contemporary Jewish Religious Thought and the Challenge of Solidarity." *American-Arab Affairs* 30 (Fall 1989): 60.

Farsoun, Samih K., and Jean M. Landis. "The Sociology of an Uprising: The Roots of the Intifada," in Jamal R. Nassar and Roger Heacock (eds.), *Intifada: Palestine at the Crossroads* (New York: Praeger, 1990).

Feuerlicht, Roberta Strauss. *The Fate of the Jews: A People Torn Between Israeli Power and Jewish Ethics* (New York: Times Books, 1983).

Galtung, Johan. *Nonviolence and Israel/Palestine* (Honolulu: University of Hawaii Institute for Peace, 1989).

Gotlieb, Yosef. *Self-Determination in the Middle East* (New York: Praeger, 1982).

de Grazia, Sebastian. *The Political Community* (Chicago: University of Chicago Press, 1948).

Halberston, Malvina. "Self-Determination in the Arab-Israeli Conflict: Meaning, Myth, and Politics." *Journal of International Law and Politics* 21 (3) (Spring 1989): 465–487.

Hallaj, Muhammad. "Breaking the Stalemate: A Palestinian View." *Journal of South Asian and Middle Eastern Studies* 14 (1) (Fall 1990): 83.

Kelsay, John. "Islam and the Distinction Between Combatants and Noncombatants," in James Turner Johnson and John Kelsay (eds.), *Cross, Crescent, and Sword* (New York: Greenwood Press, 1990).

Kennedy, R. Scott. "The Druze of the Golan: A Case of Nonviolent Resistance," in Robert L. Holmes (ed.), *Nonviolence in Theory and Practice* (Belmont, CA: Wadsworth, 1990).

Kool, V. K. *Perspectives on Nonviolence* (New York: Springer-Verlag, 1990).

Laila, Muhammad Abu. "Islam and Peace." *The Islamic Quarterly* 35 (1) (1991): 62.

Legrain, Jean-François. "The Islamic Movement and the Intifada," in Jamal R. Nassar and Roger Heacock (eds.), *Intifada: Palestine at the Crossroads* (New York: Praeger, 1990).

Lerner, Michael. "The Occupation: Immoral and Stupid." *Tikkun* 3 (March/April 1988).

"The National Conference of Catholic Bishops, Policy Statement on the Middle East," reprinted in *Journal of Palestine Studies* 19 (2) (Winter 1990): 170–184.

"Nonviolent Action from a Social-Psychological Perspective." *Sociological Inquiry* 38 (1) (Winter 1968).

Peretz, Don. *Intifada: The Palestinian Uprising.* (Boulder, CO: Westview Press, 1990).

Przetacznik, Frank. "The Basic Collective Human Right to Self-Determination of Peoples and Nations as Prerequisite for Peace." *Journal of Human Rights* 3 (1) (Fall 1990).

Rawls, John. *A Theory of Justice* (Cambridge: Harvard University Press, 1971).

Razi, G. Hossein. "Legitimacy, Religion, and Nationalism in the Middle East." *American Political Science Review* 84 (1) (March 1990): 69–91.

Ruether, Rosemary R., and H. J. Ruether. *The Wrath of Jonah: The Crisis of Religious Nationalism in the Israeli-Palestinian Conflict* (San Francisco: Harper & Row, 1989).

Satha-Anand, Chaiwat (Qader Muheideen). "The Nonviolent Crescent: Eight Theses on Muslim Nonviolent Actions," in Ralph E. Crow, Philip Grant, and Saad E. Ibrahim (eds.), *Arab Nonviolent Political Struggle in the Middle East* (Boulder, CO: Lynne Rienner Publishers, 1990).

Segal, Jerome M. *Creating the Palestinian State: A Strategy for Peace* (Chicago: Lawrence Hill Books, 1989).

Solomonow, Allan. "Living Truth: A Jewish Perspective," in Robert L. Holmes (ed.), *Nonviolence in Theory and Perspective* (Belmont, CA: Wadsworth Publishing Company, 1990).

Sonn, Tamara. *Between Qur'an and Crown: The Challenge of Political Legitimacy in the Arab World* (Boulder, CO: Westview Press, 1990).

Stavenhagen, Rodolfo. "Ethnic Conflicts and Their Impact on International Society." *International Social Science Journal* 43 (1) (February 1991).

Stout, Jeffrey. "Justice and Resort to War: A Sampling of Christian Ethical Thinking," in James Turner Johnson and John Kelsay (eds.), *Cross, Crescent, and Sword* (New York: Greenwood Press, 1990), pp. 3–33.

Szalay, Leonard B., and R. M. Kelly, "Political Ideology and Subjective Culture: Conceptualization and Empirical Assessment." *The American Political Science Review* 76 (4) (1982): 585–602.

Taraki, Lisa. "The Islamic Resistance in the Palestinian Uprising," in Zachary Lockman and Joel Beinin (eds.), *Intifada: The Palestinian Uprising Against Israeli Occupation* (Boston: South End Press, 1989).

Wallensteen, Peter (ed.). *States in Armed Conflict 1988* (Uppsala: Uppsala University, Department of Peace and Conflict Research, Report No. 30, July 1989).

12

Attaining Justice Through Development Organizations in India

Elizabeth Mathiot (Moen)

In recent years India's popular image has changed from one of nonviolence to violence: from the nonviolent revolution of Mohandas K. Gandhi to the assassinations of Indira and Rajiv Gandhi; religious, ethnic, labor, and separatist conflicts; police brutality; sabotage of public transportation; political riots; routine murder of infant girls and young brides; and bloody conflicts between caste Hindus and *dalits* (untouchables). Behind the overt violence stand injustice and its companion, structural violence.

Less noticed is the unfolding of a new nonviolent movement in India, led, not by a single great soul, but by thousands of grassroots organizations intended to enable India's most oppressed people to uplift themselves. These organizations, being nongovernmental and nonprofit, are in the "third" or "voluntary" sector of society. In India they are known as voluntary organizations; elsewhere they are called nongovernmental organizations (NGOs) or private voluntary organizations (PVOs).

Voluntary sector grassroots development organizations (DOs) such as these are rapidly multiplying throughout the world. Advocates of decentralized, people-centered development, in governmental and international funding agencies, are turning to them, hoping they can do what forty years of centralized, top-down, capital-centered development has failed to: produce nonviolent, just, and sustainable development. This is a good omen, for as David Korten wrote: "If transformation is to come, it must come as a consequence of voluntary action, an act of human commitment to

This chapter has been heavily edited by Paul Wehr after the author's untimely death. We believe the edited version is faithful to her insights and conclusions.

collective survival, driven by a vision that transcends the behaviors conditioned by existing institutions and culture."[1]

This chapter is about DOs in the south of India, their goals and strategies, the obstacles they face, and their power. These DOs work with the most oppressed people in India, not just the "most backward" classes, untouchables, and displaced indigenous tribes, but within these groups, the landless, those with too little land to make a living, outmoded artisans, unemployed slum dwellers, and especially women. In other words, the participants in these DO programs are so marginalized, they are barely clinging to the edge. Their goal, then, is *sarvodaya,* the uplifting of the last person.[2]

Social Context

Had Mahatma Gandhi's will prevailed, India would now be the undisputed leader of a new world order—one based on human unity and love, nonviolence, genuine democracy, and national self-reliance. But from Nehru on, India opted for what seems to be the worst of both socialism and capitalism: Euro-American–style modernization that measures success by the gross national product (GNP); gridlock bureaucracy; capital-intensive industrialization and heavily promoted consumerism; centralized planning and control, along with rapacious private capitalism; and militarism.

In some ways this strategy was quite successful. India is one of the world's major industrial nations. It has nuclear capabilities. It is self-sufficient in food. Economic growth and saving have been notably high, and among the elite there is fabulous, often extravagant and extroverted, wealth. But success came at a heavy price. India is suffering a foreign exchange crisis and is deeply in debt to other nations, the International Monetary Fund (IMF), and the environment. Many of the middle class, the majority of whom are government employees, debase themselves through corruption and sycophancy, and destroy one another to attain the symbols of modernity, wealth, and success.[3] Below them, at least two-thirds of the population lives in poverty and debt, and over half of these subsist below a poverty line of three rupees per capita per day, or about $U.S. 0.17.[4]

Things are likely to get worse, for India has recently sold twenty tons of gold to pay just the interest on its foreign debt and is going deeper in debt to the IMF.[5] The IMF generally extracts a harsh price for its loans, not in the form of high interest rates, but in the requirement for structural adjustment that generally involves deregulation, privatization, and elimination of programs especially benefiting the poor. In the long run, structural adjustment may help the elite and the national economic indicators, but the poor and lower middle class will suffer. Consequently, class, caste, and religious enmity and violence are likely to increase.

Sources of Injustice

India has a complex social structure based on economic class, gender, caste, ethnicity, religion, language, and locality. The result is a hierarchical social system that discriminates on all of these factors, especially economic class, gender, and caste, and in some places, religion. With unequal opportunity and with injustice embedded in the system, those on the bottom of these multiple hierarchies suffer greatly. Most of them are poor, uneducated, un- or underemployed, malnourished, diseased, and subject to threat and humiliation. They watch some of their children die, and know the others will live only half a life. Some of them are materially well off but because of caste or gender, they are still deprived of autonomy, full human development, and self-esteem. This is the structural violence the DOs seek to abolish. Because those on the bottom of the social hierarchy are usually more likely to experience direct physical violence also, eliminating the structural violence should help eliminate most of the shocking, physical violence as well.

According to DO officers and other development workers (DWs), India's poverty and other development failures result when social structure, culture, government, environment, and population dynamics interact to maintain and justify a multidimensional stratification system. At the bottom of the hierarchy is a very large underclass of powerless, unaware, and debt-ridden people. Their illiteracy, poor health, traditions, addictions, superstitions, fear, passivity, and internal divisions reinforce the stratification, making the powerful more so and the powerless also more so, for according to the DWs, economic, political, and brute power go hand in hand.

For development workers, the key aspects of this stratification are class, caste, and gender, which through invocation of "natural law" are used to oppress women and untouchables. (Making untouchability illegal has not rendered dalits "pure" in the minds of many caste Hindus.) Patriarchal gender ideology combines with consumerism to encourage unreasonable demands for dowry, wife murder or forced suicide and husband's remarriage to get more dowry, and as a preventive measure, female infanticide and the abortion of female fetuses.

In village India, where 70 percent of the people live, power lies with the rich farmers and landlords, village government officials, moneylenders, labor contractors, master weavers, and middle people who market the village products. Here full employment is the exception. Agricultural laborers may be unemployed half the year or more, and rarely do daily wages exceed Rs 5 for women and Rs 10 for men. Debt is inevitable because banks will not lend to resourceless people, despite government subsidies for this purpose. Moneylender interest rates range from 10 percent a month to 1 percent a day. Thus, children are sent away as bonded labor, whole families slave in quarries as indentured labor, and local initiative is thwarted by moneylenders who control the time and activities of debtor families.

Despite such cruel poverty and exploitation, the system hangs together. There is little rebellion among the oppressed, partly because everywhere remnants of semifeudal patron-client relationships and mentality persist. The resourceless can often count on employers to come through in times of most critical need, and even to provide gifts and loans for dowries, food, and clothing for festivals and ceremonies. Thus, there may be a curious form of solidarity based on the oppressed's fear and worship of the oppressor. In addition, the state of Tamil Nadu's social welfare program includes the distribution of basic clothing, a nutritious noon meal for all children, and fair price shops where households can obtain a monthly ration of sugar and kerosene, and low-income households can get staples such as rice. These forms of charity make the work of the DOs harder, for they breed dependency. Out of the rationality of poverty, people with no security may prefer the assurance of loans and handouts from government, employer, or moneylender to a movement toward self-reliance, which may cut them off from both the exploitation and the "largess" of their oppressors.

The Government

It is clear that Indian governments are part of the problem. Their antipoverty rhetoric is impressive. Excellent plans, policies, and programs are drawn up. But with politicians controlled by powerful proprietary classes, and with inefficient and corrupt bureaucracy, "failure of implementation"[6] is the norm. Politicians and civil servants benefit more by taking bribes than by following laws and policies aimed to uplift the poor. DOs condemn the hypocrisy of government—the gap between what it says about poverty and what it actually does about poverty.

Can the government change the situation? Can it overturn what Bardhan called "history's most well-entrenched and ornately elaborate ideological systems of legitimizing inequality and exploitation"?[7] It is possible. As Mahatma Gandhi said, "The revolution is easy, if the mind is made up."[8] Such massive change will require not only the resolve of the government and the governed, but also considerable vision and planning if chaos and bloodshed are to be avoided. The process is as important as the goal.

Although political and economic power appear to be highly concentrated in the central government, there is agreement that the government is losing autonomy. There is also considerable disagreement about its actual strength. It may be that even if the central government got serious about poverty alleviation, without massive mobilization of the oppressed that DOs envision, it could not take the necessary steps. Meanwhile, from the perspective of the village poor, government officials seem to hold life-and-death power.

Development Organization Goals and Strategies

Orienting Perspectives

The majority of DOs are secular in orientation. The rest are about evenly split between Christian benevolence and Gandhian nonviolence as a primary source of inspiration. Some DOs are also feminist. None are connected with a political party. Although only a few espouse socialist or communist ideals, all would have to be characterized as more or less "left" because they emphasize the need for a more equitable society and cultural change.

DO analyses of the problem generally begin with Marx; their strategies, grounded in nonviolence, reflect Gandhi. "Release, not relief" is a common theme. The great majority of the organizations seek a society based on decentralized political power and collective ownership and management of productive assets by workers. This is not small-scale capitalism as some claim because it does not allow the exploitation of workers. Neither is it large-scale socialism. Instead, it is the middle way of self-reliance advocated by Gandhi.

Definition of Development

According to one development worker, "We strongly believe and work with our faith that development can only come from 'within' and as outsiders we can help, but insiders must do the job. We believe in total development of a total person, and solutions to the problems, issues, and needs of the rural communities can be found by people themselves by their collective actions with solidarity."

Although each DO has its own fix on development, strong common themes emerged regarding what development should be.

Participatory. Projects should be "felt, designed, and implemented by the people." It may take some time before the "culture of silence" is overcome, but eventually participants should take control over their own destiny.

Emancipatory. As one DW said, "Modern society is so concerned with economic aspects of development that spiritual and moral values are apt to be neglected." DWs do not think of development entirely in terms of material growth. Instead, they speak of the full realization of human potential; the development of body, mind, and spirit; the release of physical, economic, and mental power.

Comprehensive. Just as they promote emancipation of the whole person, development workers also seek development that is not piecemeal, but comprehensive, and healing of the divisions in society.

Sufficient. DWs speak of family welfare and an adequate standard of living. They do not talk about consumption, shops full of things, or accumulating possessions. For many it is a question of "having or being." Thus, sufficiency is tied to emancipation. As one development worker wrote:

> People in affluent countries find it hard to imagine life without easy communications, innumerable gadgets, packaged food, ample furniture, and a vast choice of cosmetics. They feel sorry for those who have so few possessions, and think life would be better for them if they had more. . . . The philosopher Erich Fromm has written a book entitled *To Have or To Be?* in which he maintains that two modes of existence are today struggling for the spirit of humanity, the "having" mode, which equates success with material goods, and the "being" mode, which recognizes that the only value is what a person is. This teaching is as old as the Buddha, and it is the very heart of the Christian Gospel. . . . This is why we refuse to count success in terms of increase in material goods, in buildings, transport or equipment.

Decentralized. Currently, as one respondent said, "Development needs are determined by those at the apex. Local needs and preferences take a back seat. . . . Elite values are imposed on the common man." DWs insist that development must be a mass movement coming from the bottom, not directed from the top, and that it be designed for village needs.

Democratic. DWs say that India's "ballotbox democracy" is deceptive because "the concentration of political power goes along with the concentration of economic power" so that landlords, loom owners, and moneylenders can expect those who depend on them to vote as told. According to one DW, "People are not using their voting power without fear. This fear comes because they are weak in their economic positions." For the development workers, genuine democracy comes with decentralization, individual autonomy, and a sense of community.

Nonviolent. All the development organizations are committed to nonviolent social change; they speak of nonviolence as both a method and a goal, of creating change through a "raging but peaceful fire." According to one DW, "We must fight injustice with all our might but with mercy and compassion for both the exploited and the exploiter."

Self-sufficient. Although some of the Christian organizations engage in maintenance charity and all DOs provide emergency charity, the great majority advocate the former only for those few unable to participate in their own uplifting.

Revolutionary. "Development projects create a base to revolutionize the minds of society and establish new social values and a new social order." Most DOs are emphatic that their work must go beyond mending society's ills. Instead, they seek redistribution of power.

Indian. Development organizations desire an Indian mode of development, not Westernization. They know this goal is problematic because much of the injustice in the society is justified, maintained, and enforced through the Indian culture.

Strategies of Development

Implicit in the development organizations' goals for development is a metatheory of development, which becomes explicit in the work they do. They agree on what should be done. Broadly speaking, the goal is to unite the oppressed across boundaries of age, gender, religion, and caste to overcome exploitative individuals and classes. A nonviolent strategy in the full spirit of Gandhi would fight a more difficult battle—that of making the enemy a friend, of enabling the exploiter to change voluntarily. Some DWs are thinking along these lines, and some have even succeeded in modest ways.

As participants in DO programs become more aware of their rights and responsibilities, more self-sufficient, and more self-confident, they will develop a mass movement to demand what is lawfully due them. They will free themselves from employers and moneylenders, thus improve work and credit conditions. Beginning with the local governmental unit, the *panchayat,* they will influence government by standing for election and mobilizing to elect others who will actually serve them. Participants will be creating local, autonomous structures for savings and credit, conflict resolution, cooperative production, and critical and practical education as the building blocks of a transforming society. Whereas some of the goals can be attained with short-term projects, the entire process—from awareness to self-reliance—will take many years.

DOs also agree about specific strategies.[9] They emphasize heavily six strategic factors: awareness, empowerment, social restructuring, income generation, education, and health (including family planning).

Awareness. According to one DW interviewed, "The first step is to meet [with participants] to create unity and understanding and get rid of jealousy, greed, and narrowmindedness. We must create a cooperative mentality, through the understanding of common suffering and exploitation. At first there are barriers; we must keep going back."

Most awareness building is done through education classes employing conventional and experiential methods as well as community organizations called *sangams.* DOs also use puppet shows and street theater, movies and videos, community forums, and role playing. They focus on: the realization of individual and group strength; the possibility of solving personal and community problems from the inside and in new ways; citizen rights and responsibilities; understanding the political and economic systems; and social and cultural "evils" such as dowry, untouchability, bribery, alcohol, wife beating, superstition, expensive ceremonies and festivals, and lavish gift giving.

The ultimate goal is participants' realization that their condition is due to gender, class, and caste oppression, not fate or karma; that they have the right to a better life; and that by acting in solidarity, they can soon make improvements in their condition and eventually bring about a more just society.

Empowerment. Empowerment is the process by which participants gain confidence and self-esteem as they come to realize their own strength and power, as they come to understand they can say no to the status quo, that they can make changes, especially when they act as a body. According to one DW: "We help the members to form *sangams* before initiating development activities. The members discuss in the *sangam* meetings . . . about the type of programme that they need with a view of long-term benefits. The village level *sangam* had achieved in getting facilities like drinking water taps. . . . Their collective attempts had helped bring in themselves a sense of confidence."

The primary purpose of empowerment is the elimination of dependency, and thereby the reduction of the power of landlords, moneylenders, and the like. Subthemes are: community self-help; self-determination, self-reliance, and self-sufficiency through local institutions; dispute resolution; income-earning capacity, savings, and credit. DOs enhance the empowerment process by helping the participants deal with the system. For example, they may organize legal aid and encourage government and bank officials to do their duty. The more immediate goals and strategies for empowerment include:

1. *Organization in solidarity.* DOs advocate group efforts, people power, group identity, cooperation, community building, and peoples' movements.
2. *Leadership development.* DOs try to eliminate traditional leadership and harassment by the local elite by fostering new leadership, local problem-solving capacity, and administrative skill among the participants. Leadership development is done through special seminars and camps, nonformal education, and as part of sangam organizations.
3. *Positive self-image creation.* The goal is to remove the inferiority complex of villagers, overcome inertia, increase feelings of self-confidence and dignity, and gain assertiveness.

The primary means of organizing, developing leadership, and building self-image is through the formation of sangams, where much of the awareness work also takes place. Sangams may be communitywide, but the DWs often begin with groups that share common gender and caste identity. Then, with increased awareness, people may become willing to meet and work in mixed groups. At some point, DOs deny participation to those who insist on caste exclusivity.

Social restructuring. "[We seek] opportunity for all for a fuller richer life," said a DW quoting Gandhi. For the DOs, the goal of restructuring the society is opportunity for all and social support for those unable to do for themselves. The more immediate steps toward restructuring are land reform, decentralization, and cooperative self-management. It is acknowledged, however, that equitable restructuring cannot occur unless there is greater unity among the participants.

1. *Land reform.* Most of the participants own no land or not enough for basic subsistence, so land reform is a top priority for restructuring but not a major activity. As one DW explained, "The government only respects voluntary organizations if people are behind them; but people won't get behind them on land reform because their next meal comes from the landlord." Some DOs work for the enforcement of land ceilings, but have had little success, because, they say, politicians and government officials are among the worst offenders. Some DOs have been able to buy land, and some have been given control over Bhoodan lands, government wastelands, and land that has been made available through the Land Ceiling Act. Here development organizations generally organize collective agricultural endeavors (farming, social forestry, apiaries, dairies), and production of related products (honey, soap nut powder, herbal medicines), but opportunities are limited. To reduce land loss by small farmers, DOs fight high interest rates, seek alternative sources of credit, and try to revitalize or provide rural extension services.

2. *Decentralization.* In addition to landlords, capitalists, and money-lenders, DWs also blame "distant and indifferent officials" who do not understand the participants' situation, and, because of class and caste differences, often do not care about their plight. DOs call for planning and administration from the bottom up through sangams and see their community organizing as an essential first step. They believe industrial policy must also shift its orientation from urban, centralized, and capital intensive to rural, decentralized, and labor intensive.

3. *Cooperative self-management.* Self-employment through local cooperatives is considered essential for self-sufficiency, as is the reduction of corruption and exploitation. Moreover, when co-ops function well, important skills are learned, income is higher, and individual costs, risk,

exploitation, and debt bondage are reduced. Thus, the formation of co-ops is a central activity of the DOs. Dairy, weaving, sewing, and fiber work cooperatives are most common. Here is how one DW explained their benefits:

> Nowadays the women handloom weavers are exploited physically and economically. The sexual exploitation creates an unrest and other disturbance in their families. The indirect bondedness is also a reality. . . . Due to lack of union or organization at state level the weavers could not get the benefits of the State Welfare like: medical care, minimum wage, provident fund, standing order, permanency and job security, environment safety, disease [prevention] and hazard safety.
>
> Now people have got confident in their life to struggle for their betterment through cooperative and community action. Previously people thought that their fate and karma is the root cause for their poverty and outcaste system. Now they could get involved in the decision making and decision taking process in their activities.

In addition to work co-ops, sangams now organize cooperatives for savings and credit to evade the moneylender, and for food buying to save money. Some DOs organize housing co-ops where, after learning such skills as brick and tile making, the participants build their own houses and sometimes form labor co-ops to continue using these skills.

Income generation. Some DOs believe income generation is a prerequisite for awareness and empowerment—as one DW said, "You cannot uplift women and children if they have empty stomachs." Even if income generation is not a prerequisite for awareness and empowerment, most DOs see them as mutually reinforcing. For instance, the desire to read, write, and count becomes stronger when these skills facilitate income generation. The development organizations' goal is a stable and sufficient income and freedom from debt, within the context of traditional Indian simplicity. The benefits of greater income observed by the DOs are increased self-respect, status, autonomy, self-reliance, confidence, security, health, saving, future orientation, and planning as well as reduced labor migration and infant and child mortality, which some link with reduced fertility.

There are three general income-generation strategies: agriculture and animal husbandry, crafts and small industry, and services. The most common income-generating schemes are clothes making, dairy, fiberworks, spinning, and weaving. They draw on (a) government programs such as free sewing machines for the poorest of tailoring course graduates, or low-interest loans for animals or equipment; (b) co-ops and sangam self-funding credit schemes; and (c) consumer subsidies through sangam and co-op shops.

Education. Most of the participants cannot read, write, or count, so they are frequently cheated. The DOs' educational goals are to foster the desire to learn, encourage independence, impart knowledge for everyday life, and improve thinking skills. Problem-oriented, experiential education and participatory research are emphasized over formal curricula of government schools. DOs establish their own schools, libraries, and reading centers; hold "camps," seminars, and cultural programs; and organize "social games." In their program of nonformal education, two-hour classes are held five or six nights a week, with men teaching males and women teaching females in separate facilities. Nonformal education is aimed at adults, but children also come. Three generations struggling together over their slates is a moving scene.

Health. DOs consider health fundamental to development. Their health work includes education, diagnosis, and treatment of common disorders, prevention, nutrition programs, organization and training, family planning, and public health.

1. *Education.* The major health activity of the DOs, education includes special emphasis on maternal and child health, nutrition, alcoholism, removing the stigma of leprosy, and oral rehydration therapy. Education without other resources, however, may be in vain. Some village health workers said it really didn't matter how much they taught about nutrition because the villagers could never afford an adequate diet. "We give them medicines and lectures, and soon they are sick again; we are doing it all wrong; we should be feeding them and getting them better work."

2. *Diagnosis and treatment.* This work is done through health surveys, door-to-door outreach, small health centers, dispensaries, maternal and child care clinics, leprosy rehabilitation programs, and family planning and eye camps. Sometimes trained health workers volunteer or work for modest pay; government health workers are deployed; and self-trained DWs may do the work.

3. *Prevention.* Preventive efforts emphasize vaccination and education about the dangers of alcohol.

4. *Nutrition.* DOs provide nutrition education, assistance in home gardening, nutritious food at their child care centers, and sometimes food for sick and disabled people.

5. *Organization and training.* DOs train health education teachers and voluntary health workers for prevention and simple health care; they also organize committees to act as health advocates for the community.

6. *Family planning.* Family planning education and services are integral to maternal and child health projects. They are featured in the general health care services, and family planning is usually included in nonformal education. Some DOs hold special family planning camps.

7. *Public health.* Safe water and cooking facilities are the main goals. Nonformal and health education generally include information about

vaccinations, infectious diseases, bacterial contamination, and sanitation as well as instruction for building soak pits and latrines. All DOs encourage the use of latrines, and some engage in latrine building.

Most DOs agree that all of these health-supportive elements should occur, but there is less agreement about order of importance or sequence of development. The main question is whether income generation or awareness building should come first, though many feel they should occur together.

A cluster of strategic factors less emphasized by development organizations includes physical infrastructure, technology, and the environment. Although considered important, DOs do not emphasize them for several reasons. First, the DWs consider themselves social workers with a mission to serve people directly. Second, the government is more likely to provide infrastructure and technology than human services. Thus, even poor villages with no teachers or health care workers may have electricity and even buildings for school and health care. Third, there is the implicit assumption that if the development of the people comes first, the rest will follow. Nevertheless, because much government funding (and its coveted 10 percent administrative overhead) is for infrastructural projects like latrines, many DOs integrate them into their broader programs, and others succumb to this easier work.

In recent years, DOs are placing greater emphasis on the environment. This change is partly in response to the changing priorities of funding agencies but also reflects a growing awareness of the relationship among environmental, economic, and social well-being.

A notable aspect of DO strategy is that most of them focus primarily on women, for four reasons:

1. DOs believe women are more mature, responsible, hard-working, studious, innovative, cooperative, and altruistic than men. Thus, focusing on women will bring greater benefits.
2. Women are in the worst condition, the most oppressed, and in greatest need of attention.
3. Not only are women's projects more likely to succeed, but also public officials find it harder to resist the petitions and demonstrations of women, and even more important, funding agencies are pushing women's programs, which means easier money.
4. Despite all of the above, male development workers are still blocked by gender stereotypes, which lead them to contradict their own observations. The same male DW will speak not only of women's disadvantages and maturity, but also of men being busy at work and women being housewives with lots of idle time. Thus, women are also seen as an untapped pool of time and energy that can be utilized for development programs.[10]

Obstacles

DOs vary in experience, resources, administrative capacities, creativity, and ability to inspire participants. But even DOs that score high on all counts cannot fully enact their development strategy or successfully execute more modest programs because of the obstacles they face. Among these are the following.

Working conditions. DWs describe their work as meaningful and difficult. For most it means low wages, no benefits, long hours, personal insecurity, and, consequently, family problems. Financial problems are made more difficult by funding agencies and critics who seem to confuse employment in the voluntary sector with volunteer (free) work. Thus, funding agencies tend in their grants to allow only very low administrative overhead and wages or even refuse to allocate wages—as if DWs do not have personal needs or families to take care of. Most rank-and-file workers get Rs 300–500 per month. Rs 300 is similar to the wages of male agricultural laborers, but DWs may be working more than twice as many days in the year. Sometimes the very low pay of DWs is set by the DO leadership at less than the budget would allow. Those in higher positions get better wages, usually Rs 1000–1500, rarely more than Rs 2000—comparable to those of a government clerk, only with much longer hours and none of the benefits.

Female development workers face an additional set of obstacles from their families, society, and colleagues. Male DWs whose patriarchal attitudes and actions keep women out of development work prevent them from doing their best work and from achieving leadership positions, and make their lives difficult through sexual harassment, a double work day, and lower wages.[11]

Funding. DOs need money for salaries, overhead, and programs. Because program participants are destitute, and those with discretionary income generally do not support this kind of work, most DOs must turn to governmental and foreign funding agencies, which then both deliberately and unwittingly shape the programs they fund. Few DOs can pull together enough financial support from these agencies to launch the holistic approach they advocate. Governments tend to fund "safe" projects like literacy and latrines that will alleviate the worst aspects of poverty but not attack it at its source.

Foreign funding agencies tend to be both rigid and fickle. They insist that DOs design programs to fit their categories. They also jump from one development fad to another, making it very difficult for DOs to be innovative, to match their programs to the particular conditions of the area they serve, or to plan very far ahead.

Further, preparing a grant application is costly in time and money. To air mail an inquiry costs a day's wage of most development workers, and three copies of a proposal may cost more than a month's salary. Two to three years may pass before a decision is made, and by then the budget is obsolete and the project handicapped.

Agency visitors or local consultants create additional expenses (often insisting upon star hotels, travel by taxi, and even "gifts" and women) that must be covered out of DW pockets or through creative accounting. According to most development workers, Indians who work as paid funding agency staff or consultants are troublesome because they may bring to this work the same problems that constrain other spheres of Indian life: competition, corruption, jealousy, and favoritism based on caste, religion, locality, language, or politics. Some make recommendations on the grounds of favoritism or, as one DW said, "just sit in Madras or Bangalore and make decisions according to gossip and rumors." Some insist upon bribes. Many DWs described "bitter experiences" with self-serving DWs acting as funding agency consultants, but they will speak out only anonymously: "There are some very big fish in India eating the small fish [he names some]. . . . They have contact with the funding agencies and influence them; so only they receive the funds and the small organizations are in their clutches." "Funding agencies have a consultant, or intermediary [she names some] who are well connected abroad, and who don't care about rural poor. Instead they demand fees for recommending grants—Rs 5–7000 in advance." "Even the consultants don't evaluate; they just collect bribes." "Consultants do cruel things; they collect applications but only forward those that bribe."

Government control. Government requirements for DO registration, reports, and audits are considered burdensome and threatening. According to one DW, "There is no real volunteerism. Instead agencies are instructed by the government which requires six-month financial statements, yearly reports, audits, and registration renewal." Although such formalities may serve a useful purpose, they are also seen as an indirect threat and means of control because they can be used as an excuse to block a DO from receiving foreign funds. According to DWs, "The government wants us to do the work to avoid bureaucratic problems, but also wants us to be in its clutches, so we can't question politicians"; "The government accepts health and socioeconomic programs, but if we work to disturb oppressive structures, the government won't cooperate."

In other words, the government values DOs as mediating structures,[12] not social change agents. The desire to both further and control DOs is evident in the Seventh Plan for 1985–1990, which gave them an important place in the development process but simultaneously exercised further control through the establishment of registered State Consultative Groups and a code of conduct for DOs receiving government funds. These proposals for greater oversight were heavily opposed and were not implemented.

There are further governmental constraints, as local officials must approve projects to be funded by higher levels of government. This requirement presents even more opportunities for corruption. Moreover, it may hold back the entire development process, for if local politicians support local lawlessness, exploitation, and discrimination, the more successful a DO is in opposing such practices, the less likely it is to get local government approval.

Local opposition. DOs may face considerable opposition at the local level. Mentioned most often are moneylenders, landlords, and rich farmers, panchayat officials and ward leaders, members of high castes, and even large DOs. Mentioned less often are bank officials, toddy-shop owners and other merchants, those engaged in illegal operations, and left-wing parties. According to DWs:

> Power groups threaten people who act with freedom. Since the poor depend on the power groups for work, loans, government benefits, they cannot participate easily. The landlords, politicians, and village administrators will send out goondas [thugs] and can even stop government funds."
>
> "The landlord is like a god to village people; political party leaders are middlemen for government politicians; if people become free, the elite will be biased against them."
>
> ' Politicians and local teachers lend money and so have power; . . . they tell people not to participate and sabotage our work."
>
> "Left[ist] politicians give big trouble; they think they will lose ground with the people because they can't compete with us. [They] discuss development organizations and say bad things—that we are CIA and antirevolutionary."

Even churches may oppose DOs that move from charity and relief to awareness and action. Methods used by local opposition to control or drive them out range from harassing participants to murdering DWs.

Consequences. Despite the many idealistic, altruistic, talented, and hardworking DWs, a work context such as this is bound to have a degrading effect on the organizations, the workers, and their work. Funding difficulties, low wages, local opposition, hard working conditions, and lack of opportunity to advance may drive out good workers and draw in less dedicated and competent people. Even the most dedicated workers may lose motivation. In every step of the way, from getting funding to having the books audited, or even just getting a parade permit, there are opportunities for corruption.

Even the goal of nonviolence is compromised. By eschewing the violence of armed revolution, DOs remain enmeshed in the status quo.

Simultaneously trying to undermine it and use it for their own ends, DOs must often cooperate with the status quo, and thereby legitimize its violence. I am not advocating physical violence, which always seems to create more problems than it solves. I do believe, however, that structural violence is as destructive and immoral as physical violence and should be equally avoided and loathed by those who preach nonviolence.

In fact, DOs commit violence when, by necessity or design, they exploit their own workers or those who work for DO enterprises; discriminate on the basis of caste, religion, or gender; or sabotage the work of other DOs. Much of this could be changed if DWs were to use their own techniques of awareness building and empowerment. However, the main reason DOs commit structural violence, I believe, is the context within which they are operating, which tends to degrade and corrupt their workers. Often the only way to get things done is to play by the rules of the very system they are trying to change.

Critics are quick to point out DOs' hypocrisy and failure without understanding the roots of the problems. DOs can improve themselves, but given their worthwhile goals and difficult and often hostile work context, they also need assistance in forming a secure, stable organizational base that sustains altruism and makes the desire to serve others a viable goal. They need more power.

Analysis of Development Organization Power

Social power is generally assessed through the analysis of political economy. Delineating India's political economy is a fairly new endeavor filled with disagreement.[13] Moreover, analysts have ignored gender, the perspective of the "radically disadvantaged,"[14] and grassroots movements. Such ignorance is not surprising because, in India and in the development literature, DOs are primarily analyzed within the social-sectorial framework.

Social Sectors, Sectorial Power

Until recently, sectorial analysts have divided society into three sectors—government, for-profit, and voluntary. A distinguishing feature of each sector is said to be its predominant form of power—the power of the prince, the merchant, and the citizen,[15] or, as Kenneth Boulding has put it, threat, exchange, and love.[16] Thus, governments operate primarily with threat power through law and force, businesses through economic power, and voluntary organizations through integrative power. According to David Korten, "The dominant power of each sector has an important bearing on its organizations' distinctive nature, competence, and social role."[17]

The Voluntary Sector

The word *voluntary,* and the definition of this sector by what it is not—nongovernmental, nonprofit—rather than by what it is, is a source of conceptual confusion in the study of social power. The term *voluntary action* is formally defined as "human endeavor not motivated by private gain or compulsion of law."[18] But its popular understanding creates confusion because it implies that DWs are not only self-motivated, but also independent, autonomous, and unconstrained in their work. They are called catalysts, innovators, experimenters, advocates, and critics who invigorate development processes. They may attempt all of this, but as the Indian case illustrates, they are not autonomous, independent, unconstrained, or uncoerced. Instead, they are limited by resource availability; coerced by threat, violence, and demands for bribes; constrained by regulation and culture; and opposed by every element of society that will not gain from sarvodaya, or self-help.

Another confusion is that the voluntary sector is a benevolence sector, which suggests that DWs are citizen volunteers willing to work for nothing, whose families gladly survive on poverty-level wages. This confusion makes it difficult for DO leaders to be recognized as professionals and DWs as real workers.

A corresponding misconception is that DWs are a homogeneous group of highly motivated and altruistic people engaged in a "personal search for meaningful social contribution."[19] Consequently, they are held to much higher standards than others, and when they fall short, there is disappointment. In fact, DWs are quite heterogeneous in their motivation.

Moreover, the voluntary sector is not what it is said to be, and it is what it is said not to be. DOs may not be governmental in the formal sense, but they are certainly political. Their goal is to rearrange India's power structure. DOs may not be for-profit in the formal sense, but they are certainly economic institutions. Their work involves the transfer of large sums of money, and their goal of distributive justice requires the rearrangement of India's economic structures and institutions. Further, the voluntary sector is not entirely grounded in the ethos of integration and love because its actors utilize all three forms of power. Certainly DOs possess and prefer to use primarily integrative power as they seek to benefit others. Some DWs, through acts of sacrifice and compassion, acquire the emotional power to inspire and motivate others, and on them may be conferred the powers of respect and admiration.

But there is another side to the story. DWs may threaten or may exclude on the basis of caste, gender, and religion. DOs may engage in corrupt exchange relationships to gain "profits" in the form of permits, grants, or doctored audits. Relationships within and among them may be marred by the threat or use of sexual harassment, anonymous letters, and the misleading of funding agencies. Lastly, for survival or aggrandizement, some DOs may operate businesses or, as businesses, engage in profitable exploitation of workers. Thus, greed and the destructive use of power may be found side by side with love, dedication, and self-sacrifice. Clearly there is much more to the voluntary sector than a grants economy of altruistic DOs piping money from selfless funding agencies and governments to the poor.

Coordinators and Professionals

To further guide this exploration of DOs' acquisition and use of power, I will draw upon the work of Pranab Bardhan, and also use the concept of "coordinator class."[20] The coordinator class consists of managers, planners, higher level bureaucrats, and technocrats who conceptualize, coordinate, and oversee tasks that others execute. Its members deal in technical and organizational knowledge and write rules and regulations. Although such people are generally classified as "petite bourgeoisie," "new working class," or "labor aristocracy," Albert and others insist they don't fit even modifications of conventional class categories. They are not capitalists, for they do not fund production; and they are not more privileged members of the working class, for they do not produce. Instead, they generate and control information and expertise and gain power through others' dependency on their monopoly of these resources. This is the signal class of the information age, and its members are found in all sectors of society. Rather than having a distinct form of power, the coordinator class, with its monopoly on knowledge and influence, can employ threat, exchange, and integrative power. Many in the voluntary sector are of the coordinator class, including officers of DOs and funding agencies.

Bardhan[21] shows that the concept of coordinator class is especially useful for understanding socioeconomic development in India. According to Bardhan, there are three dominant proprietary classes in India, the industrial capitalists, the rich farmers, and the professionals.[22] The proprietary classes get their way through power brokers who act as their agents in exchange for big fees in "black money," that is, corrupt money not declared for income taxes.

DOs are antagonists to these proprietary classes and the politicians who protect them. Development workers would agree with Bardhan's analysis, enriching it with their understanding of the local view. In general, DWs neither subscribe to the psychologically based modernization theory of development nor are they caught up in family planning ideology or doomsday economics that preach a simple Malthusian race between population growth and economic growth. Nor do they subscribe to the stages theory of development, for they do not blame India's poverty on a lack of resources, technology, or capability, or the absence of rationality, foresight, or entrepreneurial spirit among poor people. Instead, they speak of India as rich and unjust.

It is important to note that in this system, modern means of repression coexist and grow with the traditional means of social control, the patron-client relationship. According to Bardhan, the patron-client relationship is an asymmetrical relationship that ties the less powerful individually to the more powerful and thus prevents their organizing.

Sometimes participants in DO programs try to recreate patron-client relationships by overreliance on the DO or a particular worker. They come for loans or to settle family problems, and they expect the organization to take care of them should any problems arise. Some DWs take on the role of patron, expecting dependent participants to act as if they are "tied" to them.

Foremost among the Indian proprietary-class professionals, Bardhan believes, are the high-level civilian and military government officials—the educated elite. To protect their scarcity value (their monopoly on information and expertise), the educated elite try to keep the masses uneducated by diverting government educational investment away from them. To increase their power and corrupt income, the elite have acquired powers of licensing, permitting, and regulation. Clearly, the proprietary-class professionals are of the coordinator class.

In the case of Indian DOs, the sectorial perspective is further complicated by the predominance of the coordinator class, which operates in and interconnects all three sectors. DOs are beholden to government sector proprietor coordinator-class professionals and lower-level coordinator-class civil servants as well as the politicians who protect them. They have life-and-death control over DOs through registration, audits, regulations, and funding decisions. How can the DOs be independent or even survive if they bite the hand that feeds them?

Further, in the case of DOs, the official story (or the manifest functions) of the grants economy depicts a downward flow of resources (money, permits, influence, expertise, and information) from higher to lower levels of government, from governments to DOs, from foreign funding agencies and Indian banks to DOs, from more powerful DOs to less powerful ones, from DO officers to employees and program participants, and eventually from participants to their neighbors. Here is a web of co-ordinator-class relationships—from for-profit and government sectors to the voluntary sector, through which resources flow across and down from more to less powerful coordinator-class members.

Then there is the unofficial story, the latent functions of the voluntary sector, the underside of the grants economy. For at each point where a grant is given, there also exists the possibility (and often reality) of exchange and an upward flow of unauthorized resources: black money, gifts, flattery, allegiance, and dependence. These two-way exchanges are likely to constitute a patron-client relationship.

Although the voluntary sector in India is a prototype for more progressive and equitable social relations, it is, therefore, to some unknown extent, also modernizing the traditional way of getting things done by incorporating patron-client relationships into contemporary coordinator-class operations. The same problems remain: corruption, dependency, control, favoritism, threat. The origins of this phenomenon are not clear. Certainly the context of DO operations encourages—even requires—it in many instances.

However, DOs are also engaging in the same behavior among themselves. Some DWs try to acquire power and influence by monopolizing information about funding. They intervene in the funding process as unscrupulous agents and draw other organizations into patron-client relationships through coordinating groups. Other DOs, trying to survive or seeking an easier way, take on the role of submissive and dependent client. Some DO officers try to treat employees (especially females) and participants as clients.

There is nothing inherently immoral about the coordinator class, but when its members try to empower themselves through monopoly and corruption instead of by disseminating useful information, then there are serious ethical and practical problems. In the Indian case, coordinator-class DWs are recreating in the voluntary sector many of the problems it is trying to correct in the rest of society.

Conclusions

This is a story with an unknown ending. With all of its serious troubles, India has at least one source of hope: development organizations with both a vision and a strategy for a just and nonviolent society. But DOs do not have the power and backing they need, and it appears that their lack of resources and difficult working conditions may be taking a toll. Primarily because of their lack of power, DOs themselves get drawn into structural violence, corruption, and get drawn into a web of unhealthy coordinator-class patron-client relationships.

Nevertheless, DOs have been sometimes dramatically effective. Even when they have been unable to initiate truly transformative programs, their more limited projects are enriching the lives of many of India's most oppressed people. More children are going to school. More adults can now read, write, and do practical math; they can locate the right bus, count their change, and read the newspaper to learn what lies outside their village and nation. Everywhere you will find people who better understand sanitation and nutrition; who now grow their own vegetables; who are making new technology such as fuel-efficient, smokeless stoves. Also, you will find people who have attended and even led meetings—even outside of their village—even the women. They have successfully mobilized their village to get drinking water, latrines, schools, roads, and electricity. They have forced local authorities to shut down liquor shops; some have honed traditional skills and learned new ones and have earned higher incomes. Their meals are less skimpy and more nutritious; some have been elected to the local government; some have formed successful cooperative dairies, industries, child care facilities, fair price shops, and savings and credit societies. Most important, they are starting to ask, "Why are things as they are?"

If DOs are to continue this long process of projects evolving into transformative programs, to work in more villages in the most effective and ethical way, they must be given more backing and autonomy by Indian governments, foreign funding agencies, and middle India.

DOs have plenty of integrative power, but working with the most oppressed, they must be strengthened to where they can survive, without bowing to local opposition or being coopted by the status quo as patrons or clients.

Indian governments can help by enforcing existing policies, such as land ownership ceilings.[23] If funding agencies really want to support transformation, they will have to establish genuine partnerships with DOs, attain a greater sensitivity for their situation, find more trustworthy local agents, and pay DWs a decent wage. All of this requires a stable, long-term relationship between DO and funder, built on mutual respect and commitment. DOs must earn this trust through rigorous self-evaluation and clear communication of their goals, strategies, successes, and failures. Funders will have to look, listen, learn, and be patient.

But it cannot stop there; success cannot depend on the continuous presence of DOs and an eternal flow of funds into villages and slums. Nor can success be sustained if it is isolated. According to Korten, "Local power structures are maintained by protective national and international systems."[24] To be successful, he claimed, development initiatives must be linked into these systems. This is difficult, however, because "existing systems tend to be hostile to, rather than supportive of, such initiative."[25] Therefore, Korten suggested that these systems must be changed before development initiatives will be successful.

The next step, then, is Korten's sustainable systems development, which

> looks beyond the individual community and seeks changes in specific policies and institutions at local, national, and global levels. . . . [These strategies] may involve the NGO [i.e., DO] in working with major national agencies to help them reorient their policies and work modes in ways that strengthen broadly-based local control over resources. These strategies may also involve the creation of new institutions of significant

size to provide essential local services on a sustained, self-financing basis.[26]

Here is where those of middle socioeconomic status with their education, experience, resources, and contacts could play a valuable role as regional and national NGO leaders.

In the end, I think we are asking the wrong question. Rather than asking what it will cost to support DOs, we might instead ask what it will cost if we do not. For if Bardhan was correct when he described Indian society as "one of history's most well-entrenched and ornately elaborate ideological systems of legitimizing inequality and exploitation,"[27] the costs of maintaining the injustice of the status quo and its violent consequences are too high to measure, too great to bear.

Notes

1. Korten, *Getting to the 21st Century*, p. 105.
2. A detailed account of the research process, perspective, data, and analyses is given in the Methods Appendix of Moen, *Voluntary Sector Development*. Briefly, data are from three sources: (1) the files of Right Sharing of World Resources, a small U.S. donor agency, on thirty-three DOs in Tamil Nadu; (2) semi-structured interviews with leaders of DOs based in and around the Madurai District of Tamil Nadu; and (3) a very detailed survey of resources and time use in thirty-two landless agricultural households in the Madurai District. These data were supplemented by my broader images developed after three visits and seven months in India, during which time I held discussions with and observed the work of over thirty DOs throughout India. Other supplementary information included annual reports and other publications of these DOs.
3. By focusing on problems, I do not want to leave the wrong impression about Indian people. For every instance of brutality, corruption, and indifference you will find many more of kindness, honesty, and generosity.
4. When the poverty line was calculated in 1990, a kilo of subsidized rice cost Rs 4–5, the local bus fare was about one-half a rupee, and an aerogramme cost Rs 5.
5. Tefft, "India Deals with Economic Crisis."
6. Gupta, "The Political Economy of India."
7. Bardhan, *The Political Economy of Development,* p. 82.
8. Gandhi, *Constructive Programme*, p. 19.
9. The consensus is not entirely wholesome. Whereas the goals and strategies of many DOs are shaped by study, experience, and funding agency guidelines, some do not have a clue about what they are doing or why. Still, they fit the pattern because they are influenced by other DOs or just do whatever is most easily funded.
10. These contradictions are explored in Moen, *Voluntary Sector Development,* where I substantiate that: (1) few, if any, of the participants are housewives; (2) women do more work and have less leisure time than men; (3) men are more likely to spend time and money in self-serving ways such as going to the tea shop and cinema, purchasing snuff and tobacco, and watching television. I conclude that DOs' gender strategy has serious flaws. First, it is women-centered rather than

feminist. That is, although they seek to end the harshest cruelties toward women, DOs are concerned more with how women can benefit society within patriarchal culture and norms. Second, the strategy is both patriarchal and antimale. That is, while DOs avoid significantly disrupting the patriarchal norms and customs constraining both men and women, they consider men too degenerate to create positive social change or even participate in their own uplifting. A winning strategy would enable women to achieve freedom from male dominance, permit men to be more mature and responsible, and allow both to become partners in development.

11. The situation of female development workers and its consequences for DO work are analyzed in detail in Moen, *Voluntary Sector Development.*

12. Berger and Newhaus, *To Empower People.*

13. See Bardhan, *The Political Economy of Development;* Frankel, *India's Political Economy*; Herring, *Land to the Tiller*; Kohli, *The State and Poverty;* Rudolph and Rudolph, *In Pursuit of Lakshmi*; Basu, "State Autonomy"; and Gupta, "The Political Economy of India."

14. Basu, "State Autonomy," p. 483.

15. Nerfin, Drabek, and Ahooja-Patel, *World Economy in Transition.*

16. Boulding, *The Economy of Love and Fear*; *Three Faces of Power.*

17. Korten, *Getting to the 21st Century*, pp. 96–97.

18. Van Till, *Mapping the Third Sector*, p. ix.

19. Khan and Thomas, "Role of Voluntary Agencies," p. 6.

20. Albert et al., *Liberating Theory.*

21. Bardhan, *The Political Economy of Development.*

22. Bardhan excluded landlords from the proprietary classes because he believed their numbers are no longer significant. He may underestimate the staying power of landlords in Tamil Nadu, where DWs nearly always refer to the oppressor of landless agricultural laborers as landlords, though they include wealthy farmers in this category. Although the remaining landlords may not fit Bardhan's proprietary class of rich farmers who generate their wealth from profitable cultivation and bonded labor, they are certainly a major exploitative class.

23. Earlier, I stated that even if the Indian government got serious about poverty alleviation, it could not take the necessary steps without the massive mobilization of the oppressed, DOs envision. Now here I say DOs must have the cooperation of the government. This is not a contradiction, but an acknowledgment that sarvodaya may not come without mutual reinforcement. It may not progress in linear but in pendular fashion.

24. Korten, *Getting to the 21st Century*, p. 120.

25. Ibid.

26. Ibid.

27. Bardhan, *The Political Economy of Development*, p. 82.

Bibliography

Ahooja-Patel, Krishna, Anne Gordon Drabek, and Marc Nerfin (eds.), *World Economy in Transition: Essays Presented to Surendra Patel on His Sixtieth Birthday* (Oxford and New York: Pergamon Press, 1986).

Albert, Michael, Leslie Cagan, Noam Chomsky, Robin Itahnel, Mel King, Lydia Sargent, and Holly Sklar, *Liberating Theory* (Boston: South End, 1986).

Anheier, Helmut K. "Indigenous Voluntary Associations, Nonprofits, and Development in Africa," in Walter Powell (ed.), *The Nonprofit Sector: A Research Handbook* (New Haven: Yale University Press, 1986).

Bardhan, P. *The Political Economy of Development in India* (Delhi: Oxford University Press, 1984).

Basu, Amrita. "State Autonomy and Agrarian Transformation in India." *Comparative Politics* (1990): 498–500.

Berger, Peter, and Richard Newhaus. *To Empower People: The Role of Mediating Structures in Public Policy* (Washington DC: American Enterprise Institute, 1977).

Boulding, Kenneth. *The Economy of Love and Fear* (Belmont, CA: Wadsworth Publishing Co., 1973).

———. *Three Faces of Power* (Newbury Park: Sage Publications, 1989).

Das Gupta, Jyotirindra. "India: Democratic Becoming and Combined Development," in Larry Diamond, Juan Linz, and Seymour Martin Lipset (eds.), *Democracy in Developing Countries, Volume 3, Asia* (Boulder, CO: Lynne Rienner Publishers, 1989).

Etzioni, Amita. *The Active Society* (New York: Free Press, 1968).

Gandhi, M. K. *Constructive Programme* (1941, 1945) (Ahmedabad: Navajivan, 1989).

Garilao, Ernesto. "Indigenous NGOs as Strategic Institutions," in Krishna Ahooja-Patel, Anne Gordon Drabek, and Marc Nerfin (eds.), *World Economy in Transition: Essays Presented to Surendra Patel on His Sixtieth Birthday* (Oxford and New York: Pergamon Press, 1986).

Gupta, Akhil. "The Political Economy of Post-Independence India." *The Journal of Asian Studies* 48 (4) (November 1989): 787–797.

Frankel, Francine R. *India's Political Economy, 1947–1977* (Princeton: Princeton University Press).

Herring, Ronald J. *Land to the Tiller* (New Haven: Yale University Press, 1983).

———. "The Lessons of Early Capitalism." *IDS Newsletter* 6 (3) (Summer 1989): 3.

Khan, M. Z., and M. E. Thomas. "Role of Voluntary Agencies in Rural Development." *Social Change* 19 (1) (March): 3–12.

Kohli, Atul. *The State and Poverty in India* (Cambridge: Cambridge University Press, 1987).

Korten, David C. *Getting to the 21st Century* (West Hartford, CT: Kumarian, 1990).

Moen, Elizabeth. *Voluntary Sector Grass Roots Development in Tamilnadu* (Gandhigram: Gandhigram Rural Institute, 1992).

Powell, Walter (ed.). *The Nonprofit Sector: A Research Handbook* (New Haven: Yale University Press, 1986).

Rudolph, Lloyd, and Susanne Rudolph. *In Pursuit of Lakshmi: The Political Economy of India* (Chicago: University of Chicago Press, 1987).

Smith, David H. "Four Sectors or Five? Retaining the Member-Benefit Sector." *Nonprofit and Voluntary Sector Quarterly* 20 (2) (Summer): 137–150.

Tefft, Sheila. "India Deals with Economic Crisis." *The Christian Science Monitor* (July 3, 1991): 7.

Van Til, Jon. *Mapping the Third Sector* (New York: The Foundation Center, 1988).

13

Justice Without Violence: Theoretical Synthesis

Heidi Burgess & Guy Burgess

The studies in this volume illustrate a variety of ways in which people who believe themselves to be victims of acute injustice can seek remedies without resorting to violence. Some of these are cases of traditional nonviolent direct action, but other approaches are described as well. Thus, the picture being drawn is multifaceted and complex—and broader than that of most other nonviolence and justice literature.

In order to give the project some cohesiveness, the project team started with an initial theory of nonviolence based on alternative sources of power. This theory utilized Kenneth Boulding's trichotomous conception of power, which states that power derives from three sources: threats, exchange, and love (that is, the integrative system).[1] These methods of persuasion can be used either singly or in combination to alter power structures and, therefore, to persuade one's adversaries to behave differently.

As the project developed, however, our theoretical approach broadened considerably. In addition to examining the interaction of threats, exchange, and love as we initially planned to do, we realized that many aspects of the conflict context were important as well. These factors included the nature of the injustice, the characteristics and goals of the opposing groups, the historical context, psychological and structural factors in the societies involved, and the presence and nature of intervention from outside groups. These factors interacted with strategic and tactical considerations and the response of the dominant group to determine the degree of success of any particular nonviolent effort.

The analysis was complicated by the problem that all of the variables of interest were interrelated, so that a change in any one, including the so-called dependent, or outcome, variables, can cause changes in the independent, or input, variables. The case studies themselves, as well the analysis presented below, are first attempts to illustrate how some of these interrelationships work.

Readers will note that many of the categories of variables discussed below are equivalent to those discussed earlier in Chapter 2, although others are not. We learned as we went along that some variables that we had not originally identified were important, while others that we had expected to be significant did not appear so. In still other instances, we simply were unable to get enough information from these case studies to shed light on some of the original questions, which are thus absent from the concluding chapter.

Nature of the Injustice

At the outset, we were forced to grapple with the meaning of *justice*. The term means different things to different people, and disparate belief systems have equally valid, but varying views of what constitutes justice, so we declined to impose a common definition in all cases. Rather, we decided to examine only situations of such profound injustice that few would challenge the assertion that it was taking place. The source or nature of the injustice, however, varied considerably from case to case.

Our review of the literature, the theoretical work of Kenneth Boulding and Doug Bond, and our case studies all suggest that the nature of the injustice plays an important role in determining which nonviolent strategies are most likely to be effective. In particular, we have identified the following four features as being important.

Economic Versus Political Injustice

One important distinction was the degree to which complaints were politically or economically based. Political injustice involves violations of individual liberties similar to those covered by the U.S. Bill of Rights (for example, freedom of speech, freedom of religion, right to due process, protection from cruel and unusual punishments, and the right to vote in free democratic elections).

In contrast, economic injustice involves the failure to provide citizens with the minimum necessities of life, especially in cases where a society's elite lives in relative luxury. Violations of these rights can result either from the maldistribution of wealth or a society's overall poverty—or both.

Boulding observes that there are two views of economic justice. On the one hand there is the belief, underlying most market economies, that people should get what they deserve and, therefore, inequality of incomes is desirable and to be expected. A competing view is that the world's resources should be shared equally. This is the avowed idea of the communist, and to a lesser extent, the socialist world.

Given the political will, dominant elites can remedy political rights violations relatively easily (as was seen in Eastern Europe). Maldistribution problems can also be corrected, though this is more difficult since it requires dominant groups to make significant economic sacrifices. In contrast, efforts to remedy economic injustice stemming from societywide poverty, inadequate human and physical capital, limited natural resources, or other resource factors can be time consuming and difficult, as the experiences of Eastern Europe, Nicaragua, and India demonstrate. Nevertheless, such economic shortfalls are generally perceived as "unjust" by the victims, and remedies are often sought, either through violent or nonviolent means. If a challenging group makes demands that are beyond the control of the dominant group, however, the likelihood of their success is, obviously, very low.

According to Stephen Thomas, Eastern Europe and the Soviet Union have made rapid progress in diminishing political injustice over the last few years, but economic injustice remains severe and may even increase as political justice is attained. China, on the other hand, has achieved a remarkable degree of economic justice for a poor nation with the lowest amount of arable land per person of any nation in the world. The cost of this economic success, however, is a continuing high level of political injustice.

In his chapter Boulding outlines another approach that parallels our distinction between political and economic rights. For him, these concepts offer both opportunity and danger. For example, political rights and freedoms, while highly desirable, threaten to produce anarchy if pursued too far. Economic rights involve the just distribution of resources. But here, the danger is that those who are supposed to enforce justice will instead enforce tyranny and gross inequality.

Legitimated Injustice Versus Tyranny

Another important distinction is that between legitimated injustice and tyranny. In the case of tyranny, which often, though not always, involves outside oppressors, the subordinate group clearly understands the illegitimate and exploitative nature of its relationship with the dominant group. Such tyrants have to employ a domination strategy based on terror and military force in order to maintain their position in the face of widespread hatred. The best example of tyranny described in our case studies was the domination of the Soviet republics and Eastern Europe by the Soviet military and the KGB. In such cases the dominant group is viewed as so illegitimate that the oppressed can be expected to rise up in instant revolt should they ever perceive a significant weakening of the ability of their oppressor to carry out its threats. This is what happened in Eastern Europe when Gorbachev made it clear that Soviet tanks would no longer support the region's communist regimes.

At the other end of the spectrum is legitimated injustice, which arises when a national belief system sanctifies and rationalizes the domination of some groups by others. As Elizabeth Mathiot (Moen) observed in India, the subordinate group may, to some extent, believe that its subordinate position is justified. "There is little rebellion among the most oppressed [people in India], partly because everywhere remnants of semifeudal patron-client relationships and mentality persist."[2] This, Moen asserts, leads to a "curious form of solidarity based on the oppressed's fear and worship of the oppressor."[3] In such circumstances, Moen argues, heightening the awareness of injustice and the possibility of achieving an improved situation is a critical first step in any nonviolent campaign for justice.

In other cases, such as South Africa, the dominant group may rationalize the legitimacy of its dominance, even though most of the subordinate group views it as illegitimate and tyrannical.

Boulding observes that declines in legitimacy are often associated with the rise of expectations and unfulfilled promises. This, he suspects, is one of the principal causes of the collapse of the communist world.[4]

Majority Versus Minority Domination

Successful nonviolent action must also take into account the difference between injustice perpetrated by a majority on a minority, and injustice inflicted by a minority on a majority. When a minority is oppressed by a dominant group with grassroots majority support, the majority of the population is much more likely to view the injustice as legitimate and to dispute the notion that the minority group is being unjustly treated. This is the situation that characterized the extreme poor studied by Moen in India. To a lesser extent, Thomas feels that it also characterizes the majority Chinese view of the persecution of a relatively small and radical Chinese student population.

Similarly, the Israeli government has enjoyed fairly strong legitimacy with the dominant Jewish population of Israel. Until recently they were able to resist the intifada's demands for Palestinian self-determination. However, the intifada succeeded in splitting Israeli public opinion regarding the justification of continued occupation and repression of the Palestinians. This division in public opinion undoubtedly played a major role in Israel's decision to seek a peace accord with the Palestinians in the fall of 1993.

In other cases, the majority may be suppressed by a relatively small, minority elite. This was the case in the control of Eastern Europe by the Soviet Union and its client governments and was also the case in South Africa. In such cases, the domination is much less likely to be viewed as legitimate by the subordinate group. This recognition of injustice is necessary to stimulate pressure (either violent or nonviolent) for change.

Internal Versus External Domination

Injustice can be perpetrated either by external occupying powers or by a dominant elite within a particular country. For example, the Soviet Union was an external power dominating Eastern Europe; the Chinese elite that perpetrated the Tiananmen Square Massacre had internal origins. Hybrid cases are also possible. For example, in South Africa the external British Empire eventually led to an internal South African white elite.

Characteristics of the Dominant and Subordinate Groups

In addition to the nature of the injustice, the characteristics of the dominant and subordinate groups and the relationship between those groups was also important in determining the nonviolent groups' strategy and outcomes. Of particular importance were the nature of the ruling regime, the sources of the regime's power, the size and level of organization of the subordinate group(s), the dominant and subordinate groups' legitimacy, and the racial/cultural similarities or dissimilarities between the groups.

Nature of the Ruling Regime

Many casual observers of nonviolence assume that nonviolent action works better in democratic contexts than it does under authoritarian regimes. The assumption seems to be that democratic regimes have a higher tolerance for dissent; authoritarian regimes would be more likely to repress any nonviolent challenge to governmental authority. Although such repression did occur in China, it was not effectively applied in many other nondemocratic systems we studied (for example, those of Eastern Europe and the former Soviet Union). However, considerable repression did occur in the formal democracies of South Africa, India, and Israel. Thus the cases studied here seem not to support the hypothesis that democracies facilitate effective nonviolence more than do authoritarian regimes.

Several of our authors (Scarritt, Moen, Arabajan, Bond, and Burgess) did note the inverse effect, however. Nonviolent action does seem to stimulate demands for increased democratization of authoritarian regimes. James Scarritt's study of Central and Southern Africa suggests such an effect, as does Moen's study of India and Zaven Arabajan's analysis of changes in the USSR. Thomas, too, suggests that this was true in China. Though the 1989 movement was crushed, it seems likely to have sowed the seeds of further demands for political change.

More important than democratization, perhaps, is a regime's commitment to socioeconomic justice and at least some civil and political rights protection. The most successful case of negotiation presented in this volume was that used in Nicaragua, involving the Sandinista government, which was not formally democratic. However, the Sandinista regime was committed to socioeconomic justice and a certain degree of civil and political rights protection as basic principles. China, too, was strongly committed to socioeconomic justice, but was not at all interested in granting civil and political rights. Negotiation failed in that case, indicating perhaps that some economic and political rights are important for successful nonviolent change, though formal democracy, per se, is not.

Sources of Government Power

Another factor of importance to nonviolent change is the strength and character of the dominant group's power. Sharp presented a theory of power as it relates to nonviolent direct action that seems to apply very well to several of our cases.[5] Power, Sharp wrote, derives from six sources: authority, human resources, skills and knowledge, intangible psychological factors, material resources, and sanctions.[6] When the dominant group in a society possesses high levels of these factors, their power is strong and they are able to influence others to strengthen it further. However, a shortage of one or more of these sources can decrease the ability to influence others, which will further reduce the dominant group's power. A feedback system is thereby produced, which can eventually lead to the collapse of the ruling elite. This dynamic seems to have been illustrated in a number of the cases presented in this book, particularly Eastern Europe and the Soviet Union.

Dominant Group Legitimacy

The Communist elites in the Soviet Union and Eastern European countries apparently lacked the necessary combination of human and material resources, skills, and knowledge to enable them to deliver the socioeconomic benefits they had promised. This lack of effectiveness, coupled with corruption and incompetence, diminished government legitimacy and, consequently, the Communist Party's power. For instance, writing about Poland, Edelstein says that the Polish centralized economy was completely ineffective and incompetently run. It lacked the flexibility to incorporate technological change and consequently was unable to deliver a high quality of life for Polish citizens. Economic incompetence, he says, was compounded by political incompetence.

> [F]rom Wladyslaw Gomulka to Edward Gierek to Wojciech Jaruzelski, the official leadership lacked political skill. . . . Of Gomulka, Brown wrote . . . "He possessed neither intellectual ability, nor political flair; nor administrative nor economic expertise. Scouring the whole East European scene these last forty years it is difficult to find a leader less competent."[7]

Loss of legitimacy of the dominant group appears to be a key criterion of challenge group success in many of our cases. The rapid fall of the Eastern European and Soviet regimes was largely due to the loss of governmental legitimacy. The Chinese government, to the contrary, enjoyed a relatively high degree of legitimacy based on its socioeconomic success. This success enabled it to repress the student movement and still retain power and some legitimacy, which was, as Thomas suggests, somewhat tarnished after the Tiananmen Massacre.

Subordinate Group Characteristics

Also important were the characteristics of the subordinate group in our studies. Key factors included: (a) relative size of the protest groups; (b) level of organization of the groups; and (c) legitimacy of the nonviolent movement and its leadership.

Size. Many students of nonviolent action have found the size of the subordinate group to be an important determinant of nonviolent action, for example, Kuper[8] and Oppenheimer.[9] They argued that nonviolence is more successful if the challenge group is relatively small; if the challenge group is too large, it will threaten the dominant group to the degree that change will be more difficult.

Our findings lead us to question this hypothesis. Although small nonviolent groups may generate less fear, and, therefore, are less likely to be repressed, they are also more likely to be ignored. Large movements supported by major portions of the population, as in Eastern Europe and the Soviet Union, for example, fared much better than smaller movements with less support by the general population, such as the one in China.

Level of organization. Another theoretical proposition is that the challenge group needs to be well organized, with clear goals, strategies, and tactics in order to be effective. This hypothesis does seem to be supported by our cases, although the evidence is somewhat ambiguous.

The Polish Solidarity movement was very well organized, had good communication, well-defined objectives, and the means to attain them. The popular resistance to the Soviet Communist Party was less well organized. Most of the new parties developed clear strategies and tactics and had reasonably clear goals, but they did not all work together or share goals for the future. Nor did they have a clear image of what "democracy" really was or how they wanted to structure an alternative society.

The Chinese student democracy movement was even less organized. The student activists in the 1989 movement did have a simple strategic plan based on classical nonviolent techniques. But much of the protest was spontaneous, planned on the square, as events evolved. Lack of consensus about goals was a serious problem. Although most of the students wanted

enhanced civil and political rights, there was little agreement about movement objectives. Some leaders called for the abolition of the Communist
Party and removal of the ruling elite. Others probably would have settled
for a reform-minded party under the leadership of Zhao Ziyang, who was
willing to make some concessions toward civil and political rights. But
none of the democracy movements in China have had a clear vision of
what should replace the current system.[10]

Tactical disagreement and disorganization can even be blamed, in
part, for causing the Tiananmen Square Massacre. According to Thomas's
analysis, many of the student groups on the square were ready to leave by
June 3, as it became clear that the military was likely to move in soon with
force. But others, especially those who had recently come to the square
from afar, were unwilling to leave. It was mostly those outsiders who were
still in the square on the night of June 3 when the tanks rolled in.

Challenge Group Legitimacy

Another key variable in our cases appears to be the legitimacy of the challenging group and its leadership. Just as legitimacy is critical for the dominant group to maintain power, so it is for the group challenging that
power. In Poland, Lech Walesa and Solidarity had far more legitimacy
with the Polish population than did the government. In Russia, Boris
Yeltsin brought a high level of legitimacy to the democracy movement.
The strength of this legitimacy was demonstrated in the failed 1991 right-
wing coup attempt in which the general population and the military supported Yeltsin, not the Communist Party elite.

Many advocates of nonviolence suggest that the challenge groups'
avoidance of violence increases its legitimacy. In his chapter on the Middle East, for instance, Kazak observes that the intifada won international
sympathy and support, as well as support within Israel itself, by maintaining a largely nonviolent stance. Israel's violent repression of the intifada
further enhanced the legitimacy of the Palestinians and diminished the legitimacy of the hard-line Israeli government. This dynamic clearly illustrates Sharp's concept of political jiu-jitsu.[11]

Group Similarities and Differences

In addition to the characteristics of each of the conflicting groups, the similarities and differences between the groups in conflict appeared to be important in determining outcome. As has been suggested previously by Oppenheimer, if racial or cultural differences between groups are great, the
nonviolent group will be perceived as "foreign, strange, subhuman or uncivilized."[12] This perception makes repression easier and successful nonviolent action more difficult. Several of our cases suggest this idea. For

example, Moen observes that in Tamil Nadu, India, women and untouchables are perceived as lesser beings. They are treated as objects to be exploited—even murdered—as best suits the dominant group or individual's needs. Untouchable children, she says, are sent away to serve as bonded laborers, whole families slave in quarries, women are murdered so the husbands can remarry and get more dowry, and female infanticide and aborting of female fetuses is common. Despite judicial and extragovernmental efforts to change these conditions, they have proven to be highly persistent.

Kazak finds a similar problem in the Middle East, where belief systems perpetuate intergroup hostility. Belief systems not only influence societies, nations, and cultures to behave differently, but often, he says, they cause a sense of superiority or hostility toward those with opposing belief systems. Therefore, in multicultural societies, the potential for culturally legitimated unjust treatment of minorities is very high.

Historical Context

The historical context was another important factor determining the nonviolent options chosen and how well they worked. Again there were several features of interest, the first being the history of violence and nonviolence in the society.

The Role of Violence

One might assume that societies with a strong history of violence would tend to continue to use violence in their current struggles, and those with a history of successful nonviolence might be expected to use that approach more often. The findings of our case studies do not support that assumption. Arabajan, for instance, writes about the Soviet Union: "Traditionally, beginning in the Middle Ages, social conflict in Russia was waged with violence and accompanied by chaos and bloodshed."[13] The current socioeconomic and political upheavals are not unprecedented, he says, but rather have occurred (in other forms for other reasons) several times before in Russian history. Thus the current situation is deeply rooted in the country's history and traditional political structure. One might therefore have expected the Soviet people to turn again to violence to achieve their political goals.

This resort to violence has happened to some extent, especially in the southern republics, where violence has been severe. However, Arabajan observes that in May 1991, Soviet citizens were increasingly opposed to the use of violence for political ends. Increasing numbers of people had been turning to demonstrations, strikes, and other nonviolent alternatives to force the government to change its policies and structure. The outcome

of the summer 1991 attempted coup and the relatively peaceful disman-
tling of the Soviet political structure seems to support this contention.

Other cases in this volume also seem to negate the importance of a
history of violence in the choice of challenge group strategies. Violence
has long characterized the Israeli/Palestinian conflict, yet the intifada has
turned, in part, to nonviolence in recent years to promote the Palestinian's
cause.[14] Nicaragua, too, has emerged from a long history of violent repression and resistance to a culture and political structure more concerned
with healing and forgiveness.

These cases seem to correspond to Zielonka's observations about
Poland: "Violence abounds in modern Polish history, and the Polish people have given widespread support to armed resistance, especially where it
counters military invasion by a foreign power. One could even say that
armed resistance was, in a way, cultivated by Polish culture and tradition."[15] Yet Solidarity turned to nonviolence, Zielonka argued, for three
reasons. First, there were tactical considerations—they thought it would
achieve the desired goals with far fewer casualties. Second, there were
doctrinal issues (nonviolence better corresponded philosophically with the
goals of self-government and grassroots participation). The third reason
was ethical. Nonviolence better reflected the Christian concepts of social
love and justice than did violence. These factors, Zielonka stated, are far
more important in the choice of a resistance strategy than are history and
the tradition of violence in a culture.

Belief Systems

Although a society's history of violence did not seem to determine the
choice of violent or nonviolent strategies in our cases, cultural belief systems did seem to play an important role. As discussed earlier, belief systems help determine if particular actions are considered unjust or legitimate. When actions are perceived as illegitimate, resistance or rebellion
is much more likely.

Belief systems also help determine whether resistance that occurs will
be violent or not. Some value systems provide a moral justification for the
use of violence; others encourage nonviolence and constrain violent response. For instance, in discussing Nicaragua, Paul Wehr and Sharon Erickson Nepstad stress that a variety of normative pressures have encouraged the use of nonviolence over violence. The Sandinista revolution, they
say, "was gentle, as such movements go. Reason not coercion, conciliation
not division, nonviolence not violence were to be guiding principles for
transforming society."[16] While such principles were not always followed,
Wehr and Nepstad say, the Sandinistas made a good-faith effort to do so.

Among the normative pressures that restrained violence in Nicaragua,
religious values and the participation of women were extremely important.

As an example of religious values tempering violence, Wehr and Nepstad point to Father Miguel D'Escoto, the Nicaraguan foreign minister in the mid-1980s, who led a nonviolent campaign of fasting, prayer, and walking to "rise up against war, repression, hatred, violence, external intervention."[17]

In his chapter on the Palestinian conflict, Kazak, too, focuses on the importance of belief systems in determining conflict strategies. "An examination of the ideological and sociopsychological patterns of different cultures," Kazak asserts, "suggests that each culture promotes and nurtures different violent or nonviolent attitudes and behavior."[18] Thus, he suggests, some cultures or belief systems may encourage nonviolent responses to injustice; others may encourage violence. Despite the high level of violence used by all the major religious groups in the Middle East, Kazak observes that Christianity and Judaism also contain strong justifications for the use of nonviolent techniques.

"[Do] unto others as you would have them do unto you" is a basic Christian precept, Kazak argues, that translates into the dictum that "thou shalt never use force against others."[19] Similarly, "while Judaism does not appear to require a commitment to nonviolence in order to fulfill its precepts, it so sharply curtails the use of violence that nonviolence becomes more often than not the only meaningful way to fulfill a life dedicated to truth, justice, and peace."[20]

Islam focuses on these issues within the context of jihad. As Kazak explains, in Islamic scholarship jihad can mean either the use of military action and efforts to expand the sphere of Islam (what is commonly referred to in the West as "holy war") or it can refer to a moral effort of self-purification.[21] Sheikh Mahmud Shaltut, a leading Muslim scholar, argued that the Qur'an does not condone violence, as is commonly thought.

> [P]eople would do well to learn the Qur'anic rules with regard to fighting, its causes and its ends, and so come to recognize the wisdom of the Koran in this respect: Its desire for peace and its aversion against bloodshed and killing for the sake of the vanities of the world and out of sheer greediness and lust.[22]

Thus, jihad is not necessarily violent and may, in fact, support and encourage the nonviolent approach of the intifada. However, Kazak maintains that radical Muslims preach the revolutionary character of jihad, not its spiritual aspects. They believe the idea that jihad refers to a struggle for self-control against temptation to be a myth, deliberately spread by Westerners in an effort to weaken the Muslims' will to fight. The difference of opinion on this central Islamic concept is a source of considerable conflict within Islamic society—and is a key factor determining strategy to be used in the Palestinians' struggle against Israel.

Belief systems, combined with the social, legal, and political structures of a society, play a major role in determining that society's threshold
of violence. If that threshold is high, nonviolent techniques are more likely
to succeed. If the threshold is low, however, successful nonviolent strategy
must involve efforts to use and strengthen nonviolent components of the
society's belief systems.

Changing belief systems is not easy. Kazak observes that many Arabs
view nonviolence as a Western idea and they reject it on that basis. To
succeed in the Middle East, he argues, nonviolence must be justified
through indigenous (that is, Christian, Jewish, and Muslim) belief systems,
not one imported from the West.

Violence Escalation

Our cases suggest that the escalation of violence causes yet more violence.
Once violence breaks out and lives are lost, the motivations of all parties
shift dramatically away from abstract conceptions of justice and toward
the more immediate goal of self-defense and the emotional demands of revenge. Boulding referred to this as the "sacrifice trap": "If people can be
persuaded to make sacrifices for something, their identity becomes deeply
involved with it and they find it extremely hard to admit to themselves that
their sacrifices have been in vain. Consequently it is easy to persuade them
to make more sacrifices."[23] If one were to admit that the use of violence
was a mistake, one must also admit that lives lost and sacrifices made were
pointless or counterproductive. This is an extremely difficult step to take
emotionally and politically. Thus, violence tends to beget violence. Nonviolent strategies, however, can break the escalation spiral. Although the
more threatening of these strategies may still evoke a violent response,
students of nonviolence argue that it will be less severe than the response
to violent confrontation.

Unpredictability of Violence

In the project's initial formulation we viewed the selection of violence and
nonviolence as simple rational choice. We assumed the oppressed would
examine alternative strategies for correcting fundamental injustices and
pick the one with the best cost/benefit ratio. Our goal was equally simple—to ensure that nonviolent options were on the activists' agenda. Kenneth Boulding reminded us, however, that resorting to violence is a complicated and largely uncontrollable process. Boulding has provided a rich
vision of both the evolutionary changes that lead to justice conflicts and
the complex and unpredictable forces leading to violence.

Given that the resort to violence has irreducible random elements,
Boulding suggests that successful nonviolent strategies must work to limit

a broad range of stresses that could lead to violence should events take an unfortunate course. Paul Wehr and Sharon Nepstad's violence-limiting mechanisms, discussed below, offer a practical guide to limiting such stresses.

Structural Factors

Structural factors are a key determinant of the level of violence in justice conflicts. Some political, legal, or economic structures can encourage the use of violence, on the part of either challenge groups or the state. Others can inhibit it and encourage nonviolent response to injustice. Several examples of each of these situations were examined by the authors in this book.

Constraints on Violence

In their chapter on Nicaragua, Wehr and Nepstad describe the "violence-inhibiting, conflict-moderating, justice-producing constraints" that operated in Nicaraguan society during the decade of Sandinista control. These include: (1) institutional constraints, (2) normative restraints, and (3) the innovative use of conflict management.[24]

Institutional constraints on violence included the political and legal systems of the Sandinista state. The Sandinista Constitution guaranteed human and civil rights and judicial grievance procedures. Although there were some attempts to restrict political opposition, open repression, Wehr and Nepstad say, was rare. The political costs of such opposition were too great.

Socioeconomic structures created by the Sandinistas also contributed to the nonviolent resolution of conflicts. The national health, agrarian reform, education, and basic needs programs measurably reduced social inequality. These programs also provided mediating organizations that could respond to justice grievances and resolve problems before violence broke out.

A third set of structural factors limiting violence were the integrative affiliations and organizational linkages encouraged in Sandinista Nicaragua. "There were cross-cutting religious, political, and social ties that bridged existing cleavages."[25] These linkages limited the tendency to respond with violence in conflicts and facilitated the use of what Wehr and Lederach elsewhere referred to as *confianza* mediators.[26]

Scarritt's analysis of Africa also refers to the importance of structural factors in determining violent and nonviolent response to actual or threatened injustice. Levels of discrimination and demographic and ecological stress are among the factors Scarritt suggests cause rebellion. Shifting coalitions also, he says, contribute to a feeling of insecurity among groups and tend to cause a high level of protest, most frequently nonviolent.

Although the Soviet Union placed many constraints on nonviolent action in civil protest, it also constrained violence in some instances. Arabajan refers to both cultural and structural constraints on violence in the Baltic states of the Soviet Union, which he suggests have a higher "level of development and political culture" than did the Soviet southern republics, where violence was the predominant response to injustice. Although violence was culturally accepted and politically encouraged in the southern republics, it was unacceptable in the Baltic region, where governments and people relied instead on nonviolent direct action and parliamentary procedures.

Constraints on Nonviolence

Social and political structures of a society can also constrain nonviolence. The Soviet political system contained a great number of institutional constraints on nonviolence, which were slowly overcome in the late 1980s with continued public pressure and governmental liberalization. Before glasnost, any speech, literature, or organization hostile to the Soviet state or communist rule was severely repressed. Dissidents were active, but they could neither gain strong popular support nor effect meaningful change. With glasnost and perestroika, however, people were able to talk and associate more freely, and dissenting views were more openly voiced.

Yet significant changes came not only from popular pressure, according to Arabajan, but through the parliamentary process. The monopoly of the Soviet Communist Party was eliminated in 1990 when Clause 6 of the Soviet Constitution was repealed. After that, all registered political parties were legal.

Nevertheless, Communist control of the media, the army, the KGB, the courts, and huge amounts of property limited the power of the other political groups until after the August 1991 coup, which further discredited the old guard and led to its demise in late 1991.

The Indian case also illuminates structural limitations to successful nonviolent change. India has a very complex social structure that discriminates on the basis of class, gender, caste, ethnicity, religion, language, and locality. "Those on the bottom of these multiple hierarchies," Moen says, "suffer greatly." The bottom of the hierarchy, she says, is made up of a "very large underclass of powerless, unaware, and debt-ridden people. Their illiteracy, poor health, tradition, addictions, superstitions, fear, passivity, and internal divisions reinforce the stratification, making the powerful more so and the powerless also more so."[27]

Additional obstacles to nonviolent change in India include difficult conditions for development workers with long hours, low pay, personal and organizational insecurity, lack of project funds, excessive government control, local opposition from moneylenders and landlords, and the consequent lack of commitment of the development workers themselves.

Outside Influence and Intervention

A common factor in our cases was the influence and intervention of external parties in the justice conflicts. This could facilitate or impede nonviolence, depending on the nature of the intervention and the intervenor. However, the influence did not always operate as intended because of larger international conflicts and other intervening factors.

Complicating Conflicts

Justice conflicts can be dramatically intensified when other major conflicts are superimposed upon them. For example, during most of the 1980s, the U.S.-Soviet cold war was played out in Nicaragua and other Central American countries as a "proxy war." This situation greatly intensified and prolonged these conflicts and made their resolution exceedingly difficult.

Wehr and Nepstad see U.S. intervention in Nicaragua as one of the main obstacles to nonviolent conflict resolution there. Political and economic destabilization from the outside, they report, was a major stimulator of conflict, as was the constant militarization going on in Nicaragua from 1980 through 1988. This militarization was a function of the U.S./Soviet military competition being played out in what Wehr and Nepstad call "proxy" wars. This dynamic also occurred in the Palestinian-Israeli conflict, which was not only a conflict of Middle Eastern belief systems, but also one in which U.S. and Soviet interests were at odds. This dynamic was also true in the Palestinian-Israeli conflict, where Soviet and U.S. interests were also at odds.

Withdrawal of External Support for the Dominant Group

The international context was also critical in Eastern European justice struggles, though in a different way. Before perestroika, most of the Eastern European governments were kept in power by a Soviet presence. Once Gorbachev removed this threat, the regimes' ability to survive quickly deteriorated.

A similar dependence on outside support has characterized the Israeli-Palestinian conflict. U.S. support of the Israelis has facilitated their continued hard-line stand against Palestinian autonomy. The United States in 1992 began to withhold some support to get Israel to modify its stance regarding settlement in the West Bank and Gaza Strip. This modification is likely to have contributed to Israel's decision in the fall of 1993 to sign a peace accord with the Palestinians. Although it is still unclear whether this peace will hold, the accord signifies a major change of position on the part of Israel regarding the occupied territories.

International Opinion and Sanctions

Another form of outside influence on justice conflicts was the effect of international public opinion and diplomatic pressure. In some cases this pressure involved public censure; in others it involved imposition of economic and political sanctions. Although the perception of many economists and political scientists is that external sanctions are largely ineffective in forcing governments to change repressive and aggressive policies, the analysis of sanctions in South Africa by Kaempfer et al. suggests otherwise. These authors acknowledge that sanctions "seldom inflict major pain on the target economies." However, sanctions can affect interest groups' ability to mobilize internal and external support. Therefore, Kaempfer et al. argue that "even sanctions with weak economic impacts on the target country can nevertheless induce political changes there, although not necessarily in the directions preferred by the sanctioners."[28] The last phrase is critical. The authors conclude that sanctions may have had a short-term positive effect on antiapartheid efforts in South Africa, but over the long term, sanctions diminished the incomes of South African blacks, thereby stifling the antiapartheid movements.

Despite this negative finding, Kaempfer et al. also observe that sanctions do have what they call a "signal" or "threat" effect that works independently of their income effects and may even be more important than the latter in inducing policy changes. The "signal" effect can change how people assess the costs and benefits of supporting a challenge group. Each person has a "private threshold"—the level of population-wide support that a group must have before he or she is willing to openly support the challenge group. "Depending on the distribution of private thresholds across the population," Kaempfer et. al say, "it is possible that a switch by one person from supporting the government to supporting an opposition interest group can create a bandwagon effect leading to majority support for the opposition to a very high level in the population."[29]

In this way, Kaempfer et al. suggest, sanctions and other forms of foreign intervention can help interest groups mobilize collective action by lowering the threshold necessary for a bandwagon effect. However, they caution, sanctions can also increase support for the ruling group if they cause the population to rebel against foreign interference in national affairs. Therefore, Kaempfer et al. conclude that sanctions should be applied only with caution because haphazard application may be ineffective or even counterproductive by "lowering the political effectiveness of the 'right' group within the target polity."[30]

Public opinion and sanctions also played a role in the unfolding events in China. Public support—both within and outside of China—stimulated the demonstrations, according to Thomas, and influenced the government to delay its suppression of the student movement. The students were well aware of the impact of publicity and timed their demonstrations to maximize that effect. (For instance, one demonstration was held during Gorbachev's visit, when many foreign news correspondents were already there.)

However, public awareness and international pressure were unable to stop the government from its eventual use of massive force. The publicity may have also hurt the students' efforts in the long run, since the international sanctions after the massacre have tended to hurt the reform-minded Chinese intellectuals and business people more than the government. This reinforces the idea postulated by Kaempfer et al. that sanctions must be applied carefully to be sure that they are really having the intended consequences.

A more complicated example of the role of outside intervention is presented in Wehr and Nepstad's analysis of Nicaragua. Some people would argue that the U.S. support of the Contras was international support of a protest group, but this support was primarily intended to encourage violence, not nonviolence. However, other international intervention was nonviolent. This external, nonviolent intervention was a key to the resolution of Nicaraguan conflicts.

The regional peacemaking program of Esquipulas II and the international movement of solidarity with the Nicaraguan people were both influential in bringing peace with justice to Nicaragua. Esquipulas removed the Sandinista-Contra war from the U.S.-Soviet competition while pushing the Sandinistas and their opponents to a negotiated settlement. The Esquipulas agreement of 1987 outlined a series of steps that were designed to resolve the Nicaraguan conflict without violence. These steps included: demilitarization of the conflict through cease-fire agreements; refusal of support for and use of territory by insurgents; national reconciliation through negotiation, amnesty, and repatriation of refugees; democratization; ending states of emergency; protecting human rights; and continued regional consultation. The international movement of solidarity with the Nicaraguan people also brought "volunteers; material, technical, and financial aid; and pressure from external support organizations on behalf of nonviolence and justice."[31]

External Influence Through Funding

Another type of external influence is discussed by Moen. She found that in India, external funding organizations often control what development organizations can and cannot do. Foreign funding agencies, Moen says, tend to be "both rigid and fickle. They insist that DOs design programs to fit their categories. They also jump from one development fad to another, making it very difficult for DOs to be innovative, to match their programs to the particular conditions of the area they serve, or to plan very far ahead."[32] Corruption and discrimination on the basis of caste, religion, locality, language, or politics also plague the grant system.

Protest Group Objectives

Another major category of variables of interest are the objectives of the
protest group. Two ultimate objectives are possible—one is total and permanent separation of the conflicting groups; the other is continued integration with a modified power relationship.

Permanent Separation as a Goal

In cases of external occupation, where the subordinate group has independent sources of support, the challenge group's objective can be to force their
oppressors to withdraw permanently and leave them alone. Although this
can be done in a number of ways, most analysts of nonviolence and civilian-
based defense suggest that nonviolent threat is most effective in such instances.[33] Integrative and exchange strategies, they suggest, are more likely
to break down the internal solidarity necessary to maintain an effective resistance. Threats do tend to generate a negative response and risk conflict
escalation more than the "softer" strategies do. However, if total withdrawal
and separation are achieved, this effect may not be a continuing problem.

However, a heavy reliance on threat may be unnecessary. As Boulding
argues, the benefits of occupation for the occupier are usually relatively
meager. Therefore, a protest strategy offering a modest amount of resistance is likely to alter the occupier's cost/benefit structure in favor of its
withdrawal. However, use of threats by the resister may generate such hostility that the occupier continues the occupation for vengeance or to save
face rather than from self-interest.

The separation option is more problematic in cases where the dominant group has nowhere to go. Attempts to push the oppressors "into the
sea" will generate all-out resistance. Such appears to be a problematic aspect of the Palestinian-Israeli conflict. It also seemed to a be major motivation behind hard-line white resistance in South Africa.

If the goal of the challenging group is to overthrow the ruling regime
or dominant group without geographical separation, it must expect
stronger opposition than with more moderate objectives. It will also have
to depend heavily on threat as a mechanism of action, as neither negotiation nor integrative tactics are likely to succeed toward a zero-sum outcome (that is, whatever one group wins, the other must lose). Because
threats are likely to generate stronger repression than exchange or integrative strategies, all options should be considered carefully.

Integration

In situations where the subordinate and dominant groups have little choice
but to coexist, strategies that rely upon the integrative system and exchange

are likely to generate a less hostile and polarized response.[34] Threat-based alternatives, on the other hand, will likely escalate the conflict to a point where they may be counterproductive.

This would seem to be true in the case of China, India, and Nicaragua, where the opposing groups must continue to live together. It is also most likely true in the Israeli-Palestinian conflict. An independent Palestine would certainly have considerable contact with Israel. To the extent that psychological hostility can be lessened between these peoples, the probabilities of peace in the region are increased.

Vengeance/Retribution/Punishment

Often the dominant group is guilty of acts that, by any reasonable standard, are criminal and deserving of punishment. Still, it is much easier to resolve conflicts if a settlement is offered that all parties can live with. If the goal is vengeance or punishment, rather than a relatively simple end to injustice, the dominant group is more likely to harden its resistance. This tendency suggests that there may be a trade-off between demands for punishment and the speed with which one moves toward a more just society.

The degree to which protest groups are pursuing a long-term, sustainable solution rather than a quick fix also has important tactical implications. Subordinate groups may be able to mobilize threat power to achieve victory over the short run, but it is likely that the use of that power will create long-term instability and a backlash potential that will require liberated groups to maintain an expensive and dangerous threat capability indefinitely.

Strategy and Tactics

In addition to the conflict context, group characteristics, and goals, other major determinants of protest outcomes are the strategic and tactical choices made by the subordinate group. The degree of strategic and tactical planning varies considerably with the challenge group; many do consider their strategy and tactics before acting. The first decision they must make is whether to engage in violent or nonviolent resistance.

Principled Versus Pragmatic Nonviolence

Some groups decide to use nonviolence out of normative considerations (this is termed "principled nonviolence" in the literature). Others opt for nonviolence for pragmatic reasons—they expect it to be more successful than violent action.[35] Our cases illustrate both, with pragmatic nonviolence much more common than principled, and the two coexisting in several cases.

Much of the nonviolent response to conflict in Nicaragua, for instance, was based on principle. (Wehr and Nepstad refer to this as a "normative factor.") In some cases the Sandinistas did employ violent options, but they were considerably restrained. They more often turned to nonviolent conflict resolution to heal past wounds and cleavages in their war-torn society.

The Palestinian intifada, Kazak argues, also bases its use of nonviolence on both principle and practicality. Advocates of the nonviolent strategy of the intifada base their choice, in part, upon pacifism and traditional religious values of the Palestinian people. But the intifida has pragmatic roots as well. "Confronted with superior force," Kazak writes, "one has few options. Either one build one's own forces to achieve superiority, one is destroyed, or one neutralizes the superior force by using nonviolent techniques."[36] The Israeli military was sufficiently powerful that a military confrontation was unlikely to succeed. Since the Palestinians would not accept being destroyed, the only option left was nonviolence. The recent Palestinian-Israeli peace accord demonstrates the degree of success of this option. Even if the peace does not hold, the fact that the accord was signed in the first place is a strong indication of the degree of success the nonviolent strategy had in changing the power relations between those groups.

Pragmatic and principled nonviolence are also found together in Moen's analysis of Indian development. Only a quarter of the development organizations she examined cited Gandhi as a primary source of inspiration. However, all of them grounded their strategies in nonviolence and other Gandhian principles to some extent. Moen quotes one development worker: "'We must fight injustice with all our might but with mercy and compassion for both the exploited and the exploiter.'" All the DOs, Moen says, "are committed to nonviolent social change; they speak of nonviolence as both a method and a goal, of creating change through a 'raging but peaceful fire.'"[37]

Power Strategy Mix

Once challenge groups decide to respond to injustice nonviolently, they must choose their strategy and tactics. Such choices are intended to alter the balance of power between groups. Once the relative power of the subordinate group increases to equal or surpass that of the dominant group, the subordinate group will prevail.

In severe justice conflicts, the subordinate group appears to be at an extreme power disadvantage. However, the differential may be less than it seems. As Sharp pointed out, power is granted through the cooperation of low-power groups and individuals. If this cooperation is withdrawn, the ruler can be overthrown.[38]

In *Three Faces of Power*, Boulding suggested that power is exercised in three distinguishable forms—threats, exchange, and love. Each of these approaches can be used to manipulate the power structure to increase the power of the subordinate group.

Threats, violent and nonviolent, take the form "you do something I want, or I'll do something you don't want."[39] They are negative modes of persuasion and are hostile, even if they are not violent. Threats can be met with submission, flight, counterthreat, or defiance, and, depending on the response, can either be withdrawn or carried out.[40] But threats are something of a bluff—they work best if you don't have to implement them. If people easily submit, they can be quite cost effective. If people resist, however, the cost of carrying out the threat can rapidly alter the threatener's cost/benefit ratio.

Exchange, in Boulding's theory, is basically bilateral negotiation, a relationship in which "you do something I want and I'll do something you want."[41] Unlike a threat, exchange is a positive relationship that fosters cooperation. An offer of exchange can be refused, but it is unlikely to generate hostility, as do threats. Exchange-based solutions were pursued in Nicaragua and in Hungary. In both those cases, the justice grievants stopped short of demanding the heads of those in power and were willing to negotiate solutions to the justice problems that would benefit all sides.

In China, however, the students were demanding massive changes that could have eliminated the power and privilege of the ruling group. Although many movement leaders indicated a willingness to tolerate a reformed Communist Party under the leadership of Zhao Ziyang, their demands were seen by hardliners as too extreme for negotiation.

Love, Boulding's shorthand for the integrative system, is even more positive than exchange. It can be characterized by the statement "you do something for me because you love me"[42] or, in our words, "I'll do something for you because I like you, not because I expect you to do something for me in exchange or fear you might hurt me if I don't." Love has been largely ignored in the academic literature on power and conflict, but Boulding argues that it is the most significant source of power, as it underlies legitimacy. In Boulding's words, "Without some sort of legitimacy, neither threat power nor economic [i.e., exchange] power can be realized in any large degree."[43] This idea corresponds to Sharp's notion of power being based on consent.[44]

One promising way of using the integrative system in justice conflicts is what we term "hypocrisy mobilization." This tactic involves appeals to the dominant group's own belief systems, which often support universal justice in principle though not in practice. When confronted with clear evidence of a gap between principle and practice, the dominant group theoretically has to respond or repudiate its own values. This strategy is not foolproof, but it can get the dominant group to correct the injustice because they believe *they should,* not because they are being forced to do so. This was a primary tactic of U.S. civil rights activists. This strategy may also permit South African blacks and Palestinians to make profitable use of the dominant group's legal systems.

Subordinate groups can combine threats, exchange, and integrative strategies to alter the power structure of a conflict in their favor through what Wehr and Nepstad call a "power strategy mix." This mix must be carefully balanced:

> We would argue that in a conflict, the less violent the mix of power strategies, the more successful the challengers will be in achieving justice. There must be, in such a strategic mix, sufficient threat to escalate change-producing conflict. That threat, however, need not take the form of violent action. On the other hand, the love, or integrative, inclination cannot be too strong or creative conflict will not occur. The exchange in the mix is the means by which threat and integration are kept at sufficiently moderate levels to permit movement toward justice-oriented change.[45]

Although challenge groups routinely mix strategies, certain conditions may be necessary for the right mix of threat, exchange, and conciliation to emerge. In the Nicaraguan case, Wehr and Nepstad identify institutional, normative, and experiential factors that inhibited violence and led to a workable balance of the power strategies. This balance did not come quickly, however. It was preceded with an overreliance on threat and sanctions. Neither approach was effective. By 1984, the Atlantic Coast resistance was scattered, and the Contras were defeated. Both groups then altered their strategy by reducing their emphasis on threat and initiating negotiations (that is, exchange). The result was an autonomy agreement for the Atlantic Coast and a Sandinista-Contra cease-fire, which was followed by agreements on elections, demobilization, and reintegration.

The importance of exchange in the power strategy mix is also noted by Bond. While neither he, nor many other nonviolence theorists, consider negotiation to be a technique of nonviolent action, Bond agrees that exchange "offers the 'power of balance,' a build-in correction process through which opposing parties can learn about and adjust to each other."[46]

Wehr and Nepstad suggest that the Nicaraguan experience provides a model for other challenge groups built around the concept of the power strategy mix. Rapid movement to violence with a heavy reliance on threat was counterproductive for the Sandinistas, the Contras, and the indigenous peoples, Wehr and Nepstad argue. All three groups paid heavily for this strategy in terms of lives and homes lost, and in terms of loss of control to external (U.S. and Soviet) powers.

The most important requirement for attaining justice, Wehr and Nepstad maintain, is for "opponents to be flexible and diligent in using available conflict-moderating resources and to create them where they do not exist. The Nicaraguans used institutional constraints [on violence], normative inclinations toward conciliation, and conflict management" together to attain justice.[47] Even though Wehr and Nepstad acknowledge that Nicaraguan conditions will not be reproduced elsewhere, they believe that much of the conflict-moderating experience there has general applicability to other justice conflicts.

The Palestinian struggle presents some aspects similar to the Nicaraguan conflicts. First is the heavy reliance on threat and negative sanctions characterizing the Palestinian resistance prior to the intifada. As in Nicaragua, this strategy led to much loss of life and suffering but did not succeed in winning concessions from the Israelis. Second is the mixture of principled with practical nonviolence used by the intifada and the juxtaposition of violence and nonviolence within one conflict setting. Third is the nonviolent power strategy mix.

Although pressure to use violence remains strong in the Palestinian-Israeli conflict, the intifada's espousal of nonviolence remains. The Palestinians, Kazak contends, have gained more support and trust within Israel than they had previously enjoyed. This trust has caused a significant split in Israeli public opinion regarding the continued occupation of the West Bank and the Gaza and may eventually lead to complete Israeli withdrawal from those lands.

Another illustration of the power strategy mix can be seen in Arabajan's analysis of the Soviet Union. There, change issued from a dynamic juxtaposition of nonviolent threats and sanctions with the parliamentary process, playing off and influencing one another. "Serious mass nonviolence started in early 1989, when the election campaign for the Congress of People's Deputies of the USSR had begun."[48] This election resulted in growing mass political participation and influenced the form of demonstrations. Especially important, Arabajan contends, was the permission to telecast congressional proceedings on radio and television. As a result of this decision, people could see, hear, and assess their deputies for the first time. The result was a significant increase in the popularity of the opposition.

Following the 1989 Congress, which was broadcast on radio and television, many new political parties were formed, benefiting from the new mass political activity. They were hampered, however, from effective organization by the Soviet Constitution, which forbade formation of opposition parties. Public pressure forced the removal of this restriction in February 1990, after which all political parties became legal. Juxtaposition of parliamentary and popular action brought about many of the subsequent changes and continue to interact as forces for change in the still unstable situation in Russia. As in the Middle East, the "final" outcome of this nonviolent movement has yet to appear.

A different power strategy mix is noted in Thomas's analysis of China. There, students relied heavily on exchange and integrative strategies. The students frequently based their appeal on moral virtue, calling for peaceful change and pointing to real problems, such as lack of government responsiveness, official corruption, and inflation. Their moral appeals generated support for large numbers of "previously quiescent Beijing officials and citizens—including police, soldiers, bureaucrats, teachers, journalists, and middle-level officials,"[49] according to Thomas.

When moral appeals alone did not work, exchange was pursued. The government, however, refused to negotiate, and the democracy movement was at least temporarily suppressed with the June 1989 massacre. However, Thomas does not think that the pressure for political change was thereby eliminated.

> As is well known, the students lost the June battle. They were driven from Tiananmen Square and then from the country. Many of their leaders were expelled from the party and imprisoned. It is possible to argue, however, that by losing the battle in a principled manner, the students have set the stage for winning the war. Chinese are probably less supportive of anti-student actions by the government since the bloody suppression.[50]

Over the long term, Thomas predicts the students are likely to prevail. If the government continues to provide economic growth and avoids further violent repression of its own citizens, the political system in China is likely to slowly evolve into a more democratic polity. If the economy fails, however, the Communist party may be overthrown, as occurred in 1989 in Eastern Europe. "Such radical change," Thomas predicts, "would probably be precipitated by yet another round of mass protests, led by students and supported by a still larger percentage of China's urban population."[51]

Timing and Pacing

Another tactical consideration is the timing and pacing of nonviolent action. The Soviet and Chinese cases illustrate well the importance of proper timing in a nonviolent struggle. Many of the protests in the USSR were timed to coincide with the First Congress of People's Deputies. Subsequent protests responded to later parliamentary processes. This interplay was choreographed by several influential leaders, for example Boris Yeltsin, who was able to manipulate both the masses and the political process in his favor.

Obviously, democracy movement leaders in China were not as successful. The key distinction between the cases seems to be the substantial difference in legitimacy that the two governments had among their populations, but the timing and pacing of the protests might also have been a factor. In China, the students did time their protests for maximum visibility. However, they did not back down until after the Tiananmen Massacre. Had they exited the square earlier (as the Beijing students had advocated shortly before June 3), they might have regrouped and continued their effort without the massive Tiananmen defeat.

Pacing nonviolent action is also an important consideration. In justice conflicts, the demands of subordinate groups are likely to require a dramatic restructuring of society. The more abruptly and definitively such demands are made, the more likely the dominant group is to feel threatened and pressed to respond with repression, escalation, and violence. Fast-moving movements may also ask their already impoverished members to make sacrifices they cannot afford. Kaempfer et al. note that the sacrifices required by the imposition of external sanctions on South Africa led to a decrease, rather than an increase, in antiapartheid protest activity.[52]

Yet, there are also dangers in moving too slowly. People will not sacrifice for a movement unless they believe that it will produce change. With lack of movement momentum, it is all too easy to be a free rider deciding to let others make the sacrifices, knowing that one will still enjoy the rewards of a successful movement. The key is to stimulate the bandwagon effect without outrunning the movement's grassroots support.

Dominant Group's Response

Although success of a challenge is difficult to define, one clear aspect of it is the dominant group's response to the challenge of the subordinate group. This response can range from violent repression of the challengers to complete capitulation or collapse of the dominant group.

Violent Repression

Nonviolent challenges to a policy or government often may yield a violent response from the dominant group. The challenge group is then faced with the choice of maintaining nonviolent resistance, becoming violent, or withdrawing temporarily from the conflict. Without major outside support, armed response to repression is almost certain to lead to defeat and even greater intergroup hatred. If outside support is available, violent response is more likely to be successful, though only if the goal is separation and independence. If continued interdependence of the conflict groups is required, the resulting animosities will complicate the process.

One alternative response to violent repression involves scrupulous adherence to nonviolent principles with protest actions planned to illuminate the most outrageous forms of injustice for sympathetic international observers. This approach helps explain why the relatively nonviolent intifada has been more successful in mobilizing outside pressure on Israel than has the terrorism some Palestinians have pursued for so many years.

The third possible response to repression is withdrawal from the conflict. This choice was made by the Chinese students who met overwhelming violence at Tiananmen Square. However, as was noted earlier, such repression may not defeat the movement. The government's action increased the movement's legitimacy nationally and globally, while diminishing its own. Thus, while the students lost the battle, they may still win the "war."

Nonviolent Repression

Dominant groups can also resist demands for change in nonviolent and legitimate ways. They can, for example, simply ignore the opposition, as in India, where the development workers are seen as largely irrelevant by the central government. They are not numerous or powerful enough to be considered a serious threat, so they are neither repressed nor accommodated—except at times through funding decisions.

But forms of mild repression occur in India, especially at the local level, where development workers and organizations threaten the status quo, especially the power and privilege of the dominant individuals and groups. Usually the threat is not credible; therefore the repression is not strong. Development workers are not generally aided by the powerful, but are coopted or thwarted by a corrupt system of local leaders and moneylenders who maintain an iron grip on the poorest sectors of Indian society. In situations of mild, nonviolent repression, a challenge group's resort to violence is likely to be extremely counterproductive. What is needed instead are nonviolent actions that clearly focus the attention of international sympathizers on specific injustices.

Accommodation and Cooptation

Repression may also be hidden or disguised. Dominant parties can employ a strategy of *apparent* accommodation while utilizing other ways of maintaining their position. This strategy can coopt many protestors and outside sympathizers. Also used is the divide-and-conquer strategy by which different protest groups are played off against one another.

Still, nonviolent dominant group response is more desirable than violent repression. It may open the door to a continuing series of incremental changes that, if aggressively pursued by subordinate groups, can lead to significant change and overall strengthening of the integrative system. Such accommodation and cooptation efforts usually require the dominant group to recognize the validity of protestor complaints. Continued challenger pressure can limit the ability of the dominant group to develop more subtle and creative domination strategies.

Negotiated Settlement

Although negotiation is not often included in studies of nonviolence, usually a negotiated agreement is the ultimate goal after nonviolent groups use threats or other means to increase their relative power. Negotiation can, at times, be used without threats as well, when subordinate groups understand their strengths and use these directly in the negotiations to improve their power position.

Settlements were negotiated in Nicaragua between the Sandinistas and their opponents and in Hungary before 1989, when the government tried to accommodate the demands of the people, rather than resisting change as did the Polish government. In Nicaragua, negotiation was successful, although the Sandinistas were later removed from power through the electoral process. The Hungarian government, too, was eventually overthrown, despite its efforts to adjust to change through negotiation.

Capitulation

The other end of the response continuum is complete capitulation or collapse of the ruling group. This outcome can happen surprisingly quickly, as in Eastern Europe and the Soviet Union. However, the fall of the ruling regime may not bring success to the protest movement if the government replacing the old regime does not remedy the injustices of the past or replaces them with new ones. The insinuation of old leaders into new regimes, "old wine in new bottles," is a common problem, as we saw almost immediately in Rumania and Bulgaria and somewhat later in Czechoslovakia.

Measures of Success

Dominant group responses to protest may facilitate challenge group goals or hamper them. Other factors unrelated to those responses, such as external pressure or socioeconomic conditions, may contribute to or inhibit "success." But what is "success" in the context of justice conflict?

In one sense, nonviolence can be said to "work" when it attains particular short-term goals of the challenging group. These goals might be simply to make a point in a publicly visible way, to recruit new participants, to increase its cohesiveness, or to win a particular concession from the dominant party. To measure such an outcome, one must first determine what the short-term goal of a particular action was and whether or not that goal was attained. However, participants often disagree about the goals of a particular activity. Some may desire and expect significant concessions, while others would be pleased with a simple public acknowledgment of their grievances.

Success might also be measured by the attainment of major long-term change, such as the overthrow of an oppressive regime (as occurred in Eastern Europe) or the implementation of major structural changes (as was sought in China and India). Here one is tempted to say that the nonviolent movements in Eastern Europe and the Soviet Union succeeded, while the movement in China failed. But that is probably too simple. China may not illustrate failure, but rather a short-term setback. China has already experienced three democracy movements since 1978, each temporarily repressed, but stronger than its predecessor. Despite the apparent failure of the 1989 movement, many social and political forces are now aligned in favor of democratic change:

> The Chinese leaders' dilemma is similar to that of leaders in South Korea, Taiwan, and other developing countries. If Chinese leaders do not keep the door open to foreign markets and technology, their economy will stagnate, leading to failing economic and social justice and massive political protest. If the door is kept open to external trade and its consequent foreign influences, leaders may be subject to increasing demands by internal political movements and to international pressures for democratic reforms, as in the industrializing countries of East Asia.[53]

Thus, Thomas suggests that further nonviolent action and consequent social change is highly likely in China in the coming years.

In contrast, Joel Edelstein argues that the revolutions in Eastern Europe are not shining examples of successful nonviolent action. In some, Edelstein observes, the changes were brought about from the top down, not the bottom up. And with time, it appears that many leaders and control structures have not changed. They are, however, examples of successful nonviolence in the sense that neither challengers nor dominant groups used violence in the process.[54]

Another criterion of success is sustainable change. Even in the most successful of the movements presented in this volume, the potential they create for stable democracies with viable economies is not clear. Crane Brinton[55] has suggested that few revolutions result in much beyond an exchange of elites. Justice is not better served, he argued, for society overall. There have been so few nonviolent revolutions as yet that it is difficult to tell if their consequences are more hopeful. But clearly, many Indians are not better off under Indian rather than British rule. Whether the Poles, Hungarians, or Russians will be better off after the fall of communism remains to be seen.

Relative transaction cost is another important measure of success. Many advocates of pragmatic nonviolence suggest that it is better than violence because it costs less, both economically, and, more important, in terms of human life and suffering. The cases studied here seem to support this contention.

Conclusions

Ideally, we would like to be able to look at our cases and say, "When a, b, and c, are true, then a particular nonviolent strategy or tactic will work; when c, d, or e are true, then others will be required; and when e, f, and g are true all will fail." Given the complexity of dominant/subordinate relations, the large number of independent variables, the small number of cases analyzed, the complex interaction between independent and dependent variables, and the difficulty defining success, we cannot yet make any statements that strong. We have, however, been able to tentatively test many hypotheses and have generated a number of new ones not considered at the beginning of this effort. Some of the findings that appear to us to be particularly interesting, and, hence, worthy of further inquiry, include the following.[56]

Nature of the injustice. Nonviolence may be the most effective approach in a wide diversity of justice problems, but our cases suggest that the nature of the injustice has a significant effect on the likely outcome of nonviolent action. As we can see in the cases examined here, political injustice seems easier to remedy than economic injustice. Despite the political success of nonviolent revolutions in the former Warsaw Pact countries, none has overcome its national economic problems with a new regime. Most countries, in fact, appear to be suffering as severe if not worse economic woes with the new governments than with the old. Few scholars in the West find this surprising (one would expect the transition from socialism to capitalism to be very slow and difficult). However, the reformers in East European countries appear to find the task of achieving economic justice to be considerably more difficult than originally expected.

What this implies for would-be nonviolent activists is not clear. It certainly is not meant to imply that violent change would be more successful. But it might imply that in cases of economic injustice, when the source of the problem is less maldistribution and more an ineffective economy overall, the goals of nonviolent action should be gradual change, rather than pushing for changes so vast that the economic system cannot survive at all.

Nature of the ruling regime. Both the literature and logic suggest that nonviolent action would be more likely to be successful in democratic societies than in autocratic ones. Although our sample was small, this hypothesis was not confirmed in these cases. The inverse, however, was suggested: Many of the authors found that nonviolent action tends to stimulate demands for increased democratization of authoritarian regimes.

Sources of power. These cases highlight the importance of Gene Sharp's six sources of power: authority, human resources, skills and knowledge, psychological factors, material resources, and sanctions. Authoritarian regimes may rely heavily on sanctions to maintain control, but these cases clearly illustrated that there is more to power than sanctions. Dominant groups need control of the other factors, as well, if they are to withstand nonviolent challenges.

Dominant group legitimacy. Perhaps the most important variable closely related to power is legitimacy. The more the dominant group had legitimacy with a majority of the population, the more difficult and less successful nonviolent action seemed to be. The more the dominant regime lacked legitimacy and the challenge group had it—with its own members as well as with the general population, within and outside the country—the more successful the latter's efforts were at achieving change.

Subordinate group characteristics. Most of our findings about subordinate group characteristics confirmed those found in other literature—with one exception. Although some analysts have found that nonviolence is more successful if the challenge group is relatively small, our findings seem to contradict that view. In our cases, bigger was better—the larger the size of the challenge group, relative to the population of the society overall, the higher the apparent chance of success.

Historical context. We expected that the societal history of violence or nonviolence would play a significant role in determining the willingness of a challenge group to use nonviolence in its current struggle. Once again, we found our assumption was wrong. Societies with long histories of violence—for instance, Poland, the Soviet Union, and the Palestinians—have all successfully adopted and used nonviolent strategies in their efforts to attain justice in recent struggles. However, India, which has a strong tradition of nonviolence, has in many ways become a violent nation that seems to have eschewed the teachings of Gandhi in its modernization.

Belief systems. The history of violence or nonviolence may not be as important as we originally thought, but the belief systems of a culture do appear to have significant impact on challenge group strategy. As Kazak finds in his study of the Middle East, members of a challenge group must believe in nonviolence themselves, not have it imposed on them from some external source, if they are to effectively adopt a nonviolent approach to justice struggles.

Constraints on violence. Another key idea, which has not appeared widely in the literature, is Wehr and Nepstad's concept of violence-moderating constraints. Societies with institutional, normative, or conflict management constraints on violence are much more likely to be able to implement non-violent solutions to justice problems than are societies without such constraints. We agree with Wehr and Nepstad's final statement, which says that "what appears most important is for justice opponents to be flexible and diligent in using available conflict-moderating resources and to create them where they do not exist."[57]

Power strategy mix. Another key idea expressed most directly by Wehr and Nepstad, but echoed by many of our other contributors as well, is the concept of the power strategy mix. In Nicaragua, Wehr and Nepstad observed that a careful balance of threats, exchange, and integrative strategies can be more effective than any strategy used alone. Other cases in this volume illustrate the same point. For instance, several of our cases examine the utility of negotiation (that is, exchange)—a concept that is heavily stressed in the conflict management literature, but seldom appears in non-violence writing. Although we would agree, as Bond argues, that negotiation used alone does not constitute nonviolent direct action, it certainly does constitute a nonviolent approach to justice problems. However, given the usual power disparities between the opposing groups in these justice conflicts, negotiation must be supplemented with integrative and threat-based strategies in an appropriate power strategy mix to be successful.

Conflict escalation. The conflict management literature focuses considerable attention on the pros and cons of conflict escalation; however, the nonviolence literature does not. Clearly, escalation of a conflict can be beneficial at some times and detrimental at others. Even when potentially beneficial, however, escalation is dangerous as it generally increases anger and hatred and may therefore encourage the opposition to heighten its resistance to the challenge group's demands.

One benefit of nonviolence is that it tends to escalate conflicts more moderately than violent approaches to justice problems. If challenge groups are seen to be rational and reasonable, they are likely to be taken more seriously than if they are seen as irrational fanatics. Similarly, if challenge groups make demands that are simply impossible to meet, that circumstance is likely to escalate the conflict and cause the resistance to be stronger than it would be if the demands were less extreme.

Clearly, more research will be needed to fully answer our primary research questions: *What* forms of nonviolence work to remedy injustice, *when, how,* and *why?* The next few years should be an especially productive time for this research since so much nonviolent action has recently taken place. Analysts will now be able to follow unfolding events to assess the long-term consequences of these nonviolent movements. This analysis will tell us much more than we now know about the ability of nonviolence to advance the causes of social, economic, and political justice.

Notes

1. Boulding, *Three Faces of Power.*
2. Moen, Chapter 12.
3. Ibid.
4. Boulding, Chapter 3.
5. Sharp, *The Politics of Nonviolent Action, Part I.*
6. Burgess and Burgess summarize Sharp's theory of power more extensively in Chapter 1 of this book.
7. Edelstein, Chapter 6.
8. Kuper, *Passive Resistance.*
9. Oppenheimer, "Towards Understanding Nonviolence."
10. Thomas, Chapter 8.
11. Sharp, *The Politics of Action, Part III.*
12. Oppenheimer, "Towards Understanding Nonviolence."
13. Arabajan, Chapter 7.
14. This is not to say *all* Palestinians support nonviolence. Many, especially the more radical members of the Hamas faction, reject nonviolence as "Western," while believing violence is the only way to obtain either honor or justice.
15. Zielonka, "Strengths and Weaknesses," p. 93.
16. Wehr and Nepstad, Chapter 5.
17. Ibid. Here Wehr and Nepstad draw on McManus and Schlabach, *Relentless Persistence*, p. 159.
18. Kazak, Chapter 11.
19. Ibid. Kazak attributes this assessment to Stout, "Justice and Resort to War."
20. Kazak, Chapter 11. Kazak is quoting Solomonow, "Living Truth," in this passage.
21. Kazak, Chapter 11.
22. Ibid. Cited from Muhammad Abu Laila, "Islam and Peace."
23. Boulding, *Ecodynamics*, p. 206.
24. Wehr and Nepstad, Chapter 5.
25. Ibid.
26. *Confianza* mediators are third parties known and respected by all disputants, though they may not be impartial as is expected in the Western model of mediation. See Wehr and Lederach, "Mediating Conflict."
27. Moen, Chapter 12.
28. Kaempfer et al., Chapter 10.
29. Ibid. See also Kuran, "Preference Falsification" and "The East European Revolution."
30. Kaempfer et al., Chapter 10.
31. Wehr and Nepstad, Chapter 5.
32. Moen, Chapter 12.
33. See, for instance, Sharp, *Civilian-based Defense*; Boserup and Mack, *War Without Weapons*; and Wehr and Nepstad, Chapter 5 in this book.

34. This hypothesis is reviewed more extensively in Burgess and Burgess, "Intractable Conflict."

35. See Burgess and Burgess, Chapter 1 in this book, for a further discussion of the meanings of principled and pragmatic nonviolence.

36. Kazak, Chapter 11.

37. Moen, Chapter 12.

38. Sharp, *The Politics of Nonviolent Action, Part I.*

39. Boulding, *Three Faces of Power*, p. 25.

40. Doug Bond persuasively urges us to explicitly distinguish between threats and sanctions; Boulding lumps the two together. Bond argues there is a significant difference between a threat that is withdrawn when the threatener's bluff is called, and a threat that is translated into action in the form of either violent or nonviolent sanctions against the threatened party. We agree, and consider this in the following analysis.

41. Boulding, *Three Faces of Power*, p. 27.

42. Ibid., p. 29.

43. Ibid., p. 109.

44. Sharp, *The Politics of Nonviolent Action, Part I.*

45. Wehr and Nepstad, Chapter 5.

46. Bond, Chapter 4, referring to Torbet, *The Power of Balance*, p. 41.

47. Wehr and Nepstad, Chapter 5.

48. Arabajan, Chapter 7.

49. Thomas, Chapter 8.

50. Ibid.

51. Ibid.

52. Kaempfer et al., Chapter 10.

53. Thomas, Chapter 8.

54. Edelstein, Chapter 6.

55. Brinton, *The Anatomy of Revolution.*

56. This summary does not imply that other topics are unworthy of further inquiry. We are simply highlighting those that strike us as being especially interesting, either because they are counterintuitive or because they make an important, new, and different contribution to the literature.

57. Wehr and Nepstad, Chapter 5.

Bibliography

Boserup, A., and A. Mack, *War Without Weapons: Non-Violence in National Defense* (New York: Schocken Books, 1975).

Boulding, Kenneth. *Ecodynamics: A New Theory of Societal Evolution* (Beverly Hills, CA, and London: Sage Publications, 1978).

———. *Three Faces of Power* (Newbury Park, CA: Sage Publications, 1989).

Brinton, Crane. *The Anatomy of Revolution* (New York: Vintage Books, 1965).

Burgess, Guy, and Heidi Burgess. "Intractable Conflict and Constructive Confrontation." Conflict Resolution Consortium Working Paper #91–6, University of Colorado, Boulder, 1991.

Kuper, L. *Passive Resistance in South Africa* (New Haven: Yale University Press, 1957).

Kuran, Timur. "Preference Falsification, Policy Continuity and Collective Conservatism." *Economic Journal* 97 (September 1987): 642–665.

————. "The East European Revolution of 1989: Is It Surprising that We Were Surprised?" *American Economic Review* 81 (May 1991): 121–125.

Laila, Muhammad Abu. "Islam and Peace." *The Islamic Quarterly* 35 (1) (1991): 62.

McManus, P., and G. Schlabach. *Relentless Persistence: Nonviolent Action in Latin America* (Philadelphia: New Society Publishers, 1991).

Oppenheimer, M. "Towards a Sociological Understanding of Nonviolence." *Sociological Inquiry* 35 (1965): 123–131.

Sharp, Gene. *The Politics of Nonviolent Action. Part I: Power and Struggle* (Boston, MA: Porter Sargent Publishers, 1973).

————. *The Politics of Nonviolent Action. Part III: The Dynamics of Nonviolent Action* (Boston, MA: Porter Sargent Publishers, 1973).

————. *Civilian-based Defense: A Post–Military Weapons System* (Princeton, NJ: Princeton University Press, 1990).

Solomonow, Allan. "Living Truth: A Jewish Perspective," in Robert L. Holmes (ed.), *Nonviolence in Theory and Perspective* (Belmont, CA: Wadsworth Publishing Company, 1990).

Sonn, Tamara. *Between Qur'an and Crown: The Challenge of Political Legitimacy in the Arab World* (Boulder, CO: Westview Press, 1990).

Stout, Jeffrey. "Justice and Resort to War: A Sampling of Christian Ethical Thinking," in James Turner Johnson and John Kelsay (eds.), *Cross, Crescent, and Sword* (New York: Greenwood Press, 1990), pp. 3–33.

Torbet, William R. *The Power of Balance: Transforming Self, Society, and Scientific Inquiry* (Newbury Park, CA: Sage Publications, 1991).

Wehr, Paul, and John Paul Lederach, "Mediating Conflict in Central America," *Journal of Peace Research* 28 (1) (1991): 85–98.

Zielonka, J. "Strengths and Weaknesses of Nonviolent Action: The Polish Case." *Orbis* (Spring 1986): 91–110.

Index

Jiu-jitsu: moral, 69; political, 19, 64, 69, 264; social, 19
Judaism, 221, 222, 267
Justice: commensal, 48; criminal, 48; definition of, 8, 48, 227, 258; distributive, 8; procedural, 8; production of, 82, 269; social, 29, 81, 87, 89, 161, 165, 166, 169–171, 180, 183, 184, 284; universal principles of, 13

Kadar, Janos, 104–106, 108, 109, 112, 117
Kelman, Herbert, 73
King, Martin Luther, Jr., 13, 14, 16, 56
Korten, David, 233, 248, 253
Krenz, Egon, 114, 115
Kruegler, Christopher, 26
Kuper, Leo, 17, 25–27, 263
Kurds, 217

Lakey, George, 21, 22, 26, 61, 65
Leadership: in China, 152, 161, 277; in Czechoslovakia, 115–117; development in India, 240, 241; in Hungary, 108; independence from traditional, 30; of nonviolent group, 27, 111; quality of, 25, 107, 110, 262; in USSR, 130
Lebanon, 45
Legitimacy, 38, 221, 261, 280, 282; basis of, 106; of challenge group, 17, 264; in China, 147–161; of communism, 47, 53, 55; of dominant group, 262, 286; in Eastern Europe, 100, 101, 104, 105, 112; loss of, 51, 53, 55, 107, 119, 263; of opposition leadership, 27; role in integrative system, 13, 51, 277; in USSR, 51
Liberation theology, 81, 89
Li Peng, 155, 158
Lofland, John, 61
Love: and Christianity, 29, 221, 266; definition of, 277; in Gandhian nonviolence, 14, 18, 22; Solidarity's belief in, 29, 266; source of power, 10, 12, 13, 51, 86, 95, 248, 257, 276–278. *See also* Integrative system
Loyalty, 51

Mack, Andrew, 18, 22, 27

Manifest behavior, 61
Manipulation: discrete, 21
Mao Zedong, 149–151, 153, 155
Marx, Karl, 46, 53, 56, 89, 237
McCarthy, Ronald, 17, 18, 24–26
Mechanisms of action, 2, 16, 20, 21, 60, 62–70, 73–75; violent, 67
Mechanisms of change, 2, 16, 20, 21, 43, 60, 70–74; defined and described, 70–72
Media: role in nonviolent action, 17, 27; and sanctions, 192
Mediation, 84, 96
Meyerding, Jane, 22
Middle East belief systems, 220, 221
Mightiness as source of violence, 47
Militarization, 82, 91, 96, 271
Miller, W. R., 17, 65
Minorities at Risk Project, 167, 169, 171–173
Moldova, 144
Monarchy in Russia, 127
Mozambique, 45
Multiethnic coalitions, 166, 172–174, 179, 184
Muste, A. J., 14

Nagy, Imre, 104
Nationalism, 46, 110, 126, 128, 144, 145, 224, 227; national liberation, 224; and violence, 56
Negotiation, 7, 10, 12, 16, 20, 262; in China, 157, 159; in Hungary, 104, 109; Israeli/Palestinian, 226; in Nicaragua, 84–86, 88, 92, 93, 95, 261, 273; in Poland, 111, 113
New Forum, 114, 118
New Zealand, 45
Nicaragua: Atlantic Coast resistance, 82–84, 95, 96, 278; Conciliation Commission, 84; National Autonomy Commission, 83; National Autonomy Law, 83, 86, 91; National Reconciliation Commission, 92; U.S. intervention in, 12
Niebuhr, Reinhold, 50
Noncooperation, 22, 27, 63, 65, 70, 99; Gandhian, 18, 22; Sharp's, 18, 20
Nongovernmental organizations (NGOs), 233
Nonintervention, Soviet, 113, 117

About the Contributors

Zaven Arabajan is a research fellow in the Institute of Oriental Studies and Department of General Theoretical Problems, Section of Social Problems, at the Academy of Sciences in Russia.

Lynne Bennett is a graduate student in the Department of Economics at the University of Colorado, Boulder.

Doug Bond is Director of Research for the Program on Nonviolent Sanctions at Harvard University.

Kenneth E. Boulding was one of the leading scholars in peace research and conflict resolution for at least thirty years. His many works include *Conflict and Defense: A General Theory, Stable Peace,* and *Three Faces of Power.*

Guy Burgess and Heidi Burgess are a husband-and-wife team who codirect the Conflict Resolution Consortium and, with Paul Wehr, also codirect the Justice Without Violence Project. Sociologists by training, their career has led them through a series of interdisciplinary projects.

Joel Edelstein is professor of political science at the University of Colorado at Denver.

William Kaempfer is a professor of economics at the University of Colorado at Boulder.

Amin M. Kazak is a Lebanese political scientist now working at the University of Colorado and the University of Denver.

Anton D. Lowenberg is a professor of economics at the University of California at Northridge.

H. Naci Mocan is a professor of economics at the University of Colorado at Denver.

Elizabeth Mathiot (Moen) was a University of Colorado sociologist who studied and worked extensively among the very poor of India in conjunction with the Quaker Right Sharing of World Resources Program.

Sharon Erickson Nepstad is a sociology graduate student at the University of Colorado at Boulder.

James R. Scarritt is a professor of political science at the University of Colorado at Boulder.

Stephen C. Thomas is a political scientist from the University of Colorado at Denver.

Paul Wehr is one the Justice Without Violence project's codirectors and chair of the Department of Sociology's Social Conflict Concentration at the University of Colorado at Boulder. In recent years Wehr has been studying conflict management and peaceful change in Central America.

About the Book

Justice Without Violence investigates nonviolent ways—both successful and unsuccessful—of confronting acute political and economic injustice around the world.

A well-integrated mixture of theoretical analysis and case studies (from Asia, Africa, Europe, Latin America, and the Middle East), the book examines nonviolent direct action, political action, economic sanctions, and social movements as alternative remedies in the struggle for justice. The authors thus address the basic questions that underlie current debates in international politics over the use of preventive diplomacy, humanitarian intervention, and international enforcement action as alternatives to violence.